PLAYBACK+
Speed • Pitch • Balance • Loop

Transcriptions • Lessons • Bios • Photos

25 GREAT JAZZ GUITAR SOLOS

Featuring Legends of Jazz Guitar, Including Charlie Christian, Wes Montgomery, Pat Metheny, Joe Pass, Kenny Burrell, Django Reinhardt, Jim Hall, Grant Green, John Scofield, and Many More

by Paul Silbergleit

AF009452

To access audio visit:
www.halleonard.com/mylibrary

Enter Code
"4877-8004-6298-3886"

ALSO AVAILABLE:

100 Jazz Lessons
(book/2-CD)
HL00696454

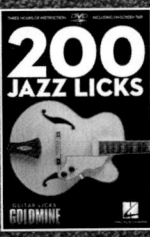
200 Jazz Licks
(DVD)
HL00320931

25 Great Blues Guitar Solos
(book/CD)
HL00699790

Cover Photo Credits:
Charlie Christian © Jan Persson Archive CTSImages, Joe Pass © Retna Ltd., Wes Montgomery photo courtesy Photofest,
Mike Stern © Retna Ltd., Django Reinhardt © Alamy, Jim Hall © Raymond Ross Archives CTSImages

ISBN 978-1-4584-5393-8

7777 W. BLUEMOUND RD. P.O. BOX 13819 MILWAUKEE, WI 53213

Copyright © 2015 by HAL LEONARD CORPORATION
International Copyright Secured   All Rights Reserved

For all works contained herein:
Unauthorized copying, arranging, adapting, recording, Internet posting, public performance,
or other distribution of the printed or recorded music in this publication is an infringement of copyright.
Infringers are liable under the law.

Visit Hal Leonard Online at
www.halleonard.com

Preface

The guitar has a rich, colorful, and ever-growing place in the story of jazz, America's greatest art form. With an incredible array of sounds, styles, and personalities, guitarists have been there contributing to the genre's development from the beginning. The tones of the original Mississippi Delta bluesmen wove their way into the language of the music at its inception, early acoustic pioneers laid a foundation for solo performance and accompaniment, and rhythm masters like Freddie Green drove the swinging momentum of the big bands. But since the swing era, the instrument has grown into a leading improvisational role, its players wailin' for all the world to hear, and that's where our ongoing legend begins.

When, over three quarters of a century ago, Charlie Christian first plugged in his Gibson with the Benny Goodman Sextet, a new door was opened for guitar soloists everywhere, and the melodic ideas he put forth at horn-player volume influenced even the horn players who were in the process of inventing bebop. Through the 1940s, Oscar Moore demonstrated the tastefulness with which the newly amplified axe could blend into an intimate trio setting. And meanwhile, an utterly passionate and virtuosic solo voice, one whose acoustic flights of fancy would inspire so many devotees of the African-American music called jazz, had emerged from the Gypsy encampments of suburban Paris in the form of Django Reinhardt.

In the aftermath of the bop revolution, iconic figures such as Barney Kessel, Jimmy Raney, and Tal Farlow carried forth the Charlie Christian spirit, and adapted the vernacular of saxophonist Charlie Parker and trumpeter Dizzy Gillespie to the guitar, each in their own unique manner. The wizardly Johnny Smith raised the bar for six-string precision and reached a new audience with his relatively subdued style, while Herb Ellis kept a traditional sense of swing alive, well into modern times. Kenny Burrell's bluesy melodicism resonated with the hard bop vibrations of the 1950s and beyond, and Jim Hall began his intrepid investigations of electric guitar quietude that have spoken so loudly to generations of jazzers.

When Wes Montgomery arrived on the scene near the end of that decade, the jazz world was once more turned upside down by a guitarist, through the sheer rhythmic force and improvisational brilliance of his work, not to mention his amazing right-hand thumb technique and use of octaves and chordal textures in soloing. Wes represented a milestone for the instrument, preparing its place in the post-bop environment of modern jazz, and leaving a legacy for all subsequent players to reckon with. Still, a yet earthier approach was manifested by Blue Note Records favorite Grant Green, his often deceptively simple phrases laced with a profound and soulful sense of time and touch. Nashville studio ace Hank Garland took a break from his usual hit-making sessions to briefly show his great flair for swingin' on standards. And soon a young George Benson would cut his teeth in the soul jazz domain of organist Jack McDuff's band, already displaying his plentiful chops, years before attaining huge success in a more popular vein with both voice and guitar.

The amazing Joe Pass came into his greatest notoriety in the 1970s, expertly holding down the fort for old-school jazz while the first wave of jazz-rock fusion passed through, and setting a new standard for solo guitar performance along the way. Pat Martino followed up on the Wes impulse in cutting-edge fashion, making some of the most transcendent and influential statements yet heard. Modernists like John McLaughlin, John Abercrombie, Pat Metheny, John Scofield, and Mike Stern, reconciling their rock-generation roots with their love of jazz, began to open up the sonic landscape of the whole style through their electronic explorations, and have long shown great ingenuity in their blending and blurring of genres. Emily Remler, within her tragically short life, carried the torch of Wes into the 1980s and helped make inroads for female instrumentalists in the business. Current masters such as Peter Bernstein and Bobby Broom continue building on the tradition of straight-ahead jazz guitar, in their 21st century way, and the highly influential Kurt Rosenwinkel keeps widening the aural palette of the music.

These are the artists whose ingenious and beautiful improvised creations are represented here, with full detail, analysis, and technical tips, along with bios, pics, and sound-alike audio recordings. So start reading, start playing, and enjoy your hands-on experience with the solos of the jazz guitar greats!

Acknowledgments

Special thanks to Dan Flynn, Jay Mollerskov, Bob Monagle, Ric Probst, and the musicians for their great input and support.

About the Audio

The accompanying audio for this book includes all 25 solos performed note for note with a full band. The time code shown at the start of each solo transcription indicates the point at which the solo begins in the original recording. To access the audio online, for download or streaming, visit **www.halleonard.com/mylibrary** and enter the code found at the front of this book.

All music on the accompanying audio performed by:

Guitar: Paul Silbergleit

Tenor saxophone: Eric Schoor

Piano: Mark Davis

Keyboards: Dan Trudell

Bass: Jeff Hamann

Drums: David Bayles

Recorded, mixed, and mastered by Ric Probst/Remote Planet Recording, at Tanner-Monagle studios in Milwaukee, WI.

Contents

PAGE	SONG	GUITARIST
1	I've Found a New Baby	Charlie Christian
6	Embraceable You	Oscar Moore
10	The World Is Waiting for the Sunrise	Django Reinhardt
16	Lullaby of Birdland	Barney Kessel
23	Spring Is Here	Jimmy Raney
28	Like Someone in Love	Tal Farlow
35	East of the Sun (And West of the Moon)	Johnny Smith
40	Lyresto	Kenny Burrell
47	Relaxin'	Hank Garland
54	Full House	Wes Montgomery
64	Jean de Fleur	Grant Green
73	Benny's Back	George Benson
79	Orange, Brown and Green	Herb Ellis
87	Days of Wine and Roses	Pat Martino
95	Whisper Not	Jim Hall
103	Lover Man (Oh, Where Can You Be?)	Joe Pass
109	You Don't Know What Love Is	John Abercrombie
116	Nothing Personal	Pat Metheny
123	East to Wes	Emily Remler
132	Nardis	Mike Stern
142	Swing Spring	John Scofield
152	No Blues	John McLaughlin
159	The Acrobat	Peter Bernstein
168	If I Should Lose You	Kurt Rosenwinkel
177	I Thought About You	Bobby Broom
185	Conclusion	
185	About the Author	
186	*Guitar Notation Legend*	

I've Found a New Baby 1941

Charlie Christian

© CTSImages

"So take heart, all you starving guitarists… you play damned fine music, but now you've got a chance to bring the fact… to the attention of the world."

—Charlie Christian
(on the implications of amplification)

In the realm of jazz guitar, Charlie Christian was at the start of many things. He did more than anyone else to bring widespread awareness to the electrified instrument in its early years, forever establishing it as a solo voice and liberating his fellow players from a rhythm-only role on acoustic. Through his hot lines and warm, neck-position pickup tone, he was a direct and primary influence to nearly all the major bop-oriented guitarists who followed in his wake, including Barney Kessel, Herb Ellis, Jimmy Raney, Tal Farlow, Kenny Burrell, Jim Hall, Wes Montgomery, Grant Green, and George Benson. The reverberations of his musical advancements were felt not only by those playing on six strings, but through the jazz world as a whole, as he contributed early on to the development of the bebop language. And his presence as a third African-American member of clarinetist Benny Goodman's band helped to break the mold of musical segregation in his time.

Born into a musical family on July 29, 1916, in Bonham, Texas, Charles Henry Christian grew up in Oklahoma City, gaining a wide exposure to music through the program at his school, the blues tradition of the Southwest, the experience of busking with his father and older brothers in a strolling string band, and the opportunity to hear top-flight players who would come through town. Among these was the uniquely brilliant tenor saxophonist Lester Young, a key influence on Christian as well as on countless other budding jazzers. From a young age, he acquired skills on various instruments, learning trumpet, piano, and bass in addition to guitar, while also showing proficiency at baseball and billiards. Still in his teens, he befriended and influenced another future pioneer of the electric guitar: bluesman T-Bone Walker.

By age 18, he worked in his brother Edward's band (The Jolly Jugglers) and began touring regionally with groups such as the Alphonso Trent Sextet (as a bassist) and later the Anna Mae Wilburn Orchestra. His reputation as a guitarist grew, and after time spent in places like Kansas City and St. Louis, he was back in Oklahoma City leading a jump band as a pianist when Eddie Durham came to town with the Count Basie Orchestra in 1937. A notable big-band trombonist, composer, and arranger, Durham is also credited with being the first significant jazz musician to perform and record on the electric guitar. Christian met him, heard the newly amplified version of the instrument, and was captivated, procuring one for himself shortly thereafter.

Christian soon went on the road again with the Al Trent Sextet, but this time as an electric guitarist, honing his abilities as an out-front soloist rather than a strictly rhythm player and traveling as far north as Bismarck, North Dakota for a stint at the Dome. It was here that he was heard by future notable guitarist Mary Osborne, then 17 years old, who was blown away by the single-note lines that originated from a guitar with the clarity and fluency expected from a

I've Found a New Baby

tenor sax. Christian was an admirer of Django Reinhardt, even if not a disciple, and around this time he could be heard mixing note-for-note transcriptions of the Gypsy great's solos in with his own electrified improvisation.

His new sound caught the ear of many others, including piano luminaries Teddy Wilson and Mary Lou Williams. At the urging of Williams, jazz promoter John Hammond went out of his way to hear Christian, now back in Oklahoma City again in August of 1939 and performing with a local group. Hammond recognized the genius in his playing right away and arranged for him to fly to Los Angeles for an audition with famous bandleader Benny Goodman, who was skeptical and had to be coaxed to go along with the idea. When they all met days later at an L.A. recording studio, the "King of Swing" remained unimpressed—to top things off, Christian showed up in a purple, green, and yellow outfit with a wide-brimmed hat and pointy shoes, helping Goodman to dismiss him as an "impossible rube."

Hammond (as he himself remembered it) didn't give up, and he conspired with bassist Artie Bernstein to sneak Christian and all his gear onstage that same night between sets at Goodman's restaurant gig. The clarinetist was highly displeased when he saw what had transpired and called the standard song "Rose Room" to pose what he thought would be a stumper for the naive-looking guitarist. But when it was his turn to solo, Christian took off and, far beyond showing that he knew the tune, rolled on for chorus after chorus of fresh, inspired, and virtuosic improvisation. If there had been doubters, everyone in the room was a convert, including pianist Fletcher Henderson, vibraphone legend Lionel Hampton, and not least of all the leader himself, who promptly hired the electric guitarist, marking the beginning of the Benny Goodman Sextet.

For just short of two years, Christian was onstage and in the studio with both Goodman's Sextet and Orchestra, and occasionally with others, creating the amazing recordings that would become his legacy. After his first serious session in September 1939, with an all-star lineup under Hampton's leadership, he began laying down the famous Goodman numbers for which he is best known, such as "Flying Home," "Seven-Come-Eleven," "Rose Room," "Gone with 'What' Wind," "I've Found a New Baby," and "Good Enough to Keep (Air Mail Special)" with the small group, as well as "Honeysuckle Rose" and his tour-de-force guitar feature "Solo Flight" with the big band—all with noteworthy solo statements from the guitar. Probably to a greater extent than he was given credit for, Christian contributed to the writing of the groups' original tunes. He also cut some sides with blues singer Ida Cox and had the chance to perform and record with his long-time hero Lester Young, initially in the context of Hammond's second Spirituals to Swing concert at Carnegie Hall on December 24, 1939.

While in New York City with Goodman, Christian became a regular at the after-hours jam sessions at Minton's in Harlem, where pianist Thelonious Monk and drummer Kenny Clarke were part of the house band and trumpeter Dizzy Gillespie a frequent guest. This was a hotbed for the formation of bebop, the harmonically and rhythmically more complex style of jazz that was soon to revolutionize the music, and these were some of its main progenitors. Christian was on the same page with this crowd, able not only to grasp their innovations, but to influence the scene himself with an ahead-of-his-time sense of phrasing and note choice. Informal live recordings made at the club in 1941 (and released in the years since under various album titles) give special insight into his stretched-out, trailblazing improvisations, especially through his multiple choruses on "Swing to Bop" (which used the chord changes to Eddie Durham's "Topsy").

Christian had received a tremendous boost in income upon joining Goodman (from $7.50 to $150 a week) and was inclined to live it up with booze, pot, and general partying, in addition to all the jamming and his busy professional schedule—all this despite frequent illness, a diagnosis of tuberculosis, and warnings to take it easy. In June of 1941, he collapsed and was admitted to the Seaview Sanitarium on Staten Island. He would occasionally sneak out to indulge in his vices (if someone else didn't sneak them in), and on March 2, 1942 he succumbed to his condition.

A friendly and generally soft-spoken person, Christian was a revolutionary voice on his instrument and an outspoken advocate for its players. In his lifetime, he was honored with the *DownBeat* Readers Poll award for best guitarist three years in a row (1939–41), and long after his death, he was inducted into both the *DownBeat* Jazz Hall of Fame (1966) and the Rock and Roll Hall of Fame (1990)—fitting tributes for a jazz guitarist whose monumental contributions went so far beyond jazz and so far beyond the guitar.

Many a jazz guitar legend got their first inspiration hearing Christian on his 1939–1941 recordings with Benny Goodman, some of the greatest of which are assembled here.

I've Found a New Baby

How to Play It

The January 1941 session in which Charlie Christian recorded this solo found him in a star-studded small-group lineup including bandleader Benny Goodman on clarinet, big band icon Count Basie at the piano, Basie's revered drummer Jo Jones, and trumpeter Cootie Williams of Duke Ellington Orchestra fame. It is among the most highly influential statements with which he would set the guitar world (as well as the jazz world) on its ear, and in it he displays elements of both the swing environment from which he emerged and the soon-to-arrive bebop movement he helped to launch. The strong quarter-note pulse plus syncopated accents of swing are evident as he begins, along with a very plain-as-day approach to the Dm chord at hand. But starting with the end of measure 4, we get a taste of the fluent eighth-note lines, replete with extended chord tones and chromatic connections, that would characterize bop.

Oftentimes the line that Christian plays to bring out a particular chordal sound lies right where we might grab a pertinent chord shape on the fretboard. In both measures 5 and 8, for example, he treats the dominant 7 chord as a 9 chord, giving us G9 and A9 respectively, by using his single-note run to outline a common 9 chord shape (one that would have its root on string 5). Notice that he adds a 13th tone each time when he hits the highest note of the phrase on string 1 (though in both these cases, the second note of the measure is a chordal 5th on string 4—generally absent from that common guitar voicing, but part of the complete arpeggio). In the earlier instance (measure 5), Christian plays quickly and fluidly across the top four strings with a move that can take some practice to execute. Carefully let your index finger *roll* from string 3 to string 2 here, positioned almost as if you were barring a Dm chord at fret 10, as you sweep the pick across.

The chromatic motion we hear towards the end of measure 5 (E–E♭–D) or early in measure 7 (D–D♭–C), and elsewhere throughout this solo, is very bop-like in its nature. But interestingly, his harmonic treatment of A7, which will lead to Dm in a V–i movement, harkens back to the earlier era in which he came to fame—i.e., he treats it like a natural dominant with a natural 9th and 13th (B♮ and F♯, respectively). A later jazz soloist would likely alter these tones to create an A7♭9 or ♯9 (perhaps with a ♭13th as well) when a dominant chord resolves to minor in this way. He does indeed sometimes give the altered treatment to a dominant 7, as in measure 14, where the D♭ at the very end of the bar implies a C7♭9.

As the bridge of the song begins at measure 17, we again hear a natural dominant sound for A7, along with an even more straightforward use of tones from a chord voicing to create the melodic line—this time involving the A9 shape in fourth position (which looks like a C♯m7♭5 rooted on string 5), followed by notes found directly in A7 or A13 in fifth position. Also at this point in his solo, Christian increases the intensity with greater density, bringing us towards the end of the eight-bar section with a longer, more continuous line before using an interesting tone coloration leading into measure 24—the same G played twice in a row but on different strings. In measures 25–27, he swings more simply again with some basic D minor tones, as he did at the very beginning and in measures 9–12. Note the use of B♮ (string 1, fret 7)—the 6th in a Dm6 chord—which can be found in the D Dorian mode or D melodic minor scale (as opposed to the B♭ found in D natural minor).

Now Christian further lets loose with another exciting stylistic element of his playing—the blues influence, exemplified here by the very down-home-sounding figure in measures 28 and 29. Here he slides up to and down from an F on string 2, bouncing it against an A or B note, alternately, on string 1, all in a repetitive, syncopated rhythm (the whole thing occurs in units of one-and-a-half beats, against the 4/4 meter). To get the feel of this little riff, practice slowly and get used to the alternation between strings and between the two notes on string 1. Also keep in mind that the main thing happening on string 2 is the note F, even if the E below it is heard for brief moments, and the exact time values vary. After concluding this gesture, Christian gives us a rhythmically and harmonically well-defined resolution to F (the tonic chord in the actual key of the tune) and finally to Dm (the prominently heard relative minor) once again.

Vital Stats

Guitarist: Charlie Christian

Song: "I've Found a New Baby" (also appears as "I Found a New Baby")

Album: Columbia single 36039, 1941—Benny Goodman Sextet Featuring Count Basie (*The Genius of the Electric Guitar*, 1987—Charlie Christian)

Age at time of recording: 24

Guitar: Gibson ES-150 or ES-250

Amp: Gibson EH-185 or EH-150

I've Found a New Baby

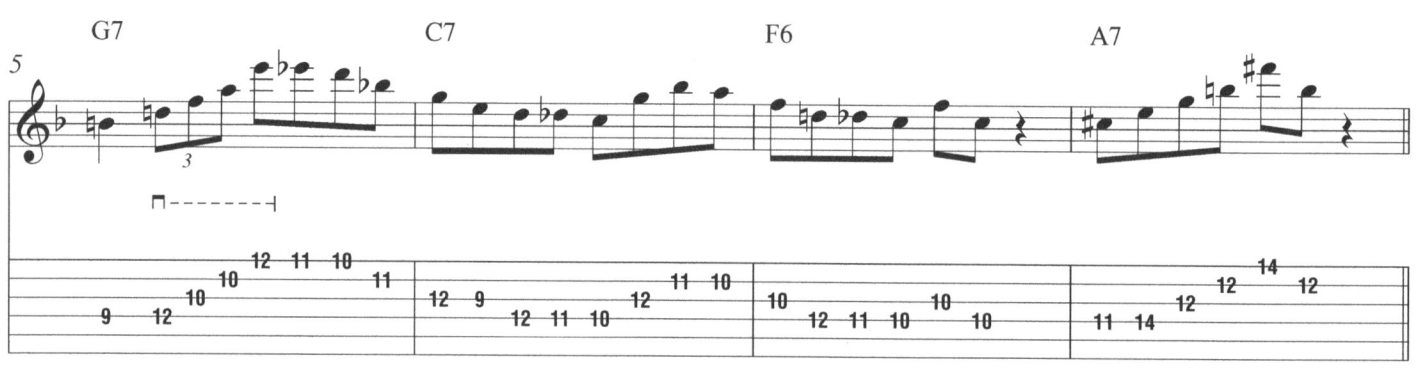
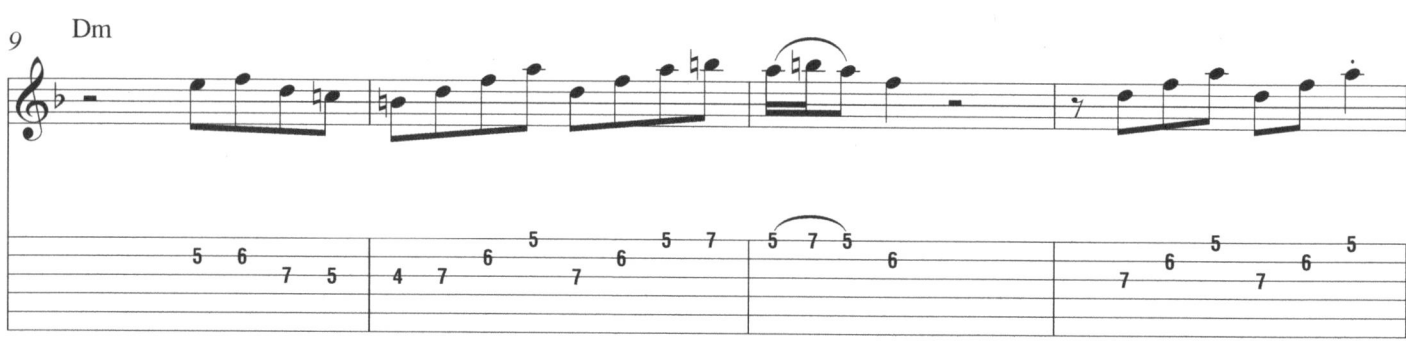
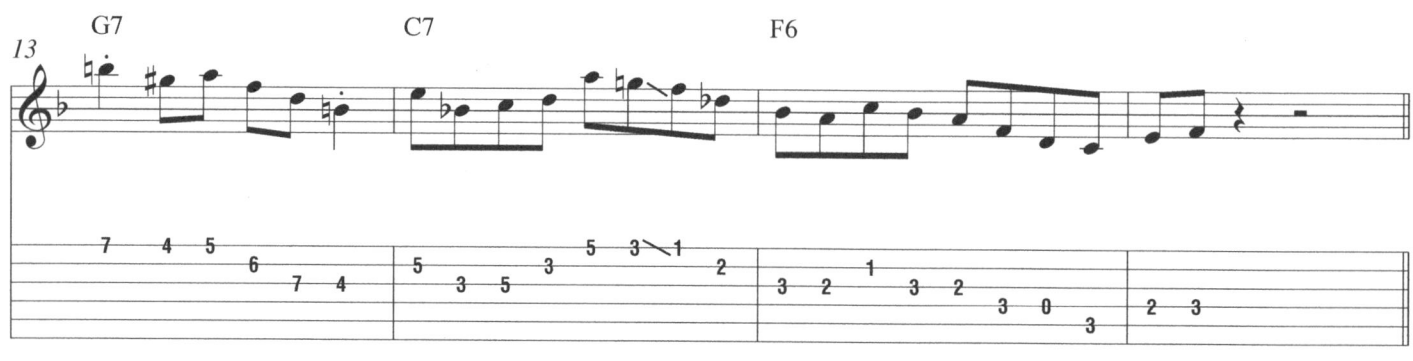

Words and Music by Jack Palmer and Spencer Williams
Copyright © 1926 UNIVERSAL MUSIC CORP.
Copyright Renewed
All Rights Reserved   Used by Permission

I've Found a New Baby

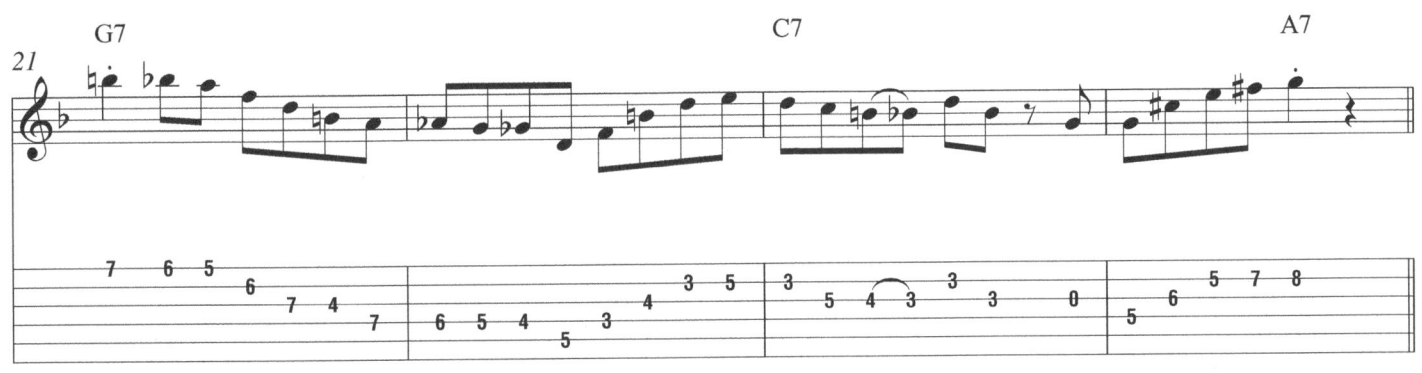

Embraceable You 1944

Oscar Moore

"He had one of the greatest harmonic conceptions of any guitarist I've ever heard."

—Kenny Burrell (on Oscar Moore)

© Ray Avery CTSImages

In 1937, a young Nat King Cole put together a drummer-less trio in Los Angeles with himself on piano (and occasional vocal) along with bass and guitar. The intimate but swinging sound of this particular lineup was a new thing for most listeners and caught on with jazz aficionados and the general public alike. The bassist was Wesley Prince—the guitarist, Oscar Moore. Through his ten years in the limelight with the King Cole Trio, Moore set the standard for tasty guitar playing in this kind of small-group setting, shifting seamlessly from accompaniment to solo roles while always augmenting the delivery of the song.

Oscar Frederic Moore was born on December 25, 1912 in Austin, Texas and began learning guitar as a child.

Jumpin' at Capitol *offers an excellent sampling of the many fine sessions Moore played with the Nat King Cole Trio from 1943–1947.*

By the age of 18, he was playing professionally in the company of his older brother Johnny throughout the Southwest. After moving to Los Angeles in the mid-1930s, Oscar picked up good work in the recording studios and played with the likes of vibraphone great Lionel Hampton and piano virtuoso Art Tatum before joining Nat's trio (originally the King Cole Swingsters).

Taking some influence from both contemporary innovator Charlie Christian and early jazz guitarist Eddie Lang, Moore went his own route in exploring the various textures required of his instrument in the trio (going electric in 1941). He was needed alternately to play driving four-to-the-bar rhythm guitar, short fills either together with or independently from the piano, sustained chords that would mesh with the piano for a lush timbral blend, and improvised solos (often with a very limited span of the tune in which to make his statement). He did each of these beautifully in a manner that spoke at once of a swing era aesthetic and of his own unique, forward-looking approach, perfectly fitting the format of the group all the while.

The King Cole Trio enjoyed growing success on stage, on the air, and in record sales, signing with Capitol Records by 1943 (now with Johnny Miller on bass) and creating a long line of hits—from Cole's original "Straighten Up and Fly Right" through such iconic performances as "Route 66" and "The Christmas Song" (the latter with the addition of strings). This period brought much attention to the fine playing of Moore, who won awards from *Metronome* and *Esquire* magazines in addition to top honors as a guitarist in the *DownBeat* Readers Poll four years in a row (1945–1948). He influenced younger players like Barney Kessel and Kenny Burrell and saw the publication of a transcription book based on the trio recordings (*Oscar Moore Guitar Solos*, Capitol Songs, 1946).

Embraceable You

By 1947, an increasingly popular Cole wanted more singular control of the venture on the business end and was soon to head in a more commercial musical direction altogether. Moore left (Irving Ashby being his notable replacement) and reunited with his brother, together with pianist/singer Charles Brown, in Johnny Moore's Three Blazers. This group, of similar makeup to the Cole trio (though with more of an R&B bent), had some hit records of its own but soon faltered after Brown left to pursue a solo career. Moore continued doing Los Angeles studio work in the early 1950s and eventually made a few records under his own name. These included *Oscar Moore Quartet* (a 1954 10" LP), featuring West Coast pianist Carl Perkins and alternately involving drum set or bongos, and the classy but quizzical *Presenting Oscar Moore* (1957), a duo effort with bassist Leroy Vinnegar and overdubbed guitar accompaniment, initially released only on reel-to-reel tape.

But by and large, Moore's career would fade following his departure from Cole, and after 1957 he would not record again until asked back into the studio to make *We'll Remember You, Nat* (1965), a guitar-piano-and-bass tribute album to his old bandleader, who had just passed on. In his later years, Moore worked as a bricklayer in Los Angeles, and he passed away himself on October 8, 1981, an underrated figure in the development of jazz guitar.

How to Play It

Though recorded shortly after the time of Charlie Christian's work, Oscar Moore has his feet a bit further back in the swing era with this beautiful interlude on the Gershwin ballad. Soloing on the first half of the song's chord progression (after a one-and-a-half-bar pickup), he gracefully mixes guitaristic slides and bends, pretty chordal arpeggios, both ballad and swung rhythms, and profuse references to the melody.

His very first phrase echoes the shape of the vocal line on the words "my sweet embraceable you" (especially where they first occur in the song). The repeated-note motif at the end of this—heard in the three C notes early in the first full pickup measure—is taken up again and again throughout his solo (usually preceded by a higher note), reflecting the frequent appearance of this melodic shape in the song itself. From the last half of measure 9 into measure 10, he plays as if singing along on his guitar to the corresponding part of the tune ("just one look at you"). He similarly quotes the melody again in measure 13 ("you and you alone").

Key to playing this solo successfully, or appreciating it fully, is a recognition of the sensitive touch used to create dynamic contrast and the patient pacing that results in a very song-like use of space. Play softly through parts such as the end of measure 3 or the beginning of measure 7, saving some emphasis for spots like the first note of measure 6 or the quick back-and-forth slide in measure 8 (also, at this last point, be prepared to jump up the fretboard!). Notice how Moore often brings a phrase to a complete conclusion, leaving real breathing room before the next idea, as in the beginning of measure 4 or the end of measure 5.

Chordal arpeggios figure prominently in Moore's solo. His 16th notes in the last half of measure 4 build an $E°7$, which here is essentially the same as $C7♭9$ without the root. Two measures earlier, through the first half of measure 2, he gets away remarkably well with tones of $Cm7$ over the official $G♭°7$ chord in the progression (indeed, either of these chords could function as a transition from the previous $E♭6$ to the upcoming $Fm7$). Most of measure 5 is filled with $Fm7$ tones, and the first chunk of measure 6 (through the second $C♭$) consists of $D♭9$ chordal members. The sweep-picked G minor triad found in measures 7 and 11—really part of an $E♭maj7$ arpeggio—is a romantic touch that exemplifies the ballad-playing flavor of the era.

The arpeggio figure that begins with the dramatic slide in measure 8, running through the next two beats and into measure 9, is particularly interesting. Besides its sudden attack and jagged shape (which requires some good mapping out of your fingering on the fretboard), its note content brings out a typical harmonic coloration of the times. After the first five 16th notes outline a $B°7$ chord (part of $G7♭9$), and the $E♭$ that follows turns our $G7$ into an augmented chord, we hear the striking appearance of $A♮$ towards the end of this measure and just into the next. By the time Cm is at hand, landing on this lower A brings out a color tone of the chord, the 6th. But the anticipation of this sound at the end of measure 8 gives the effect of the $G7$ having a natural 9th instead of flatted 9th, which would be unusual for a later jazz soloist when leading thusly from a dominant to a minor chord.

Embraceable You

(Charlie Christian often used a similar approach—see his treatment of A7 chords on "I've Found a New Baby.") Also noteworthy regarding this phrase is that Moore actually plays it earlier in the same recording, prior to the guitar solo, as a fill between Nat's vocal phrases. He shows here that he is drawing heavily on some "pet licks," both in terms of such recurring ideas, and by the repeated use of one particular string bend throughout this performance (F# on string 2 bent efficiently up to G).

Rhythmically, he picks his way through the leisurely tempo with a degree of relaxed looseness and various basic divisions of the beat. The eighth-note triplets, especially with the quarter-plus-eighth rhythm found at the end of measure 1 and elsewhere, give the impression of a slow swung-eighth-notes texture, while even eighths, such as those at the end of measure 3, settle calmly into the ballad rhythm. The swung 16ths in measures 4, 8, and 14 give a momentary suggestion of double-time feel.

A particularly pretty—and tricky—spot in this solo is his brief chordal excursion in measure 12, in which he slides up on the first string into a D—and then further to E♭ and back to D again—while strumming the rest of a rootless Cm6/9 chord on the three strings below before sounding Cm6, Cm7, and F7♭9 (these latter two also rootless). This takes a firm attack on the B♭ at the end of measure 11, with the pinky sliding up from it strongly into the next notes on string 1. As the pinky reaches the D, the index and middle fingers fret the notes on strings 2, 3, and 4, and the picking hand carefully strums through those three strings alone.

Vital Stats

Guitarist: Oscar Moore
Song: "Embraceable You"
Album: Capitol single 20009, 1944 (recorded 1943)—King Cole Trio (*Jumpin' at Capitol: The Best of the Nat King Cole Trio,* 1990)
Age at Time of Recording: 30
Guitar: Gibson L-5 with bar (Charlie Christian) pickup
Amp: Gibson EH-150

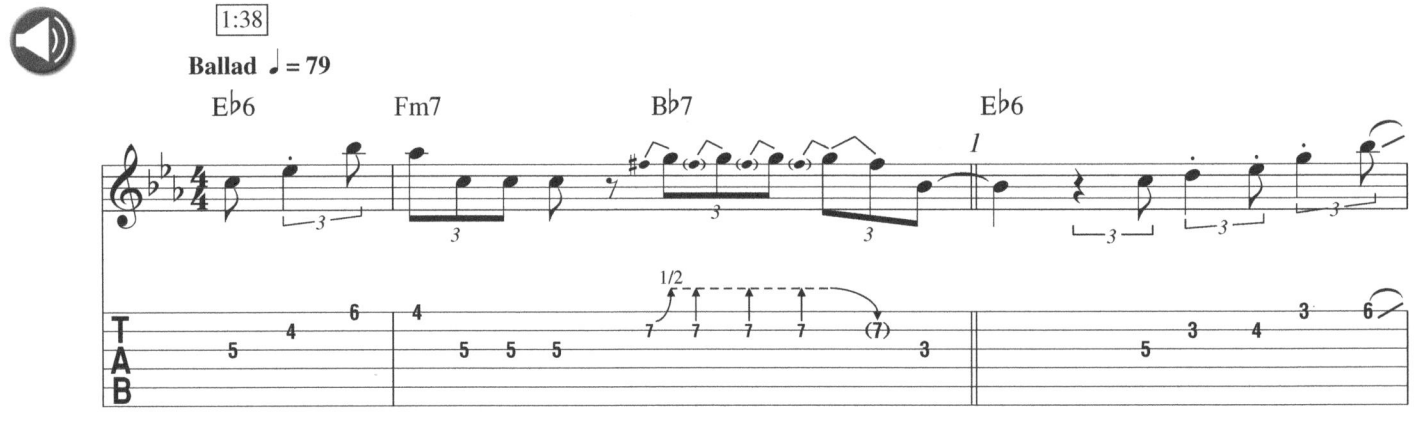

*Played as swung 16th notes.

Music and Lyrics by George Gershwin and Ira Gershwin
© 1930 (Renewed) WB MUSIC CORP.
All Rights Reserved   Used by Permission

Embraceable You

The World Is Waiting for the Sunrise 1949

Django Reinhardt

Django. To many ardent followers, the very name implies a whole genre of music. He holds a unique place in jazz, having blended it with the sounds of the Romani (commonly known as Gypsy) culture from which he came and, together with the Quintette du Hot Club de France, having created the first—and arguably biggest—European contribution to this American art form. He preceded Charlie Christian and the age of amplification in demonstrating single-note guitar virtuosity, and his fiery melodicism has inspired generations of players, including Christian, Joe Pass, and Wes Montgomery—whether or not they directly emulated his style.

On January 23, 1910, Jean "Django" Reinhardt was born in Liberchies, Belgium. His family moved around quite a bit through his early childhood, after which he grew up in various encampments outside of Paris. Here he learned on his own to play violin, banjo, guitar, and *banjo guitar* (a hybrid of the two), influenced stylistically by elder musicians within the Gypsy community and performing professionally by his teen years. His fledgling career had seemed to be going alright when, on the night of November 2, 1928, a fire broke out in the caravan he shared with his pregnant wife. She escaped unharmed, while he suffered massive burns, almost completely losing the use of his left-hand ring finger and pinky and nearly a leg as well. He had a long and painful recovery (during which it took him a year to even walk again) and began to retrain himself on the guitar—incredibly using only the index and middle fingers to fret his blazing melodic runs and the other digits only sparingly to assist with his rich, driving chordal work.

Photo by William P. Gottlieb / Courtesy Library of Congress

He also soon discovered jazz and was particularly inspired by the music of Louis Armstrong, as well as the work of Duke Ellington and the playing of guitarist Eddie Lang and his violin cohort Joe Venuti. On the Parisian scene of the early 1930s, he met his own musical soulmate in French jazz violinist Stéphane Grappelli, and in 1934 they formed the Quintette. From then until 1939, the group would record prolifically and tour Europe and Britain—its most popular and influential incarnation

> *"Django Reinhardt was the greatest guitarist that ever lived."*
> —Les Paul

The World Is Waiting for the Sunrise

Reunited in early 1949 for an Italian tour, Django and Grappelli recorded these last cuts together in Rome with local musicians Gianni Safred on piano, Carlo Pecori on bass, and Aurelio De Carolis on a lone snare drum.

involving a lineup of three acoustic guitars (one of them played by Django's brother, Joseph "Nin-Nin" Reinhardt), bass, and violin. Drawing on American standards like "Dinah" and "Honeysuckle Rose," as well as original tunes such as "Djangology" and "Tears," they combined chunky swing rhythm with a European romanticism and produced the seminal sounds of gypsy jazz (or *jazz manouche*, with a reference to a French branch of the Romani people). Reinhardt also worked with vocalists such as Jean Sablon and visiting American jazz greats like saxophonists Benny Carter and Coleman Hawkins.

The quintet was in England when World War II broke out in Europe, and Grappelli stayed in Britain, while Reinhardt hurried back to France, which fell under German occupation the next year. The Nazis officially frowned on jazz and lethally persecuted the Roma along with the Jews, but Django and his music managed to survive. Some German officers were fans and offered a degree of conditional protection to the culture and its musicians. During this time, he reformed the Quintette with a clarinet in place of violin (and drums in place of a third guitar), wrote some of his most famous tunes (including the dreamy "Nuages" and "Manoir de mes Rêves"—a.k.a. "Django's Castle"), and enjoyed a high degree of popularity. He also remarried and saw the birth of his son Babik, who would become a prominent guitarist in his own right. And yet, his situation was precarious, and at times he moved around with his family to ensure their safety, even trying to escape the country.

After the war, Reinhardt reconnected with Grappelli, and in late 1946 left for a U.S. tour with Duke Ellington. He was warmly received by a Carnegie Hall audience and befriended by American fans and fellow guitarists such as Les Paul, Barney Kessel, Remo Palmieri, and Johnny Smith. However, the venture was plagued by guitar troubles (in the absence of his own special Selmer acoustic), the falling-through of West Coast bookings, and a lower level of notoriety than he was expecting, and this would be his only trip to the States. Back in France, Django fell more than ever into erratic, free-wheeling ways, often disappearing when it was time for a show. Still, he played with various groups, dabbled in electric guitar, appreciated the bebop innovations of Charlie Parker and Dizzy Gillespie, and made special appearances with Armstrong and Gillespie. In 1951, he settled in the little village of Samois-sur-Seine, from which he could easily go fishing or make a gig in Paris. Sadly, he died in 1953 of a brain hemorrhage shortly after collapsing outside his home.

He has been lovingly memorialized by, among so many other things, the jazz standard "Django," written by pianist John Lewis and originally recorded by the Modern Jazz Quartet (without a guitar even on the session). His most direct influence is seen today in the ever more popular sub-genre of gypsy jazz and in the work of current guitarists like Frank Vignola, Martin Taylor, and Biréli Lagrène (himself of Manouche Romani heritage). But the impulse of his spirited style still echoes through the worlds of guitar, jazz, and modern music altogether.

How to Play It

In a good ol', Hot Club-style, up-tempo, swingin' romp, Django burns through two choruses of this joyous 32-bar standard. His solo, full of cookin' eighth-note runs that outline the chords with much the same approach as his American jazz counterparts, is also replete with decorative elements of his own. He hits the ground running, taking off from a chromatic turn in his pickup measure (enclosing the principal note G with tones a half step away on either side) into a rapid scalar ascent. The following phrases in measures 5–8 show some European flair, with their expressive (though not necessarily jazz-derived) timing and a particular flavor of hammer-on/pull-off embellishments.

Given Django's permanent injuries on his fretting hand, any of the linear material here is, of necessity, playable even while using only the index and middle fingers. But most of us will do well to use more of our available digits! In order to

The World Is Waiting for the Sunrise

achieve his extraordinary ratio of facility to fingers, he had to become extra-adept at quick stretches and changes of position, repeated use of one finger along a string, and even diagonal motion of a finger (from one string to the neighboring fret on the next, as could be used between the second and third notes of measure 10). He often favored diagonal fretboard patterns, such as the shape that develops from measure 9 into measure 10, or even more so from the end of measure 14 to the start of measure 16. Sometimes, there could actually be a technical advantage for the rest of us in playing such patterns with the same physical limitations. For example, in the similar diagonal climb of measure 47, if we use the middle finger for the last note on each string (as opposed to ring or pinky), the index finger is more easily ready for its spot on the next string.

In any case, much of this solo is indeed fast and technically demanding, and nothing beats slow, careful practice to get your fingerings down initially. If you are aiming for an authentic Django sound and playing on an acoustic, an instrument with a cutaway is very helpful for reaching the upper frets with sufficient agility (especially in spots like measure 42). "Gypsy jazz" guitars per se are designed along the lines of the Selmer Maccaferri he used. These are widely available on the market today and heavily favored by many devotees of the style. But even on a conventional steel-string, you can try picking close to the bridge for a more Django-esque tone.

In measures 49–56, he beautifully demonstrates an important aesthetic skill for improvisers of any stripe: how to play something slow in a fast-tempo setting. Here, his sparse lines float languorously over the band's driving quarter-note pulse with plenty of breathing space in between. He ultimately lays way back behind the beat for the last phrase of this section before rejoining the vigorous pace of the prevailing rhythm. The timing and feel of these slower gestures is just as important to the overall flavor of the solo as the speed of all the eighth-note runs.

The melodic content here shows a mixture of approaches and stylistic impulses along the way. Chordal arpeggiation is frequently used to very plainly fit the harmonic progression, with Fmaj9 traced in measure 9, Cmaj7 in measure 11, a Dm triad in measure 41 (fits Fmaj quite neatly), and a Cmaj triad in measures 43 and 49. The double-stop gesture of measures 23–24 brings out E7 in a classic, old-school manner, the diminished scale material of measure 47 implies a G7♭9, and the A♭ at the ends of measures 42 and 58 highlights the change to Fm. The descent of measures 45–46, as well as the slower climb of measures 53–54, gets more chromatic and invokes some of the flavor of Reinhardt's Manouche background. More striking yet in that vein are the passionate chromatic decorations and pronounced vibrato of measures 34–37. His landing on the ♭5th tone of E7 at the end of measure 55 is reminiscent of bebop usage, while inflections of the blues (less of an at-home territory for Django than for most jazzers) are heard clearly in the bendy, blue-note-laden closing phrase of measures 61–63 and also in the note choice of measures 29–32.

He announces the conclusion of his feature with two startling hits on a C9 chord (remember that he would often actually use a disabled finger to assist with chords), preceded briefly by some stopped-string rhythm.

Vital Stats

Guitarist: Django Reinhardt
Song: "The World Is Waiting for the Sunrise"
Album: *Djangology* (2002) [CD Release—original LP did not have this track from 1949]
Age at Time of Recording: 39
Guitar: Selmer Maccaferri
Amp: none

The World Is Waiting for the Sunrise

Words by Eugene Lockhart
Music by Ernest Seitz
Copyright © 2015 by HAL LEONARD CORPORATION
International Copyright Secured   All Rights Reserved

The World Is Waiting for the Sunrise

Lullaby of Birdland 1953

Barney Kessel

"I don't want people to say, 'That guy plays a lot of guitar,'... I want them to say, 'Barney Kessel really made me feel good.'"
—Barney Kessel

One night in 1940, 16-year-old Barney Kessel was playing a gig on electric guitar at an Oklahoma City dance hall 150 miles from his hometown of Muskogee. He had heard the legend of Charlie Christian through older musicians in the area who knew the great soloist in his formative years. And he had heard Christian's musical message through Benny Goodman recordings, such as "Flying Home," becoming enthralled and obsessed with the revolutionary improvisations of his fellow Oklahoman guitarist. He looked up to see his hero, visiting home during a break from the Goodman band, watching him play. Over the next few days, the two would get together to jam and to talk music, leaving young Barney with invaluable impressions of the early electric genius and direct advice from the master on how to carry on the craft.

Born October 17, 1923, Kessel became indeed the first major disciple of Christian's style, maintaining the insistently swinging feeling, but ultimately adding to it a high degree of the newly developed bop language and a rounded approach to guitar that involved beautiful chord-melody and accompaniment work in addition to his solo lines. Over the course of his extensive career, he played with a veritable who's-who list of jazz greats and of pop music icons as well. He struck out on his own for Los Angeles while still in his late teens and by and by made the scene, touring and recording in the mid-1940s with the bands of Chico Marx (of Marx Brothers fame), Les Brown, Charlie Barnet, Artie Shaw (in both his Orchestra and the more improv-heavy Gramercy Five group), and Christian's old boss Benny Goodman.

At the invitation of jazz promoter Norman Granz, he appeared in the 1944 short film *Jammin' the Blues* alongside such giants as tenor sax man Lester Young and trumpeter Harry "Sweets" Edison. He was the only white member of the band on this occasion, as had often been the case for him while coming up in Oklahoma, but here his "appearance" was obscured in shadow to disguise that fact (at the insistence of the studio). In 1947, he played

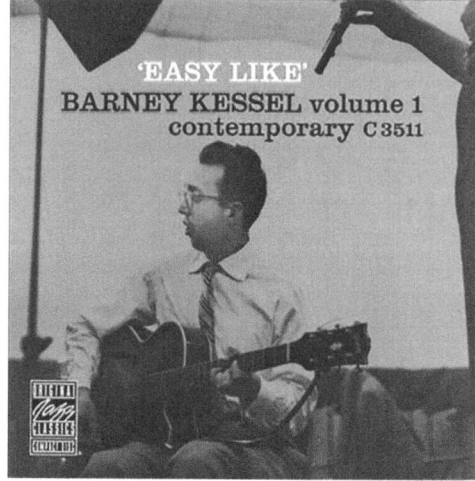

The original 1954 10" LP Barney Kessel Vol. 1, comprised of his earliest cuts as a leader from late 1953, was soon re-released as a 12" with the addition of tracks from a 1956 small-group session and given the subtitle Easy Like.

Lullaby of Birdland

on a noteworthy Los Angeles session led by bebop luminary Charlie Parker for Dial Records, on which the great alto saxophonist's famous tune "Relaxin' at Camarillo" was introduced. After some time sticking mostly to studio work at home in L.A., he went on the road again to tour from 1952 to 1953 with the Oscar Peterson Trio—and along with it, Granz's *Jazz at the Philharmonic* show—replacing Irving Ashby and preceding Herb Ellis in the piano virtuoso's drummer-less group, which included top-flight bassist Ray Brown.

In 1953, Kessel began making a string of recordings as a leader on the Contemporary label which would cement his reputation as an all-time superstar of jazz guitar. Prettily played standards, such as "Tenderly" and "That's All," were mixed in with cookin' originals like "Vicky's Theme" and appropriately, "Salute to Charlie Christian." He also made a widely acclaimed series of late-1950s trio records with Brown on bass and Shelly Manne on drums, under the name the Poll Winners (reflecting the *DownBeat* and *Playboy* jazz polls they had each in fact just won). These would help set the norm for generations of guitarists in such a trio setting, in which their instrument covers virtually all chordal and melodic duties.

Meanwhile, his general recording career took off. Among his jazz-oriented credits, he appeared on numerous titles by vocal great Billie Holiday, laid down the famous accompaniment to singer Julie London's million-selling 1955 rendition of "Cry Me a River," took part in Ella Fitzgerald's revered *Songbook* sessions in the late 1950s, and joined tenor sax legend Sonny Rollins for 1958's *Sonny Rollins and the Contemporary Leaders*.

By the beginning of the 1960s, his output was interspersed with jazz-lite theme albums like *Kessel Plays Carmen* and *Breakfast at Tiffany's*. Throughout the decade, he was part of the elite set of first-call studio musicians that came to be known as "The Wrecking Crew," and as such, played guitar and electric bass on innumerable pop records and soundtracks for film and television, occasionally having a hand in the composing and arranging duties as well. He worked in this capacity with names like Elvis Presley, the Beach Boys, the Monkees, the Righteous Brothers, and producer Phil Spector, and on TV shows such as *Star Trek* and *Perry Mason*.

Gibson honored him in 1961 by issuing a Barney Kessel signature model—a double-cutaway electric archtop—but it didn't catch on very well with the guitar-buying public or with its namesake (neither did an earlier Kessel model made by Kay) and was discontinued in the early 1970s.

He teamed up with good friends and fellow guitar veterans Herb Ellis and Charlie Byrd to form the Great Guitars in 1973 (with the additional support of bass and drums), a format in which they would continue to perform and record into the 1980s. On his own albums such as 1969's *Feeling Free* and 1988's *Red Hot and Blues*, he continued to explore new territory, bringing in more modern sidemen like vibraphonist Bobby Hutcherson, drummer Elvin Jones, and pianist Kenny Barron. A stroke in 1992 ended his playing career; he died of a brain tumor on May 6, 2004.

How to Play It

In his energetic, swingin', two-chorus outing on George Shearing's classic tune, Kessel mixes a high degree of standard diatonic material (that is, fitting neatly into major, minor, or related scales) with more blues-inspired gestures. This contrast is apparent right within the first eight-bar section of the solo, along with a few other key aspects of his improvisational approach: repetition or development of melodic shapes, bop-styled outlining of the chord changes through largely eighth-note lines, and not being shy about getting a little on top of the beat or giving the strings a good thwack with the pick!

The song is fundamentally in A♭ major, even though the chords at the start of each A-section strongly suggest the relative key of F minor. He plays through the first two measures with tones from an F melodic minor scale, executing a line that highlights the movement of the note F to an E♮ as G7 heads to C7. This is the motion of a chordal 7th to the 3rd of the next chord within a circle-of-fifths type of progression (wherein the chord roots move down in perfect 5ths, as in G to C to F, etc.)—a staple of melodic movement through standard changes. Like so many straight-ahead jazz soloists, Kessel uses this 7th-to-3rd harmonic transition again and again, whether indirectly (as in measure 2, with the D in between these tones) or directly (as in the middle of measure 4, with the A♭ of B♭m7 leading straight to the G of E♭7). But in measures 5–8 he takes a different tack entirely, as he slides into or out of a ♭3rd tone (shown here alternately as B♮ or C♭) on top of the

Lullaby of Birdland

chiefly A♭ major tonality, infusing his solo with a twangier sound and simulating the bendy-ness of the blues. Note that Kessel himself was insistent on the use of the ear rather than on theory while improvising, as are many great jazz musicians. Our analysis is an after-the-fact look at what makes these lines work.

The very first tones of the solo are echoed at the end of measure 2 and again at the end of measure 24, where in each case another phrase starts with a similar pickup before continuing in its own direction. Kessel is fond of building on a melodic motif in this way, such that many a musical idea seems to be reflected or answered by the next one (if not further down the line). We see this also from the end of measure 8 through the first half of measure 12, where he follows the first pair of short phrases with another pair, using nearly the same two melodic shapes but higher notes from within F melodic minor. He then begins the bridge of his first chorus with a repeating four-note pattern that nearly fills measures 17–19, constantly shifting downwards in pitch with the notes changing to reflect the chords (notice how the notes A, C, G♭, E♭, and F that appear in measure 17 represent the 3rd, 5th, ♭9th, 7th, and root, respectively, of the F7♭9 chord, with other chords receiving similar treatment). By the end of this chorus, he is full throttle back into bluesy territory, throwing in plenty of blues scale references with the ♭3rd, ♭7th, and "blue note" D♮ interspersed among tones of A♭ major in measures 28–31, all in a snappy, punctuated rhythm.

Kessel then ups the excitement with a device that nearly turns his small group into a little big band: a four-bar chord-melody figure he uses at the beginning of each of his three remaining A-sections (at measures 33, 41, and 57) to create a "shout" chorus, giving himself a *sendoff* for the improvised lines in between, as the horns of a larger group might do for a soloist. He plays it a little loosely in the spirit of the moment, with the downstrokes and upstrokes of typical right-hand strumming motion and without 100% of the same tones sounded every time. But an important technical tip for playing it in each instance is to leave the middle finger and pinky on strings 3 and 2, respectively, during the Fm7 parts (most of the first and third measures of the figure).

Along the way through this second chorus, we hear more of the blues flavor with his insistent repeated sliding into a double stop in measures 45–46, and he gives us another classic example of repeated shapes through changing chords in the first half of the bridge (measures 49–52). Here the motif appears initially as the A♭–A♮–F–E♭ sequence used on F7, before being echoed with a uniform four-note pattern through the next three measures, starting with the C that leads into measure 50. The shape, easily visible on the fretboard, moves up with each chord change in such a way that its tones always fit neatly into the new harmony. Charlie Christian's home-state torch bearer wraps up his solo with a nice, simple, diatonic line leading down to an E♮ to go with the C7, which will propel us back into F minor territory as the next chorus begins.

Vital Stats

Guitarist: Barney Kessel

Song: "Lullaby of Birdland"

Album: *Vol. 1: Easy Like*, 1956 (recorded 1953)

Age at Time of Recording: 30

Guitar: 1940s Gibson ES-350 with Charlie Christian pickup

Amp: 1940s Gibson BR-3

Lullaby of Birdland

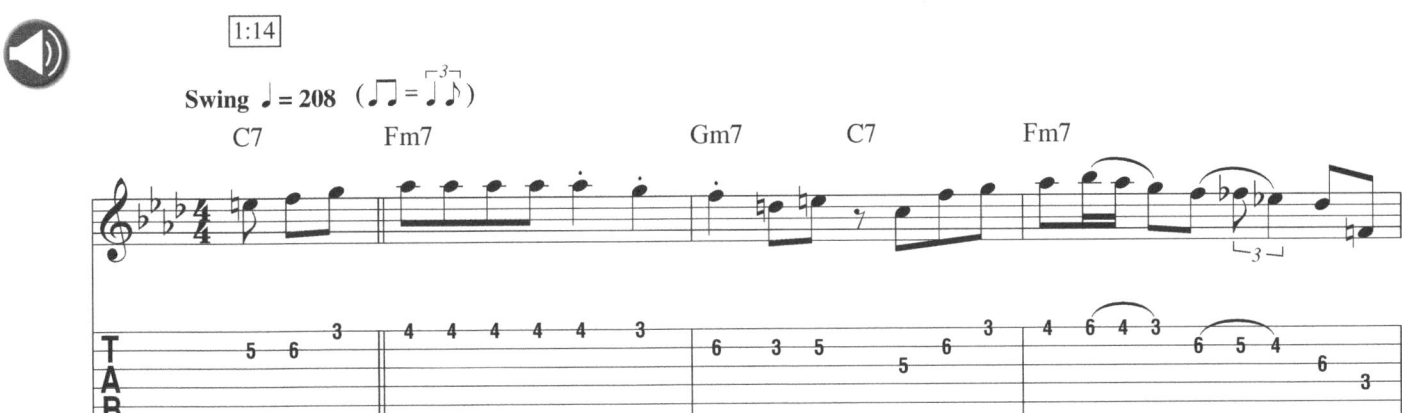

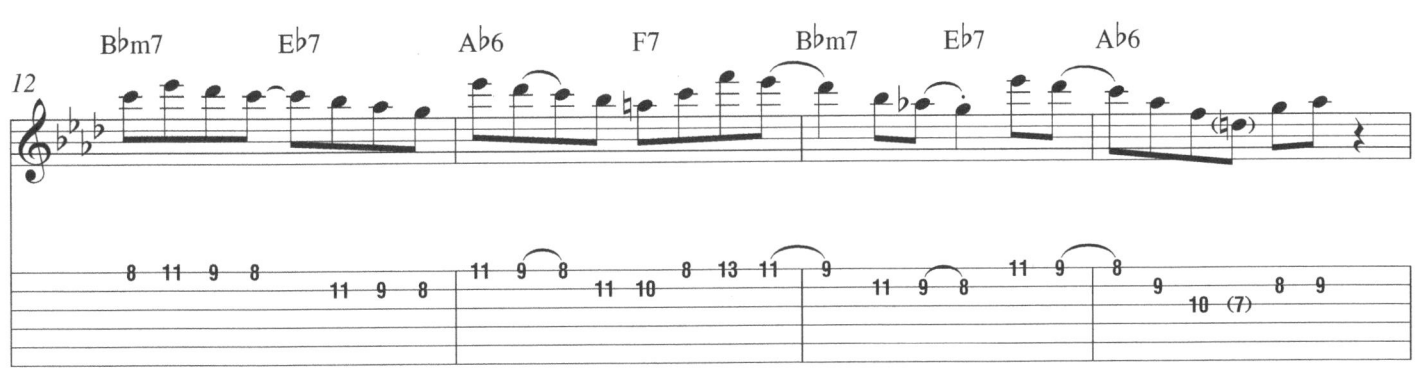

*Played behind the beat.

Words by George David Weiss
Music by George Shearing
© 1952, 1954 (Renewed 1980, 1982) EMI LONGITUDE MUSIC and ABILENE MUSIC LLC
All Rights for ABILENE MUSIC LLC Administered Worldwide by IMAGEM MUSIC LLC
All Rights Reserved International Copyright Secured Used by Permission

Lullaby of Birdland

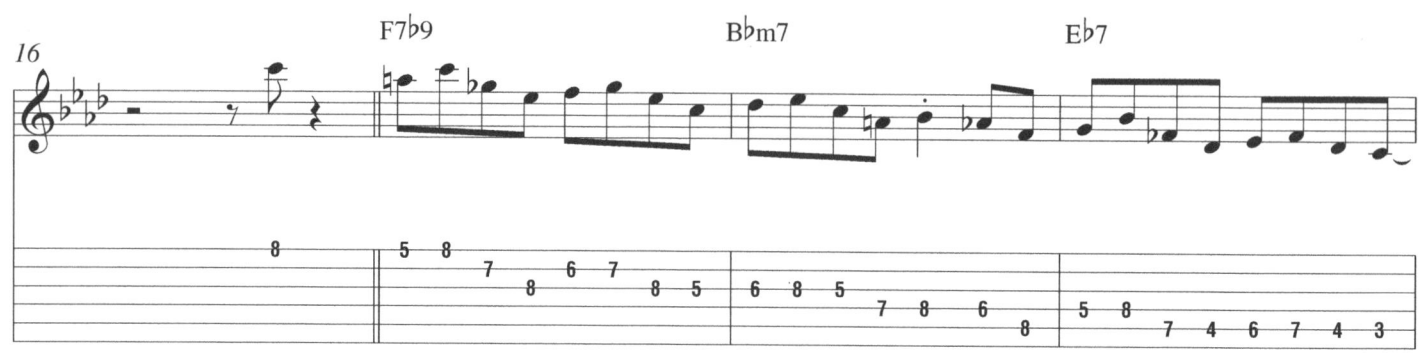
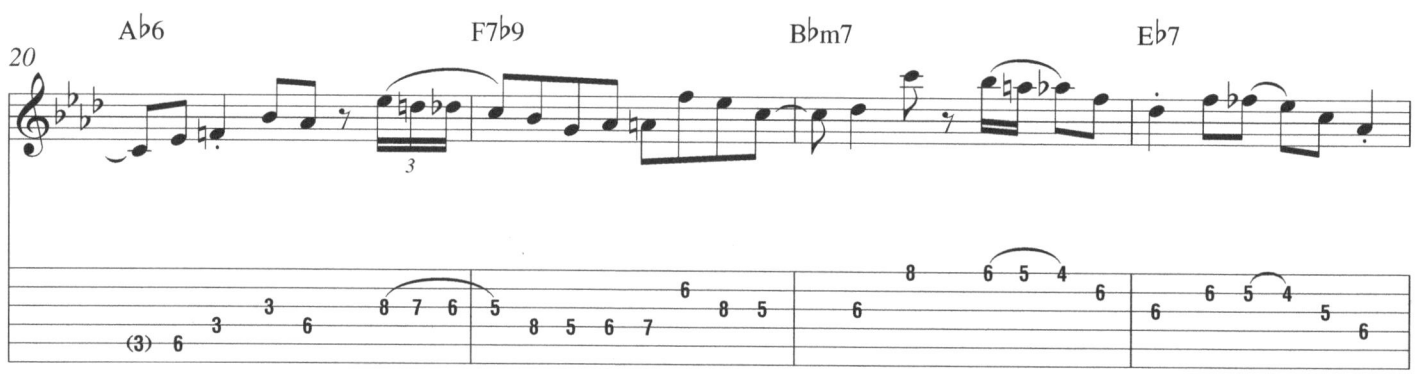
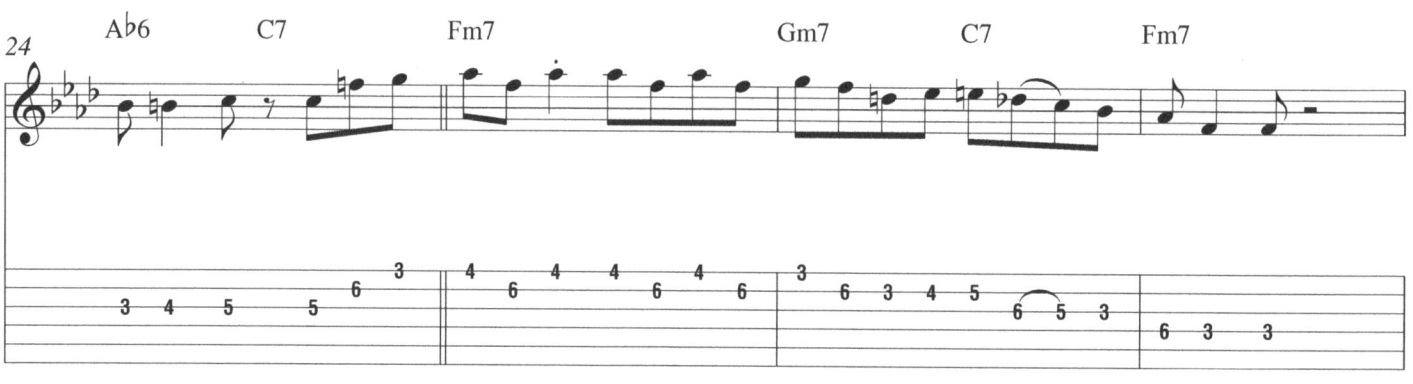
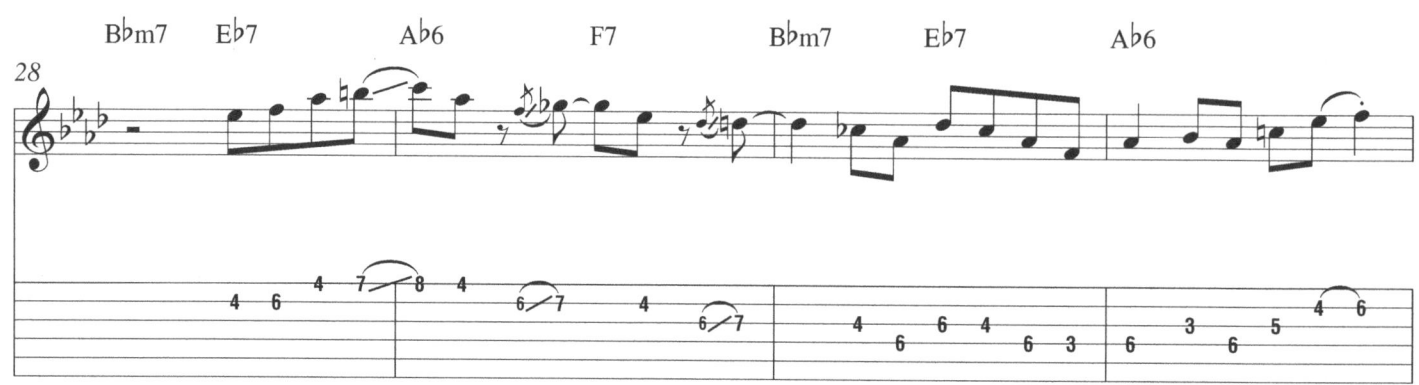

Lullaby of Birdland

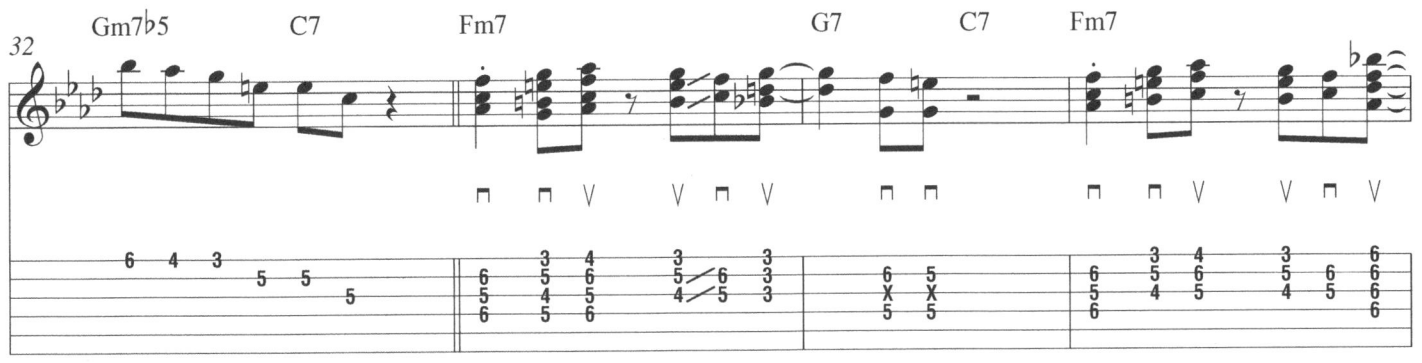

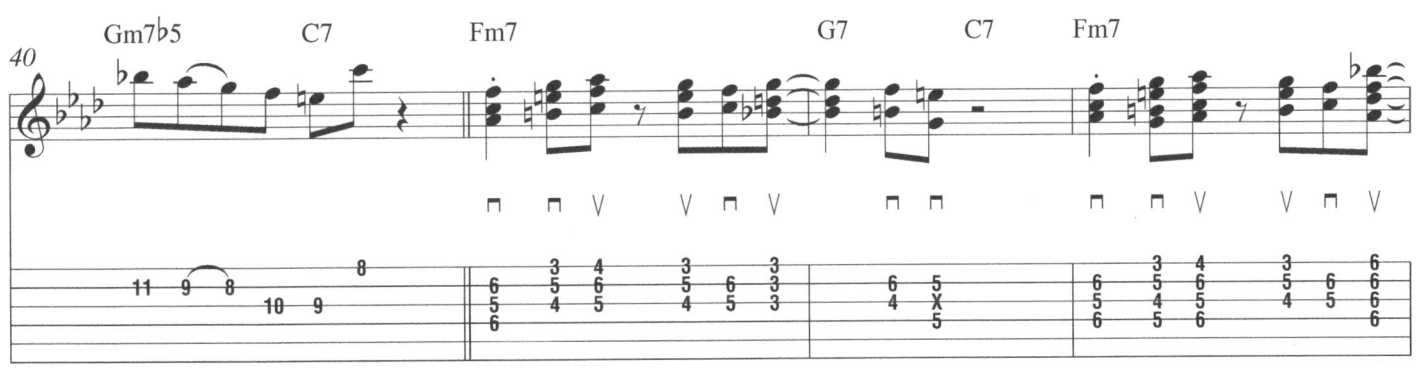
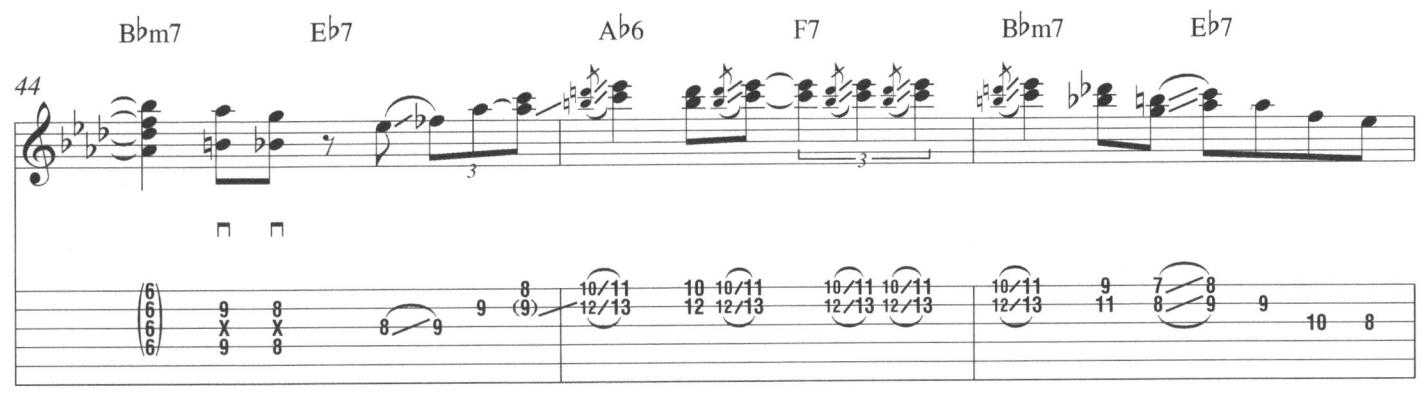

Lullaby of Birdland

Spring Is Here 1955

Jimmy Raney

© Burt Goldblatt Estate Archives CTSImages

Categories can be problematic in jazz, as in any artistic field. Jimmy Raney was one of the first major guitarists to be fully steeped in the language of alto saxophonist Charlie Parker, pianist Bud Powell, and other founders of the bebop movement and yet is considered by many the quintessential "cool school" player, belonging to a style marked by a mellower, laid-back approach. Indeed, while essentially playing bop lines in a bop setting, and certainly capable of digging in aggressively on his instrument, he brought a new degree of lyricism, relaxedness, silky-smooth tone, and subtlety to jazz guitar.

Hailing from Louisville, Kentucky, James Elbert Raney (born August 20, 1927) was one of many guitarists to experience a musical epiphany upon hearing the sound of Charlie Christian. As a young player on his first serious gig, with the big band of clarinetist Jerry Wald in 1944, he found a mentor and future collaborator in bandmate Al Haig (the early bop piano master) and got in-person exposure to the budding bebop scene in New York, including guitar innovators Chuck Wayne and Barney Kessel. After some further time cutting his teeth in Chicago, he moved back to New York long-term, joining the forward-looking Woody Herman band in 1948. He had better soloing opportunities the next year under bandleader Artie Shaw, but while still with Herman he formed a friendship with another great musical partner: then up-and-coming tenor saxophonist Stan Getz.

Getz was the perfect counterpart for Raney. Both were attuned to the phraseology of Charlie Parker and the like while preferring a softer-edged approach on their own instruments (Getz himself would often be labelled as a "cool" player). The quintet they formed in 1950 (under Getz's name, and initially with Haig on piano) was state-of-the-art, bringing Raney to widespread attention and serving as a model for small jazz groups with guitar in a largely second-horn kind of role. Their great recordings of 1951–1952 included tunes like the classic "The Song Is You" and the guitarist's cookin' original "Parker 51."

Raney played with the trio of vibraphonist Red Norvo from 1953 to 1954, following in the footsteps of his guitar buddy Tal Farlow (himself one of the vanguard of true bop guitarists, yet with a very different sound and feel). Also in 1953, he began making records under his own name, starting with *Jimmy Raney Plays*, a quintet date involving pianist Hall Overton (with whom he had begun composition studies) and Getz, who appeared in the credits as Sven Coolson

"You've gotta learn all that stuff, and then you gotta put it out of your mind when you're improvising… the best stuff comes from the instincts and the unconscious."

—Jimmy Raney

23

Spring Is Here

due to a conflicting contract. After a couple of early 1954 sessions from a European tour, he continued with *Jimmy Raney Quartet*, on which he made the unusual move of overdubbing a second guitar line on each melody, *Jimmy Raney Quintet* (the recording debut of alto sax great Phil Woods), and *Jimmy Raney: 1955*. These albums contained both beautifully played standards and creative original music and helped win him the *DownBeat* Critics Poll for guitar in 1954 and 1955.

Further into the 1950s, his notable recordings included work with trombonist Bob Brookmeyer and fellow guitarists Kenny Burrell and Jim Hall—the latter being a fellow pioneer of the introspective side of the instrument, with whom he'd record again in 1964—as well as his own classical- and jazz-influenced "Suite for Guitar Quintet" (not released until 1972 on *Strings and Swings*). He also held down a regular club gig, painted, and started playing cello. But from there into the 1960s, he wound up doing more commercial studio work and Broadway shows (which he largely did not enjoy) in order to get by and support a family. He resisted suggestions to commercialize his own music, became disheartened with the business, was more and more beset with the difficulties of alcoholism, and moved back to his native Louisville later in the decade.

Raney faded from the world scene for some years while trying to recover, but came back strongly in 1972 with acclaimed appearances in New York and eventually another string of excellent recordings, including the aptly titled *The Influence* (1975, with bassist Sam Jones and drummer Billy Higgins) and *Live in Tokyo* (1976, with Jones and drummer Leroy Butler). These would raise the bar for guitar trio performance, with the live album especially displaying more than ever his passionate side on its selection of standard tunes. Other releases from later years include *The Master* (1983), *Wisteria* (1985), and *But Beautiful* (1990), which find the influential master in a groove with his famous understated sound, a new degree of maturity, and more modern sidemen such as pianist Kirk Lightsey and bassist George Mraz. Towards the end of his career, he still managed to play at a high level despite a gradual but serious loss of hearing from Ménière's disease. He passed on due to heart failure on May 10, 1995.

Within his own family, Jimmy Raney took his initial plucked-string musical inspiration from his mother, an avid player of the ukulele, but he also passed it down in a big way: his son Doug (born 1956) is a fine and well-recognized jazz guitarist in his own right, having toured and recorded with his father—on *Stolen Moments* (1979) and *Raney '81*, among other titles—as well as creating a substantial discography as a leader himself, working with the likes of Kenny Barron, Joey DeFrancesco, and Chet Baker.

How to Play It

The tasteful, fluent melodiousness of Raney's style is exemplified in his graceful one-chorus statement on this Rodgers and Hart classic. In the two-bar solo break that follows the melody (prior to the top of the chorus), he begins with a line shaped around the tones of G6—one that could've come out of the Charlie Christian playbook—though delivered here with a mellower sound and a more subtly swinging feel. The flowing, legato approach continues with elements of elegance like the multi-note slur at the beginning of measure 2 and the very relaxed, non-sudden slide at the start of measure 5.

Notice how often Raney, when playing on or leading into a Gmaj chord of some sort, uses the note sequence E–E♭–D as part of his line, like we first hear at the end of the first pickup measure (the three notes in a row on string 2). There are many instances where he uses half-step motion in a similar way, which is characteristic of the bop language, but this particular chromatic move down from the 6th of the key (E) to the 5th (D) is the common gesture from which the *bebop major* scale was derived (a major scale with an extra tone between the 5th and 6th).

True to his bop orientation, he brings out the chord changes perfectly throughout his solo, and this is demonstrated nowhere

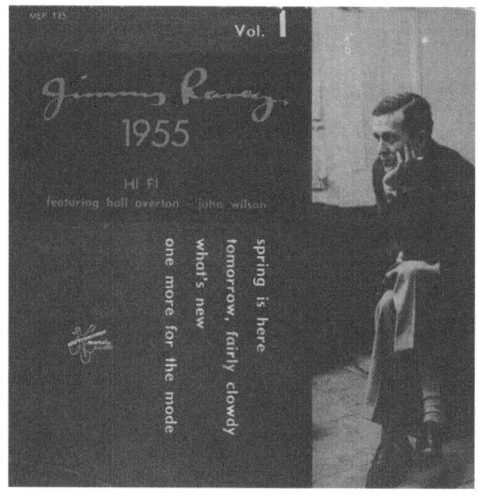

The 10" LP Jimmy Raney: 1955 *was made with a quintet featuring trumpeter John Wilson and pianist Hall Overton.*

Spring Is Here

better than in the long, well-developed phrase of measures 10–13. After encircling the tonic G with mostly step-wise motion through a G major scale in measure 10, he relates to the Am7 in measure 11 by traveling straight down and back up its chordal arpeggio (a favorite device of his) and then connecting to an exemplary minor ii–V–i idea over the F#m7b5–B7–Em7 sequence in measures 12–13. A couple of inadvertent double stops along the way only help to bring out the sound of the impending B7 with its chordal 3rd (D# on string 3 sounded below the principal note)! He accentuates the altered colorations of B7 by reaching C as his highest note (b9th) and moving into the F# (5th) from a half step below (b5th or #11th) at the end of measure 12. With this, his line takes on a plaintive songfulness and a Bach-like quality in its concluding shape.

Of special harmonic interest are the very first changes to "Spring Is Here." The song begins, in both halves of the form, with the particular repeated movement of a °7 chord to a major chord on the same root (the tonic of the key, G in this case). Raney's treatment of G°7 seems to imply an F# triad that resolves up a half step to G in the next measure—compare especially the end of measure 3 to an F# barre chord shape at the second fret. The tones on strings 3 and 2 here could be the 3rd and 5th degrees of either F# or G°7 (and could accordingly be called either A# and C#, or Bb and Db). If we add to them an F#, the tone found here on string 1, the F# major sound follows clearly enough—and we could consider this F# to be a major 7th added for color to the G°7. It could also be arrived at through use of the G whole-half diminished scale, which contains all the basic G°7 tones and then some.

Profuse arpeggio tones continue elsewhere in the solo, with a straight-up basic E7 chord spelled out in measure 23 landing on the 3rd of Am7 on beat 1 of the next measure. From here, we get a nice triplet figure that suggests F13#11 as a particular version of F7—compare the notes on beat 3 and immediately on either side of it to an F9#11 chord shape in the seventh position (or F13 in the same area). These tones could relate to Cm(maj9) as well, and indeed the harmonic move to F7 here is really akin to landing on Cm, the minor iv chord in the key. To play the beginning of this phrase, slide on string 3 with the middle finger and then roll onto string 2 with the flat part of that finger, leaving the index free to catch string 1, fret 7. You could substitute the ring finger on string 2 instead of rolling, but in any case the index should be free to get its note. Sweep picking is not necessary here, though we do need well-coordinated picking with a light enough touch.

In measure 27, Raney plays on the connection between A7 and Em7, with tones that seem based around an Em7 or Em9 shape rooted at the 7th fret, before sliding down to the fifth position for easy access to Am7 material. (This echoes the positioning he used, and the move he made, in measures 14–15.) Measure 28 consists purely of chord tones, as he heads straight down through an Am7 arpeggio and into D7 tones, including both the #9th and b9th, on string 2. Finally, he takes a bit of a left turn from all the harmonically specific vocabulary, throwing in some blues flavor in measures 29–30, to set up his conclusion—still in relatively gentle Jimmy Raney fashion.

Vital Stats

Guitarist: Jimmy Raney
Song: "Spring Is Here"
Album: *Jimmy Raney: 1955* (10" LP, 1955)
Age at Time of Recording: 27
Guitar: Gibson ES-150
Amp: Gibson EH-150

Spring Is Here

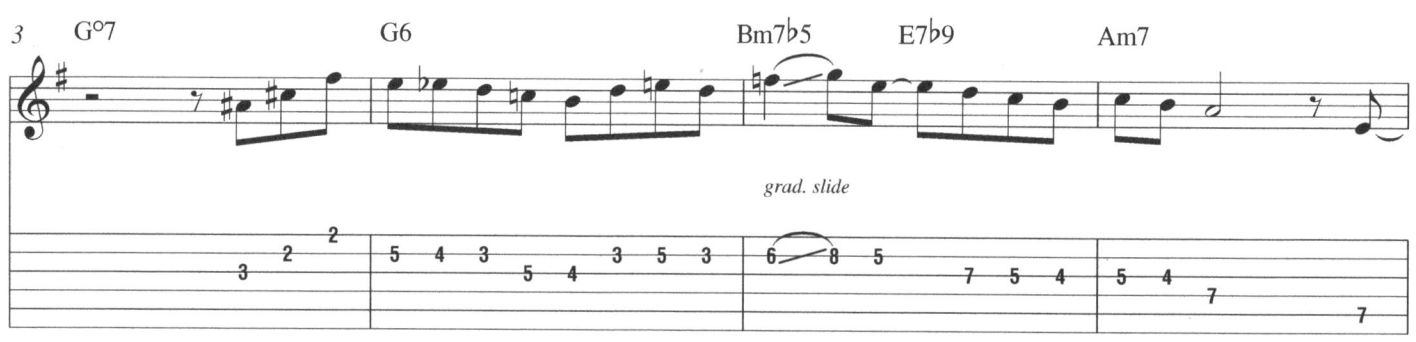
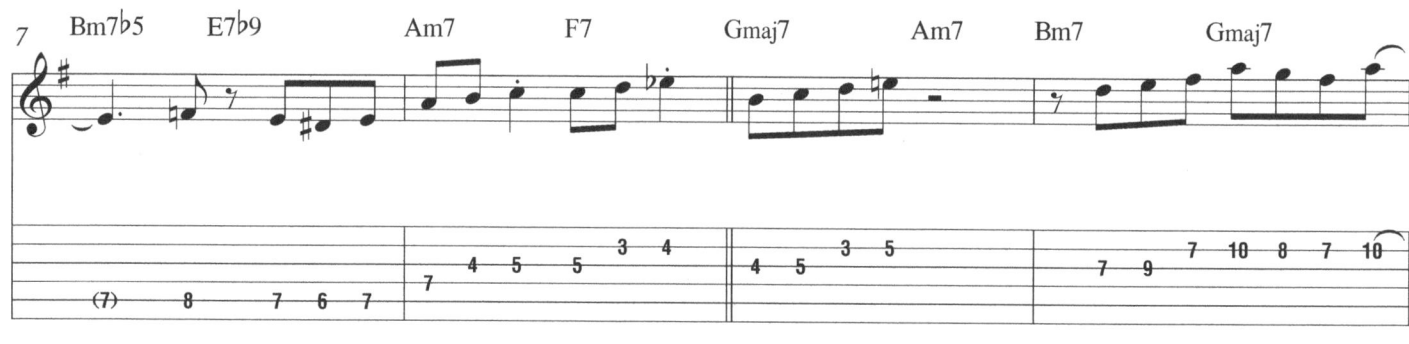

Words by Lorenz Hart
Music by Richard Rodgers
© 1938 (Renewed) EMI ROBBINS CATALOG INC.
All Rights Administered by EMI ROBBINS CATALOG INC. (Publishing) and ALFRED MUSIC (Print)
All Rights Reserved   Used by Permission

Spring Is Here

Like Someone in Love 1956

Tal Farlow

Arriving in mid-1940s New York City while on the gig with vibraphonist and pianist Dardanelle Breckenridge, a young Tal Farlow relished the chance to hear up close his heroes of the 52nd Street scene: bebop originators like Charlie Parker, Dizzy Gillespie, and Bud Powell. The newly flowering style of jazz was largely considered the dominion of horn players (despite the early contributions of Charlie Christian), and Farlow was in the forefront of adapting its harmonic language, melodic shapes, and aggressive playing attitude to the guitar.

At the dawn of that decade, Talmage Holt Farlow (born June 7, 1921) was working at a sign-painting shop in his hometown of Greensboro, North Carolina when he first heard Charlie Christian on the radio. Having grown up in a musical family, it was the discovery of the electric single-note-soloing pioneer that truly set him in motion towards a career in jazz. He acquired an electric guitar, an amp, and every Benny Goodman record with Christian on it that he could get, and set about learning his solos note for note (taking great inspiration also from tenor saxophonist Lester Young and piano god Art Tatum).

He spent some time on the Philadelphia scene after his early work with Dardanelle and got to New York again with vibraphonist/bandleader Marjorie Hyams in 1948. But he became known to the world—and came into his own as a player—with the trio of vibraphonist Red Norvo (yes, lots of vibraphone in his younger years!), initially from 1949 to 1953, together with Charles Mingus and later Red Mitchell on bass. The group was successful, the arrangements were tight, and the tempos were breakneck, forcing the guitarist to develop a speed he had never otherwise imagined. Certainly, his famous ability to play fast, quickly reaching all over the neck of the instrument, stemmed from his inner drive and his study of bop as well as from these efforts to keep up with the band. But it didn't hurt either that he had particularly long fingers, for which he earned the nickname "The Octopus." He had fine capabilities as an accompanist in addition to his mercurial improvisational skills, and especially in drummer-less ensembles would involve a percussive chording and tapping technique on the

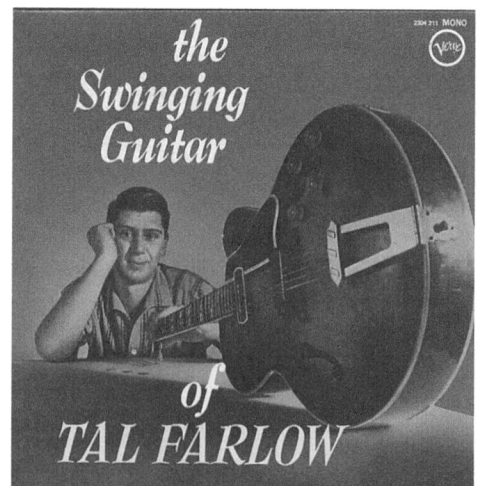

Farlow brought his own regular drummer-less trio into the studio for this May 1956 session with pianist Eddie Costa and bassist Vinnie Burke. His burnin' original "Meteor" is another highlight.

> "Tal's music came from his essence, which was unique and marvelous. There's really no other way to describe it."
> —Jim Hall

strings. After Norvo, he played briefly with clarinetist Artie Shaw's forward-looking Gramercy Five group.

Farlow's own albums of the 1950s solidified his place in jazz guitar history, starting with *The Tal Farlow Quartet* (a 1954 10" LP on Blue Note), on which he was joined by fellow guitarist Don Arnone. On the album, Tal delivers a mind-boggling solo on the blistering "Lover," as well as pretty harmonics on "Flamingo." He continued with releases on the Norgran/Verve label (mostly), among them *Autumn in New York, Poppin' and Burnin'*, and *The Swinging Guitar of Tal Farlow*. His career was taking off, and *DownBeat* awarded him their Critics Poll award for best guitarist in 1956 and 1957.

But he was fundamentally a modest person and averse to the hustle and bustle of the business—so much so that in 1958, with his fame and chops at a high point, he largely withdrew from New York and the world scene, settling with his wife Tina in coastal Sea Bright, New Jersey for a quieter life of continued sign-painting and local gigs (friend and fellow guitar luminary Johnny Smith would make a similar move around this time, though for more severe immediate reasons). Through the remaining decades of his life, he would sporadically step out for tours or festivals or to make recordings such as *Up, Up and Away* (1967, with alto saxophonist/leader Sonny Criss), *The Return of Tal Farlow* (1969), and a string of albums for the Concord label starting in 1977.

In the 1970s and 1980s, he often filled in for one of his colleagues in the Great Guitars (a jazz supergroup originally involving Barney Kessel, Herb Ellis, and Charlie Byrd) and enjoyed reunions with Norvo. He could otherwise be seen in local venues sitting atop his own specialized contraption of a stool with built-in amplifier, volume pedal, and octave divider, the last of which he used for bass-line accompaniment of bass solos. (He always had a penchant for tinkering and, earlier in his career, had modified a Gibson ES-250 into a shorter-scale guitar by having part of its neck removed.) He continued performing close up to the time of his death on July 25, 1998.

A longtime Gibson endorser, Farlow was honored in 1962 with the creation of a signature model largely based on the ES-350 and inclusive of a painted scroll near the cutaway at his own insistence (during his 1951 participation in the first color television broadcast, the company had provided him with a red guitar to meet the demands of TV producers). He was the subject of the 1981 documentary film *Talmage Farlow*, which explored his choice of life away from the limelight and featured him performing with younger guitar master Lenny Breau as well as in a trio with pianist Tommy Flanagan and bassist Red Mitchell.

How to Play It

[Editor's note: Even though this solo contains a pickup phrase spanning more than four measures, these are not counted in the measure numbering so as not to complicate the numbering of the typical 32-bar form.]

Tal Farlow's lively medium-tempo, two-chorus excursion through this timeless standard is replete with the lengthy, flowing, dexterous lines one would expect from the virtuosic master. But evident here too is his great use of space, which yields a wonderfully musical effect. Notice the songful contrast brought on by him simply pausing and waiting in measures 11–13, 18–19, 32, or 49, creating spaces that are as filled with meaning as the long strings of notes around them.

He is not quite finished with his initial performance of the melody when he busts out improvising in the first full pickup measure, still paraphrasing the end of the song as he approaches a two-bar solo break (at the E♭maj7), where the head (melody) would normally conclude. His bop-line brilliance and fretboard pyrotechnics are already on display here with the snaky E♭ major-based segment leading up to his first full chorus. The elements of this line are typical of his style: after *enclosing* a G, the chordal 3rd, on string 4, fret 5 (landing on it after looping around it with nearby members of the scale or chromatic neighbor tones), he ascends through an E♭ major arpeggio to finish out the third pickup measure and then encloses the 5th (B♭) on string 1, fret 6 before a leap up to and back from a high E♭ (the chordal root, or tonic of the key) and a chromatic descent to resolve on the 3rd (a higher G now) at the end of the pickup.

Executing this passage in the manner of Farlow requires some up-and-down-the-neck agility, as he frequently makes substantial stretches and jumps to render his labyrinthine melodic ideas. After the left hand has been sitting comfortably enough in the third position, the pinky moves up quickly to cover the C at string 1, fret 8. It's a good tip to let the index finger handle both frets 5 and 6 in the

Like Someone in Love

fourth pickup measure, while the pinky reaches yet further to fret 11 for the high E♭ and a pull-off of a perfect 4th interval. Remember that he was nicknamed the Octopus!

The techniques and tone language of this opening statement show up again and again throughout the solo. Check out the almost interminable stream of eighth notes that runs from the end of measure 3 to nearly the end of measure 9 before he takes a breath! Such phrases are rich with internal rhythm and forward momentum, thanks to their contour of varied ups and downs and clever connection of chord tones along the way (their greatness does not lie in duration alone). Here too, some tricky shifting and reaching is involved, as at the beginning of measure 5—with the ring finger holding the C on string 3, fret 5 (after a pull-off by the pinky), the middle finger nudges in for the next two notes on string 4, effecting a seamless change of position mid-flight.

After biding his time through measure 12, Farlow sneaks into his next phrase quietly at first with descending eighth notes on string 1 (he will do likewise, with even more of a temporarily laid-back impression, at the end of measure 36). He then approaches the halfway point of his first chorus with a reference to the song's melody, evoked by the tones of measure 14 plus the F that follows. The last two of these notes are a half step lower than they occur in the written tune, and the E on string 5, fret 7 seems like an odd misstep until he slickly, subtly resolves it to the F a moment later. Cascading triadic arpeggios adorn his line from the last two notes of measure 20 through most of the next measure, as he descends through tones of A♭, Gm, and Fm (collectively suiting well the Fm7 of the progression).

He adds a particular decorous touch to the solo through the use of double stops, which first occur in measure 25. Let your pinky take the top note at this point, leaving the middle and index fingers to handle the descending tones on the next string as the interval expands. A whole G major triad is strikingly sounded at the tail end of measure 32 to kick off another rolling bop phrase and his second chorus of improvisation altogether. It anticipates the E♭maj7, implying a brief ♯5th on that chord (the B♮ on string 2) that quickly moves up to the more consonant 6th at fret 13.

The most extreme position-jumping occurs within the 16th notes of measure 39, beat 2. After rolling the ring finger to fret both notes on fret 6, the index is at string 1, fret 4 but quickly leaps to fret 8—before an additional stretch of the pinky to fret 11. This is followed by an abundance of pretty double stops—initially perfect 4th intervals descending along the top two strings. Barre with the pinky, middle, and index fingers for these on frets 14, 12, and 11, respectively, and then use the ring finger on string 2, again leaving the middle and index free for the string below, as the 4th intervals continue but soon expand.

To be sure, not all of Farlow's inspired playing is so dang complex or difficult. He nicely throws in some simpler gestures, like the short, hummable, descending scalar pattern of measures 1–3, the paraphrase of the melody at the end of his first chorus (measures 29–31), or the groovy comment of measures 47–48. And in a common jazz move, he wraps up with a taste of the blues in the final few measures (see Jimmy Raney's last four measures on "Spring Is Here"), using blues scale tones with the tonic E♭ sustained above, until finishing at the last moment on an E♭ major sound.

Vital Stats

Guitarist: Tal Farlow

Song: "Like Someone in Love"

Album: *The Swinging Guitar of Tal Farlow*, 1957 (recorded 1956)

Age at Time of Recording: 34

Guitar: Gibson ES-350

Amp: Gibson GA-70 (or possibly a Fender Twin or Tweed Deluxe)

Like Someone in Love

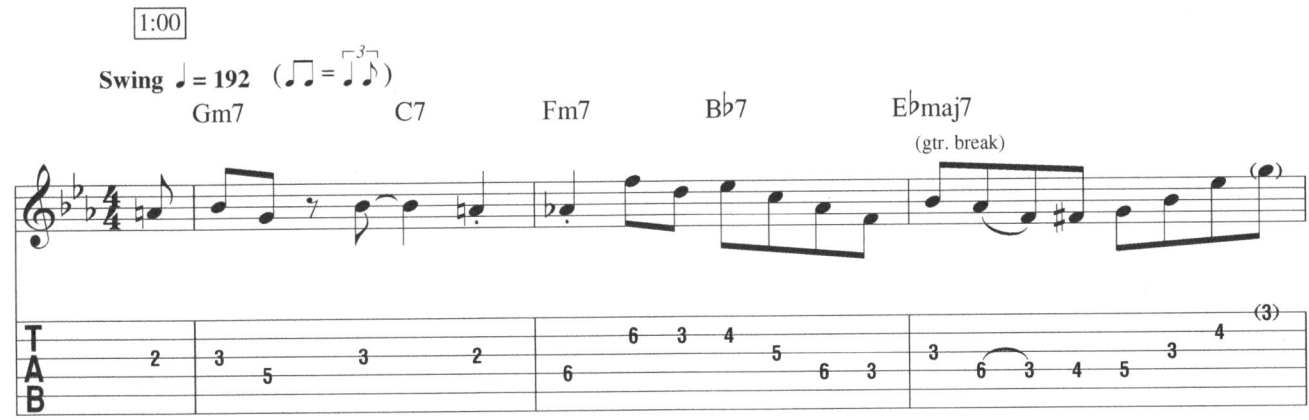
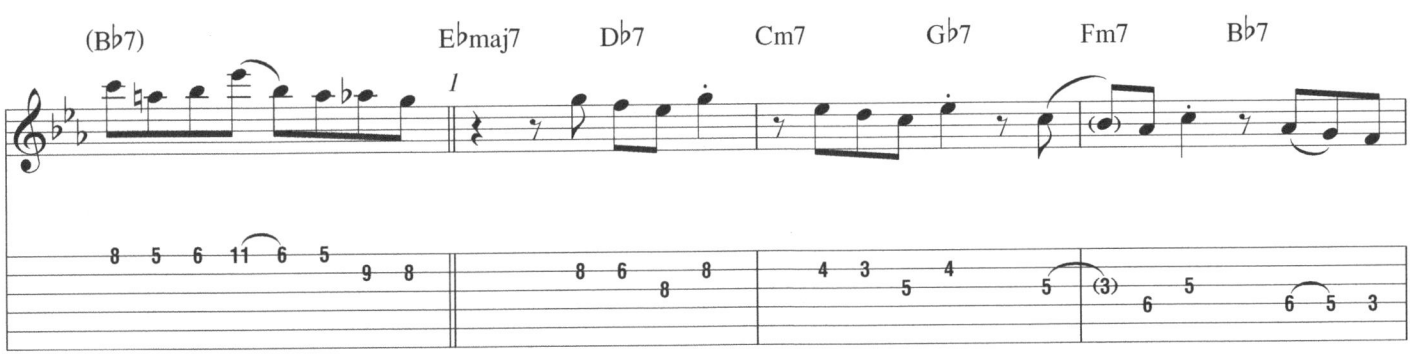

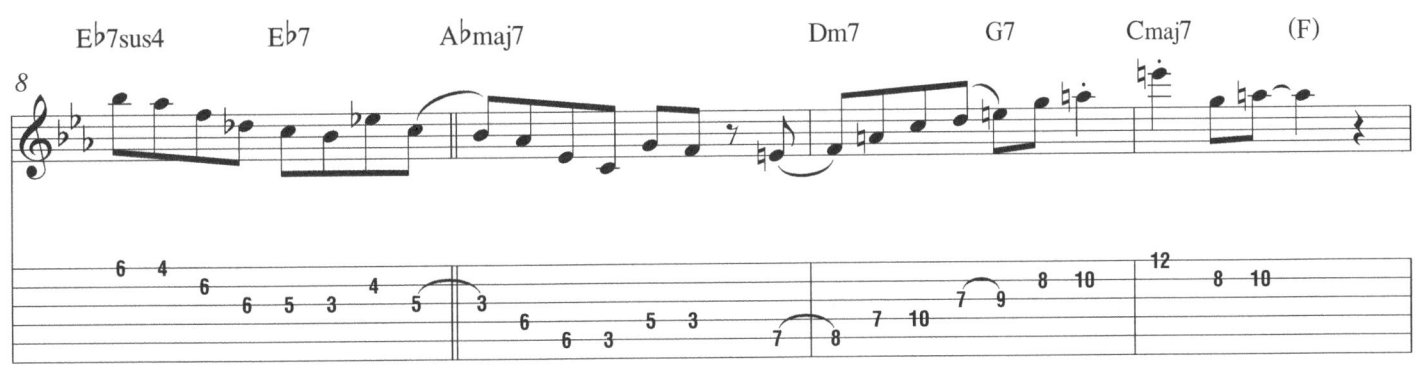

Words by Johnny Burke
Music by Jimmy Van Heusen
Copyright © 1944 by Burke & Van Heusen Inc., a division of Bourne Co. (ASCAP) and Dorsey Bros. Music, A Division of Music Sales Corporation
Copyright Renewed
International Copyright Secured   All Rights Reserved

Like Someone in Love

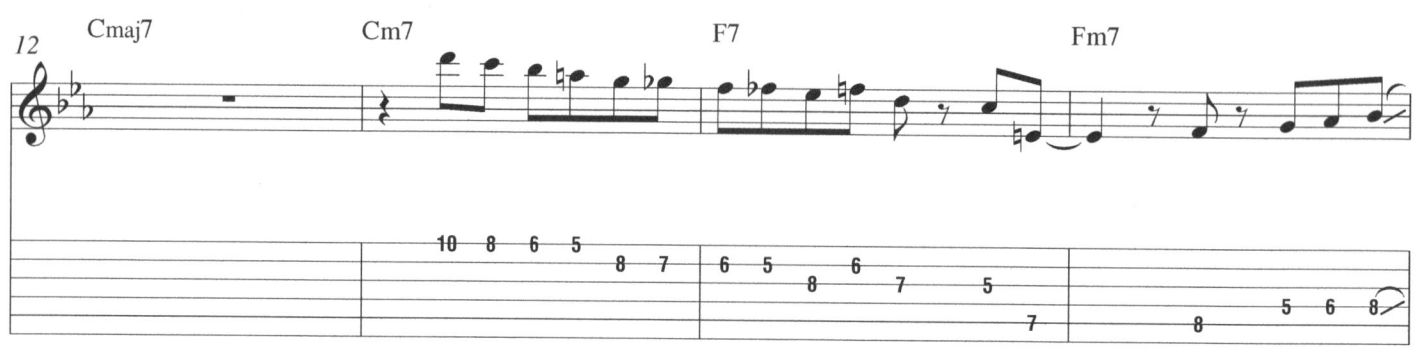
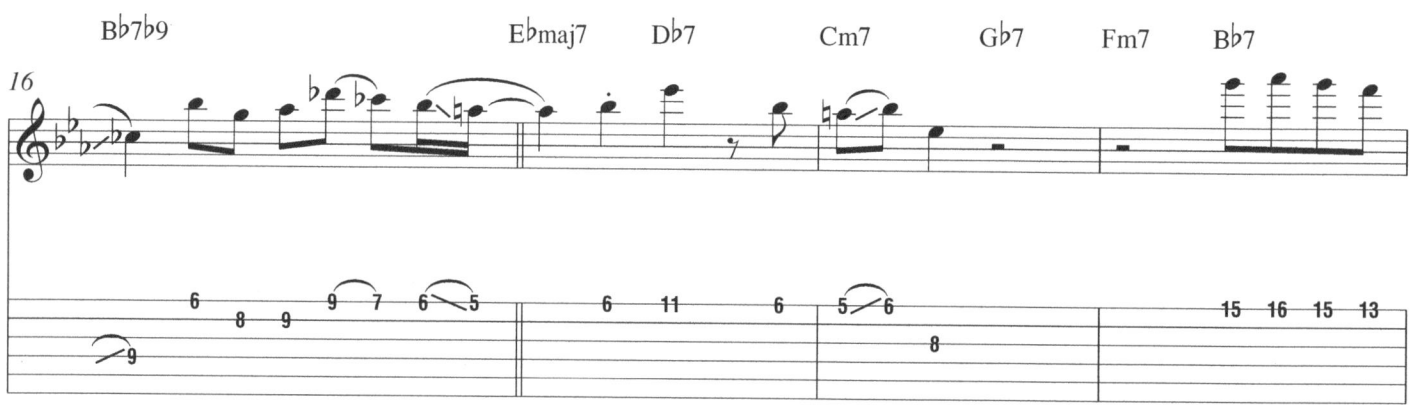
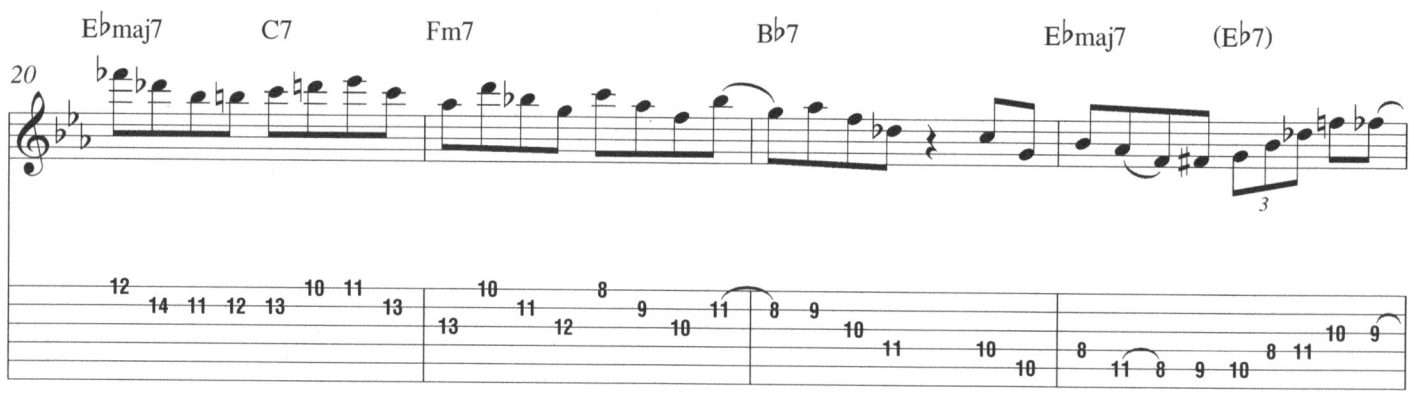
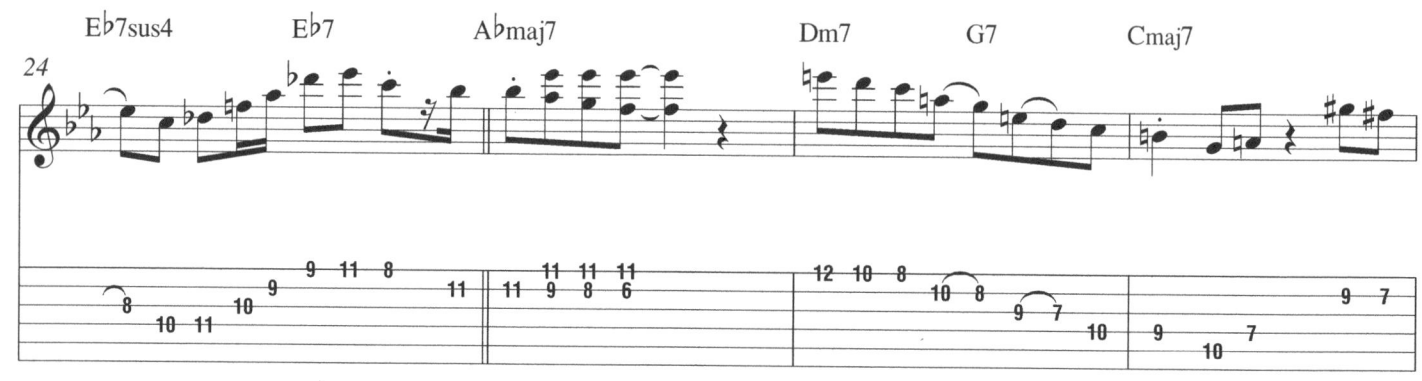

Like Someone in Love

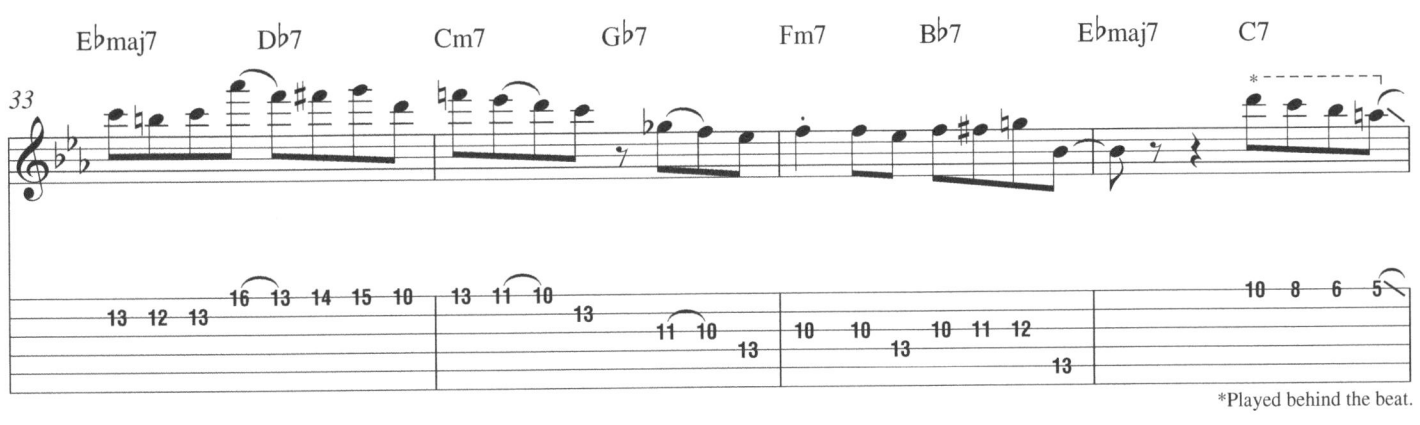

*Played behind the beat.

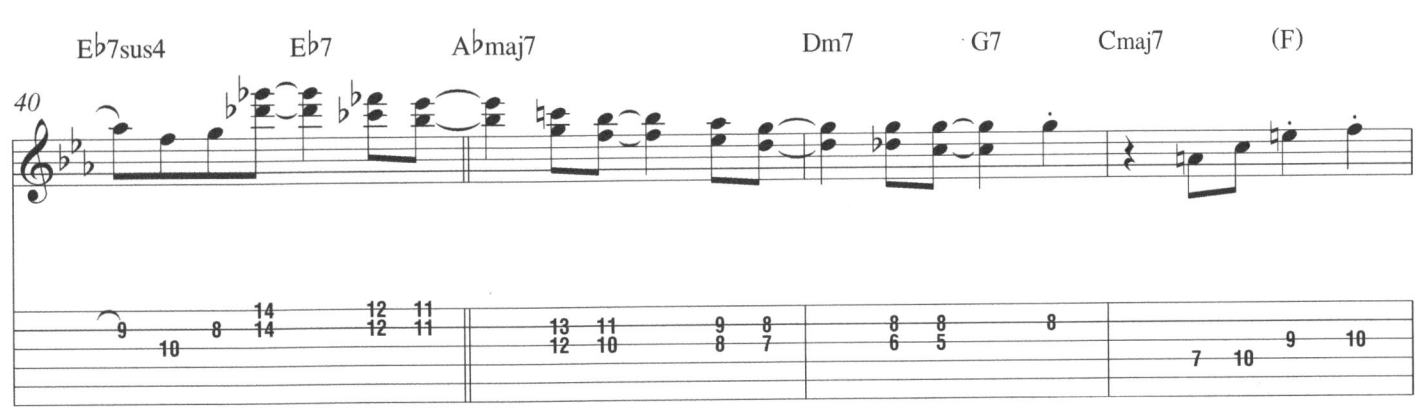

Like Someone in Love

East of the Sun (And West of the Moon) 1957

Johnny Smith

"I never considered myself a jazz player—just a guitar player who tried to supply what was missing."

—Johnny Smith (to 1999 JVC Jazz Festival audience when introduced at his own tribute concert)

© William "PoPsie" Randolph

As generations of players have been inspired by the bop-foreshadowing early electric genius of Charlie Christian, and Django has resonated in the hearts of so many with his impassioned artistry, Johnny Smith has long been considered the technical giant of the archtop guitar. His clear sound, breakneck-speed precision, and total melodic and harmonic mastery of the fretboard have been highly influential to diverse legions of guitarists, among them Pat Martino, John McLaughlin, Gene Bertoncini, Jimmy Bruno, and Bill Frisell. His musical contributions went beyond sheer skill, of course, and he delighted jazz listeners and the general public alike with his tasty, creative chordal arrangements and well-conceived lines.

Himself inspired by Christian and Django, as well as by showman and electronics pioneer Les Paul, classical master Andrés Segovia, and the big bands of his youth, John Henry Smith did not in fact claim to be a jazz player, though this was the music that most called to his heart. He understood the eclectic nature of his own musical life work and considered some of his colleagues to be more full-time steeped in the style. In any case, while he enjoyed partaking in the New York scene of the late 1940s and early 1950s, surrounded by virtuosi such as Art Tatum and Charlie Parker, he was more of the "cool school" persuasion—with his smooth tone and rather understated manner of expression—than part of the bebop movement.

Born June 25, 1922 in Birmingham, Alabama, and growing up in Portland, Maine, he managed by his teen years to become adept at the instrument without even owning one—so much so that he was sought after as a teacher by adult students (one of whom would finally give him a guitar). He also played violin and viola, and his father was a banjoist. An aviation enthusiast from early on, he joined the Army Air Corps during World War II but, with less than perfect vision, was denied military flight training. He was made to learn the cornet instead and kept stateside for various musical purposes. By 1946, he became a staff musician for NBC in New York. With a busy schedule on guitar and trumpet for countless radio (and later television) programs, Smith also worked as the guitarist for the New York Philharmonic and other major orchestras.

He found time to play in the clubs as well and recorded with the Benny Goodman Sextet in 1951. The next year, he went into the studio with his own new quintet, featuring tenor sax great and fellow NBC staffer Stan Getz, for a session that showcased their tight ensemble pyrotechnics on Smith's original "Jaguar" and yielded his hit rendition of "Moonlight

East of the Sun (And West of the Moon)

in Vermont." His seamless, close-voiced chord-melody performance of the popular ballad, together with his fast, pretty single-note runs and dexterous harmonics behind the bass solo, brought him widespread acclaim. Subsequently, he continued making his landmark albums for Roost Records, won awards from *DownBeat* and *Metronome*, packed the house many weeks of the year at the premier jazz spot Birdland, and toured as a soloist with the orchestras of Stan Kenton and Count Basie.

His discography of mostly quartet and quintet dates, with some variation in personnel (often including first-rate pianist Hank Jones), displays a wide variety of repertoire—from jazz standards and originals to mellow electric guitar renditions of Debussy or folk songs, and eventually Beatles. Of special note among his own tunes is "Walk, Don't Run," originally a swinging melody based on the chord changes to "Softly, as in a Morning Sunrise," and appearing on his 1954 10" LP *In a Sentimental Mood*. Guitar legend Chet Atkins released a somewhat countrified version of it in 1957 (with Smith's blessing), which was in turn heard and covered in 1960 by the budding instrumental rock band the Ventures, helping to launch the surf rock genre and resulting in a pop chart hit with substantial royalties for Smith.

In 1958, after the death of his second wife, and with a four-year-old daughter to take care of, he moved to Colorado Springs, Colorado, where he would reside for the rest of his life. Here he remarried, opened a music store, gave flight instruction as well as guitar lessons, overcame a finger injury from a folding airplane seat incident, and played gigs in the area. In 1961, he was very hands-on with the design of a well-received Gibson signature model (Guild and Heritage have also made Johnny Smith models). He occasionally ventured far from home for a recording session or special appearance, releasing the solo effort *The Man with the Blue Guitar* (1962) and *Johnny Smith's Kaleidoscope* (1967), among other titles, and touring internationally with Bing Crosby in 1977. His method book, *The Complete Johnny Smith Approach to Guitar*, was published in 1980 and remains a benchmark for thorough instruction of fretboard fundamentals. Eventually, he by and large quit playing guitar altogether, not wanting to continue if he couldn't keep up the high standards that required constant performance. He passed away on June 11, 2013, leaving a legacy of high standards indeed.

How to Play It

Johnny Smith's solo on the old chestnut "East of the Sun" is a paragon of technique and taste, his blazing 16th-note runs interspersed with simple, songful, swingin' phrases that complement the harmonic progression and belie his famous modesty in the area of jazz musicianship. The beginning of the two-bar solo break is marked by the conclusion of his chord-melody arrangement of the tune (with the G major triad), and from there the "blazing" commences in a dazzling flurry of notes leading up to the top of his one full solo chorus.

In executing these speediest segments—there are four of them altogether—use alternate picking, map out your fingerings well, and go over them slowly

The personnel of this September 1957 session, different than the foursome of Vol. 1, included pianist Bob Pancoast, bassist George Roumanis, and drummer Mousey Alexander.

enough at first, perhaps in smaller chunks, gradually increasing your tempo with multiple repetitions. Note that he largely takes a position-playing approach for these fast passages, staying in or near one zone of the fretboard and allowing the left hand to trace a largely scalar route with minimal shifting or reaching. At the start of this first instance, the left hand is at the second position (index finger at fret 2) and will shift between this and the third (and briefly fourth) positions with small slides and reaches. The hand positioning is more concise for the 16th notes of measure 24 (all in the seventh position) or measures 27–28 (fourth position through measure 28, beat 1, before a shift to fifth).

The dramatic ascent of measures 20–21, however, incorporates another important element of Smith's technique: the clean leap between areas of the neck. Here he starts out in the twelfth position with a figure that rises from lower to higher strings and, upon reaching string 1, jumps up to fret 15 with the index finger for the G and stretches to

East of the Sun (And West of the Moon)

fret 19 with the pinky for the high B. The notes here essentially spell out a rising Am9 arpeggio in two different octaves, the second one beginning on beat 1 of measure 21 (it's apparent that he meant to shift one fret higher on string 2 in the process of his upward jump, to hit frets 13 and 17—for a C and E—as part of that arpeggio). The initial B on string 5, fret 14 is a scalar step between chord tones.

This ability to move quickly from one fretboard position to another (often seamlessly, with no audible slide or gap) is a skill encouraged through many of the scale fingerings in his method book and shows up prominently throughout the solo. Descending from the peak of measure 21, the index finger is on string 1 fret 15 as beat 4 begins, but the ring finger grabs the next note on fret 12, in a jump down to 10th position. In a similar occurrence, as measure 6 begins, the pinky is on string 2, fret 8, and the index hops up to fret 7 on string 1 (moving to the seventh position). In the last half of measure 7, the new position is abandoned again as the pinky retakes the G on string 2, fret 8, facilitating a reach further down the same string with the other fingers.

Position-jumping comes into play in yet another feature of Smith's performance: the use of melodic patterns rendered as repeated shapes on the neck of the guitar, as in the motif that runs from measure 13 through the first half of measure 15. Initially, the index finger covers string 2, fret 8, and the pinky takes the slide from fret 11 to 12. After this, the index is used for *every picked note on string 2* (every other note, until the open string is played), in a gradual shift down the neck. Even more striking are the back-and-forth leaps starting in measure 31, where on beat 2 the hand is at the ninth position for a three-note shape on string 1, but the triplet of beat 3 continues from string 1, fret 5, with further scooting down of the index finger required on string 2. This is soon followed by a jump back up to the eighth position on measure 32, beat 3, for the same three-note shape with which we started, though a half step lower to fit B♭m7.

Measure 29 begins with Am7-friendly tones in the fourth position, but on beat 4 there is a shift to the seventh position, *even while repeating the D on string 3, fret 7* (fretted initially by the pinky, then by the index), reflecting a change of scalar orientation that anticipates the F7 and starting a similar three-beat melodic shape in a new place. In measure 10, incidentally, Smith even further anticipates the upcoming B7 that will lead to Em7 with a line that evokes B7♭9 more than the officially present D7. In the last couple of measures of the solo, he follows suit with many of his jazz colleagues by using a bluesy figure to conclude (see the end of Tal Farlow's statement on "Like Someone in Love"), largely departing from the chord-specific approach as he hangs onto the tonic G on string 2 with the pinky, slides around through blues scale material on the strings below, and finally lands on a G major sonority.

Vital Stats

Guitarist: Johnny Smith

Song: "East of the Sun (And West of the Moon)"

Album: *Johnny Smith Foursome Vol. 2*, 1957

Age at Time of Recording: 35

Guitar: D'Angelico Excel with New Yorker trim

Amp: Direct into board (with pre-amp)

East of the Sun (And West of the Moon)

*Played as even eighth notes.

Words and Music by Brooks Bowman
© 1934 (Renewed) CHAPPELL & CO., INC.
All Rights Reserved   Used by Permission

East of the Sun (And West of the Moon)

Lyresto 1958

Kenny Burrell

© Alamy

> "I want especially to be myself. All the musicians who were considered giants in jazz history, fixed, more or less, their own rules."
> —Kenny Burrell

Kenneth Earl Burrell, born July 31, 1931 into a musical family in Detroit, Michigan, is one of the most tasteful and enduring voices of straight-ahead jazz guitar. For well over half a century, he has sounded as though he were singing through his instrument, always with a strong sense of swing, a beautiful harmonic approach, and an affinity for the blues. And Duke Ellington himself famously called him his favorite guitarist.

He emerged from the vibrant Detroit jazz scene that also produced trumpeters Donald Byrd and Thad Jones, saxophonists Yusef Lateef, Pepper Adams, and Frank Foster, pianists Hank Jones, Tommy Flanagan, and Barry Harris, bassists Paul Chambers and Ron Carter, and drummers Louis Hayes and Elvin Jones, among so many other all-time jazz greats. Initially inspired by direction-setting swing era saxophonists Lester Young and Coleman Hawkins, he might have started out as a sax player himself if not for the greater cost of the axe. He certainly also took influence from jazz guitarists Charlie Christian and Oscar Moore (and later Django), as well as bluesmen Muddy Waters, John Lee Hooker, and T-Bone Walker.

By 1947, he was gigging in his hometown with Flanagan and others, and as of 1951 was leading his own group in the area. He was soon hired for his first major recording session, upon being heard by a visiting Dizzy Gillespie (also on the legendary trumpeter's studio date were vibraphone powerhouse Milt Jackson and future saxophone giant John Coltrane). Burrell has long been one to choose formal education along with jazz-club experience, and at this point he forewent touring opportunities to stay in town and attend Wayne State University, earning his bachelor's degree in composition and theory in 1955. After graduation, and some months filling in for Herb Ellis with the Oscar Peterson Trio, Burrell made his move to New York (in the company of Flanagan). His career as a performer, recording artist, studio session player, and Broadway pit orchestra member took off.

Within his magnificent discography, he has appeared on over 300 albums as a sideman with artists such as trumpeter Kenny Dorham, tenor sax legend Coleman Hawkins, organist Jack McDuff, and iconic singers Billie Holiday and Tony Bennett. *The Detroit Jazzmen* (1956) finds him in the company of fellow Motor City musicians making good in New York, while saxophonist Stanley Turrentine's *Jubilee Shout* (recorded in 1962 but released much later) provides a great example of guitar used as a third melodic voice, in unison or harmony with two horns in front of a rhythm section. Through his playing on *The Sermon* (1958) and other classics by groundbreaking organist Jimmy Smith, he helped usher in the popularity of the guitar and Hammond organ combination.

His more than 100 albums as a leader span from *Introducing Kenny Burrell* in 1956 through *The Road to Love* (2015). Some highlights along the way are *Kenny Burrell and John Coltrane* (1958), *A Night at the Vanguard* (1959) in a live trio setting, the extra-greasy *Midnight Blue* (1963) featuring his often-covered minor-ish blues, "Chitlins con Carne," and the soulful tenor sax work of Turrentine, *Guitar Forms* (1965) with jazz-orchestral arrangements by Gil Evans and some display of classical guitar chops, *God Bless the Child* (1971), *Ellington Is Forever* (1975), *A La Carte* (1983) in a duo with bassist Rufus Reid, *Lotus Blossom* (1995), *75th Birthday Bash Live!* (2007), and *Tenderly* (live solo cuts from 2007, released in 2011), to name just a few. He also helped bring wider attention to younger guitarists Bobby Broom and Rodney Jones through a 1986 live recording with his Jazz Guitar Band, released as *Generation* and *Pieces of Blue and the Blues*.

As a composer, Burrell has created extended works in addition to shorter tunes, often dealing in both music and lyrics. Among these, *Love Is the Answer*, a multi-part 1990s project with the Boys Choir of Harlem, was eventually recorded for a 1998 release, and a live recording of *The Ralph Bunche Suite* (2008), at the University of California, Los Angeles, featured many of the school's students along with seasoned pros in a large ensemble.

In recent years, he has been a full-time educator and administrator on top of his continued performances, since 1996 directing the Jazz Studies program at UCLA. Having moved to California in 1971, his teaching at the university began in 1978 with a course entitled "Ellingtonia," still running today, in which he explores Ellington's musical legacy (expressing his mutual appreciation of the Duke!). The honors that have been bestowed upon him reflect the diversity and magnitude of his accomplishments—countless jazz-poll kudos as a guitarist, signature model guitars by Heritage, an honorary doctorate from William Patterson College, the 2004 *DownBeat* award for Jazz Educator of the Year, and recognition as a 2005 Jazz Master by the National Endowment for the Arts.

How to Play It

Burrell begins his two-chorus solo with a four-bar phrase that echoes the beginning of his tune's melody, and he displays right off the bat a key feature of his personal style: he's so *melodic* that just about every other idea he puts forth sounds perfectly hummable, as if it could be a song unto itself. Along with his general melodiousness, he has a special legato fluidity to his lines, often heightened by shorter or longer slides or multiple chromatic hammer-ons and pull-offs, as seen in measures 16 (right off of a brief sweep-picked arpeggio) and 27. He frequently throws in a slight bend or vibrato at the end of a phrase, further augmenting the vocal quality of his improvisation and hinting at another important aspect of his playing—the blues element.

This gem from the Prestige catalog, pairing Burrell with the new titan of the tenor sax, was recorded in 1958 though first released in 1963. The stellar rhythm section includes pianist Tommy Flanagan, bassist Paul Chambers, and drummer Jimmy Cobb.

His feel is as hard-swingin' as anyone's yet has a certain degree of looseness, in a distinct way from that of a player like Wes Montgomery or Grant Green. This usually goes hand in hand with the very singing nature of his delivery but sometimes presents a technical challenge within the solo. Figures like the one in measure 23, or the quick triplet run in measures 57–58, are at once precise and a little loose in their execution. He exhibits great speed at these points, while still prioritizing a relaxed swing over cold accuracy. Practice these spots slowly at first, with alternate picking and a readiness to shift the left hand as needed.

"Lyresto" is a 32-bar tune that moves in a two-half structure, each half beginning with a I–vi–ii–V sequence in E♭ major (E♭maj7–Cm7–Fm7–B♭7), a very common series of chords that could be called a *turnaround progression*. This is followed by two measures on the tonic E♭maj7 and then a visit to the minor iv chord (A♭m7, here paired with the related D♭7). For the first chunk, Burrell tends to play around the fifth position, where a common E♭ major scale fingering can

Lyresto

be found, and when A♭m7 comes by he often gravitates towards the fourth (where one would play an A♭m barre chord) and third positions, drawing from mostly A♭ Dorian tones.

In measures 29–30, Burrell gives a classic demonstration of *tritone substitution*, playing over C7–Fm7–B♭7 as if each were rooted three whole steps away (and as if the F chord were dominant rather than minor). We hear clear-cut G♭ major triad tones on C7, a B major triad on F, and E major scale tones on B♭7. The result is a line that sounds a little further out than the original chords, and yet moves in the same direction to resolve at E♭maj7.

He begins his second chorus with the very cool rising motif of measures 33–38, raising the excitement by always reaching another notch higher in pitch with the couple of notes that start off the phrase in each measure (sometimes including a little slide-in or pull-off figure). Here he goes further afield with harmonic substitution, eventually departing from the official progression altogether for a moment. He treats the chord in measure 34 as if it were an altered C7, with ♯9th and ♭9th tones (quite common for this place in a turnaround progression). The B♭7 of measure 36 gets a full-on tritone sub treatment, as the notes of his line imply a Bm7, which is closely related to E7 (the tritone sub of B♭7), essentially creating the effect of an altered B♭7. The next measure finds him back home in E♭ major territory, but in measure 38 he takes a left turn and invokes a G♭m7 sound, leading down to Fm7 material in measure 39. Basically, he improvises here as if there were another turnaround progression in measures 37–40 (I–VI–ii–V, with further substitution of the ♭iii for the VI chord) instead of the two measures of E♭maj7 followed by A♭m7/D♭7. The two approaches converge by the last half of measure 40, as his tones here could fit either B♭7♭9 or D♭7.

From the pickup to measure 49 through the beginning of measure 51, he leads off the second half of his final chorus drawing most overtly from the ever-present blues side of his musical personality. These short, aggressive, minor pentatonic-based phrases smack just as much of Chicago blues as Detroit jazz! He mixes stylistic flavors for a tasty ending to the solo, showing his famous songfulness again in measures 61–62 with what seems like a romantic line from an unknown standard, briefly returning to the blues sound in measures 63–64, and concluding in a sweetly melodic E♭ major gesture with his final three notes.

Vital Stats

Guitarist: Kenny Burrell

Song: "Lyresto"

Album: *Kenny Burrell and John Coltrane*, 1963 (recorded 1958)

Age at Time of Recording: 26

Guitar: Gibson ES-175

Amp: Fender Tweed Deluxe

Lyresto

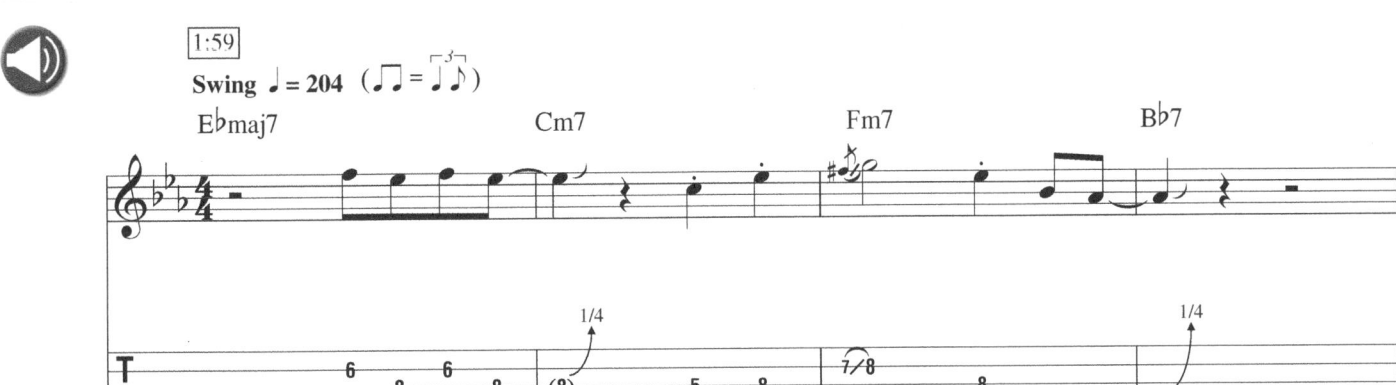
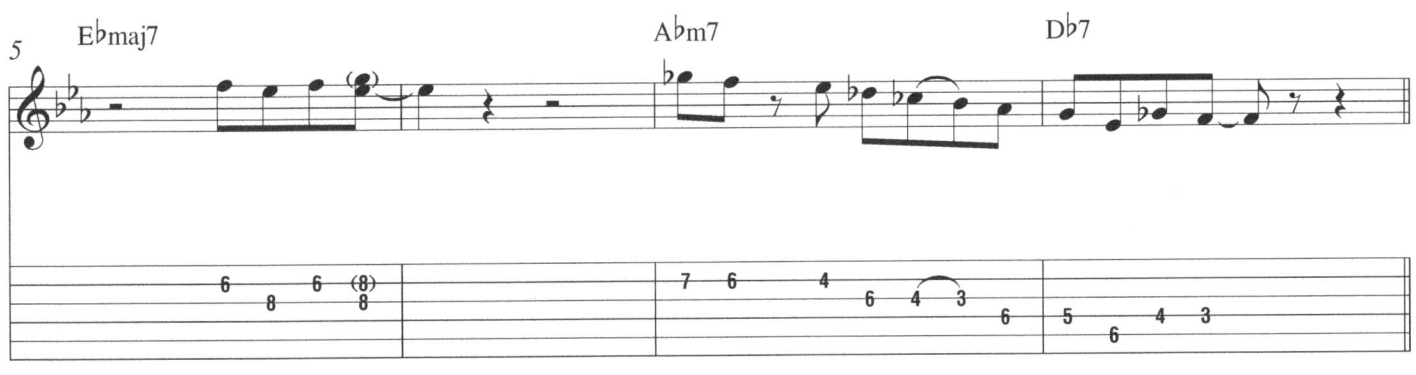

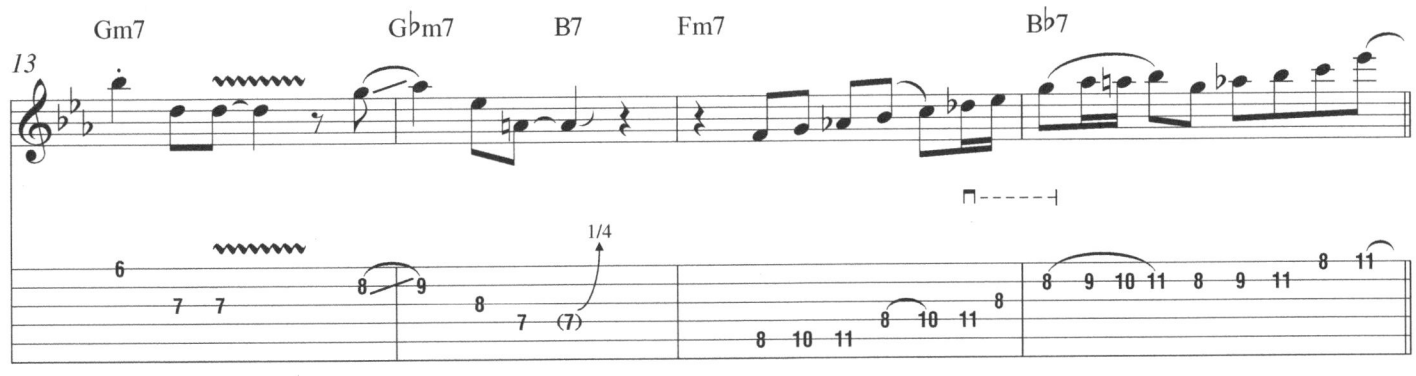

By Kenny Burrell
Copyright © 1963 (Renewed 1991) by Elliot Music Co., Inc.
All Rights Reserved   Used by Permission

Lyresto

*Played as even eighth notes.

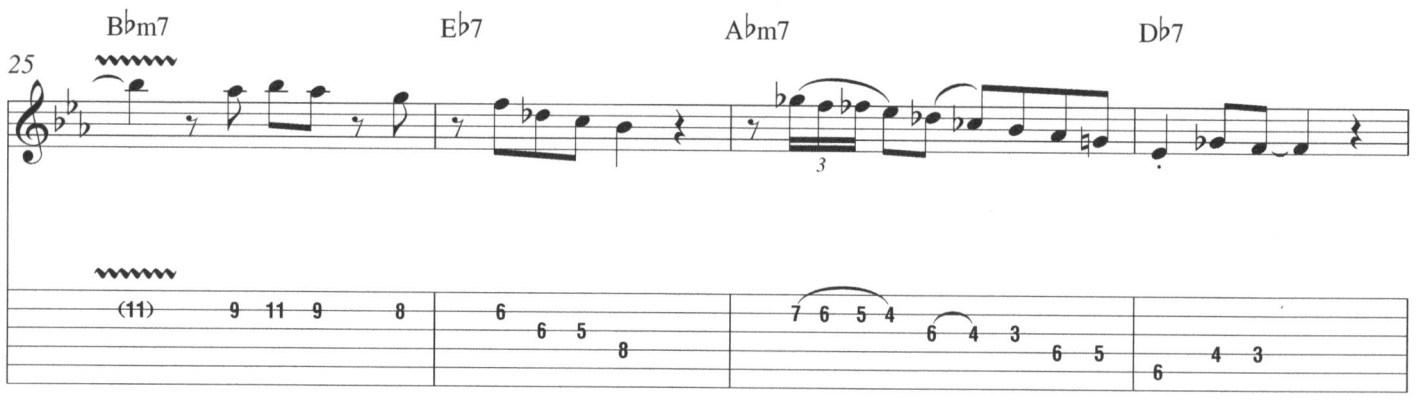
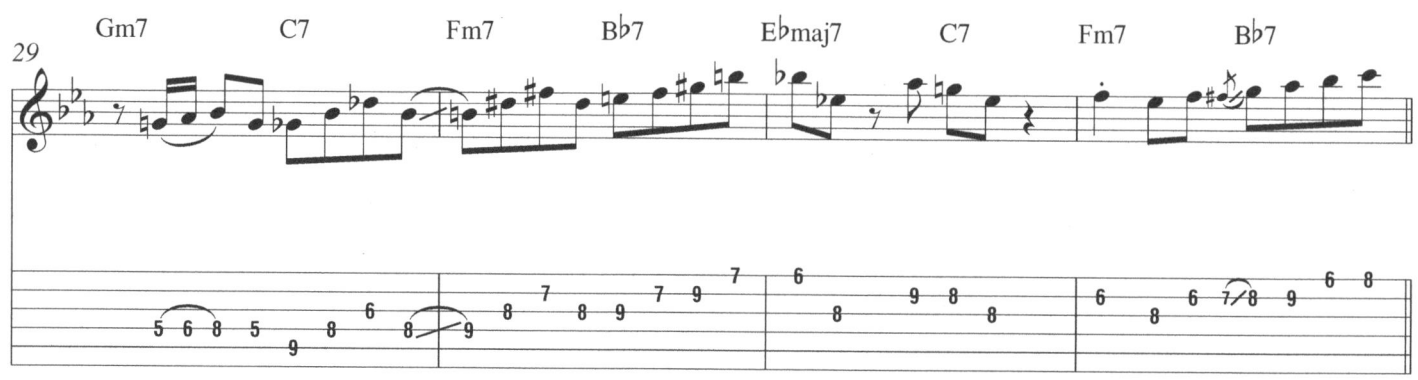

Lyresto

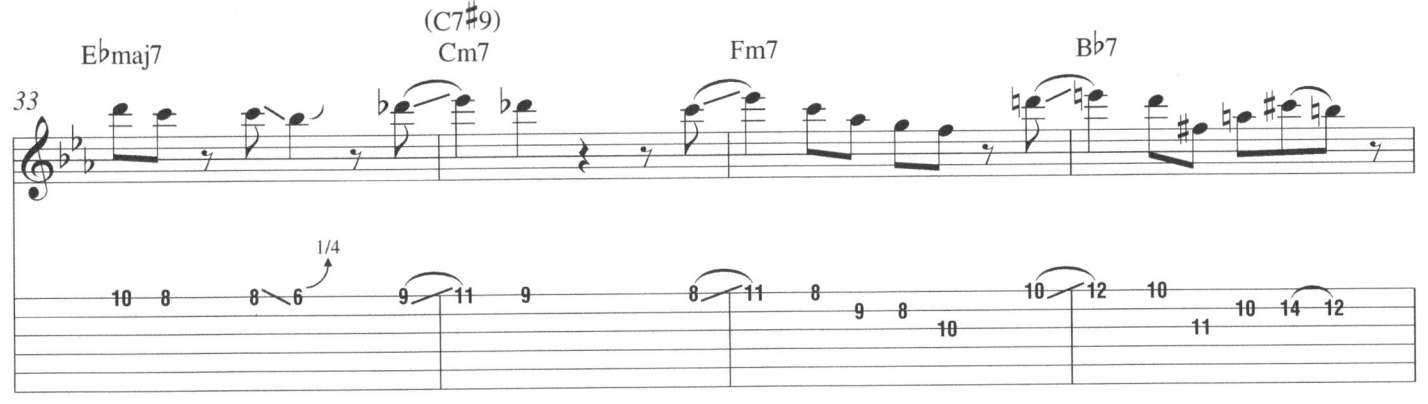

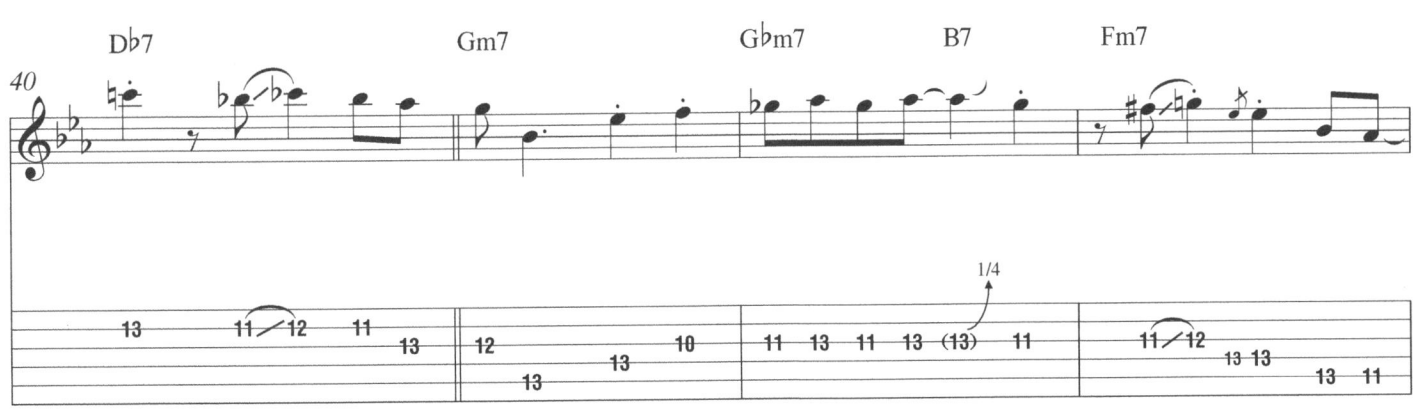
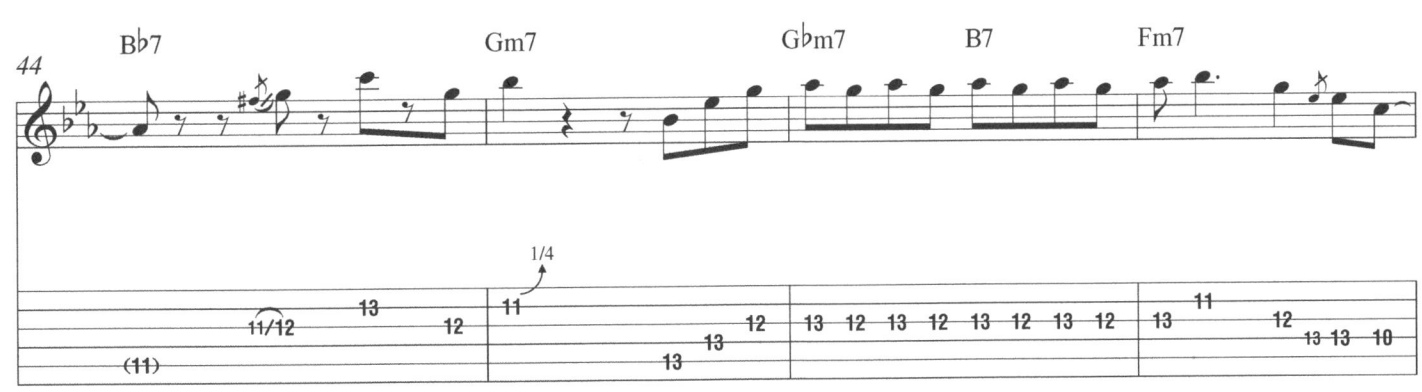

Lyresto

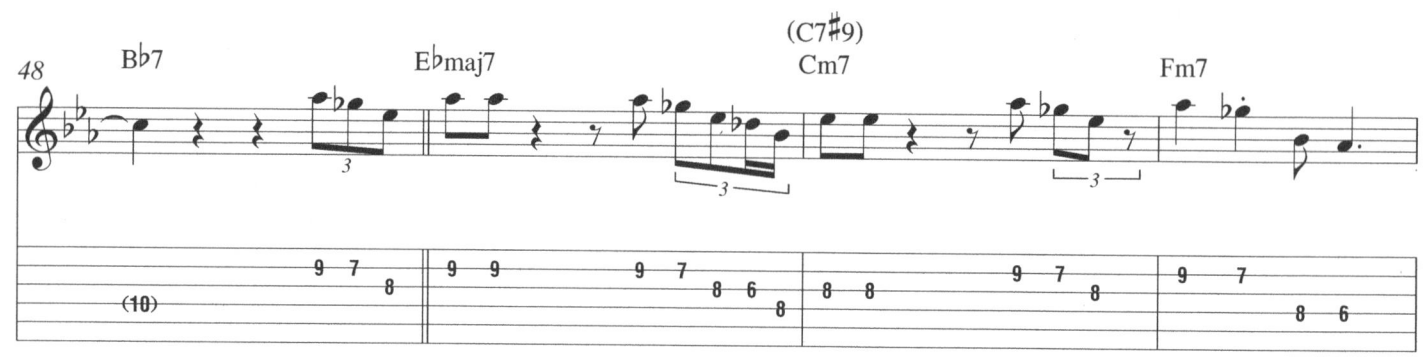
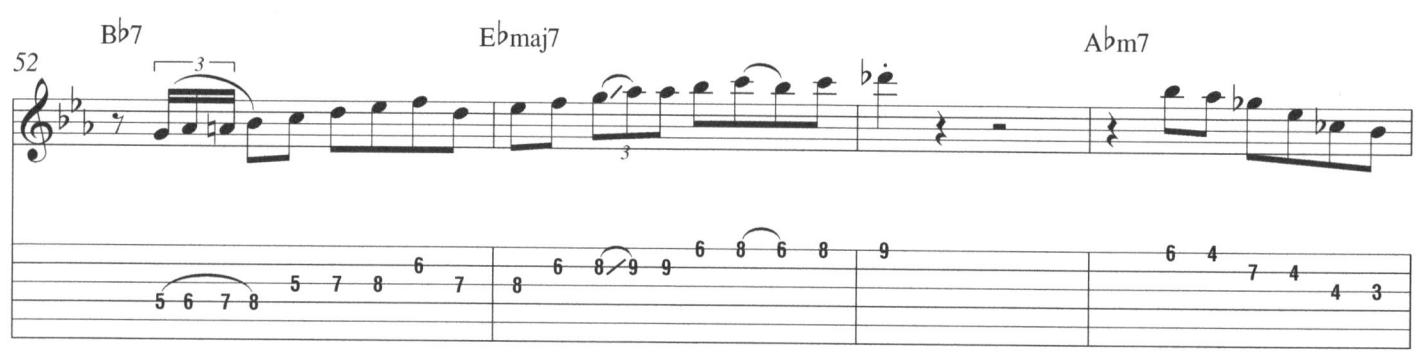
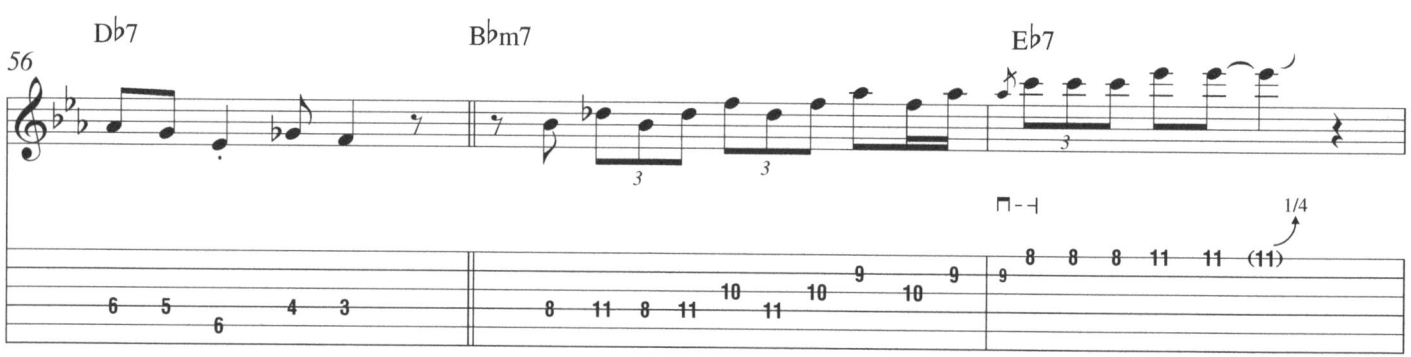

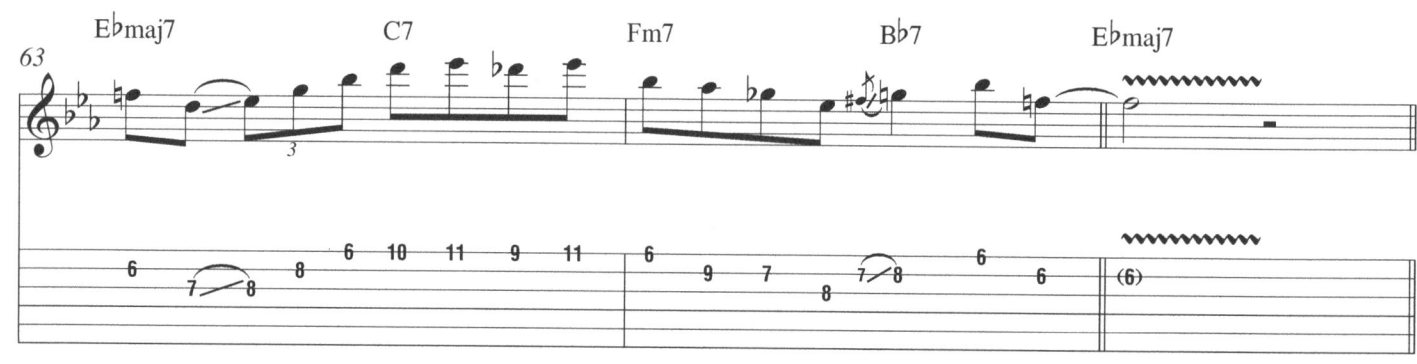

Relaxin' 1960

Hank Garland

"Go, Hank!"
—Patti Page (during Garland's solo on her 1961 hit single "Just Because")

A first-call Nashville session guitarist of the 1950s, he is remembered by venerable colleague Chet Atkins as the top guy in town. His playing graced the records of country stars such as Jim Reeves, Kitty Wells, Brenda Lee, and Conway Twitty. He performed on television with Eddy Arnold and in concert with Elvis Presley. He appears on numerous hits by Elvis, the Everly Brothers, Roy Orbison, and Patsy Cline, contributing the famous Ecco-Fonic tape-echo guitar part to Cline's 1961 hit "I Fall to Pieces." His handiwork is heard profusely every holiday season on the original renditions of "Jingle Bell Rock" and "Rockin' Around the Christmas Tree."

It may all seem a strange resume for a jazz guitar great, but Walter Louis "Hank" Garland was a jazzer at heart—and a great one at that. While not as much a household name in jazz circles as Wes, Django, or Joe Pass, he's very much a guitarist's favorite, known to insiders on the instrument as a hidden treasure in the chronicles of the music.

Born November 11, 1930, in Cowpens, South Carolina (it's hard to be any more destined for country music than that!), he moved to Nashville, Tennessee at the age of 16 to pursue the profession. Just shy of his 19th birthday, he laid down a guitar solo on his own "Sugarfoot Rag," for what became country crooner Red Foley's 1950 million-seller (with lyrics added by George Vaughn, and Garland's name appearing on the disc label as both writer and soloist). Originally an instrumental guitar piece, his iconic tune still endures as a staple of the tradition and has been covered by Jerry Reed (1979) and Asleep at the Wheel with Brad Paisley (2001), among others. Hank "Sugarfoot" Garland, along with fellow Nashville guitarist Billy Byrd, helped design the Gibson Byrdland guitar model in 1955. Named for both players, this instrument marked the introduction of a thinner variety of electric archtop, presaging the development of the semi-hollowbodies that are so versatile in their use and popular to this day.

Between his country and rock 'n' roll engagements, he listened to Django Reinhardt as often as he could and by night played jazz at Nashville's Carousel Club. While traveling to New York for the Eddy Arnold Show in the early 1950s, he took advantage of the opportunity to sit in with the likes of Charlie Parker and George Shearing, and studied with noted jazz guitarist Barry Galbraith.

In 1959, he began cutting his own albums of a jazz nature, mainly by contract with Columbia records. First out was *Velvet Guitar*, a guitar-bass-and-drums trio venture with decent enough playing, relatively short tracks, and a mix of standard and original material. In July of 1960, he participated in an impromptu recording on the back porch of a mansion as part of the Nashville All Stars, together with Chet Atkins, saxophonist Boots Randolph, 17-year-old future vibraphone great Gary Burton, and others, after their

Relaxin'

Newport Jazz Festival appearance was cancelled due to an out-of-control crowd. The resulting LP was aptly titled *After the Riot at Newport* and showed what Garland could do with more room to stretch out. But it was with *Jazz Winds from a New Direction*, recorded the next month, that he truly made his mark in the genre, startling listeners with the fluent, swingin', bop-informed sound coming out of Nashville. This quartet date involved Burton on vibes, bassist Joe Benjamin, and drummer Joe Morello of Dave Brubeck/"Take Five" fame. A subsequent session (originally issued as *Subtle Swing*) was compiled with extra material from the previous dates and released on *The Unforgettable Guitar of Hank Garland* in 1962.

Garland's brilliant career was cut short by a terrible accident in September of 1961 in which he was thrown from his car while driving near Springfield, Tennessee. After waking from a coma, he underwent numerous shock treatments that were of dubious help, and slowly relearned how to walk, talk, and eventually play the guitar, but he never quite regained the skills that allowed him to do what he had done at such a high level in so many different settings. A degree of controversy surrounds this tragic incident, as well as his relationship to the Nashville music business altogether. Garland claimed that he had co-written "Jingle Bell Rock" and was deprived of royalties, and a brother of his has suggested that the 1961 crash was no accident. The contentious side of his career and personal life is touched upon in the 2007 film *Crazy* (co-produced by Steve Vai), based on the guitarist's life story.

Some years following his injuries, he settled in Orange Park, Florida, where he lived until his death in 2004. He managed to play briefly at the 1976 Fan Fair Reunion Show in Nashville, but his unique country- and jazz-flavored voice had largely been silenced.

How to Play It

This solo provides a classic example of graceful linear playing mixed with bluesy inflections, all on a relaxed, slow-swinging groove. And a key tip for playing it well is—indeed, just as the title suggests—relaxin'!

The tempo, almost that of a walking ballad, is in the slow range for a quarter-note walking bass line (heard here throughout the solo). Garland opts to play on it not with swung eighths, which would be quite sparse at this speed, but rather with an emphasis on 16th-note lines, as if played against an eighth-note pulse (though the band never lapses into a double-time feel behind him). We most often hear a lilt to these lines, with the use of swung 16ths, but this is flexible—he plays through most of his first measure more evenly, for example. Another detail of feel and timing is the occasional slight delay in the continuance of a phrase, such as in the middle of measures 3 and 10, or perhaps more subtly before the triplets of measure 26 (this may often represent a happy joining of rhythmic expression and technical ease).

Along with scalar or chromatic movement, Garland makes great use of chordal arpeggios within his ideas, with major 7 shapes being a favorite—check out the E♭maj7 outlined on the middle four strings in measure 3 and the similar A♭maj7 in both measures 8 and 9 (from the second half of beat 2 in all cases). As measure

An influence to up-and-coming players like George Benson and Pat Martino, Garland was really put on the jazz guitar map with Jazz Winds from a New Direction *(the first studio session for a very young Gary Burton on vibraphone).*

10 begins, he moves the maj7 arpeggio up a minor 3rd to C♭maj7 (effectively the same as Bmaj7), which fits hand-in-glove with the A♭m7 chord in the progression. The first five notes of the whole solo, meanwhile, are based around an F9#11 shape in the seventh position. The beginning of measure 26 finds him leaving his fingers planted on the D♭9#11 shape in eighth position, thus sustaining those first few tones (the first finger barres strings 2 and 3 in this case—and the anticipation of D♭9 is logical enough here, given its strong relationship to A♭m7). To close out the first half of his one-chorus solo, Garland goes big-time into arpeggio-land and, from beat 4 of measure 15, descends through the tones of the first four 7th chords found in the E♭ major scale, in reverse order. That is, he plays downwards through A♭maj7, Gm7, Fm7, and E♭maj7 arpeggios (in a way that works just fine with the harmonic direction of the tune at that point). Upward sweep picking is helpful for these fast groups of descending 32nd notes.

This, the pinnacle of chordal prettiness in the performance, is followed by a slight

Relaxin'

foreshadowing in measure 17 of the sudden, aggressive blues gesture coming up. In measure 18, he lets loose with this new flavor, busting out the twangy pull-offs and tremolo picking on top of copious blues scale tones. Most striking is the pronounced plunk of the open fifth string with which he ends the phrase, unusual for Garland or just about anyone else in such a mellow, straight-ahead, key-of-E♭ jazz setting (although A♮ can be seen to fit in as the "blue note" from the E♭ blues scale). Technical tip: if you've been playing with an un-anchored right hand, as many jazzers do, that's generally fine, but this might be a good spot for bracing the heel of the hand on the bridge to get a brighter tone and more control in the tremolo picking. Also, don't sweat exact written time values for the last beat of measure 18 through the first half-beat of measure 19—the main point is to play through these notes with a fast tremolo and land in the right place.

Garland continues from here with a tasteful mix of blues scale material (mostly in measures 20 and 30–32) and chord tones, with a little reference in measure 23 to "Surrey with the Fringe on Top" (from the Western-themed Broadway musical *Oklahoma*). He finally quiets way down by the end of measure 32, ending harmoniously with tones that accentuate the move from C7 to Fm7.

Vital Stats

Guitarist: Hank Garland

Song: "Relaxin'"

Album: *Jazz Winds from a New Direction*, 1961 (recorded 1960)

Age at Time of Recording: 29

Guitar: Gibson L-5 CT with Charlie Christian pickup

Amp: Gibson GA-77

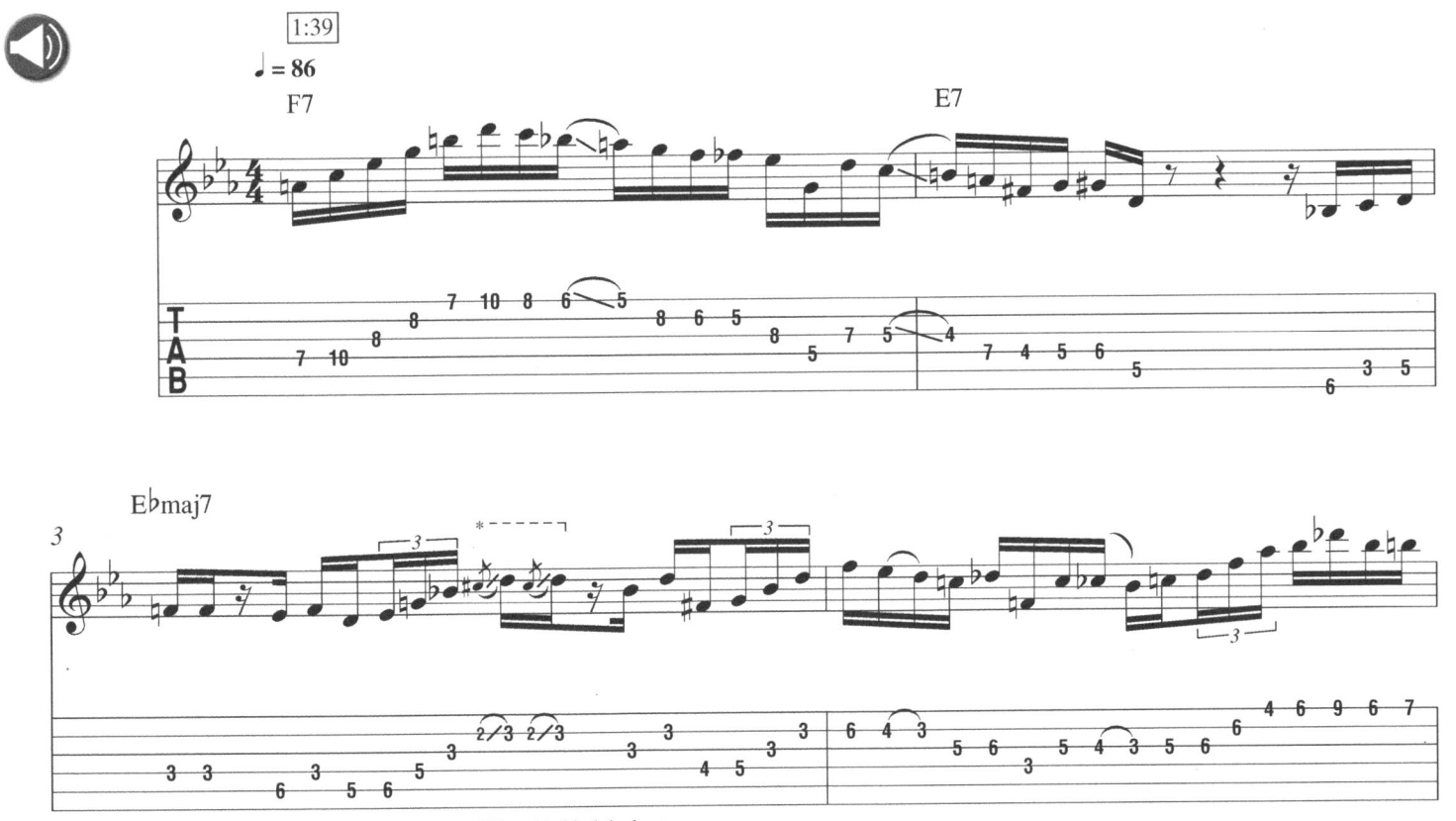

*Played behind the beat.

By Jimmie Guinn
© 1956 (Renewed 1984) EMI LONGITUDE MUSIC
All Rights Reserved   International Copyright Secured   Used by Permission

Relaxin'

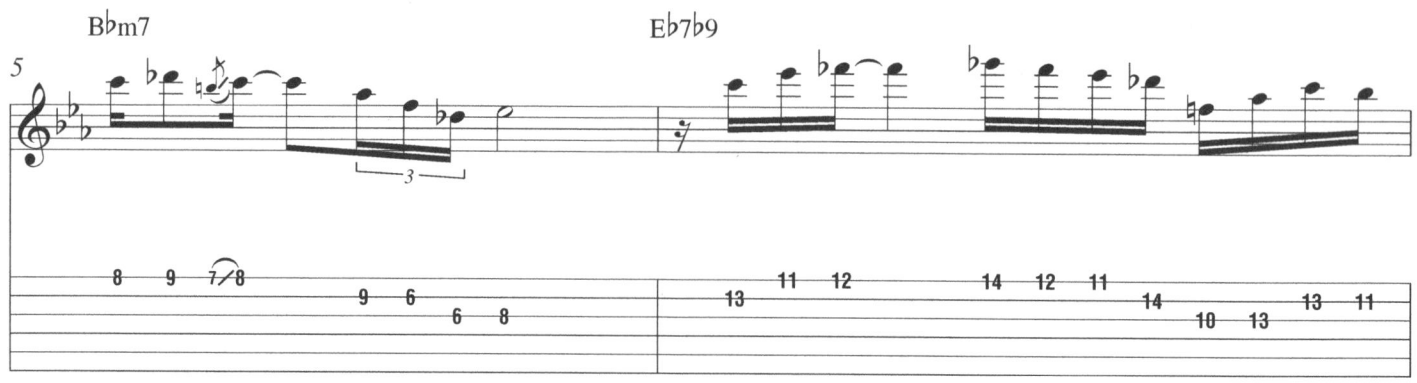

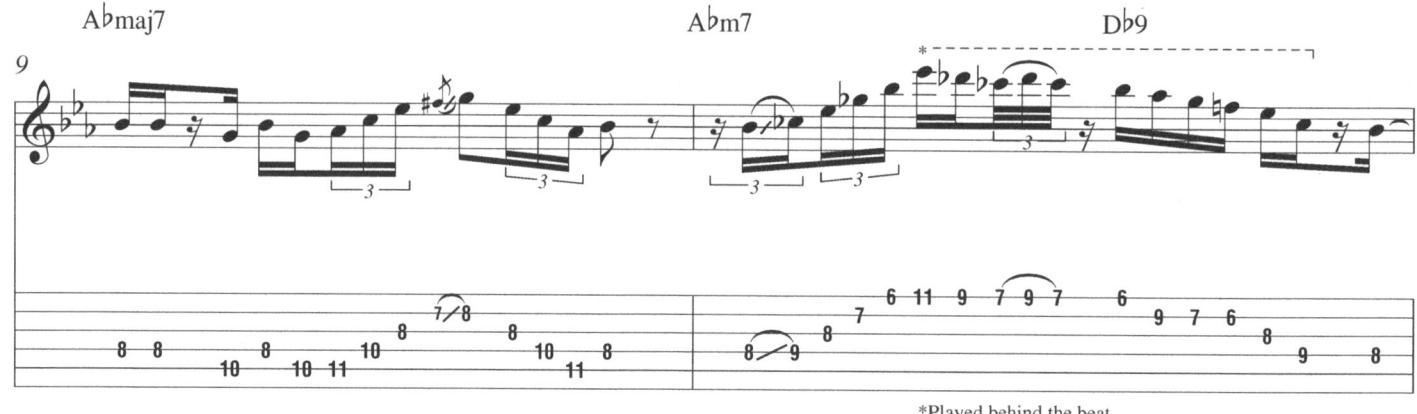

*Played behind the beat.

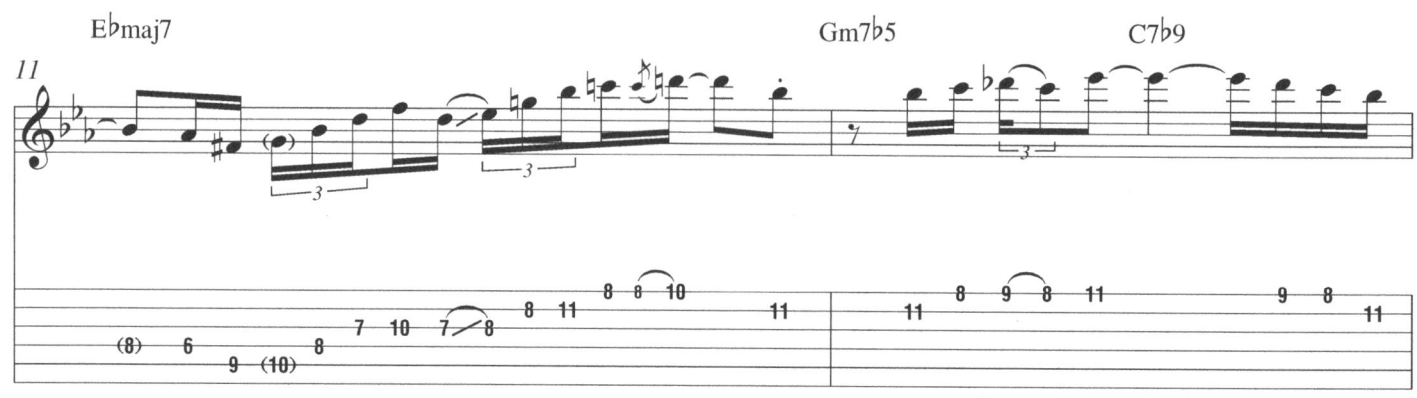

Relaxin'

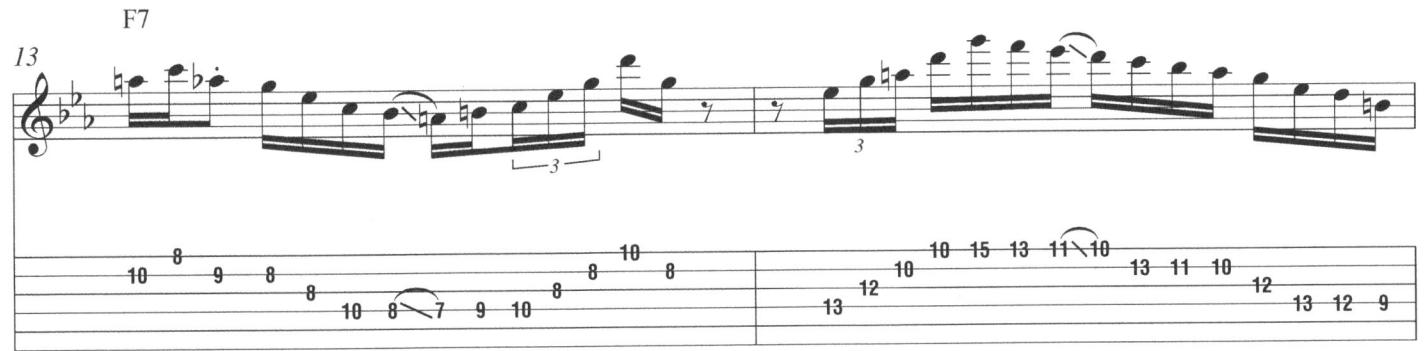
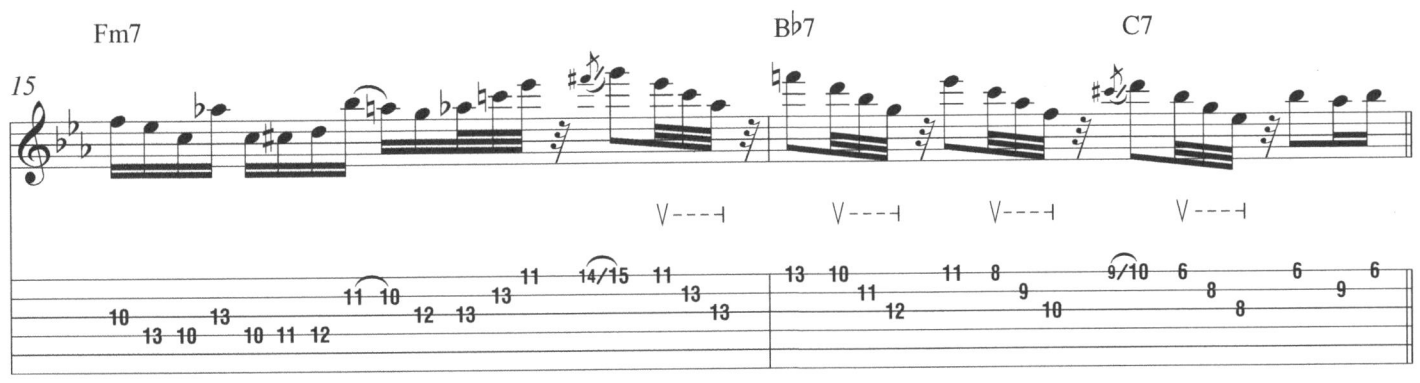
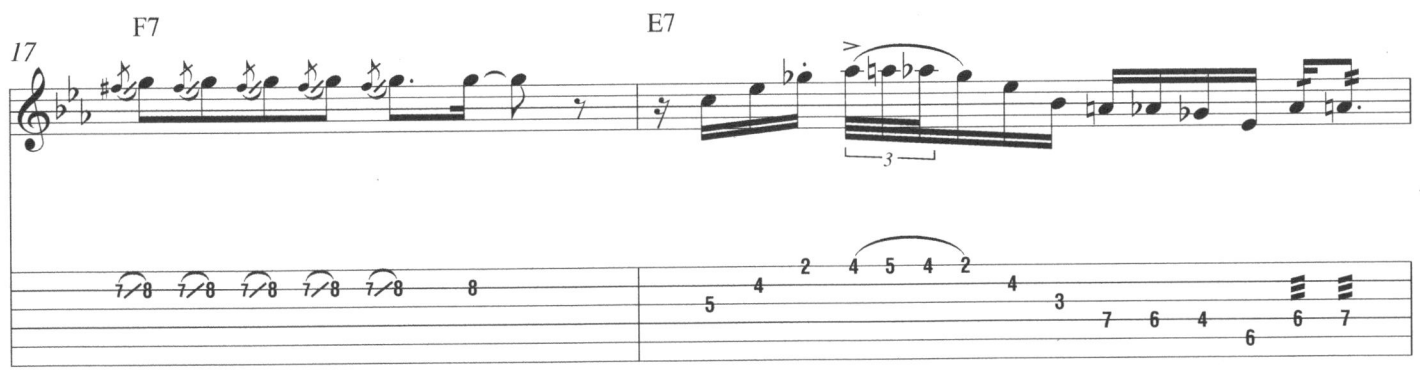

Relaxin'

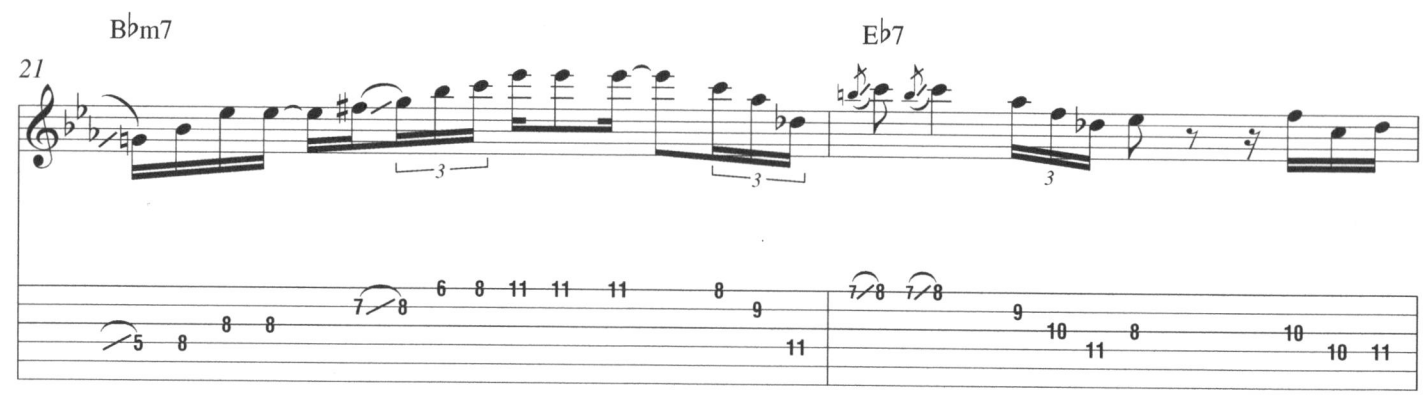
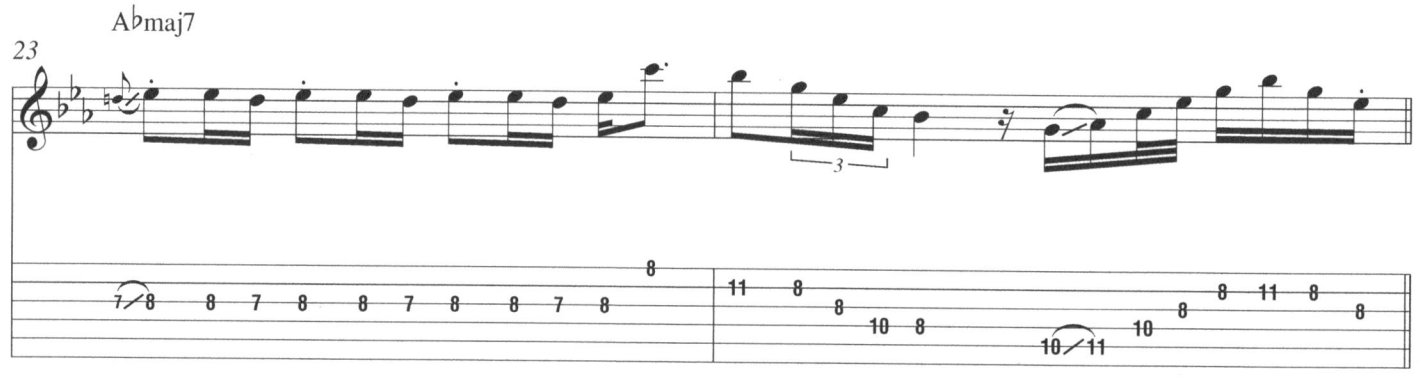

Relaxin'

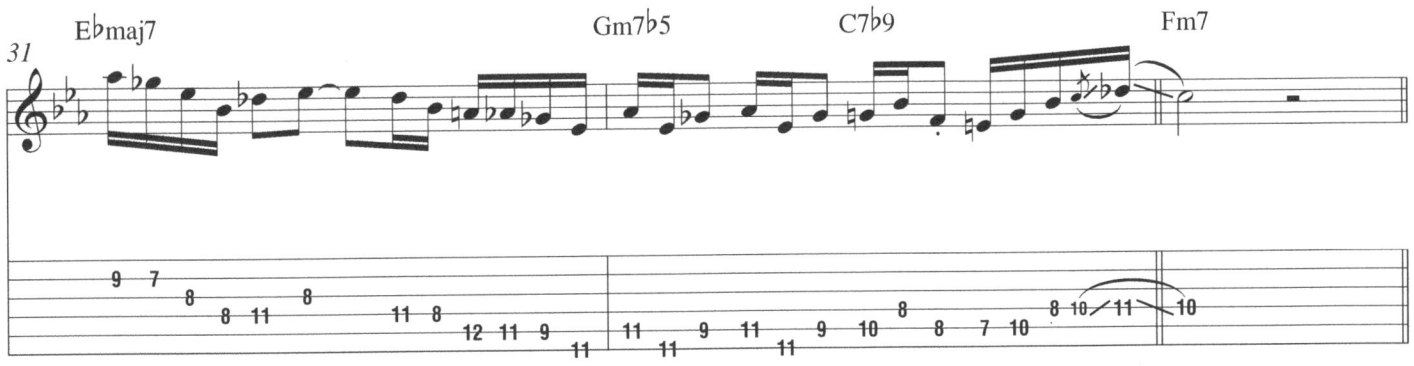

Full House 1962

Wes Montgomery

"Wes himself was like a shaman with that instrument in his hands… the smile on his face and the twinkle in his eyes were separate from [what] was pouring out."
—Pat Martino

When one name is mentioned by those in the know as the greatest jazz guitarist of all time, it is most often that of Wes Montgomery. Much has been made of his use of the thumb in lieu of a pick, as well as his trademark melody-in-octaves sound, but his contributions to the art go far beyond these specific devices. His harmonic concept, linear approach, and well-defined rhythmic feel helped bring the guitar into the post-bop era, paving the way in his own time for such giants as George Benson and Pat Martino, and profoundly influencing just about everyone else who came after him, including Pat Metheny, Mike Stern, Emily Remler, Bobby Broom, and Peter Bernstein.

Born John Leslie Montgomery in Indianapolis on March 6, 1923, Wes grew up partly in Columbus, Ohio, but came back to the city of his birth by age 17. The Indianapolis scene is historically famous as a source of leading jazz figures, with J.J. Johnson, Slide Hampton, David Baker, and Freddie Hubbard all hailing from Naptown. Wes and his brothers formed part of this milieu, as older brother Monk was a pioneer of the electric bass and younger brother Buddy a fine pianist and vibraphonist (and great composer in his own right). When Wes was 12 years old, Monk gave him a four-string tenor guitar, on which he began to get familiar with the basics of the instrument. But at the age of 19, he first heard the music of Charlie Christian and was compelled to purchase an electric guitar and amplifier, teaching himself how to play by figuring out Christian's solos note for note. Through personal preference, and lack of instruction, he soon took to sounding the strings with the thumb of his right hand, instead of with a pick or using true fingerstyle technique. He was in short time working as a musician, even if initially just replicating those copied solos on the bandstand.

His first major gig was touring with the band of famous vibraphonist Lionel Hampton from 1948 to early 1950. But Wes, already married and with children, wanted to be a family man and opted at this point for a home life in his hometown, working factory jobs by day and local gigs by night to make ends meet. By the late 1950s, his brothers were playing in California with their group the Mastersounds and had a recording contract with Pacific Jazz. Wes was brought on board for *The Montgomery Brothers and Five Others* (1958, recorded in Indianapolis with local colleagues), followed by *Kismet* (also 1958, with the Mastersounds).

But his true big break came in 1959 when legendary saxophonist Cannonball Adderley came through town and heard him with his trio at the Missile Room. Adderley reported to Orrin Keepnews of Riverside Records that here was a talent that had to be signed. Keepnews took his word for it and sound-unheard arranged to have the trio flown out to New York for a session. The first record, *The Wes Montgomery Trio* (1959, subtitled *A Dynamic New Sound*), involved organist Melvin Rhyne and drummer Paul Parker and brought Wes's playing to wider listenership. Next came *The Incredible Jazz Guitar of Wes Montgomery* (1960), with the top-flight New York rhythm section of Tommy Flanagan on piano and brothers Percy and Albert Heath on bass and drums, respectively. Now

Full House

regarded as a classic, this album introduced his signature compositions "West Coast Blues" and "Four on Six." The jazz guitar world was being set on fire with his utterly fresh, spirited, and virtuosic improvisation, as he dished out brilliantly developed solos in single-note lines, octaves, and block chords. Wes began winning awards in *DownBeat* and elsewhere and captured the attention of established players and up-and-comers alike among his fellow guitarists.

Other significant Riverside albums included *Groove Yard* (1960) with his brothers, *Bags Meets Wes!* (1961) with vibraphone great Milt Jackson, the excellent organ trio follow-up *Boss Guitar* (1963) with Jimmy Cobb on drums, and an energized live date from Berkeley, California, *Full House* (1962), which showcased his lovely chord-melody rendition of the ballad "I've Grown Accustomed to Her Face." Around this time, he would also record with Adderley and (in the company of his brothers) pianist George Shearing. His first foray into a more orchestrated context, beyond his usual small-group format, was *Fusion! Wes Montgomery with Strings* (1963—not to be confused with jazz-rock fusion in this case!), a venture that was enjoyed by Wes himself, if not so well-received by his jazz-aficionado listeners.

By 1964, Wes was working with producer Creed Taylor on the Verve label (which was no longer under the leadership of mainstream jazz enthusiast Norman Granz). Outside of another celebrated live recording, *Smokin' at the Half-Note* (1965, with the Wynton Kelly Trio), and two swingin' albums with organist Jimmy Smith plus big band in 1966, his output began to veer in a more commercial direction. Starting with *Movin' Wes* (1964) and *Bumpin'* (1965), Taylor placed him in highly arranged settings, and by 1965's *Goin' out of My Head*, he was well on his way to popular appeal with high record sales and a Grammy award. His sessions increasingly involved brass, strings, and extra percussion, as well as contemporary rhythms and frequent pop covers (the melodies of which were generally rendered by Wes playing in octaves, often with little improvisation to follow). Subsequent titles in this vein included *California Dreaming*, *Tequila*, and *A Day in the Life* (his first on the A&M label in 1967).

Wes himself looked at these projects both as a new kind of musical challenge (working in a rigorously structured framework with very literate musicians) and as a means to make a better living for his family of now seven children. But this boon also became a burden, in that his live gig audiences now expected more often to hear the cover hits, as opposed to his freely stretched-out jazz explorations. Many Wes admirers appreciate his work through this entire phase for the ever-present musicality of his interpretation, while others feel he simply sold out and created trite material by the end of his career. In any case, he was certainly a trailblazer in showing how straight-ahead guitar tone and jazz vocabulary could work within an even-eighths groove, and his own Latin-funk tune "Road Song" has become a staple of the jazz repertoire.

Montgomery died of a heart attack on June 15, 1968, at home in Indianapolis. He had been quite straight-laced in his lifestyle (although he was a cigarette smoker), and his early departure is often attributed to the exhausting work schedule he kept while paying his dues at length in Indy, and later while touring as a successful recording artist (probably exacerbated by his avoidance of airplanes). Known to be a warm and thoughtful person as well as an artistic giant, his legacy on the instrument and impact on the music cannot be overstated. The great voice of the guitar known simply as "Wes" resonates loudly through the jazz world still today.

How to Play It

With the special energy of a live session, Wes joyously swings and wails through three choruses on his lively minor-key waltz. He delivers everything with his signature in-the-pocket groove, now and then getting an extra edge of expression by holding back just slightly in the timing of a note or two—as he does going into measure 6, for example, or in the middle of measure 98 (compare its rhythm to the next two measures)—while still maintaining a very firm rhythmic feel.

Though he famously used his right-hand thumb to pluck the strings, this is a very specialized technique (occasional upstrokes included), fully developed by relatively few guitarists, and most of us will do well to use the pick for this material. Another idiosyncrasy was his total avoidance of the left-hand pinky for fretting single-note lines along with a remarkably linear approach to the fretboard. He often preferred rapid motion up and down the neck for musical ideas that could actually be played in a more concise area (where we may at times prefer sticking closer to one position). In this manner, all the single-note content of this solo can indeed be played using only three fingers of the left hand, allowing them to be somewhat angled as in violin technique (fingertips pointing slightly up the neck). But here too, we can feel free to take a more conventional route and use the pinky if it suits us.

Full House

The tune has an AABA structure, with 16-bar A-sections and an eight-bar bridge. Harmonically, the recurring Fm7 and B♭7 in the A-sections are largely treated as a pair and addressed mainly with F Dorian material, with an E♮ often thrown in (implying B♭7♯11). When the D♭7 and altered C7 are at hand, the note choice tends to be specific to each of these chords, as in measures 22–24. Chordal arpeggios come into play especially on the bridge, with, for example, the stretchy outline of B♭m7 in measure 33, the members of E°7 in measure 34 (to suit E♭7♭9), and A♭maj9 tones in measure 35 (measures 33 and 35 both seem to end with a slight miss that's one half step outside the intended chord).

By looking at a couple of key spots, we can understand much about Montgomery's fretboard movement and the way he maps out certain harmonic material. The sweeping ascent of measures 77–78 shows an elongated positioning for what is mostly an Fm9 arpeggio through two octaves. Here the ring finger (or pinky) must stretch or hop to the first G on string 2, fret 8, and at beat 2 of the next measure the index jumps up to fret 11 on string 1. For the altered C7 line starting at measure 95, beat 3, the left hand shifts up two frets for each pair of notes until there's a stretchy hammer-on at fret 11 and a reach for the grace note at fret 13. In the big descent of measures 97–102, he lays out a nearly complete two-octaves-plus of F Dorian tones, spread from the 15th to the third frets. He works his way down string 1 with a big jump to reach fret 6 in measure 99, followed by a quick visit to the eighth position for the next five notes, and then moves back down, finally landing in the third position after a bit of reaching/shifting.

Some other particularly tricky moves: in measure 36 (in the first bridge), after playing through D♭ Mixolydian tones for D♭7 in the fourth position, quickly place the middle finger on the A♮ at fret 2 to slide into the G♭ major zone. In measure 93 (in his second bridge), a big leap down from the high D♭ returns him to the bottom area of the neck for improvisation on G♭maj7 and Bmaj7, along the lines of common chord shapes or scale fingerings in that region. To avoid such an extreme jump, the notes of measures 93–94 could indeed all be played in the sixth position.

And then there are those octaves! It's a technique used by many guitarists through the history of the music, but owned by Wes more than anyone else. He makes it sound easy to play brisk melodies or improvised phrases doubled at the octave, but it requires a certainty as to where you are going with the left hand and extra-efficient repeated downstrokes from the right hand. In the first burst of these in measures 17–20, it's apparent that he covers a lot of ground on the fretboard with this technique as well. Use the index and ring fingers to fret octaves on the 6/4 or 5/3 string pairs, and index plus pinky for octaves on the 4/2 or 3/1 pairs. He occasionally uses upstrokes on upbeats (or "and" counts) within these octave lines, as in measures 145–146. Here you can see too that sometimes a note within the passage winds up not actually doubled, perhaps due to an incompletely fretted note, or a partial miss by the thumb. (Even if this is just an accident, allowing a little such latitude can ease the busy transition across strings.)

In his typical way, he uses clear-cut changes of texture at key points to help the solo build. He enters the second chorus at measure 57 with a bluesy device, playing the same note on two different strings either simultaneously (with a slide-in on one string) or alternately. His ideas are more distinctly rhythmic than linear here, as well as in many other places through the rest of the solo, with groovy repeated figures like those of measures 65–70 or his mimicking of the tune's sparse melody from measure 105 through the start of measure 110. The third chorus starts off at measure 113 with a call-and-response pattern between percussive pairs of octaves and short single-note phrases. By the second A-section at measure 129, it's all octaves until the end, with more and more slides between them, until the dramatic swoops of measures 162–165 lead to his declamatory ending on the tonic.

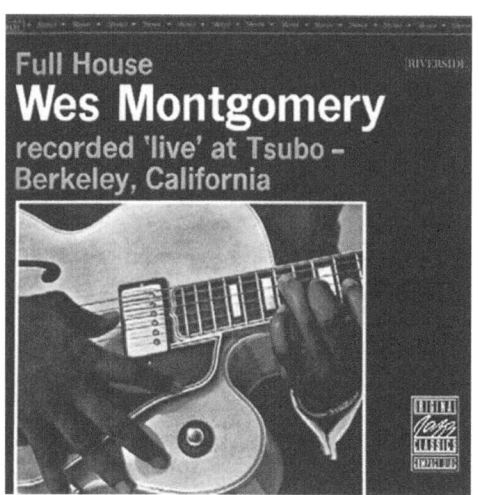

For the 1962 live date Full House, *Wes met up at a Berkeley, California cafe with tenor sax powerhouse Johnny Griffin, and Miles Davis's revered rhythm section (Wynton Kelly, piano, Paul Chambers, bass, and Jimmy Cobb, drums).*

Vital Stats

Guitarist: Wes Montgomery

Song: "Full House"

Album: *Full House*, 1962

Age at Time of Recording: 39

Guitar: Gibson L-5 with Florentine cutaway or ES-175

Amp: Fender (possibly brown-face Princeton with 12" speaker)

Full House

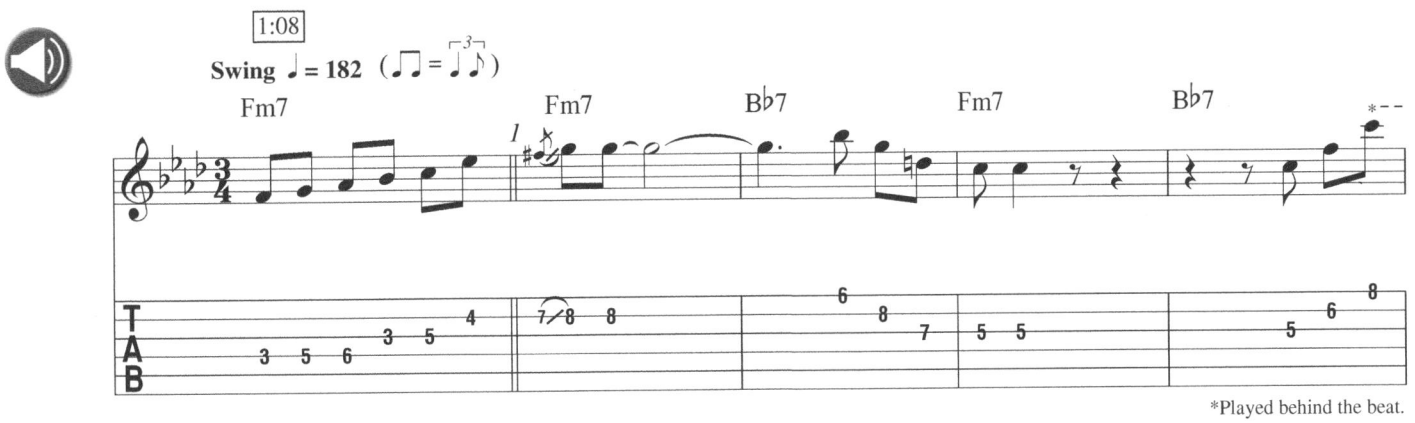
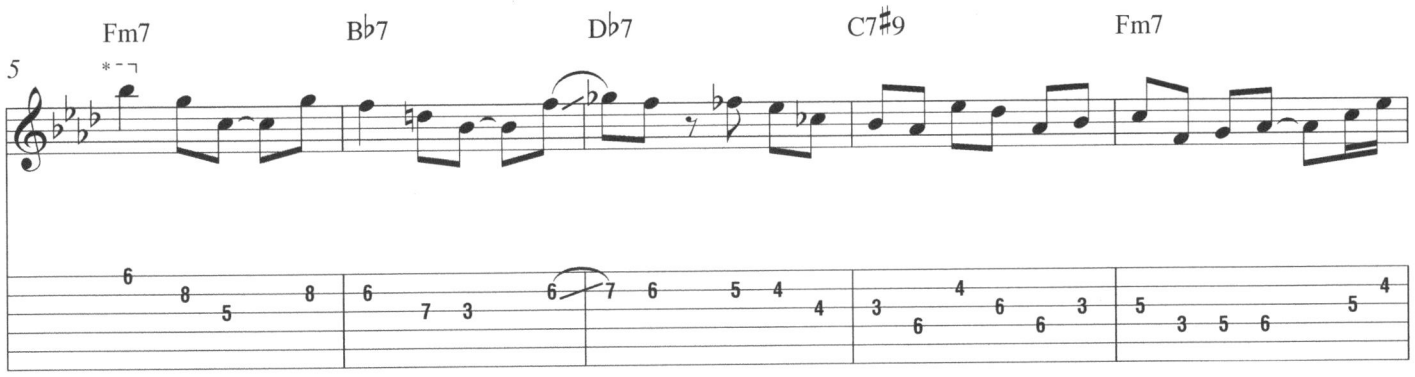
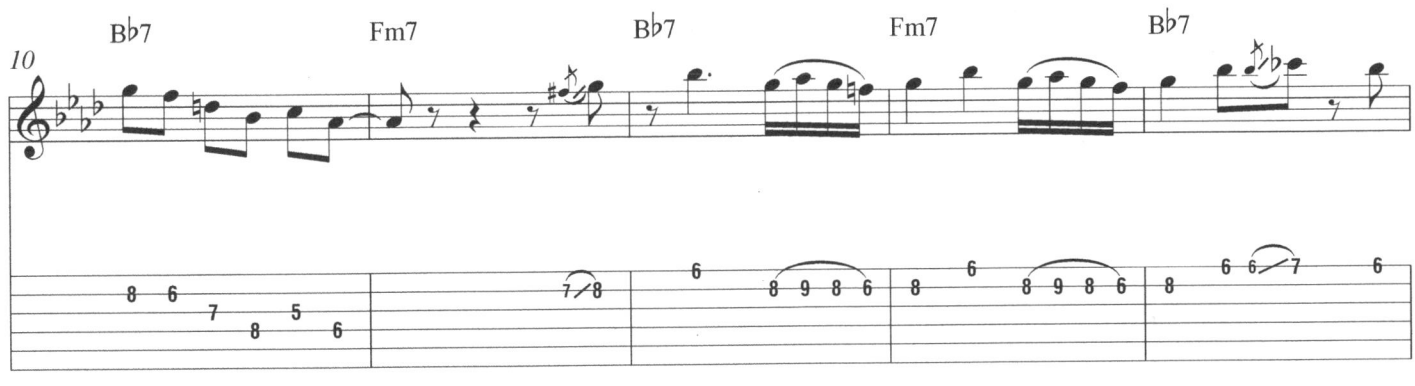
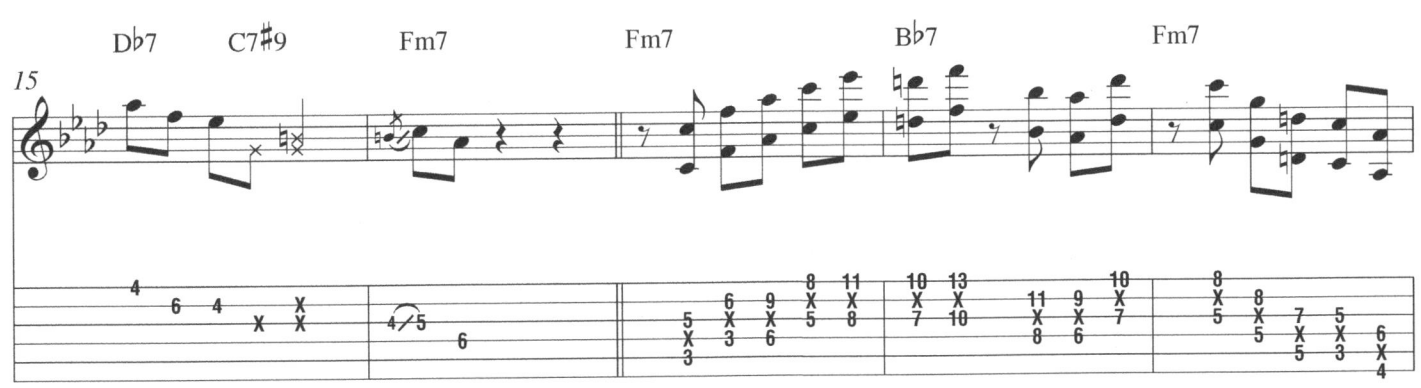

By John L. (Wes) Montgomery
Copyright © 1965 (Renewed) by TAGGIE MUSIC CO., a division of Gopam Enterprises, Inc.
All Rights Reserved Used by Permission

Full House

*Played behind the beat.

Full House

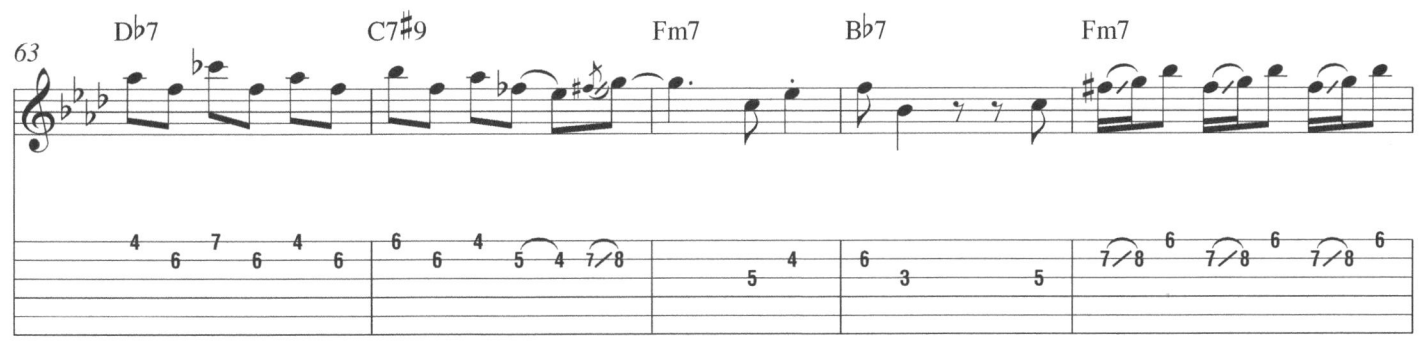

Full House

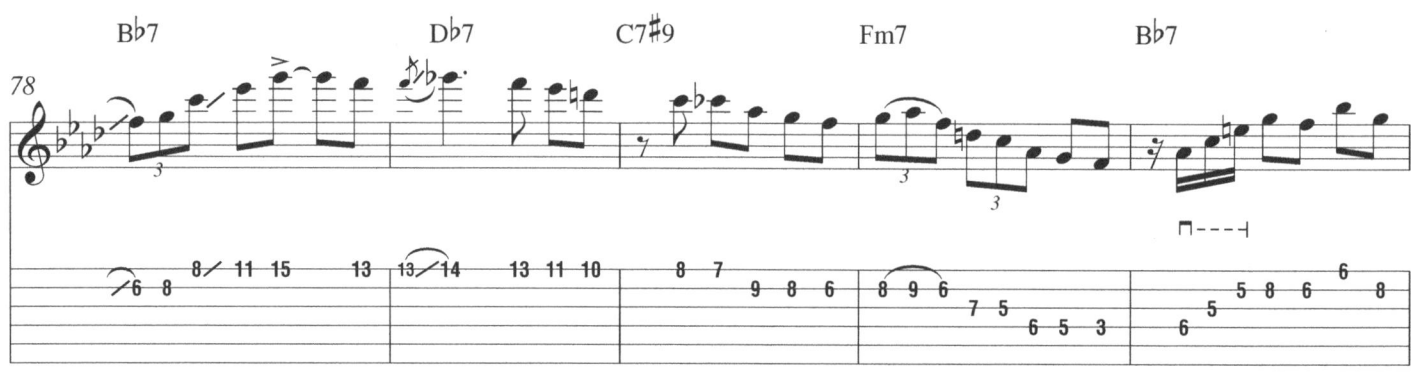
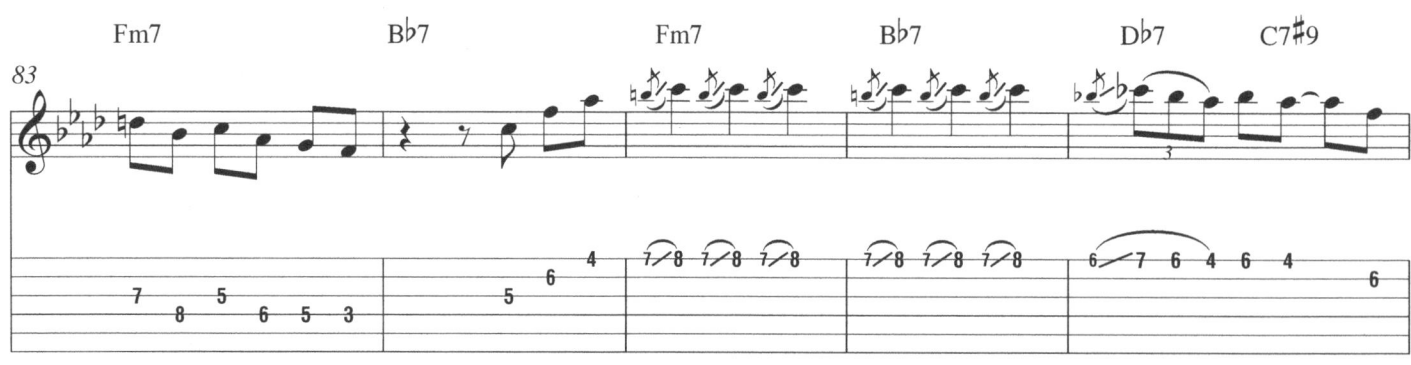
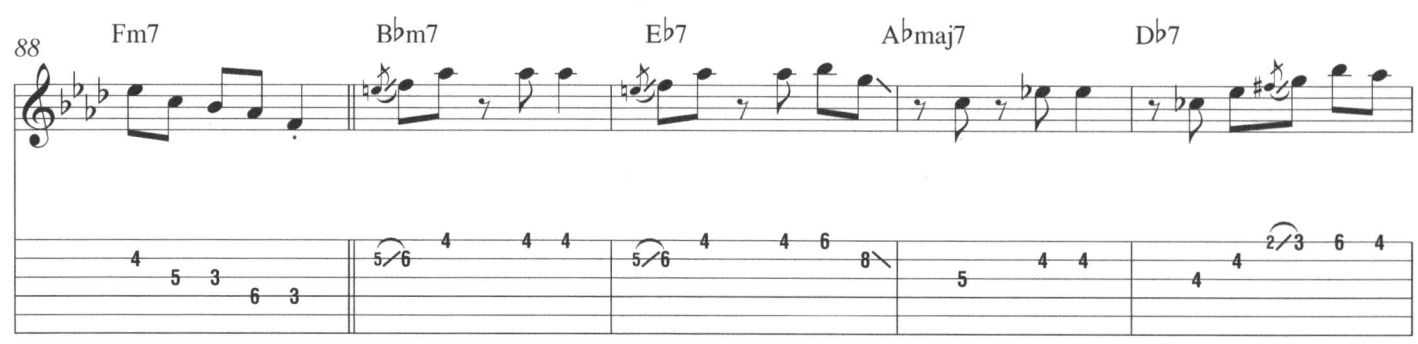

Full House

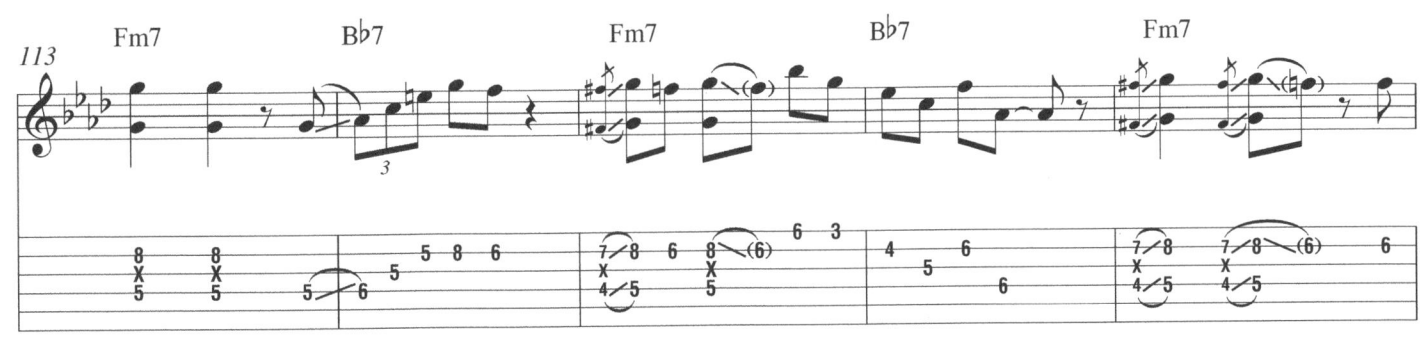

Full House

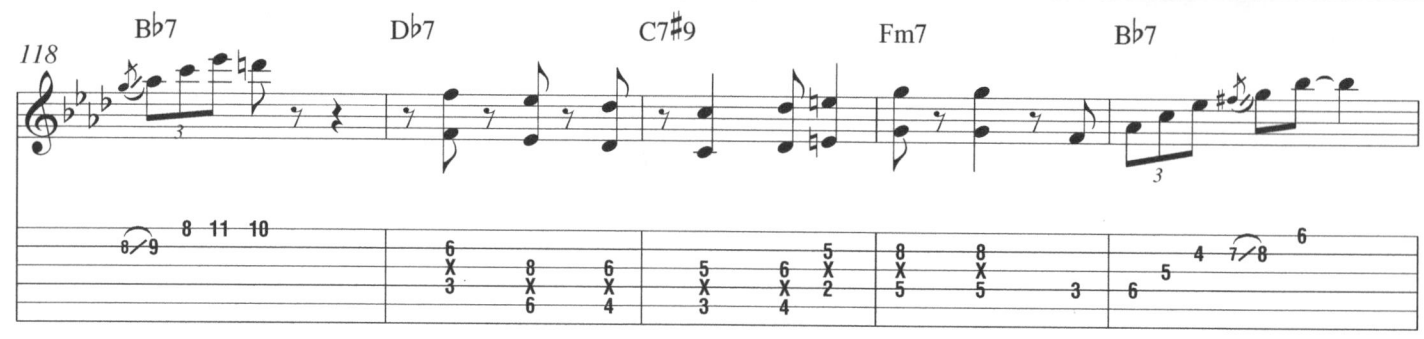
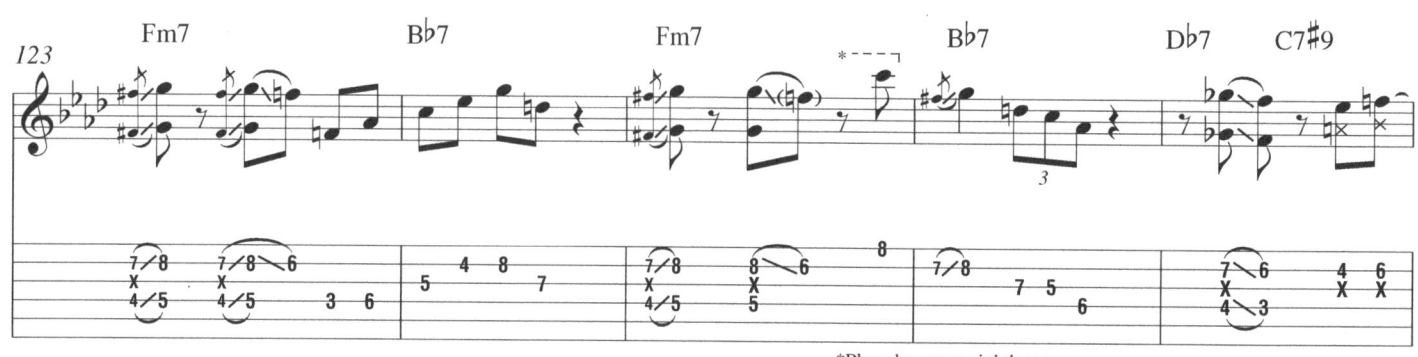

*Played as even eighth note.

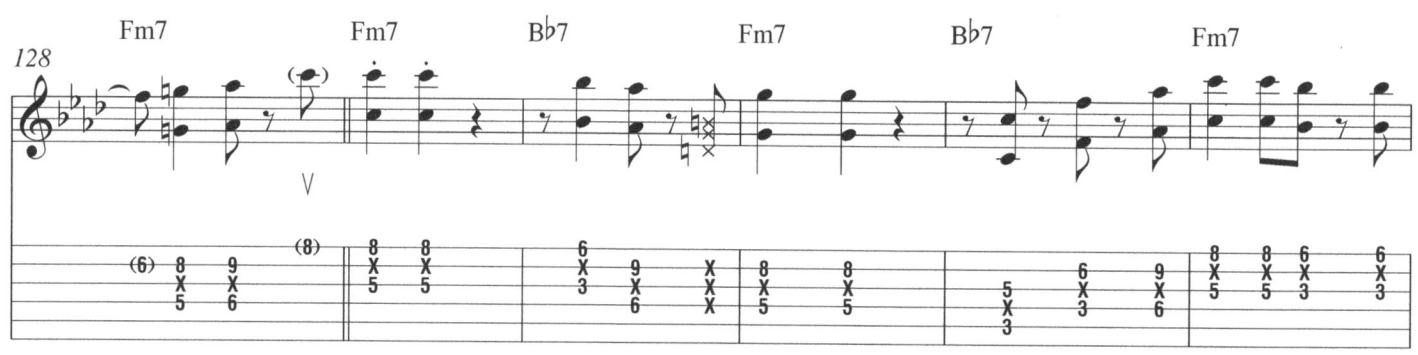
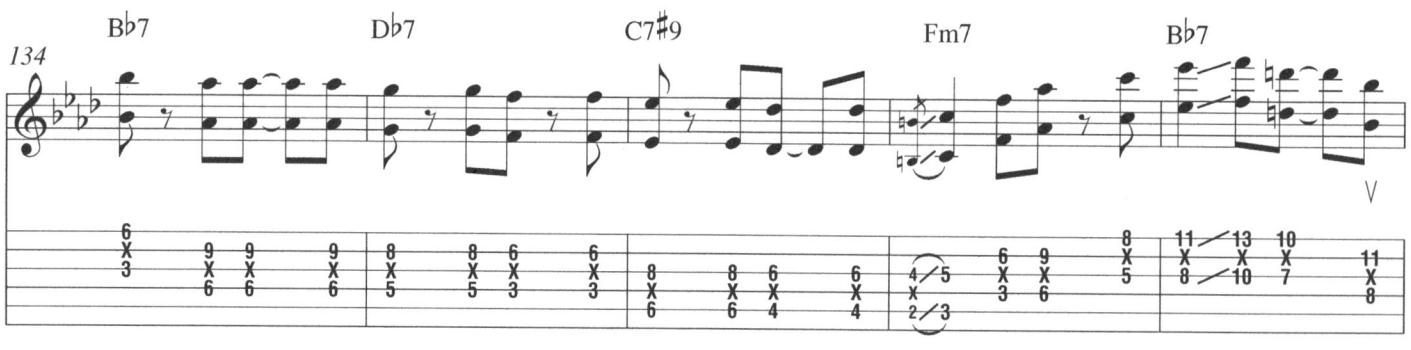
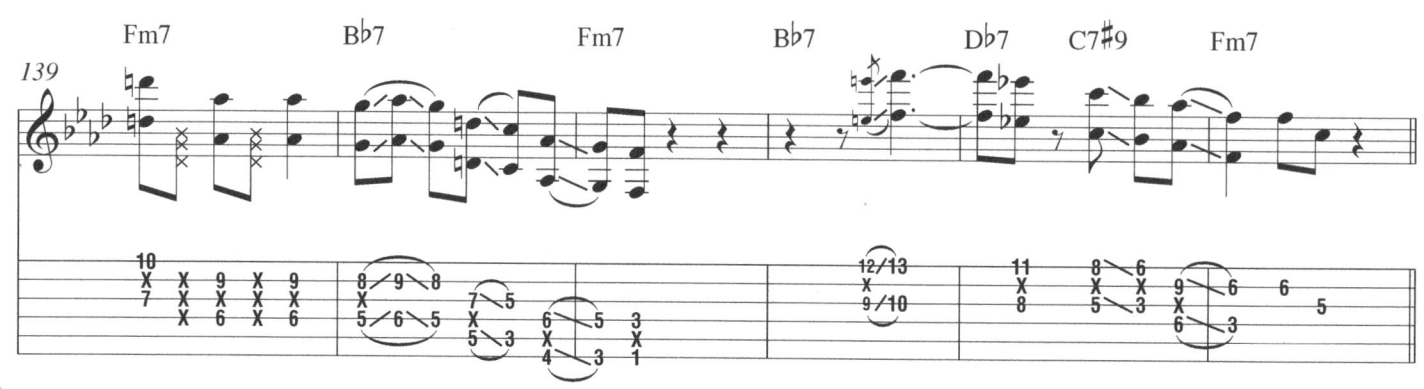

Full House

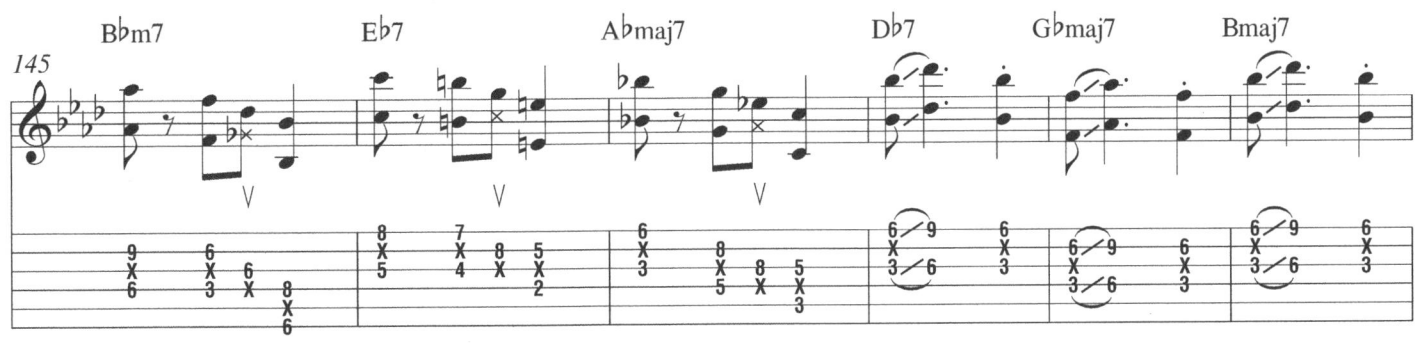
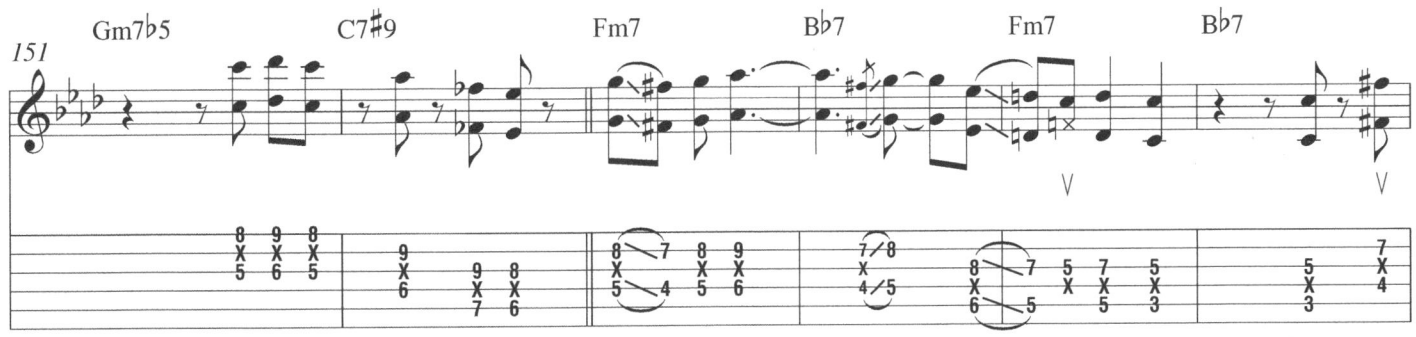
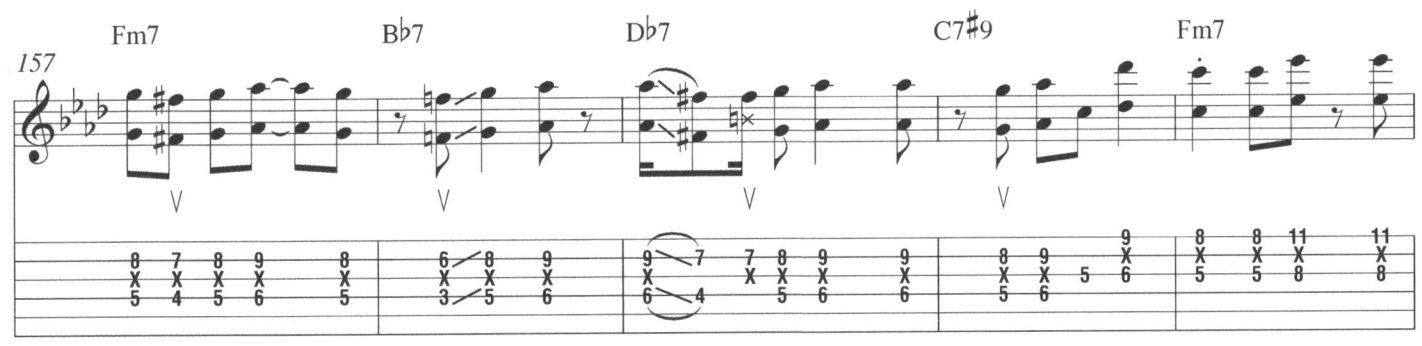
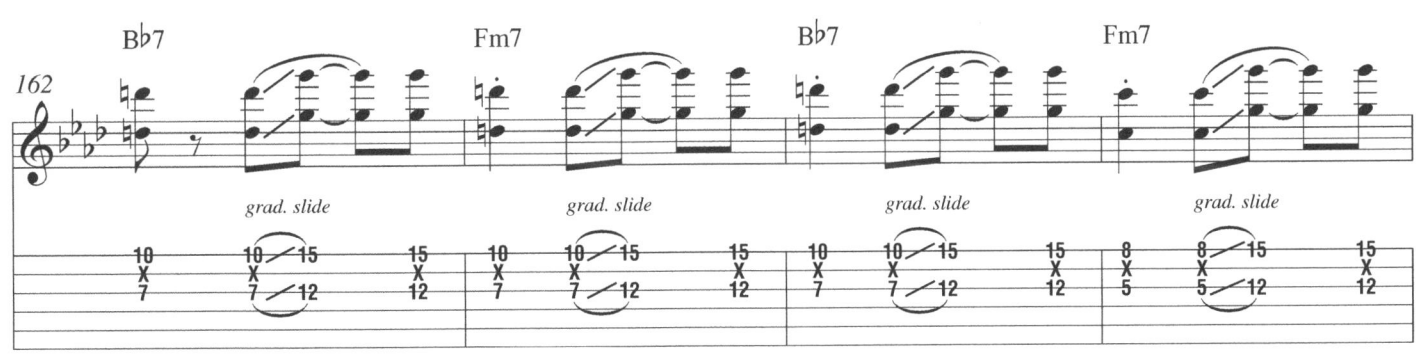
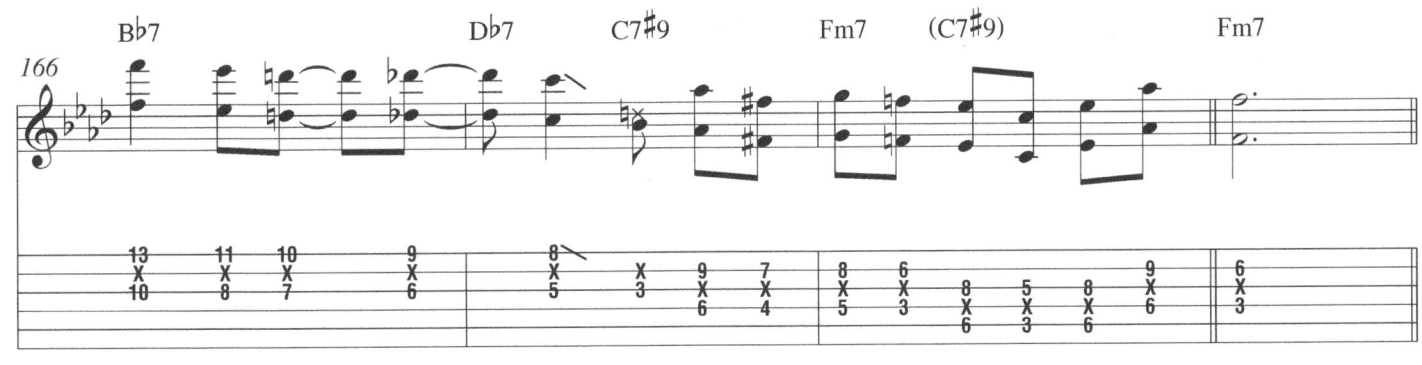

Jean de Fleur 1963

Grant Green

"I don't listen to guitar players much. I dig horn players. I was very much influenced by Charlie Parker."
—Grant Green

© Val Wilmer CTSImages

Grant Green has a unique place in the hearts of many jazz lovers, but especially musicians. While he may not have had the chops or fame of Django, Wes, or George Benson, he remains a personal favorite for a large contingent of hard-bop devotees and more recent straight-ahead jazz guitarists. Particularly resourceful in his approach to rhythm, he could move between extremes of aggressive or laid-back timing and create plentiful variations on a single phrase. He certainly had an excellent command of the instrument and of the musical language—but without the overwhelming technique and non-stop barrage of ideas heard in some of the other all-time masters, he tended more towards the aesthetic of saying a lot with a little, making powerful statements through style, feel, taste, and spirit.

Born June 6, 1935 in St. Louis, Missouri, young Grant learned blues guitar from his father and uncle (a stylistic influence that would stay with him through his career) and showed a talent for music early on. He was a class clown in grade school and frequently involved music in his antics, sneaking over to the piano or smuggling a ukulele into the classroom. By his early teens, he made enough money playing in the sanctified churches of his hometown that his parents allowed him to drop out of school. In not too long, he was asked back into his would-be high school as a musician rather than as a student—a guitarist was needed who knew enough chords to accompany the choir. Inspired by the guitar work of electric innovator Charlie Christian and smooth melodicist Jimmy Raney, he even more fervently copied the alto sax solos of bebop grandmaster Charlie Parker. He played all kinds of gigs in the area through the 1950s and gained an avid local following as an energetic young jazzman. In 1959, he was heard by famed altoist Lou Donaldson, who was impressed and arranged for him to travel to New York to meet Alfred Lion, co-founder of Blue Note Records. And thus began a great match-up of label and artist.

Blue Note is one of the most respected institutions of the jazz world, above all for their heyday of the 1950s and 1960s, when they effectively represented a whole sub-genre of the music and a pinnacle of artistic integrity—and Green is more associated with the label and its sound than any other guitarist. His 1961 debut album as a leader, *Grant's First Stand*, with organist Baby Face Willette and drummer Ben Dixon, followed a session with Donaldson (*Here 'Tis*). He became a staff musician for the outfit, ultimately recording 30 albums of his own—and nearly 40 more as a sideman—on Blue Note alone and from 1961 to 1965 was their most prolific artist on any instrument. Among the many fine titles he released in this time, *Grantstand* (1961) involved bluesy organist Jack McDuff, while *Sunday Morning* (1961) played on the gospel style with which he had grown up in St. Louis, and *The Latin Bit* (1962) featured popular south-of-the-border selections with extra percussion. His horn-like approach was quite evident on the guitar-bass-drums trio side *Green Street* (1961), where he barely played a chord even while stating a song's melody. *Talkin' About Grant Green* (1964) showcased him in a more modern organ trio setting, with innovative organist Larry Young and John

Jean de Fleur

Coltrane-drummer Elvin Jones (the three would be together again, along with other sidemen, for *Street of Dreams, I Wanna Hold Your Hand*, and Young's date *Into Something*).

1963's *Idle Moments* was a special high point, with its mix of melancholy moods and hard-swinging grooves, through a set of tastefully arranged sextet pieces. Some of his most monumental playing also comes out on *Nigeria*, recorded in 1962 with pianist Sonny Clark, bassist Sam Jones, and drummer Art Blakey, and *Matador*, a 1965 session that seems like a Coltrane record with guitar instead of tenor sax, with Elvin Jones on drums again and McCoy Tyner at the piano (neither of these titles were actually released until just after his death). His notable albums as a sideman include Hank Mobley's *Workout* (1961), Stanley Turrentine's burnin' live session *Up at Minton's* (1961), and Lee Morgan's *Search for the New Land* (1964).

Grant made his move to New York when starting with Blue Note, but it would be a few years before his young family

Here Grant was joined in the front line by modernist icons Joe Henderson on tenor sax and Bobby Hutcherson on vibes, for what is considered by aficionados to be one of the finest moments not just for him or for Blue Note, but for all of recorded jazz.

would join him there. While still in St. Louis, he had taken up the Islamic faith and was very active in the Nation of Islam. Since then, he largely maintained a commitment to the religion's dietary laws, avoiding the pork ribs that the rest of the band enjoyed after many a night of music, but was less strict about abstaining from drugs and alcohol. Substance problems and marital strife hounded him, and by the late 1960s his career took a lull and a shift. He was envious of the commercial successes enjoyed by fellow guitarists Wes Montgomery and George Benson (he and Benson especially had a friendly rivalry, and Benson became godfather to his eldest son Gregory) and was not fond of musical categories such as "jazz" that might restrict him to playing only in a certain way. After a short prison sentence in 1968 for possession, he enthusiastically began his forays into funkier territory on organist Reuben Wilson's *The Love Bug* (1969) and on his own records such as *Green Is Beautiful* (1970) and *Live at the Lighthouse* (1972). Instrumental versions of current popular tunes such as "Say a Little Prayer," "Ain't It Funky Now," and "A Day in the Life" were part of the repertoire on these sessions, as well as the Detroit funk anthem "Jan Jan."

Grant spent the last decade of his life in his adoptive hometown of Detroit, in a house on Greenlawn Street (always enjoying a play on his own name, whether in album titles, or in a green suit or Cadillac), and here he once again became a great draw on the local scene. But his health deteriorated through the 1970s. His last record was *Easy* in 1978, and early the next year he died of a heart attack after a drive between gigs in California and New York. The decade following his death saw a resurgence in the popularity of straight-ahead jazz, and his music gained new life through this trend, as well as through the use of his recorded material in the samples of acid jazz pioneers Us3, among others. His son Gregory (born 1955) has followed in his footsteps as a professional guitarist, using the name Grant Green, Jr. (not to be confused with his younger brother actually named Grant!), and the influence of Grant Sr.'s exuberant tones still looms large today.

How to Play It

Idle Moments may be, if you had to name one, Grant's most revered album, and while it indeed explores the quietude that the title suggests, his own tune "Jean de Fleur" is one of the less-idle selections from the session (it is his solo on the alternate take, released in the late 1980s, that is dealt with here). This lively setting provides a great example of the rhythmic bounce with which he could make a note or phrase come alive, as well as a chord progression that readily allows him to show his effective use of just a few melodic ideas in creating a solo.

From the start, he delivers fluid lines of eighth notes interspersed with a remarkable number of staccato tones all with a spirited sense of swing. Check out the profuse chopped-off quarter notes in measures 22–24 and 107–110, among other places. These could generally bear the risk of stiffening up one's jazz playing, but Grant sounds as if he were dancing with his fingers as he plays them, placing them with just the right feel to make the line swing even more!

Jean de Fleur

A finer point of timing is that some of his quarter notes, while not quite as short as staccato, still have a little release time—a little breath before the next tone—as heard at the end of measures 54, 56, and 58. This really stems from feeling the groove in the left hand, which may be inspired to lift off a bit at the tail end of the beat.

The tune's chord progression has many instances of parallel motion—i.e., one kind of chord or chord grouping moving around onto different roots, often in a pattern or sequence. This frequently inspires Grant to improvise through a whole chunk of the form using a single basic idea, moving it around to fit the changes and demonstrating the variety of phrasing with which he keeps it fresh. Notice how the phrase of measures 7–8 mimics that of measures 5–6, with a little abbreviation. The next six measures involve another two-bar shape played three times in a row with some modification and transposed for each new chord. Then his first bridge, beginning at measure 23, involves a four-bar melodic statement that is itself played three times in sequence (with rhythmic variation) to go with the different ii–V–I movements (B♭m7–E♭7–A♭maj7, A♭m7–D♭7–G♭maj7, F♯m7–B7–Emaj7). Grant is sophisticated in his simplicity and uses such stark near-repetition to very hip effect, achieving a sense of unity and motivic development through his two choruses.

The first section of the tune is made up of parallel dominant chords (the 13ths), and here Grant plays heavily on the relationship of minor chords (particularly minor sevenths) to dominant sevenths. Specifically, this has to do with minor (or Dorian) material rooted on the 5th of an un-altered dominant chord. This is why his very first line, which sounds as F minor as we can get, goes hand-in-glove with the B♭13 at the beginning of the progression (even as he anticipates this chord by a few beats in the pickup to his first chorus). Correspondingly, and methodically, he uses E♭ minor ideas for A♭13, A♭ minor for D♭13, F♯ minor for B13, and E minor for A13 (these "minor" lines may draw from the melodic minor scale or the Dorian mode, as opposed to natural or harmonic minor).

Within the structure of "Jean de Fleur" are also eight-bar sections, such as measures 15–22, that center around G♯m7 (with F♯m7 and Amaj7 involved as well). Here Grant gets less harmonically specific, hearing that he can gracefully skate over these changes with G♯ blues scale material and always choosing the ninth position to do so—once again, making the most out of similar melodic ideas each time, while clearly showing his bluesy side.

Hand in hand with all the parallel chord motion, this solo is a study in position playing, as Grant moves between clearly defined fretboard areas to fit each chord or ii–V–I. For D♭13, he finds himself at the sixth position in a way that relates well to an A♭m7 chord shape (rooted on the fourth string), and as the chords move down stepwise, so too he changes position, two frets down at a time. This holds true for the bridge as well, where he embraces the eighth position anytime B♭m7–E♭7–A♭maj7 comes along (measures 23–26 and 83–86)—a standard fingering for each of these chords can be found there, and his lines are built around these shapes. Here too, he moves down two frets each time this group of chords recurs a step lower. The last chords of the bridge, Gm7♭5 and C7♭9, are the ii–V of what would be a ii–V–i in F minor, and the first time around (measure 38), he pulls out one of his signature minor ii–V licks at the eighth position for the occasion.

Such position playing gives us mostly compact, ergonomic fingerings for these lines, but things get tricky by his last A-section (starting at measure 99) as his bluesy sliding in and out of high notes reaches a climax. The top notes on string 1 are slid into with the pinky, but the slide-off from any one of these does not connect to the next tone below, which is played on the same string but with the index finger. And at the end of measure 104, Grant pulls an unusual stunt with his unusually large left hand, moving down string 3 with the index while his pinky grabs the one-fret slide up into E♭ on string 1.

Vital Stats

Guitarist: Grant Green

Song: "Jean de Fleur" (alternate version)

Album: *Idle Moments*, 1964 (recorded 1963)

Age at Time of Recording: 28

Guitar: Gibson L-7 with Gibson McCarty pickup/pickguard

Amp: Ampeg Jet (or Fender Tweed Deluxe)

Jean de Fleur

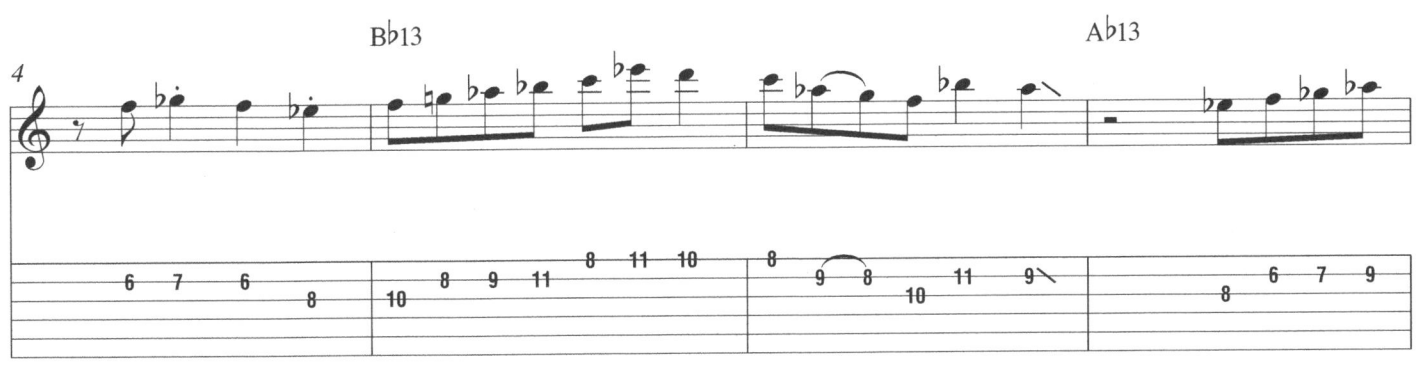

By Grant Green
© 1963 (Renewed) EMI UNART CATALOG INC.
All Rights Administered by EMI UNART CATALOG INC. (Publishing) and ALFRED MUSIC (Print)
All Rights Reserved   Used by Permission

Jean de Fleur

Jean de Fleur

Jean de Fleur

Jean de Fleur

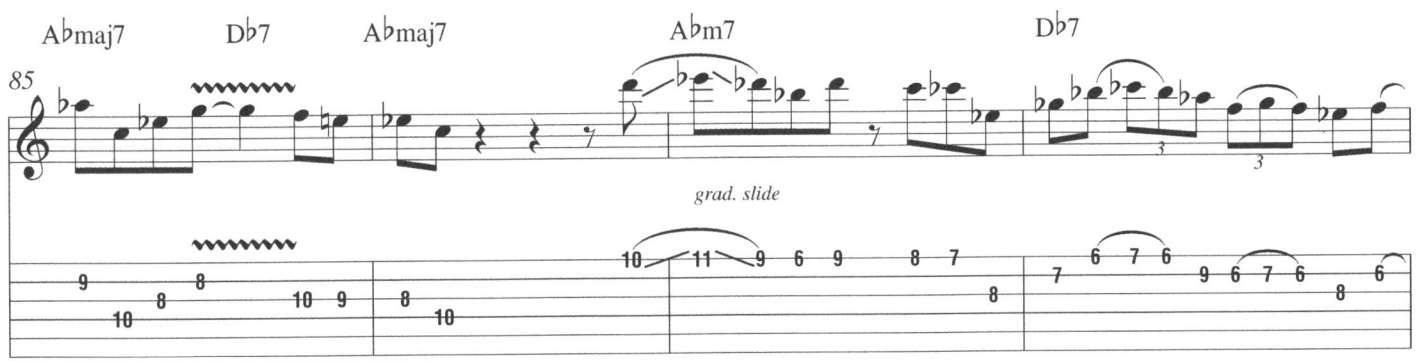

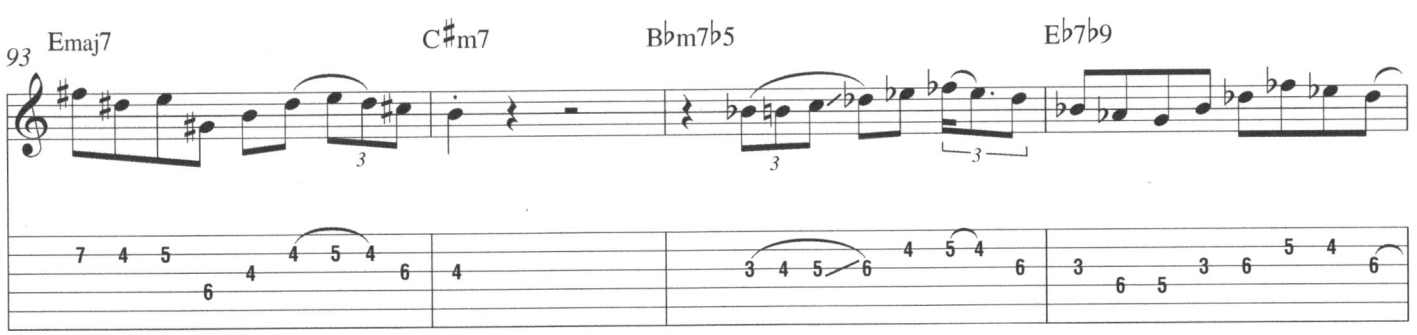
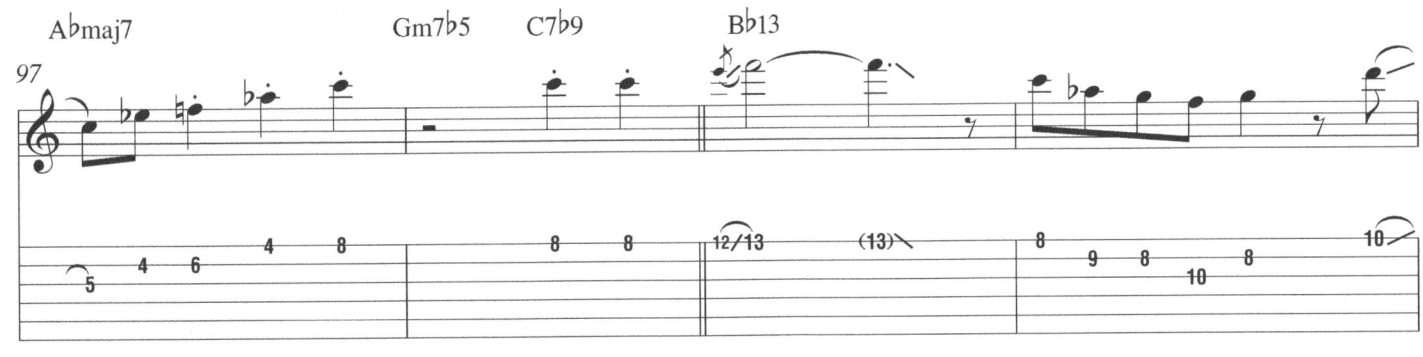

Jean de Fleur

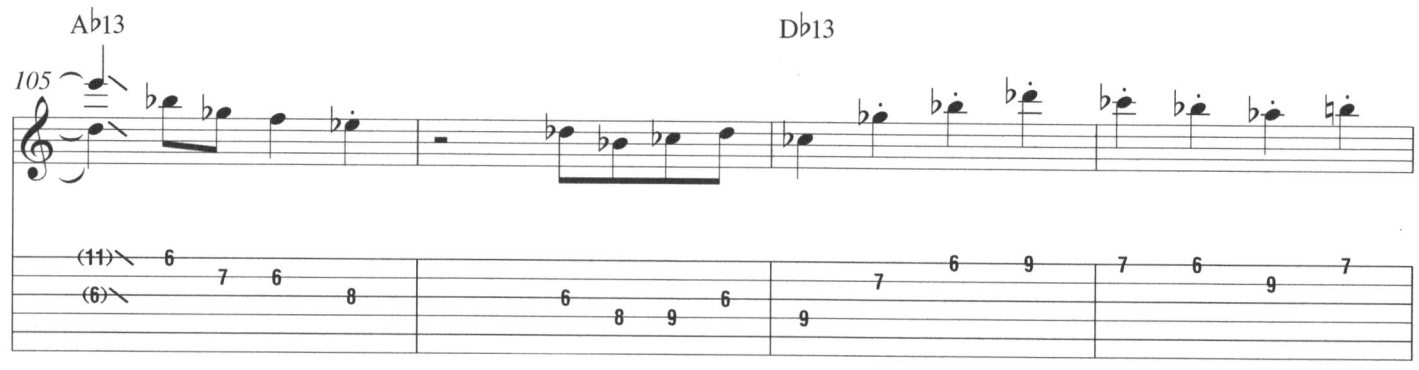
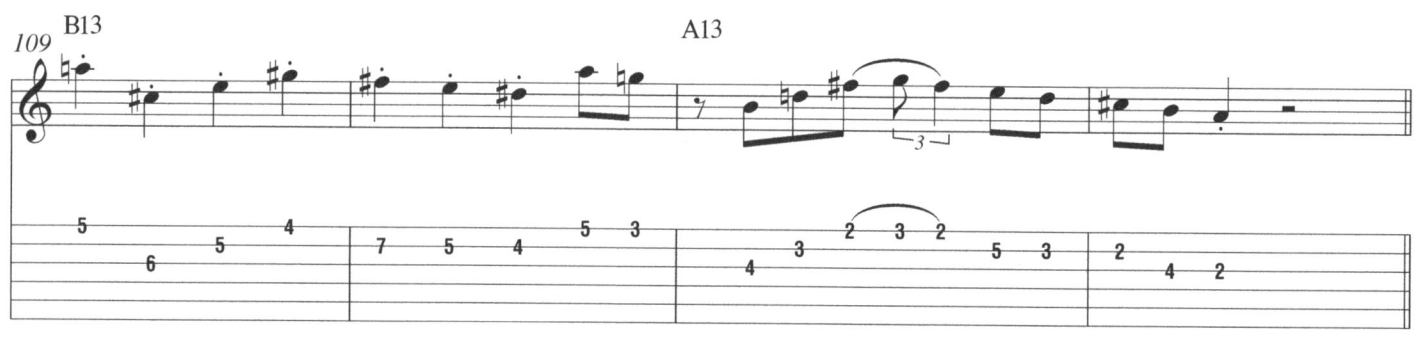
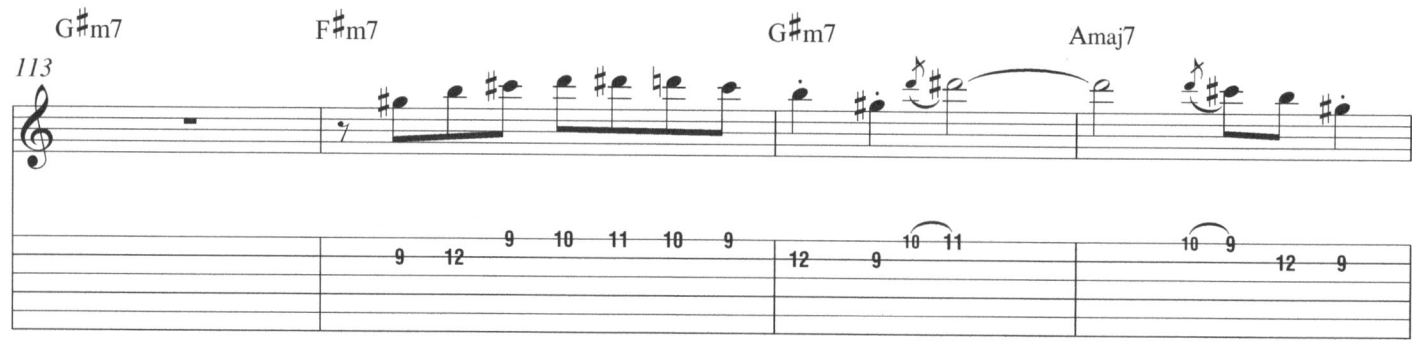
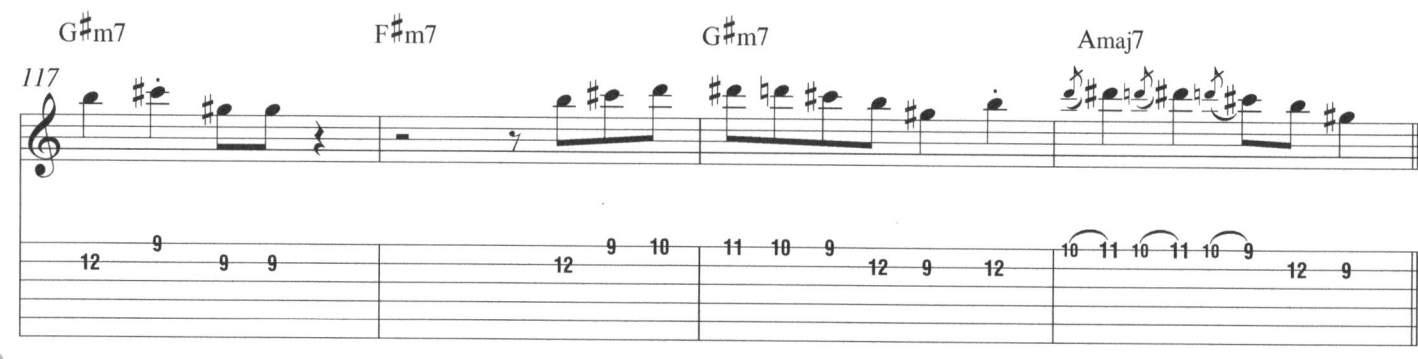

Benny's Back 1966

George Benson

"People ask me all the time whether I'd rather sing or play, but the truth is all of that is me. I'm a singer who loves to be an instrumentalist."
—George Benson

Courtesy Raúl Ranz, Wikimedia

No one fits the term "crossover artist" more spectacularly than guitarist—and vocalist—George Benson. Considered by insiders to be an artistically and technically superlative jazz player in the tradition of Wes Montgomery and Grant Green, he is also a household name among a wider public as the singer of "On Broadway" and "This Masquerade," and for top-selling instrumental hits like his version of "Breezin'." His rhythmically aggressive style, often marked by dazzlingly fast and dense material, is readily identifiable throughout all his work.

From his musical beginnings as a young child in Pittsburgh, Pennsylvania (where he was born on March 22, 1943), he was initially known more for his vocals than for his largely self-accompaniment efforts on the ukulele or guitar, making his recording debut at age 10 as Little Georgie Benson with the R&B single "She Makes Me Mad." Young Benson, as he further pursued his guitar chops, was heavily influenced by Wes, Grant, and Charlie Christian but also particularly struck by the jazz work of Nashville studio master Hank Garland. However, by the time of his first major break, touring with high-energy organist Jack McDuff from 1962 to 1965 (as a guitarist only), he was still more rooted in rhythm and blues than in jazz and had to use his sharp ears for rapid on-the-job training in the language and repertoire of the music.

His first album as a leader was *The New Boss Guitar of George Benson* in 1964, featuring McDuff on piano and organ and Red Holloway on tenor sax. This plus his other early releases, *It's Uptown with the George Benson Quartet* and *The George Benson Cookbook* (both 1966), helped to establish him as a major jazz guitarist and are still revered as some of the most raw and earthy examples of his spirited straight-ahead playing. These sides showed his gospel and blues-influenced soul jazz leanings, with some funky grooves, pop covers, and vocal tunes interspersed as of *Uptown*. He also appeared as a sideman on various titles, including several by McDuff, alto saxophonist Lou Donaldson's landmark jazz-funk effort *Alligator Bogaloo* (1967), tenor sax man Stanley Turrentine's *Sugar* (1970), and trumpet virtuoso Freddie Hubbard's *First Light* (1971). Additionally, he has the distinction of being the first guitarist to record with Miles Davis, for one track on *Miles in the Sky* (1968), a precursor to the great bandleader's out-and-out jazz-rock fusion period that was just around the corner.

Meanwhile, Benson's own records, such as 1968's *Giblet Gravy*, began to show a more pop- and funk-oriented direction, with a preponderance of contemporary rhythms and larger-group arrangements. In this regard, he became the heir apparent to Wes, who was showing the hit potential of jazz guitar crossover material but tragically died in June of 1968. Montgomery's producer Creed Taylor took on Benson, leading him to create more danceable and often highly

Benny's Back

Benson's third album as a leader is regarded as a classic, its vibrant tracks graced by the work of organist Lonnie Smith, baritone saxophonist Ronnie Cuber, and drummer Jimmy Lovelace, among others.

orchestrated material on the A&M and CTI labels. Albums like 1970's *The Other Side of Abbey Road* (with vocals and Beatles covers), *Body Talk* (1973), and *Bad Benson* (1974) involved such sidemen as Miles alumni Herbie Hancock on piano, Ron Carter on bass, and Jack DeJohnette on drums, as well as fellow guitarists like fingerstyle jazz sensation Earl Klugh and groove master Phil Upchurch.

But his popular career really took off with the release of *Breezin'* in 1976 (on Warner Brothers), which reached number 1 on the jazz, R&B, and pop charts and has to date sold over three million copies. Its instrumental title track essentially launched the smooth jazz genre and remains one of its signature tunes. The album won Best Pop Instrumental Performance at the Grammys, while the Record of the Year award went to the hit single "This Masquerade," which featured Benson's soulful voice on the melody. This track also introduced his famous technique of wordlessly singing along with his own improvised guitar lines. With a shift towards vocals, three more albums went platinum in sales: 1977's *In Flight* and *Weekend in L.A.* (a live date including his iconic voice-and-guitar rendition of "On Broadway"), and the Quincy Jones-produced *Give Me the Night* (1980). He had vocal hit singles with "The Greatest Love of All" (1977) and "Turn Your Love Around" (1981), and together with the nylon string-wielding Klugh released *Collaboration* (1987).

After years of riding a contemporary R&B and smooth jazz wave of popular success, he returned to a straight-ahead context for 1989's *Tenderly*, in the company of venerable jazz figures such as pianist McCoy Tyner, together with big band and strings. The set of standards showcased both his singing and virtuosic guitar work (including a lovely solo performance on the title track). The next year's *Big Boss Band* found him in the company of the legendary Count Basie Orchestra. In the decades since, he has moved between voice and guitar, and between pop- and jazz-flavored work, with albums such as *Absolute Benson* (2000), *Givin' It Up* (2006, with vocal great Al Jarreau), 2011's largely instrumental *Guitar Man*, and 2013's *Inspiration: A Tribute to Nat King Cole*.

Altogether, he has appeared with a vast array of musical giants, including Stevie Wonder, Dexter Gordon, Frank Sinatra, Aretha Franklin, Chet Atkins, and B.B. King. He has been honored with ten Grammys, a 2009 National Endowment of the Arts Jazz Master Award, a line of Ibanez signature models, and a star on the Hollywood Walk of Fame. He is the godfather of Grant Green's eldest son Gregory (who performs as a guitarist under the name Grant Green, Jr.) and has been a prime inspiration to legions of current players, such as Kevin Eubanks, Russell Malone, Mark Whitfield, and Bobby Broom. Benson became a Jehovah's Witness in 1979 and has felt his religion to be significant to his life and career. His book, *Benson: The Autobiography*, came out in 2014.

How to Play It

Through many a great solo, we find our jazz guitar heroes playing in a very melodic, bop-oriented sort of way through the chord changes, occasionally letting their bluesy side show through. Benson, on the other hand, seems here rather like a bluesman revealing his bebop skills. His four choruses through this 12-bar blues in C (involving a typical jazz version of the progression) are filled with a gospel- and blues-tinged exuberance and flavor, as well as some fluid lines that are more specific to the chords.

Certain recurring rhythmic figures add especially to the energized, bouncy quality of the solo. The rhythm of his first three notes, with which he kicks things off in his solo break, is used similarly at the end of measure 6 and at the beginning of measure 21, among other places. He is fond of ending a phrase with the shape found in measure 5, which is heard also in measure 42 and in the first part of measure 36 (where it is followed immediately by a segue into another line). The down-home-sounding gesture of measures 14–15 is another favorite, often played with such verve that a percussive tick of a string enters into the picture. This same basic idea comes back twice in a row in measures 24–27 (the first and third time he plays

Benny's Back

this phrase, he lands on an F, anticipating the move to an F7 chord by over a measure).

In measures 16–19, Benson further boosts the energy with a two-string device that is both blues-rooted and reminiscent of a Wes Montgomery technique (see "Full House," measures 56–62). In the midst of a steady flow of eighth notes, he plays the same note repeatedly on alternating strings, creating a cross-rhythm with the variation in tone—a *hemiola* effect with continual one-and-a-half-beat units of two eighth notes on string 2 plus one on string 3. The note eventually changes as the figure goes on, from the F of measures 16–17 to an F# by the second beat of measure 18—reflecting the move of F7 to F#°7—and finally to G (for the most part) in measure 19 to coincide with the return to C7.

Elsewhere, his lines show yet more harmonic detail. His very first phrase suggests the sound of a G7#9 or b9 during the solo break pickup before outlining the initial C chord with C major triad tones in measure 1, where his first full chorus begins. In measure 8, he moves along a very typical route into tones of A7b9 by the last two beats (the 3rd, b9th, root, and 7th) and from there into a Dm11 arpeggio idea for Dm7 (in measure 9, ascending from the chordal 3rd up through the 5th, 7th, and 9th to the 11th, then back down a notch). He also brings out the sound of A7b9 strongly in measure 20, invokes it for all of measure 44, and anticipates it from the end of measure 31 going into measure 32 with what seems like Bbm material (corresponding nicely to the altered A7). In measures 21 and 45, he imposes a D7 sound on Dm7 territory with an F# on beat 1 (the major 3rd tone for a D chord, creating a dominant sub for the ii7 of the key). A harmonically Wes-like move is his treatment of the F7 in measure 29, with minor seven material based on its 5th, C—from the pickup in measure 28 through most of measure 29, he largely spells out a Cm11 arpeggio, invoking a hip F7sus4 kind of sound. Meanwhile, more plain C major ideas, as in measures 12–13, help bring out a joyous gospel quality.

Benson moves around the fretboard with a high degree of slidy-ness—both as a means of getting to where he wants to go and as a way to add excitement with pronounced slides and fall-offs. In the long, mostly chromatic ascending run from measure 2 into the downbeat of measure 4, he finally runs out of fingers on string 1 and lets the pinky continue traveling on up the neck to frets 14 and 15, resulting in a couple of sliding grace notes along the way. Profuse half-step slides are used in his concluding statement of measures 47–48.

But a particularly snaky section is found in measures 28–36. After the initial triplet/pull-off figure, the left hand enters into a stretchy position on string 3, with the index finger reaching for fret 8 and then 7, and the ring finger taking fret 10 of string 4. The first slide on string 5 in the next measure is with the ring finger and the one right after it by the middle finger, which essentially heads down to Eb on fret 6. This finger then quickly gets out of the way as the ring finger takes over at the same spot for a slide up to fret 7, resulting in a sonic blur of notes. By the end of measure 32, he is insistently sliding down off of every tone he plays, to gutsy effect. The D on the downbeat of measure 34 is sounded with an emphatic hammer-on, before an immediate slide up off of it as well. A particular position-shifting movement is needed at the end of measure 35—after playing mainly in the third position from measure 34, beat 2, use the middle finger for the initial C on string 5, fret 3, setting up a move to the first position for the next few notes. (A similar shift is made at the end of measure 41, transitioning from mostly eighth position to sixth.)

Vital Stats

Guitarist: George Benson

Song: "Benny's Back"

Album: *The George Benson Cookbook,* 1966

Age at Time of Recording: 23

Guitar: Guild (possibly Artist Award, or Gibson Super 400)

Amp: Fender Twin Reverb

Benny's Back

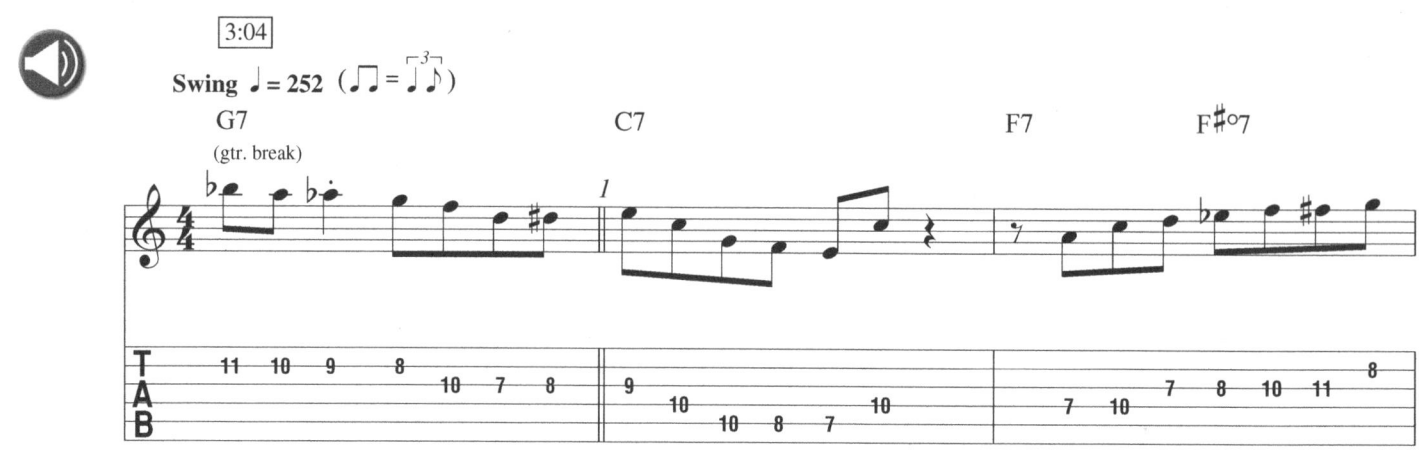
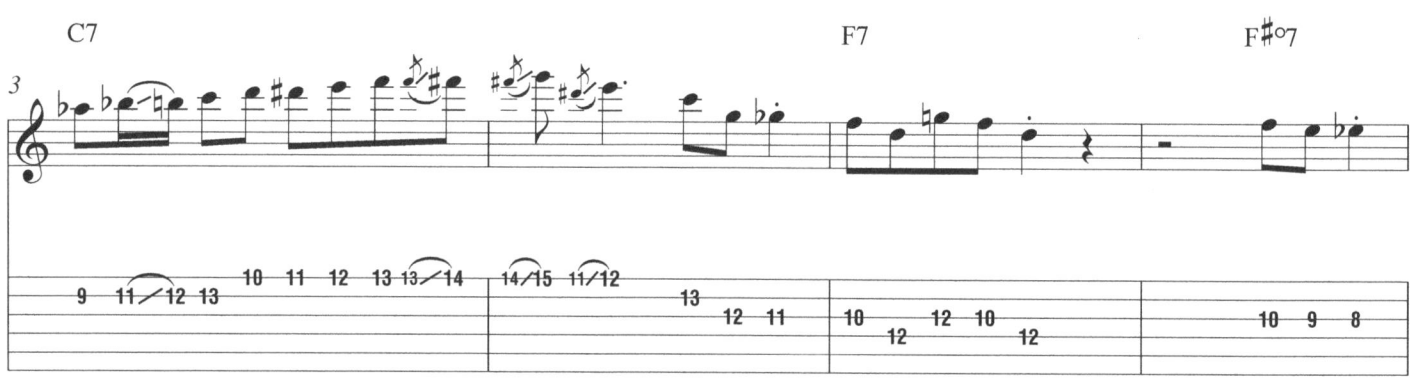
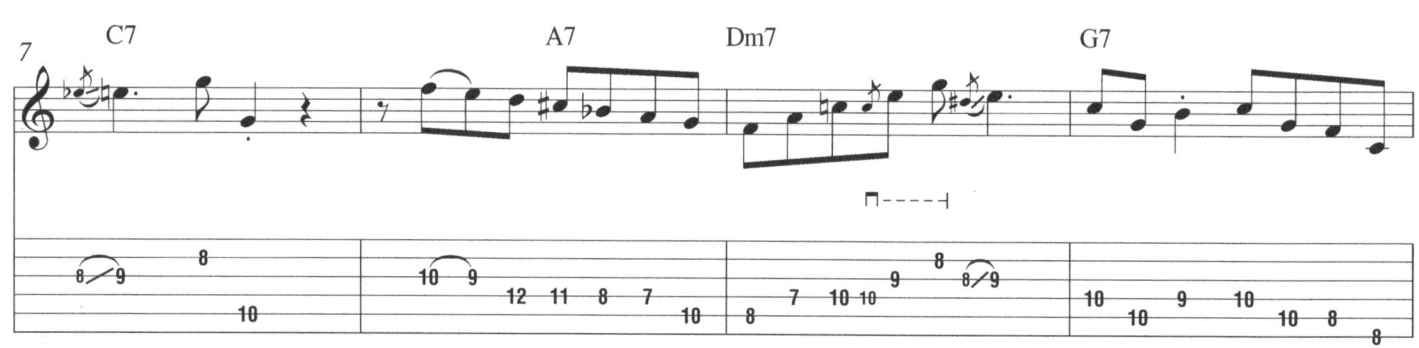

By George Benson
© 1967 (Renewed 1995) SCREEN GEMS - EMI MUSIC INC.
All Rights Reserved   International Copyright Secured   Used by Permission

Benny's Back

Benny's Back

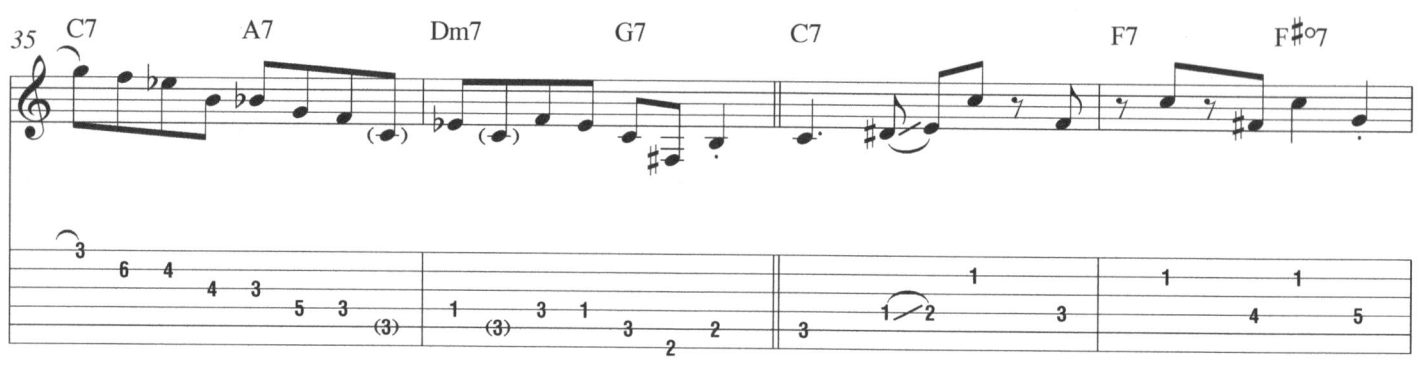

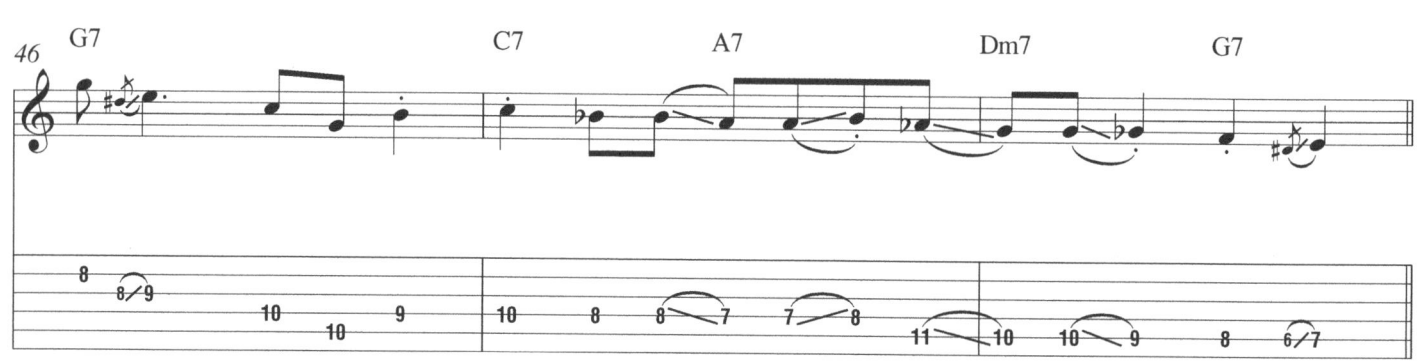

Orange, Brown and Green 1975

Herb Ellis

Born August 4, 1921 in Farmersville, Texas, Mitchell Herbert Ellis had one of the longest and most colorful careers in all of jazz, spanning more than six decades and connecting him with a plethora of all-time swingin' greats. He always retained some Texas blues influence, and even a bit of country twang, no matter how urban or jazz-dedicated the setting in which he found himself. He took up the harmonica at age three and the guitar at age eight, and never forgot the lonely sound of the train whistle near his boyhood home. Later, like so many jazz guitarists of his generation and beyond, he admired the music of Django Reinhardt but felt more directly impacted by Charlie Christian.

In 1941, he left college to make a living playing in big bands, eventually joining the popular Jimmy Dorsey Orchestra in 1945. Here, in addition to receiving opportunities as a soloist, he honed his skills especially as a rhythm guitarist in the chunky quarter-note manner of the swing era. Throughout his playing years, he would continually appreciate the chance to be an excellent accompanist, even after gaining star status as a frontman. He left Dorsey in 1947 and, together with fellow ex-band members Lou Carter on piano and Johnny Frigo on bass, formed the Soft Winds Trio for a residence at the Peter Stuyvesant Hotel in Buffalo, New York (Frigo would later become better known as a violinist). They all sang as well as played, enjoying a degree of success and winning the acclaim of fellow musicians, and are collectively credited with writing the standard ballad "Detour Ahead" (though there have been conflicting claims as to its exact authorship).

© Burt Goldblatt Estate Archives CTSImages

"The most important thing to me is the rhythm… because that's what separates jazz from other music."
—Herb Ellis

His biggest break came in 1953 when he replaced the departing Barney Kessel in the trio of piano demigod Oscar Peterson. The Trio, including the great Ray Brown on bass, toured and recorded together prolifically, becoming musically and personally tight-knit. Ellis's style fit in well with the rhythmic drive of the outfit, and at times he even filled in with percussive, bongo-like sounds by tapping on the muted strings of his guitar. As part of the family of artists managed by impresario Norman Granz (founder of Verve Records and of the world-touring Jazz at the Philharmonic concert series), they shared stage and studio with the likes of Louis Armstrong, Ella Fitzgerald, Dizzy Gillespie, Stan Getz, and Buddy Rich. Among many fine albums from this time, a standout for the trio is *At the Stratford Shakespearean Festival* (live, 1956), while Ellis made his recording debut as a leader that same year with *Ellis in Wonderland*, involving his trio-mates plus horns and drums. When he wearied of the intense road schedule and left in 1958, Peterson and Brown felt he was irreplaceable as a guitarist and went with a drummer instead to round out the lineup (that being Ed Thigpen, resulting in another revered incarnation of the band).

He continued playing with Fitzgerald for a few years after this but in large part turned to Los Angeles studio work in the 1960s and early 1970s (even though never highly confident as a reader!). In 1973, he and longtime colleague Kessel, together with Charlie Byrd, formed the Great Guitars, a specialty group that would tour and record off and on through the decades that followed, often involving Tal Farlow as a substitute (especially after the passing of Kessel in 1994). Among fellow guitarists, Ellis also had a particular affinity for Joe Pass. The two performed together as a duo and cut records such as *Jazz/Concord* (1973)—the first album for the new Concord Jazz label, together with old colleague Brown on bass and drummer Jake Hanna—and *Two for the Road* (1974), a duo session for Granz's new Pablo label. They would often run in the same circles, as Pass too worked extensively with Ella and in 1973 became the first guitarist since Ellis to join the Oscar Peterson Trio.

Ellis himself was back with Peterson for the pianist's 1970 album *Hello Herbie* and later for a reunion of the old trio (plus drummer Bobby Durham) on 1990's *The Legendary Oscar Peterson Trio Live at the Blue Note*. Through the 1970s and 1980s, he continued as a Concord artist with his own stellar titles, among them, *Hot Tracks* (1975, co-leading a quintet with Brown) and *Doggin' Around*, a 1988 live date with bassist Red Mitchell featuring hilarious cover art by Far Side cartoonist—and jazz guitar enthusiast—Gary Larson. In 1990, he was joined by a widespread pool of talent for two volumes of *Just Friends*, a tribute to his recently deceased young protegé Emily Remler. Subsequent albums included *Roll Call* (1991, with Frigo and organist Melvin Rhyne of Wes Montgomery fame) and *Burnin'* (live performances from 1998).

In 1991, Gibson Guitars created the ES-165 Herb Ellis model, based largely on the ES-175 he had so favored over the decades. The University of North Texas College of Music (his old school) awarded him an honorary doctorate in 1997. Ellis passed on at his home in Los Angeles on March 28, 2010, after a rich life of mainstream jazz, spent with generations of friends, heroes, and followers.

How to Play It

Ellis shows his colors here as both a swing-oriented jazzer in the company of like-minded musicians and a player rooted in Southwestern blues. The setting is a classic example of an up-tempo cooker on the common chord progression known as "rhythm changes" (after the Gershwin tune "I Got Rhythm," which uses the same harmonic basis). This form involves an AABA structure of four eight-bar sections per chorus in which the A-sections all revolve around the home key of B♭, starting off with

Ellis teamed up with acoustic rhythm guitar legend Freddie Green for this mid-1970s Concord session, joined also by hard-swinging colleagues Ross Tompkins on piano, Ray Brown on bass, and Jake Hanna on drums.

familiar I–VI–ii–V turnaround motion (the pattern of B♭6–G7–Cm7–F7). The bridge (B-section) moves through a cycle of dominant seventh chords, two measures each, from the harmonically distant D7 (III7), through G7 and C7, to F7, which, as the V7 chord in the key, leads us home to B♭. Ellis takes three choruses for his solo.

He starts off mainly with short, simple, down-home-sounding melodic gestures of just one, two, or a few notes, leaving lots of space in between and digging into the swing rhythm with an emphasis on beat 1 of every other measure. His harmonic strategy is clear right off the bat: he largely gives the A-sections a basic key-of-B♭-major treatment (with plenty of blues inflections thrown in) rather than playing specifically to all the harmonic movement, while on the bridge he indeed addresses the changing chords.

Phrases like the one in measures 10–11 use tones of the major scale, quite often including the 6th (the last note in measure 11) and involving a slide up into the major 3rd from a blue-sounding half step below (like at the end of measure 10,

Orange, Brown and Green

or by itself as in measure 9). When put together as in measures 30–31, this material seems both Charlie Christian-esque and country-western in its inspiration! For another blues-styled coloration, Ellis may also throw in an A♭ (the ♭7th), like at the very start of measures 13 or 33. This invokes a B♭7 sound, dominant instead of major, whether or not this chord is officially present.

His first bridge, in measures 17–24, provides a clear demonstration as to how his note choice more distinctly brings out the changes in these D7–G7–C7–F7 sections (found also in measures 49–56 and 81–88). The tones of his four-note pattern in measures 17–18 are mostly *not* found in the key of B♭ but do indeed lie within a D Mixolydian scale and relate quite well to the sound of the D7 chord (most specifically implying a D13 sonority), especially with the presence of F♯, the chordal 3rd. In measure 19, he climbs a D *minor* 7 arpeggio before coming around to land on B♮, the 3rd of G7. Then in the three-note figure of both measures 20 and 21, he *encloses* an E♮, the 3rd of C7 (circling around this note before landing on it), which gets modified into an E♭, the 7th of F7, as the figure is echoed once more in measure 23.

Ellis often maintains a sense of continuous quarter-note or swung-eighth-note groove in the motion of his right hand, even while playing shorter phrases, and this comes out in an occasional rhythmic ticking of the stopped strings, as heard in measures 20 and 25. He also shows a propensity, within his eighth-note lines, for repeated two- or four-note patterns of the kind found in measures 17–18, 27–28, 33–35, and elsewhere, which helps lend an impression of country twang to his generally smooth, low-toned jazz sound.

After keeping up a rather sparse texture through his whole first chorus (through measure 32), he ups the ante with a more dense approach, creating longer lines of eighth notes and leaving less space. The repeating figure of measures 33–34 becomes a bit loose with pull-offs and hammer-ons before entering into the overtly bluesy territory of measures 37–39, where we encounter a gutbucket combination of slides and double stops. To play the two-string lick at the end of measure 38 and just beyond, note that only one string is struck at a time, even if two notes are sustained together along the way. The sudden B♭ triad on strings 1, 2, and 3 in the sixth position (shaped like the top of a B♭ barre chord), with a half-step hammer-on into the chordal 3rd on string 3, is a favorite device of his and appears more starkly yet in measures 29 and 71.

Ellis continues with some longer phrases up in the 10th position, using a sometimes odd combination of picked notes and hammer-ons/pull-offs; practice slowly to get these lines going in the same manner. The tone material here, often involving both A♮ and A♭ (the ♮7th and ♭7th) in a row, could be summarized by the B♭ bebop dominant scale. In the last section of this second chorus (measures 57–64), he foreshadows the high energy of his third and final chorus with a sustained shake on string 2 (while rhythmically ticking on an open string 1, quickly muted by the underside of the fretting index finger) and with some pronounced half-step string bending to introduce another twangy element.

The rhythm section begins this climactic third chorus with the imposition of a bluesy B♭7♯9 sound in the piano and a B♭ pedal in the bass, right in step with Ellis's profuse bends (up to the ♭5th tone) on string 3—which can take some multi-finger muscling on thicker jazz guitarist's strings!—and aggressive accentuation of beats 1 and 3. In the line that follows, he further invokes the blues with the emphasis on D♭, the ♭3rd of the key (as on the downbeat of measure 75), before ascending chromatically in measure 77. He concludes in his last eight measures with a pair of classic, swingin', well-developed phrases of a down-home, major-plus-blues-inflections nature.

Vital Stats

Guitarist: Herb Ellis

Song: "Orange, Brown and Green"

Album: *Rhythm Willie*, 1975—Herb Ellis and Freddie Green

Age at Time of Recording: 53

Guitar: Gibson ES-175

Amp: Polytone

Orange, Brown and Green

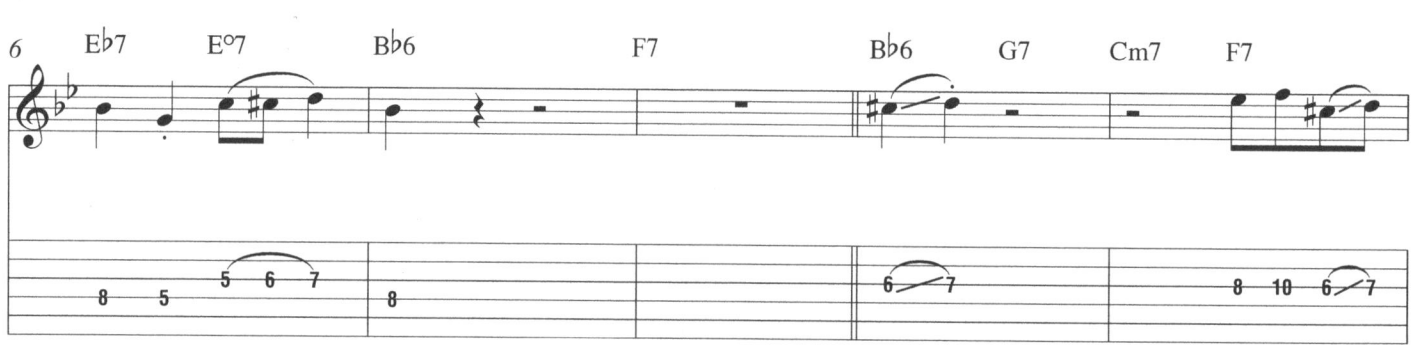
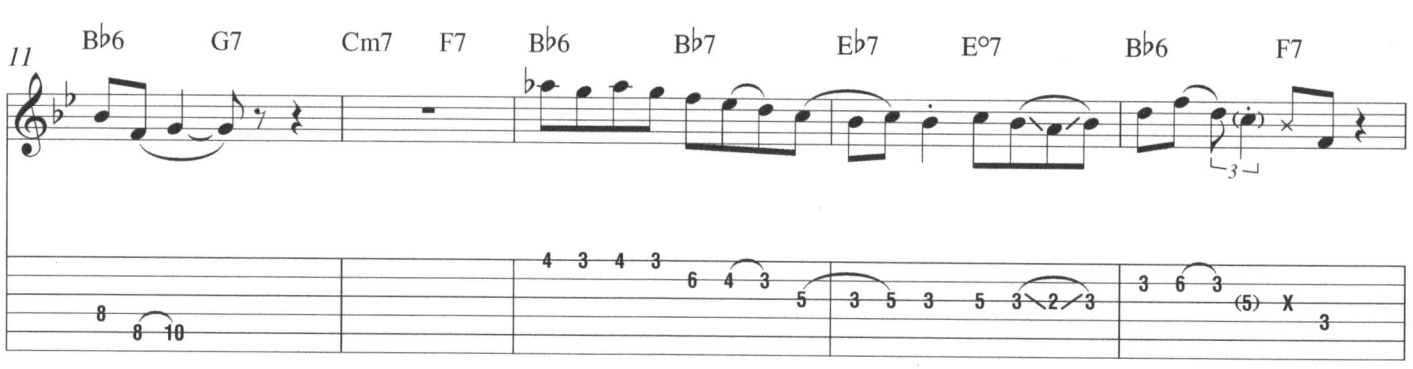

By Ray Brown
© 1975 (Renewed) Ray Brown Music
All Rights Reserved Used by Permission

Orange, Brown and Green

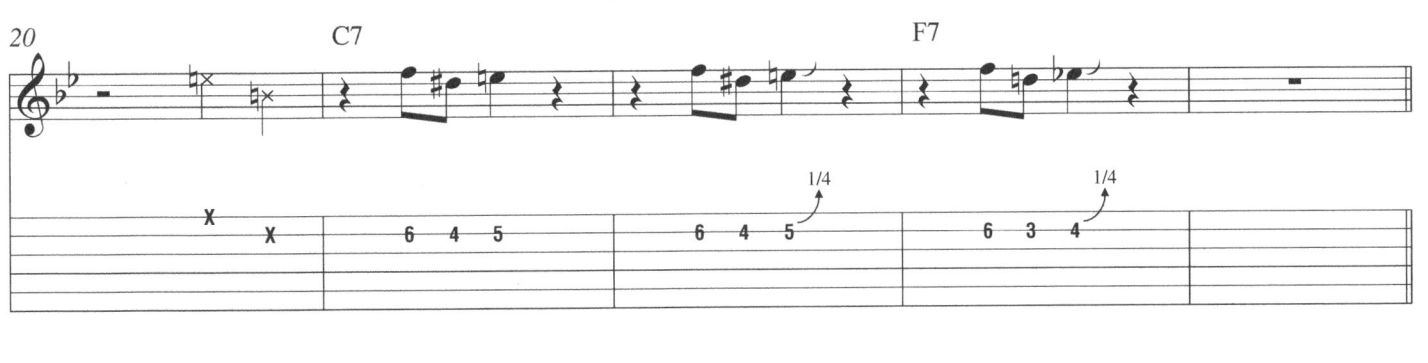
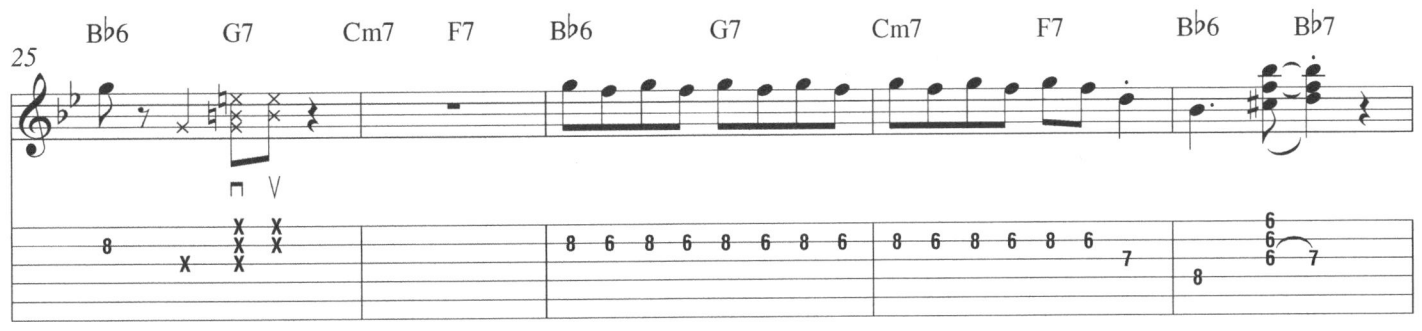
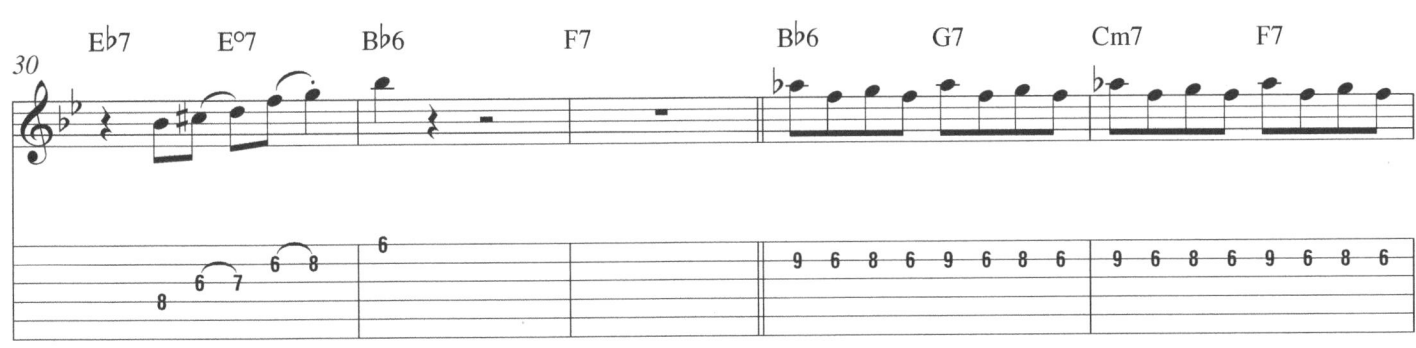
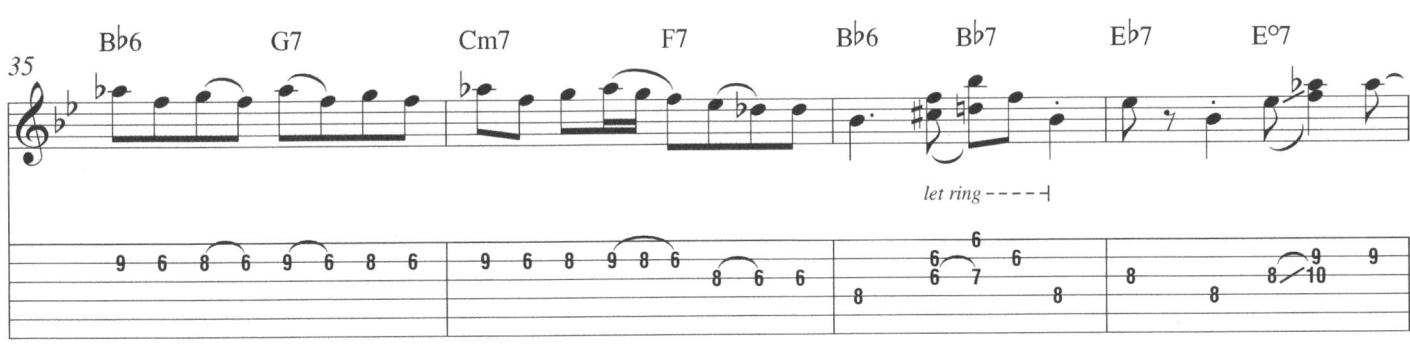

Orange, Brown and Green

Orange, Brown and Green

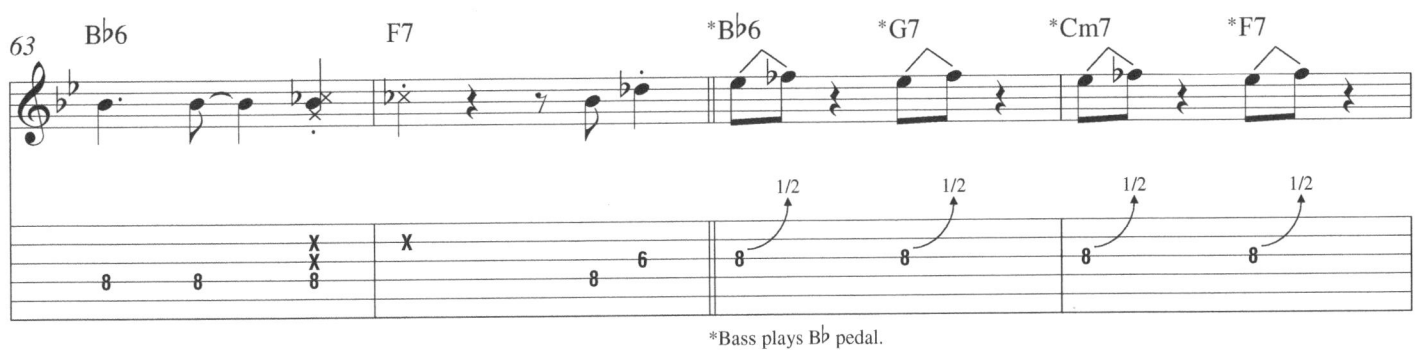
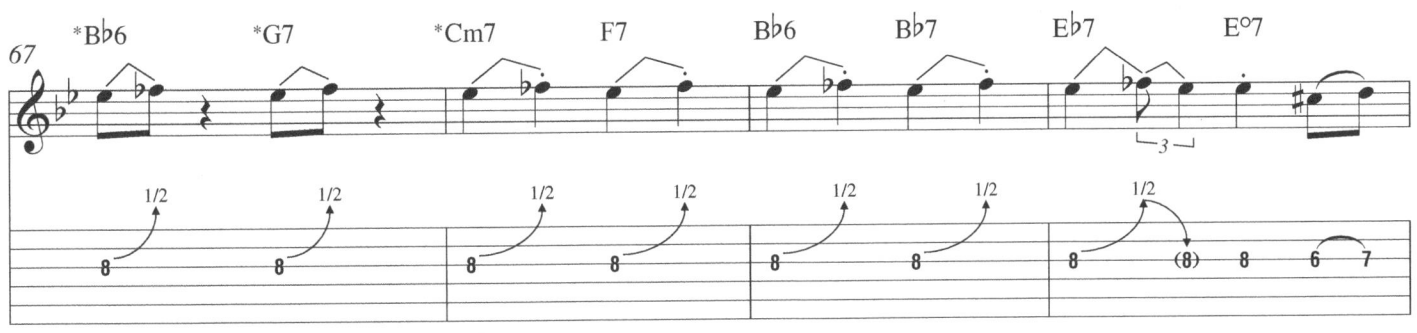

Orange, Brown and Green

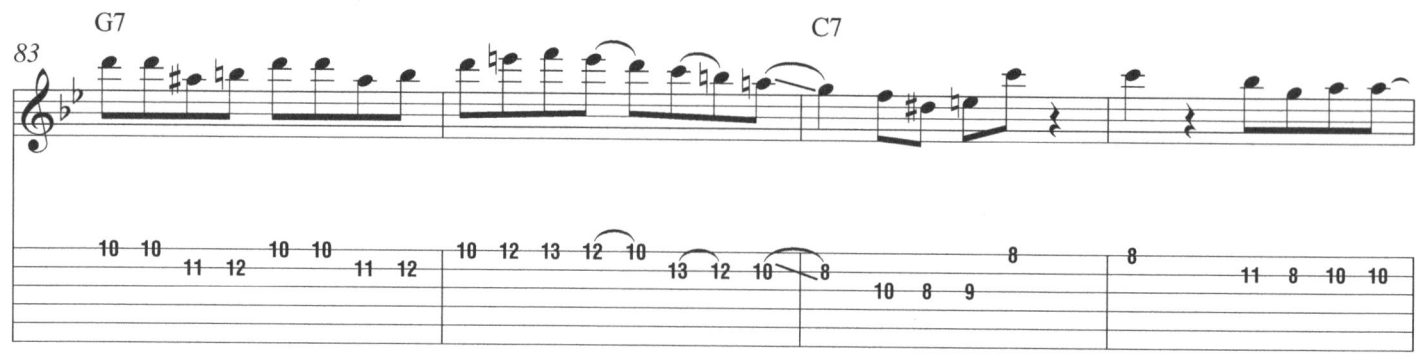
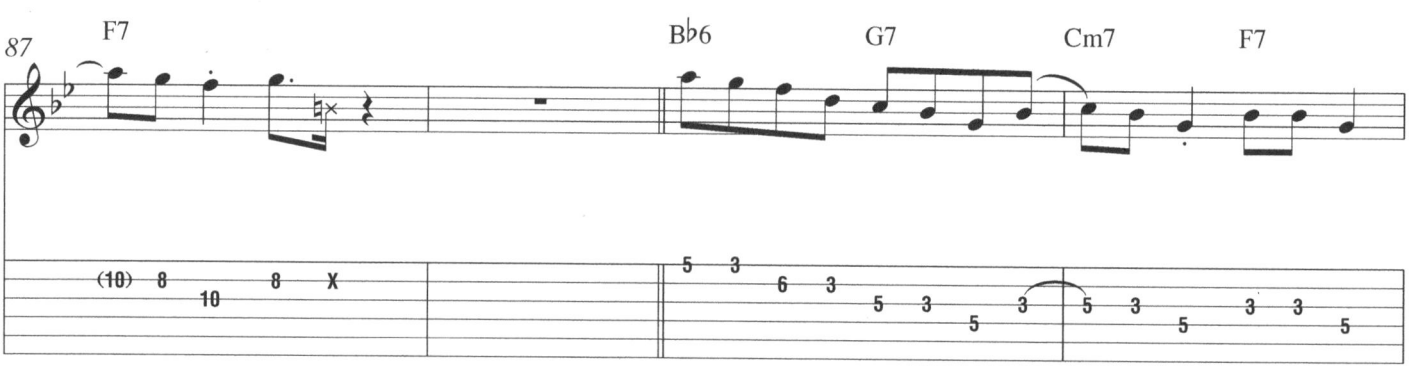

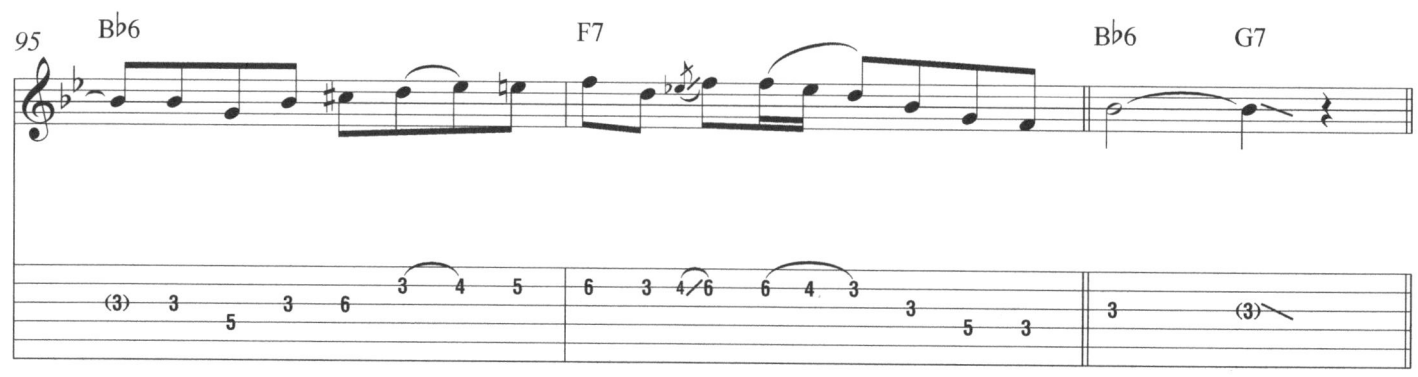

Days of Wine and Roses   1976

Pat Martino

Pat Martino stands out among jazzers as a guitarist's guitarist—one whose work has been meaningful to many listeners while occupying a special place of awe, inspiration, and influence for insiders. His burning lines of flawless melodic logic, together with his hard-swinging groove and signature percussive pick attack, have for decades set a high standard for the art. Yet beyond all his chops and savvy, he is a highly spiritual thinker who takes care to note that the guitar, for all the immediate joy it can bring, is really just a tool in the quest for self-discovery, self-expression, and deeper connection. He is also a person who has overcome tremendous adversity to be where he is today, continuing a more than half-century-long career as a performer. And in part because of this, it is more clear to him than ever that the essence of what he values in music lies not in its details, but in the people who make it and hear it, and in the relationships between them—and in its capacity to help us be awake to the present.

Born Patrick Azzara on August 25, 1944 into a South Philadelphia Italian community, he took up the instrument at age

> *"...join with us and share in the ecstasy of these creative moments, for it is here, between us that they will live."*
> —Pat Martino (in the liner notes to *We'll Be Together Again*)

12 and quickly proved to be a prodigy, practicing copiously and playing in rock 'n' roll bands with neighborhood friends (including future teen idol Bobby Rydell). His father, an amateur guitarist and singer who had briefly studied with jazz guitar pioneer Eddie Lang, encouraged him greatly in his musical pursuits. Among Pat's early guitar influences were Johnny Smith, for his precision, Wes Montgomery, for his powerful swing and spirit, and Les Paul (the namesake of his first main axe), and in short time his dad would arrange for him to meet all three at area venues. Both Wes and Les would remain his good friends for years to come. After some basic lessons and a little improvisational exploration of his own, he began to study with guitarist and local jazz guru Dennis Sandole, mentor to such all-time greats as saxophonists John Coltrane and Benny Golson and pianist McCoy Tyner.

At the age of 15, he began to venture outside of Philly as a musician (along with high school friend and future Hammond organ master Charles Earland) and wound up on the road with the big band of R&B star Lloyd Price. The formidable lineup included jazz heavies like Stanley and Tommy Turrentine, Slide Hampton, and road manager Red Holloway. While duly awestruck as to his fantastic opportunity, the very young guitarist (and only white guy in the band) wowed his elders, and was kept aboard for residencies in Harlem and Atlantic City. A few years later, he joined the organ-based group of saxophonist Willis "Gator Tail" Jackson and in 1963 made his recording debut on the tenorman's *Grease 'n' Gravy* and *The Good Life* (still appearing as Pat Azzara, though he would soon take his father's stage name of Martino). He began working with organist Don Patterson in 1964 and in 1965 replaced

Courtesy Pat Martino

George Benson in the band of organ legend Jack McDuff, getting steeped in the soul jazz sub-genre of these artists.

The year 1967 found him playing with saxophonist/composer John Handy in the counter-cultural environment of San Francisco; soon afterwards he joined up with much more conservative pianist George Shearing. He also began making his own albums on the Prestige label, starting with *El Hombre* and followed by *Strings!* and *East!*, on which he presented a mix of originals and bop repertoire while still exuding some soul flavor and tearing through classics like "Just Friends." 1968's *Baiyina (The Clear Evidence)* represented a big switch, involving Indian instruments and odd meters and reflecting the psychedelic era of LSD experimentation, as well as the influence of sitarist Ravi Shankar and Martino's pan-religious interest in spirituality.

Days of Wine and Roses

With *Desperado* (1970), he returned somewhat to his roots, though with the quizzical sound of a 12-string electric. Around this time, he also played on records by saxophonists Charles McPherson and Sonny Stitt.

In the 1970s, while his music shifted towards the use of electric piano and bass, as well as the inclusion of modal or even avant-garde selections, he cut a string of albums for Muse Records that is considered by many fans to represent an artistic high point in his catalog. The energetic *Live!* (1972) contained a hit instrumental version of "Sunny," and he paid tribute to Wes with *The Visit* (originally on Cobblestone, 1972, re-released as *Footprints*). *Consciousness* (1974) opened with a blazing rendition of Coltrane's "Impressions" and closed with a solo guitar arrangement of Joni Mitchell's "Both Sides Now." Through this point, he had often hired side musicians from the Philly scene for his own sessions, such as organist Trudy Pitts, pianist Eddie Green, bassist Tyrone Brown, and fellow guitarist Bobby Rose, generally mixed in with more widely known players. In early 1976, he recorded *Exit* and also *We'll Be Together Again*, an utterly graceful and spacious duo outing with Gil Goldstein on Fender Rhodes piano, consisting mostly of ballads (aside from the livelier, modern, extended piece "Open Road"). A new contract with Warner Brothers then led to the synthesizer-laden, stylistically diffuse *Starbright* (1976) and the high-powered, fusion-oriented *Joyous Lake* (1977), with its strong rhythm section of keyboardist Delmar Brown, bassist Mark Leonard, and drummer Kenwood Dennard, who would tour with him as a tight-knit band.

The 1976 session for Exit *marked the recording debut of pianist Gil Goldstein in the company of veteran players Richard Davis on bass and Billy Hart on drums.*

But during this time, Martino had a pronounced worsening of the headaches and seizures that had plagued him for years, due to an as-of-yet undiagnosed congenital condition called arteriovenous malformation (attempts at medical treatment had therefore been misguided and unhelpful). He soon scaled his concerts down to duets with Rose, eventually ceasing to perform altogether and joining the faculty of the Guitar Institute of Technology in Hollywood. Then in 1980 a near-fatal brain aneurysm necessitated emergency surgery, after which he suffered near-total amnesia. A difficult period followed, in which he stayed with his parents in Philly, working to reclaim memory of self, family, and guitar playing. This would require getting reacquainted with his own recordings and rediscovering the childhood joy of simple playfulness on the instrument, which itself became a healing force in his state of lost identity.

After getting back on his feet professionally into the mid-1980s, he played a live 1987 trio date in New York (albeit a bit hastily prepared), released as *The Return* (1989). He soon had another unfortunate break from the scene, however, with the passing of his mother in 1989 and his father in 1990, and an ensuing depression. But since 1994's *Interchange*, he has been on track once more as a prolific artist, touring widely and releasing such further albums as *All Sides Now* (1997, with an incredible array of guest guitarists and others), *Live at Yoshi's* (2001) with organist Joey DeFrancesco and drummer Billy Hart, and *Remember: A Tribute to Wes Montgomery* (2006), as well as reunions with the Joyous Lake band, Rose, and Goldstein.

As a teacher and composer, Martino has long mixed the theoretical with the mystical, often relating the guitar to the I-Ching, speaking of *sacred geometry* with regard to the instrument and its notes, conducting lessons and classes through philosophical discussion, and writing tunes with tones derived from the spelling of various musicians' names. He offers practical ways of viewing the fretboard in terms of *parental chord forms* from which other chordal shapes can be derived, and *minor conversion* in which various chord qualities are improvisationally approached through corresponding minor material. These concepts are spelled out in his instructional books and DVDs and touched upon in the autobiography *Here and Now!* (2011) as well. Both Gibson and Benedetto have created Pat Martino signature guitars, and the films *Open Road* (1995) and *Martino Unstrung: A Brain Mystery* (2008) have documented his remarkable story.

How to Play It

In a realm of music where so many great players draw from so much common repertoire, few standard tunes "belong" to any one artist. But in the chronicles of jazz guitar, Pat Martino has forever put his stamp on "Days of Wine and Roses" with this monumental statement, long considered a staple of serious study on the instrument. He burns and soars through two choruses of the 32-bar form with his famously well-articulated notes and lines (on famously thick strings).

Days of Wine and Roses

His melodic texture at this easy-medium swing tempo is largely based on dense, rhythmically firm 16th-note runs rather than eighth notes, but with plenty of slower-paced ideas mixed in and a pristine use of space in between.

With blazing 16ths through the initial two-bar solo break, followed by simple, sparse melodic phrases right at the top of the chorus, his entrance seems like a tip of the hat to long-time hero Johnny Smith (see "East of the Sun"). Alternate picking and a precise mapping-out of your fingerings are essential for execution of these faster segments. The solo is peppered with some of Martino's sonic trademarks—the sudden, percussive double-stop in measure 19, the aggressive-picking-plus-trill gesture going into measure 39, and various quick, back-and-forth slides of a half step, as in measures 30 or 35.

The fast and fluent lines of this solo are largely scalar in their movement, with a characteristic use of strong melodic shapes along the way. Within all the step-wise motion, he is fond of certain *enclosures*, looping around a target note with tones just below and above it. See the very beginning, where he encloses the fourth note, B♭, to launch the whole phrase, or measure 11, beat 3, in which he encircles the B♭ of beat 4. Leaps between chord tones may break up the step-by-step movement within a phrase, as with the jump from this B♭ (late in measure 11) down to D—i.e., the chordal 3rd down to a 5th for Gm7. Chromatic neighbor tones are frequently used to round out the contour of a line, often filling in the gaps between members of the predominant scale; the A♮ at the very start of the first pickup measure and the B♮ on beat 4 are exceptions to the mainly B♭ Dorian material here. Chordal arpeggios (or motion in 3rds) are often propelled from the scalar motion as in measure 29 (the E, G, and B♮ early in the measure are the 5th, 7th, and 9th of the Am7 chord) or used as the basis for a whole idea, as with the Fmaj9 tones of measure 17. Martino plays more with motion in perfect 4th intervals in measures 23 and 56, implying an E♭7sus4 and creating modern linear shapes reminiscent of pianist McCoy Tyner.

Martino tends towards particular areas of the fretboard for improvisation on specific chords in the progression, especially within the longer lines. B♭m7 (or its related E♭7) is often addressed at the fifth and sixth positions, like at the beginning of the solo or in measure 16, where his tones are based around a B♭m7 chord shape rooted on string 6 (or its corresponding Dorian scale). Accordingly, Bm7/E7 ideas might be found one fret higher, as in measures 27–28, and Am7–D7 ideas a fret lower, as in measure 29. Gm7, and C7 along with it, are frequently handled at the fifth position, revolving around a common Gm7 shape on the top four strings (or G Dorian in this position). Fmaj7 ideas might be found in this area as well (F major and G Dorian being modally related) or otherwise in the seventh and stretchy eighth positions, as in measure 17—think Fmaj7 chord shape here with root on string 5, or F major scale in this zone. D7 is at times treated as an altered dominant, especially with the presence of E♭ (its ♭9th), such as at the end of measure 4. D7♭9 is actually implied in measure 14 with the tones of beat 4, as a strong lead-in to Gm7.

Due to the often position-oriented approach, many fingerings here are concise to one area of the neck, but sometimes more movement is required. In measure 14, let the middle finger jump from fret 6 to fret 8 on string 2 to complete the line. The first half of measure 23 requires some rolling from the tip to the flat of the middle finger and pinky to play consecutive notes at the fourth and sixth frets; later in the measure a jump down to the first position is needed (facilitated by an open string 2). In measure 55, Martino shows his ability to super-accurately scoot along one string for consecutive notes, twice taking three in a row with the index finger while heading down string 3. Most of us will do better to stretch or hop with the middle finger to frets 8 and 5 here, leaving just the slide-slurred pair of notes to the index each time.

For all the brilliant strings of 16th notes, some of his slower phrases are among the tastiest of the solo and stand out with a special poignant power of their own. Check out the subdued expression as he lightly bounces down in 3rd intervals through measure 6 into measure 7 (implying Gm11 at first with notes in the key and then acknowledging the change to E♭7 with the D♭ in the new measure). And amid all the aggressive timing of these fast runs, the subtly leaned-back rhythm within segments like measures 13–15 or 44–45 has special impact. At the end of measure 31, a single high note dramatically sets the tension before we spill into the second chorus.

Vital Stats

Guitarist: Pat Martino
Song: "Days of Wine and Roses"
Album: *Exit*, 1976
Age at Time of Recording: 31
Guitar: Gibson L-5S
Amp: Fender Twin Reverb

Days of Wine and Roses

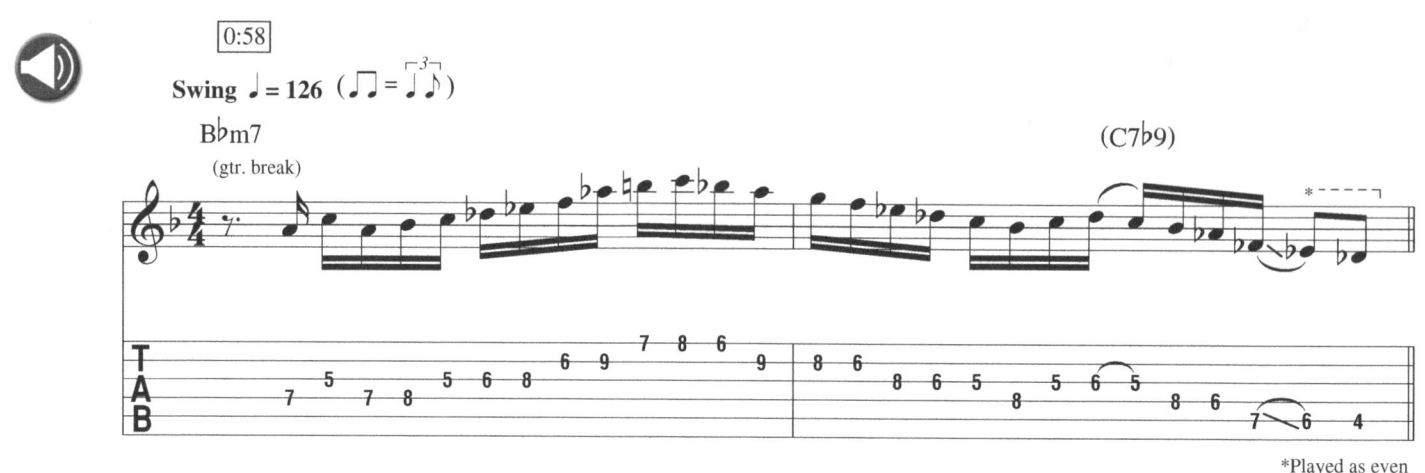

*Played as even eighth notes.

Lyrics by Johnny Mercer
Music by Henry Mancini
© 1962 (Renewed) WB MUSIC CORP. and THE JOHNNY MERCER FOUNDATION
All Rights Administered by WB MUSIC CORP.
All Rights Reserved   Used by Permission

Days of Wine and Roses

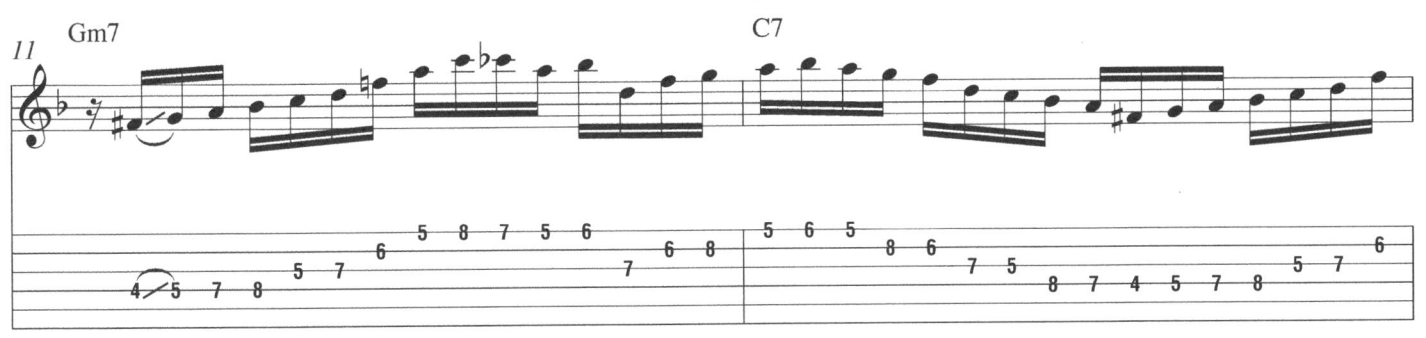

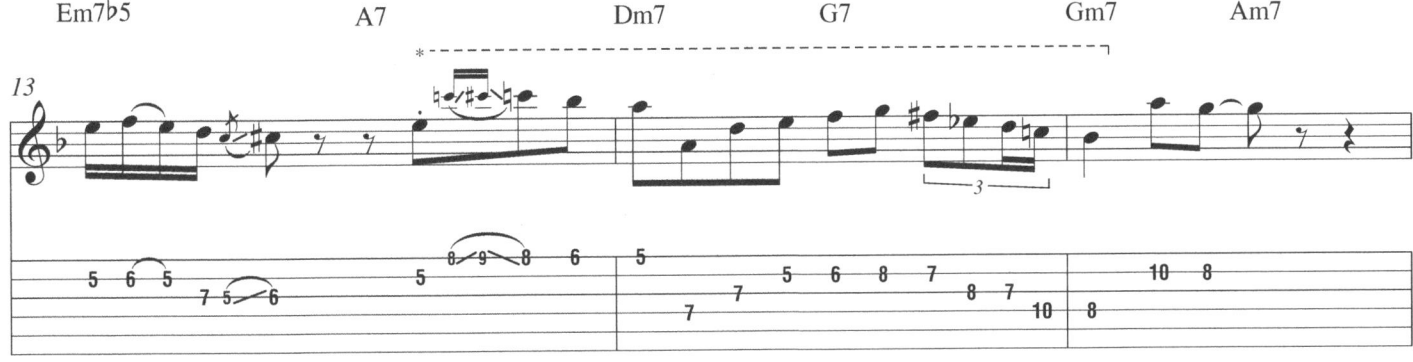

*Played behind the beat.

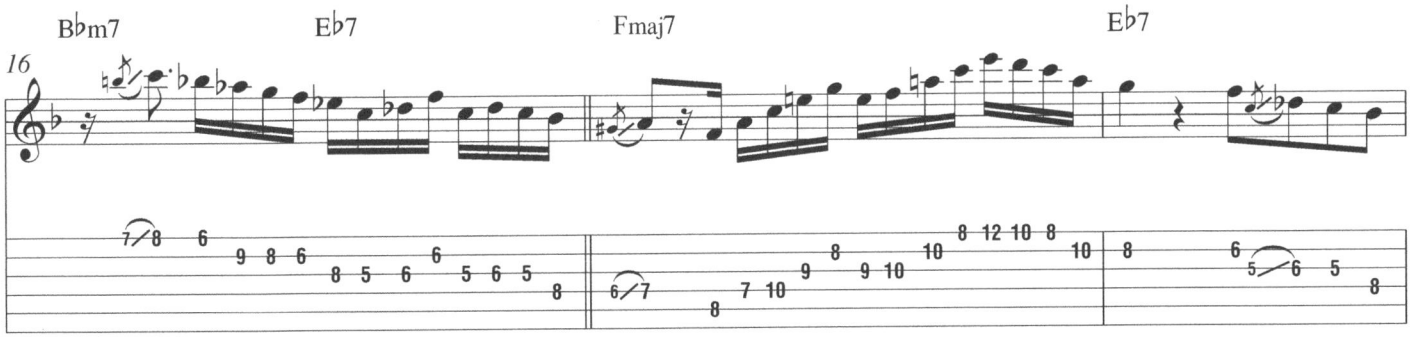

Days of Wine and Roses

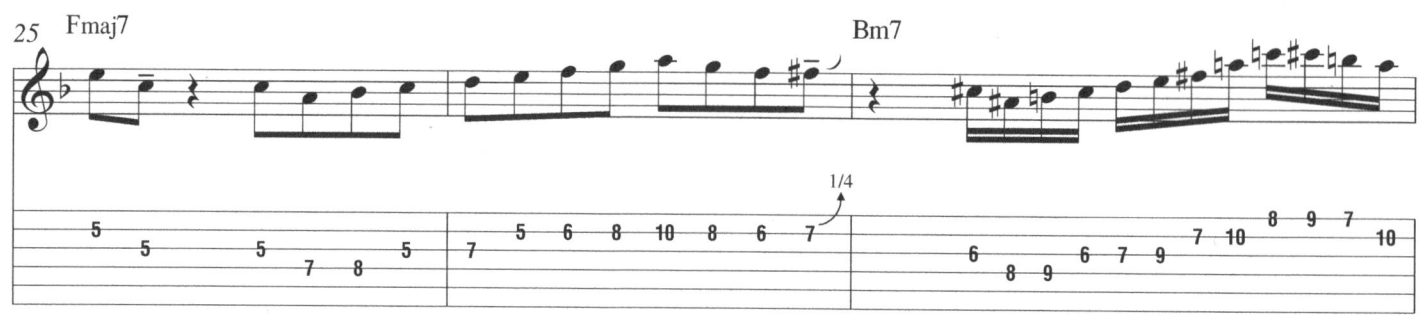

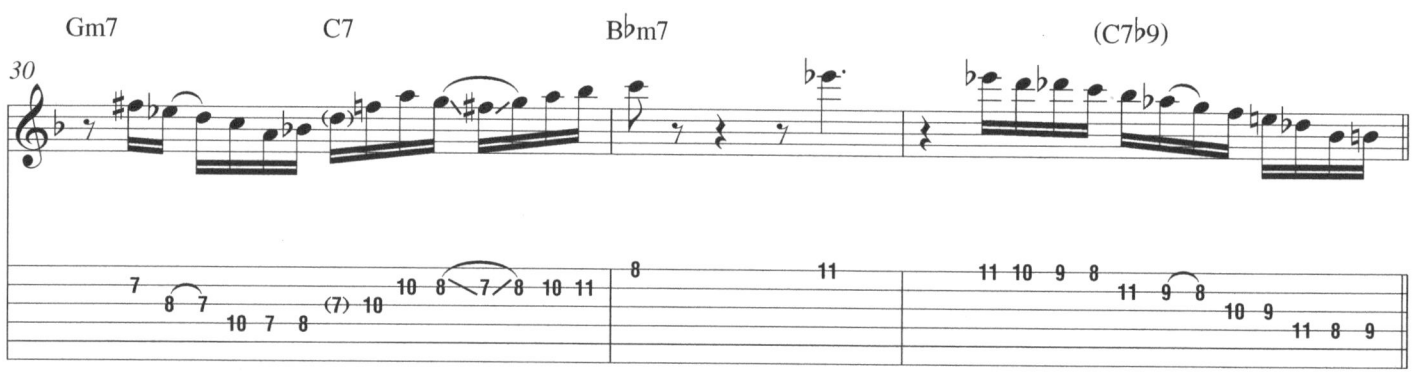
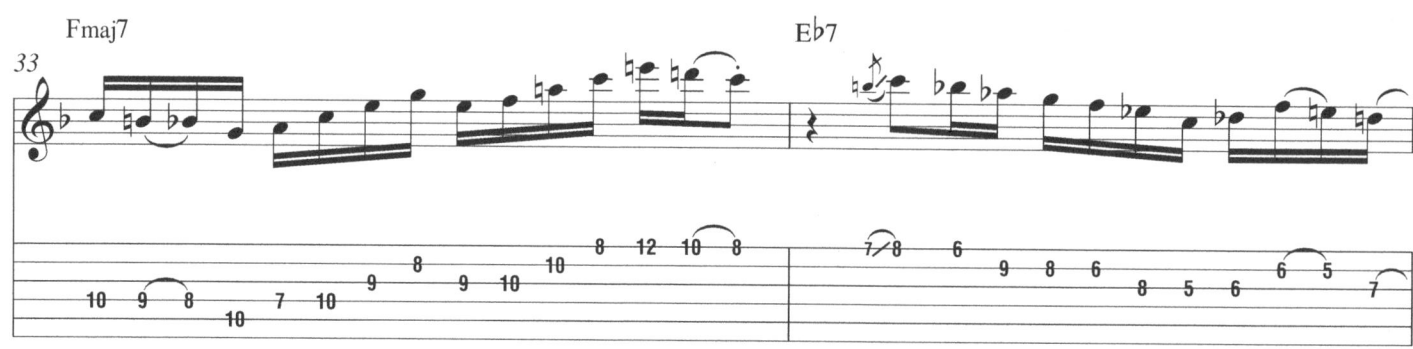
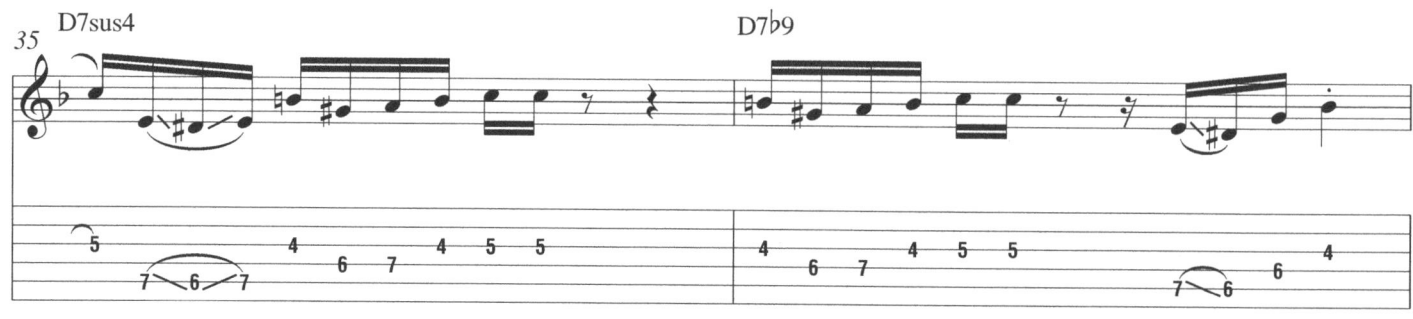

Days of Wine and Roses

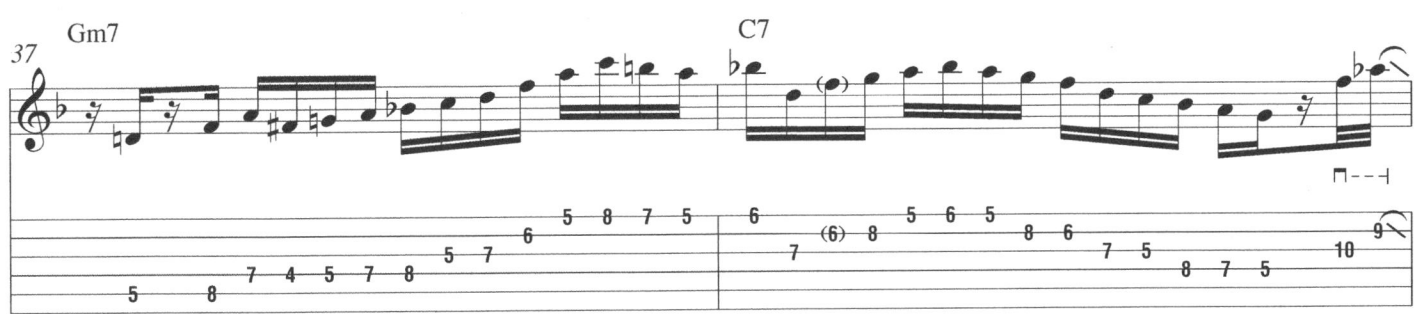

*Played behind the beat.

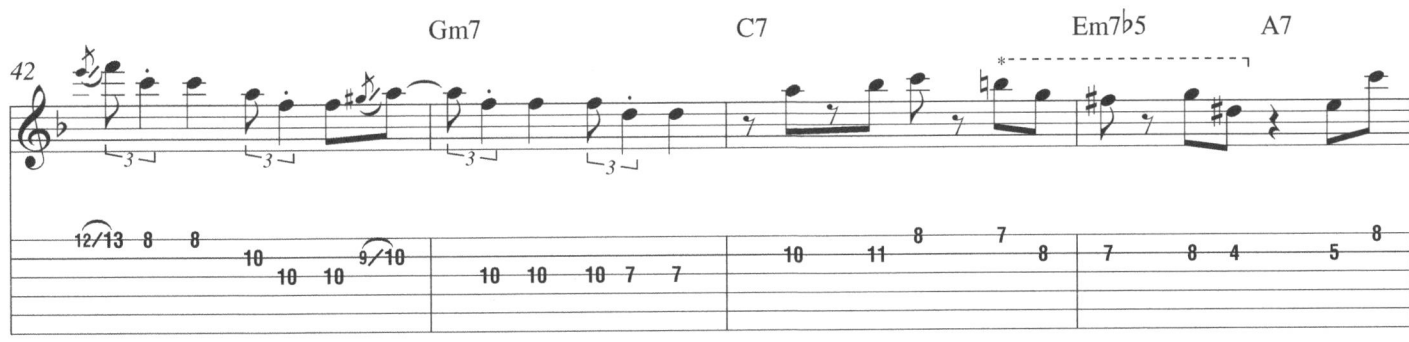

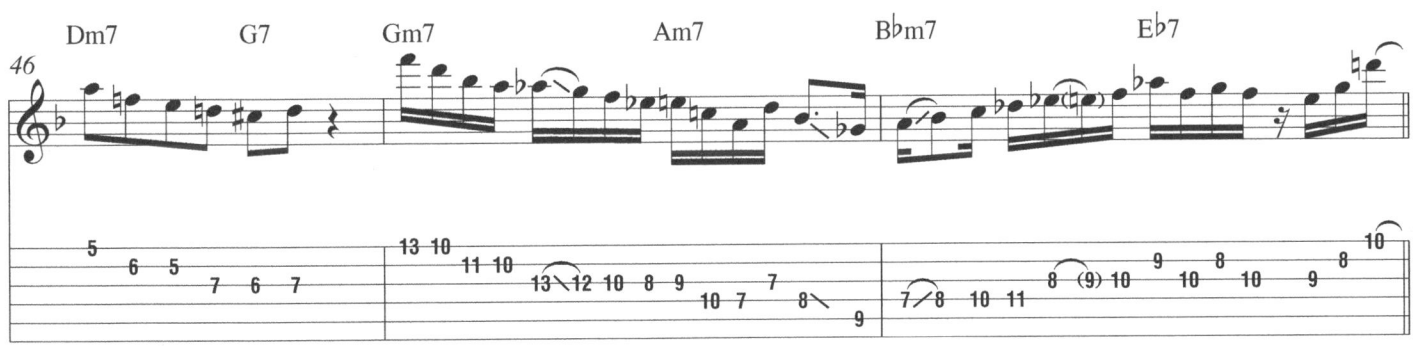

**Played as even eighth notes.

Days of Wine and Roses

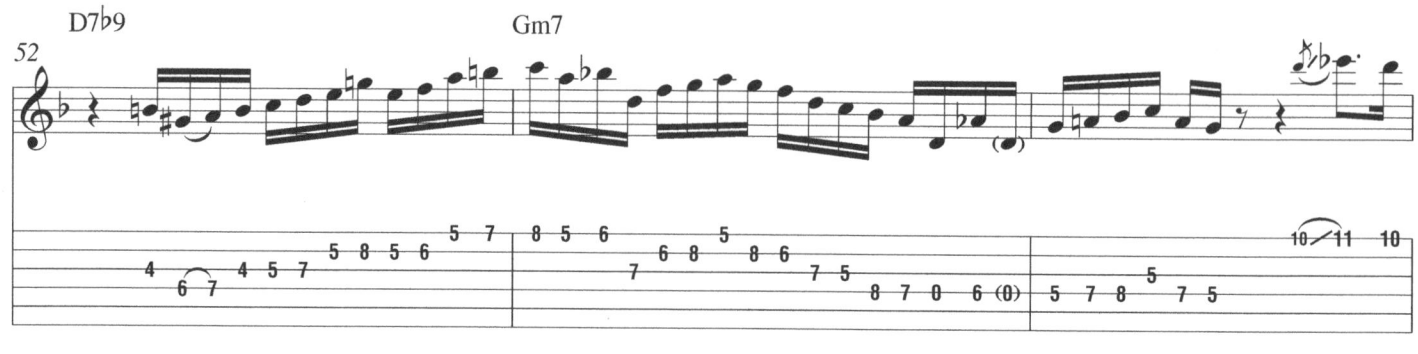

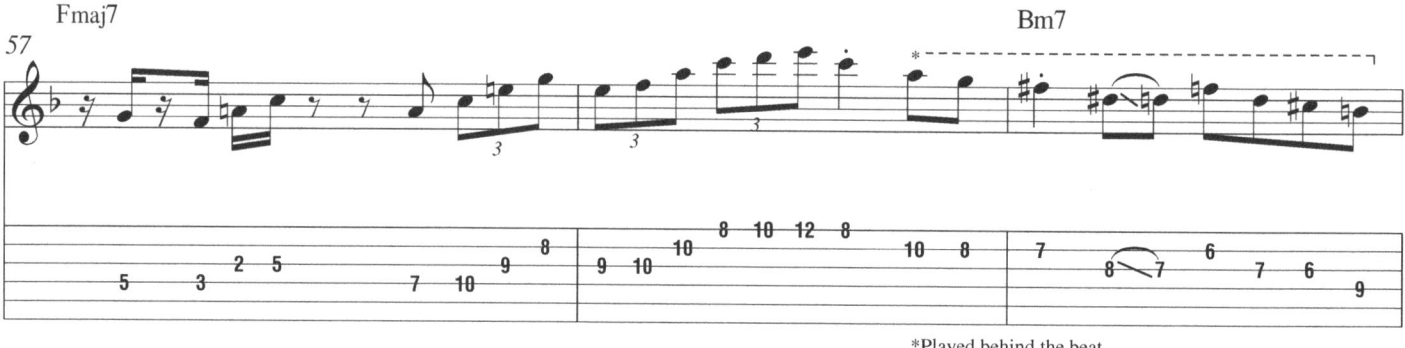

*Played behind the beat.

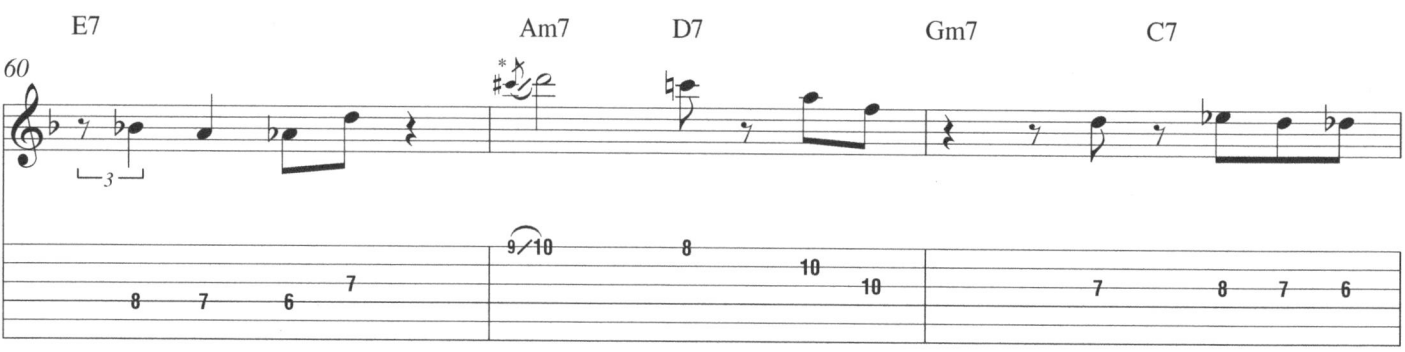
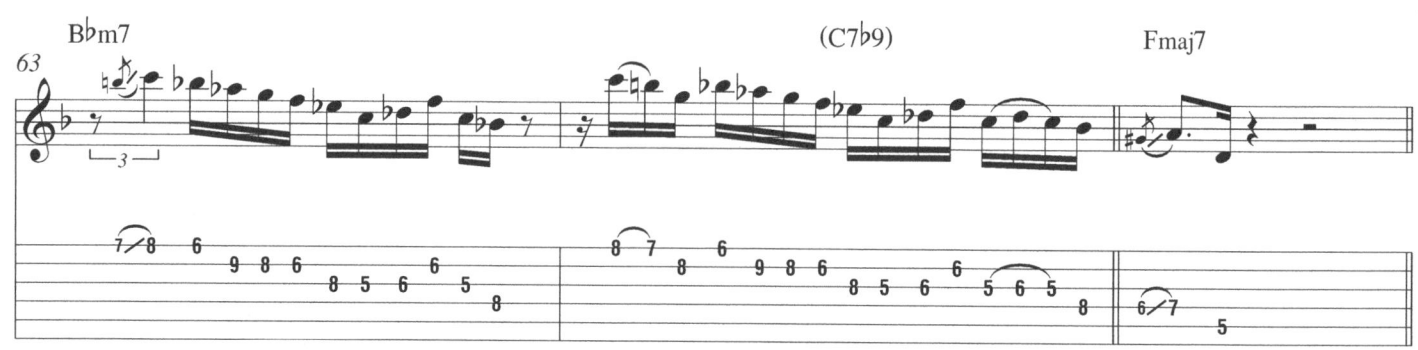

Whisper Not 1978

Jim Hall

© Ted Williams CTSImages

"If you just sort of stay open, things will happen and you'll keep evolving... I just try to stay open and literally live in the moment."
—Jim Hall

Although like so many of his contemporaries he took his initial jazz guitar inspiration from Charlie Christian, the late, great Jim Hall came to represent a whole distinct branch of the art through his lyrical, warm-toned explorations of the subtle side of the music. He has been aptly referred to as a poet or painter among guitarists—he brought a composer's sensibilities to both soloing and accompaniment, with more of a spacious, textural approach than an insistence on continuous bop lines or typical comping patterns. Having been a key influence to such diverse modern masters as John Abercrombie, Bill Frisell, John Scofield, Pat Metheny, Mike Stern, Peter Bernstein, and Kurt Rosenwinkel, he in turn acknowledged a debt to these younger stylists in his own continual development.

Born James Stanley Hall on December 4, 1930, he grew up in Cleveland, Ohio, taking up the guitar at age 10 and gigging by age 13. He attended the Cleveland Institute of Music for five fruitful years, learning theory and composition, and subsequently moved to Los Angeles, where he pursued further studies in classical guitar and big band arranging. Here he made connections on the world-class professional scene, gaining valuable exposure and experience with the intimate small groups of drummer Chico Hamilton and clarinetist/saxophonist Jimmy Giuffre. The stint with Hamilton's groundbreaking "chamber jazz" quintet (inclusive of cello and often flute), from 1955 to 1956, gave him the opportunity to contribute as a composer. Working in the drummer-less Jimmy Giuffre 3 from 1956 to 1959, he honed his slurred legato technique for melodic lines as well as his rhythm guitar skills. He recorded during this time also with pianist John Lewis, fellow guitarist Jimmy Raney, and trombonist Bob Brookmeyer, and in 1957 cut his debut album as a leader (simply entitled *Jazz Guitar*) with pianist Carl Perkins and bassist Red Mitchell.

Living in New York as of the early 1960s, Hall played in the bands of flugelhornist Art Farmer, alto saxophonist Paul Desmond, and tenor sax giant Sonny Rollins. With the piano-less quartets of these great horn players, he laid down some of the most historically signifi-

The unusual lineup on this unique 1978 session, co-led with old colleague Art Farmer on flugelhorn, was rounded out by vibraphonist Mike Manieri, bassist Mike Moore, and famously versatile rock, pop, and jazz drummer Steve Gadd.

Whisper Not

cant examples of guitar as the lone chordal instrument in a small jazz group. His innovative comping style ranged from contrapuntal lines to full, sustained chords, with smaller splashes of harmonic color in between. Particularly huge in its impact was his work on Rollins' 1962 landmark recording *The Bridge* with bassist Bob Cranshaw and drummer Ben Riley. In another monumental partnership, he joined visionary pianist Bill Evans, a kindred spirit in musical sensitivity and introspection, for two revered duo albums—*Undercurrent* (1963) and *Intermodulation* (1966)—as well as Evans' remarkably hard bop-styled quintet date *Interplay* (1962). Hall also led his own trio, and worked with the likes of Ella Fitzgerald, saxophonist Sonny Stitt, and vibraphonist Gary Burton. The mid-1960s, however, found him largely occupied in a more commercial vein, with a live television gig on the popular Merv Griffin Show.

But the remainder of his six-decade-long career was filled with creative achievement. He released the outstanding duo record *Alone Together* (1972) with bassist Ron Carter, the exemplary trio album *Live!* (1975) with bassist Don Thompson and drummer Terry Clarke, and the intriguing *Concierto* (1975) featuring Desmond, trumpeter Chet Baker, and a jazz version of Joaquín Rodrigo's famed *Concierto de Aranjuez*. Further highlights included *These Rooms* (1988) with cutting-edge trumpeter Tom Harrell, *Dialogues* (1995, involving multiple collaborations), the wildly eclectic duo effort *Jim Hall and Pat Metheny* (1999), and *Hemispheres* (2008), which paired him with modern electric guitar texturalist Bill Frisell (Hall had earlier written a quaint, funky tribute tune, "Frisell Frazzle," for *Dialogues*). Bassist Steve LaSpina and drummer Joey Baron were among his most frequent sidemen in later years.

In recent decades, Hall himself experimented with the use of effects and also more often showed his colors as a full-fledged composer. His extended writing was presented on the albums *Textures* (1996), *By Arrangement* (1998), and *Quartet Plus Four* (1999), as well as in the 2004 premiere of *Peace Movement*, a concerto for guitar and orchestra. He taught at the New School for Jazz and Contemporary Music in New York, authored instructional books including *Exploring Jazz Guitar* (1991), and participated early-on in the fan-funded ArtistShare label (from 2005). Winning top honors as a guitarist in the *DownBeat* Critics Poll no fewer than 15 times over a span of 40 years, he was also recognized with the 1997 New York Jazz Critics Circle Award for Best Jazz Composer/Arranger, a 2004 National Endowment for the Arts Jazz Masters Fellowship, and the creation of a Sadowsky signature guitar model. Jim Hall passed away in his sleep on December 10, 2013, in the Greenwich Village apartment he shared with his wife, Jane (a psychoanalyst and songwriter), and their dog, Django. He was featured in the 1998 documentary *Jim Hall: A Life in Progress* and posthumously inducted into the *DownBeat* Hall of Fame.

How to Play It

Hall's exceptionally motivic approach to improvisation, his graceful fluidity on the fretboard, and his painterly use of chord colors within a solo are all beautifully demonstrated here in this two-chorus excursion through Benny Golson's classic tune (which was also recorded by bandmate Art Farmer on a previous occasion, in the company of the composer himself).

The first three notes of Hall's statement echo the descending shape at the end of the melody (heard on the original recording just before the solo begins). He proceeds to make this shape the basis for all his ideas through the first eight measures, ultimately using it to outline the chords Dm9, Em9, Fm9, and G7#9 to match the changes in measures 7–8. The chord progression to the whole tune, in typical Golson style, moves seamlessly between the keys of C minor, G minor, and D minor, and so does Hall, with his excellent note choice throughout. Regarding the progression, it should be noted: where we see B13 and E7#9 here, as at the end of measure 5 and beginning of measure 6, these reflect specific substitutions used by his band (jazz musicians playing "Whisper Not" often play Bm7b5–Em7b5 at this point, if not the original Dm7/C–Em7b5).

Plentiful slides, pull-offs, and slight bends, along with great agility in moving between neck positions, contribute to the unique flowing quality of his lines, heard especially through the next eight measures or so. A frequent soft touch with the pick imbues them with extra dynamic sensitivity as well. Quick movement with the index finger is often needed in this section (and beyond), particularly in navigating the descent along the middle two strings. In measure 12, use the index to reach across to string 4, fret 11. In measure 14, it must reach down to fret 7 before sliding further down the fretboard, and in measure 15 it hops right over from string 3, fret 4 to a new position on string 4, fret 2.

A *pre-bend* (not terribly common among jazz guitarists) begins the pickup to the bridge in measure 16, and after some tones in the fifth position of string 3 in measure 17, the index shifts stealthily once more to string 4, fret 4 in order to continue the phrase. In measures 20–21, Hall plays with a variation on the initial three-note melodic shape. Then in measures 28–29, we get all at once a modified reference to part of the melody, our first direct taste of blues material, and the introduction of a high G-to-D pull-off figure that foreshadows the climactic point of the solo in the next chorus (besides stretching the left hand a bit).

He enters his second chorus at measure 33 with a continued blues attitude and promptly introduces another element: the use of three- and four-note chords, moving in parallel motion and interspersed with single tones. First he moves chromatically down into D7#9 in measure 34 and into E7#9 in measure 36 (substituting it for Em7b5), before launching into a dramatic passage where a high D is kept ringing atop shifting chords underneath. Keep in mind while practicing this part that he makes use of great left-hand flexibility to manage the A7 to Dm7 chunk of it, and this will be quite stretchy for many of us! Also here, in the last half of measure 38, he makes a striking move that is unusual even for the harmonically adventurous Jim Hall—after sliding down into tones of A13 on strings 4, 3, and 2, he still prioritizes the continuation of the inverted pedal D on string 1, despite its dissonance against the lower C#. A similar phenomenon occurs towards the end of measure 40, with the D played again over a G7b9b13 voicing, which includes Eb.

The grand, high pull-off figure is re-introduced going into measure 45 and is used repeatedly for the energetic peak of the solo in measure 46. Technical tip: early in measure 45, have the first finger poised to barre the top three strings at fret 10, but instead of barring, rather *roll* the finger from its flat part to the tip as you move through the notes D, A, and F. Hall starts to calm things down going into his second bridge at measure 49, soon falling into a simple, sparsely played two-note figure joined by drum accents from Gadd. His last eight-bar section begins, from the pickup to measure 57, with a nearly direct quote of the melody's A-section. A little more variation is thrown in from measure 60 onwards, and he concludes in measures 63–64 with an extension of the original descending motif, heading down through D minor pentatonic tones to ultimately land on a conclusive low C.

Vital Stats

Guitarist: Jim Hall

Song: "Whisper Not"

Album: *Big Blues—Art Farmer and Jim Hall*, 1979 (recorded 1978)

Age at Time of Recording: 47

Guitar: D'Aquisto Jim Hall Custom (or Gibson ES-175)

Amp: Polytone (or Gibson GA-50)

Whisper Not

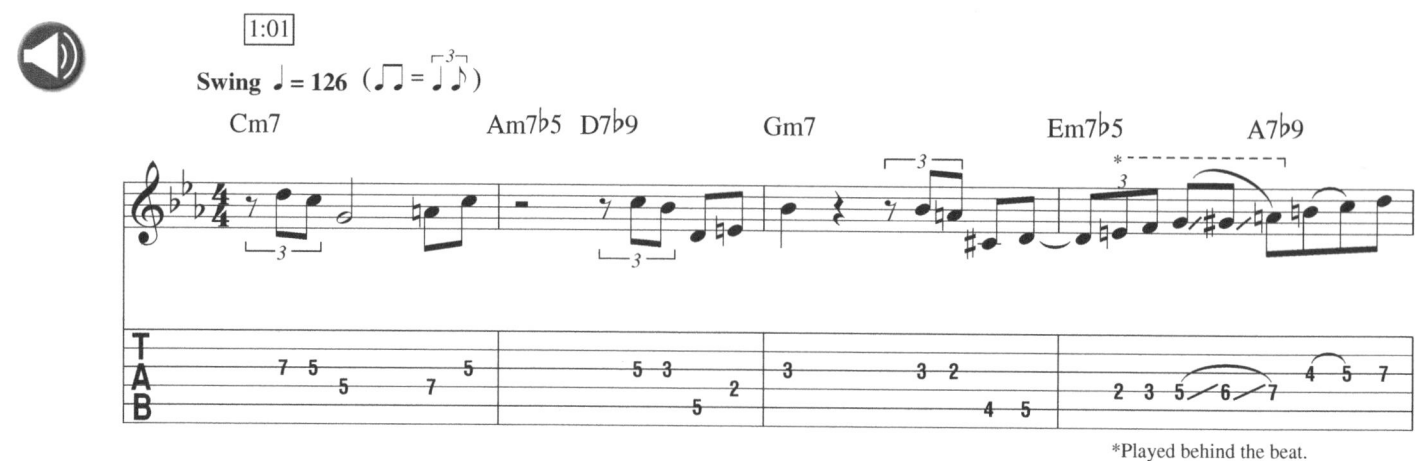
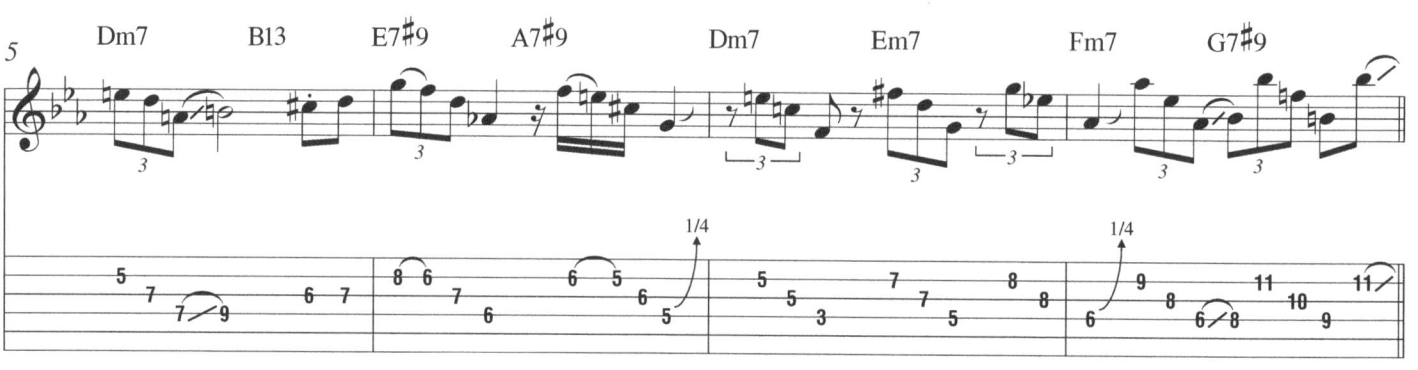
*Played behind the beat.
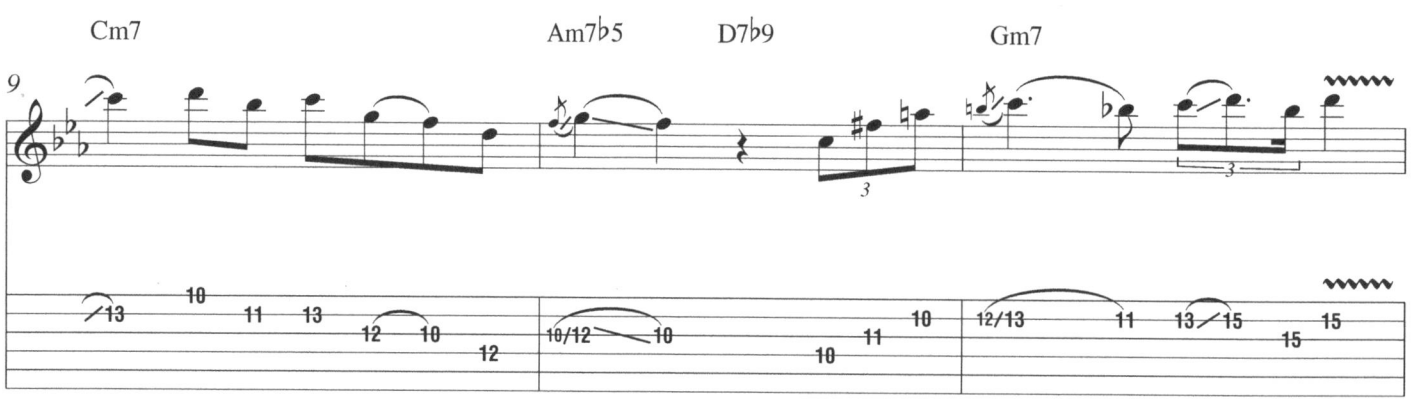
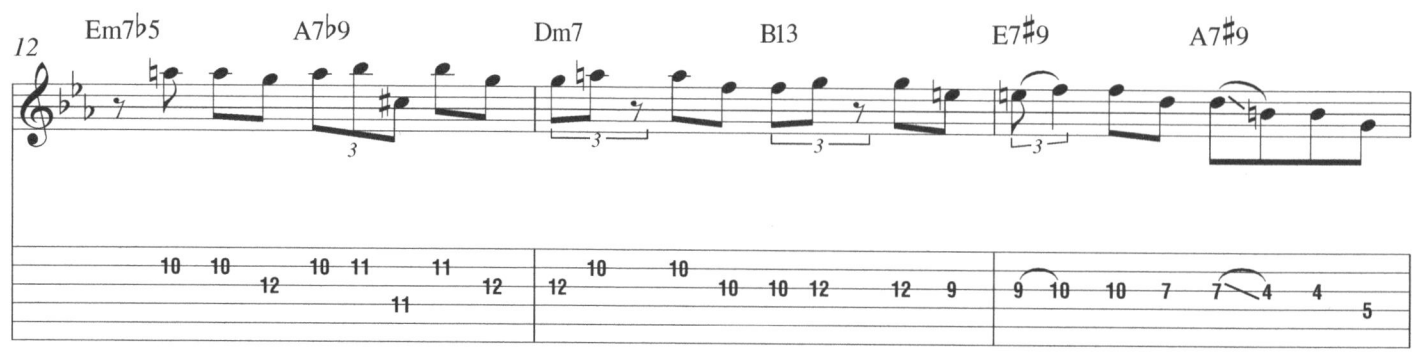

By Benny Golson
Copyright © 1956 (Renewed 1984) IBBOB MUSIC, INC. d/b/a TIME STEP MUSIC (ASCAP)
International Copyright Secured   All Rights Reserved

Whisper Not

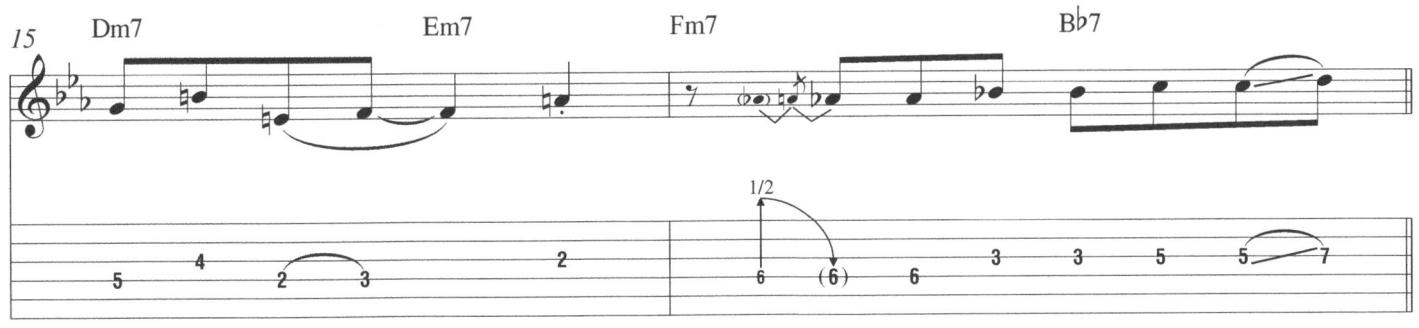

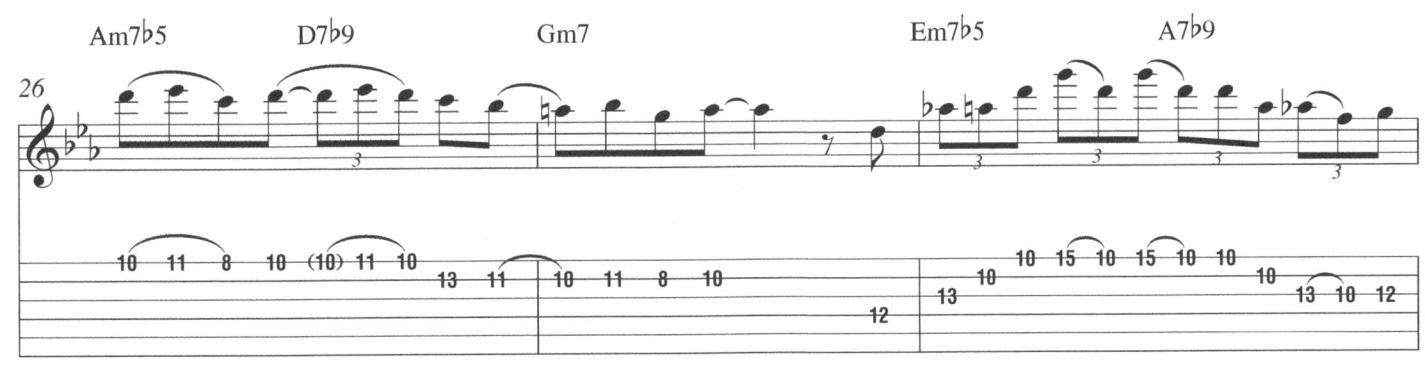

Whisper Not

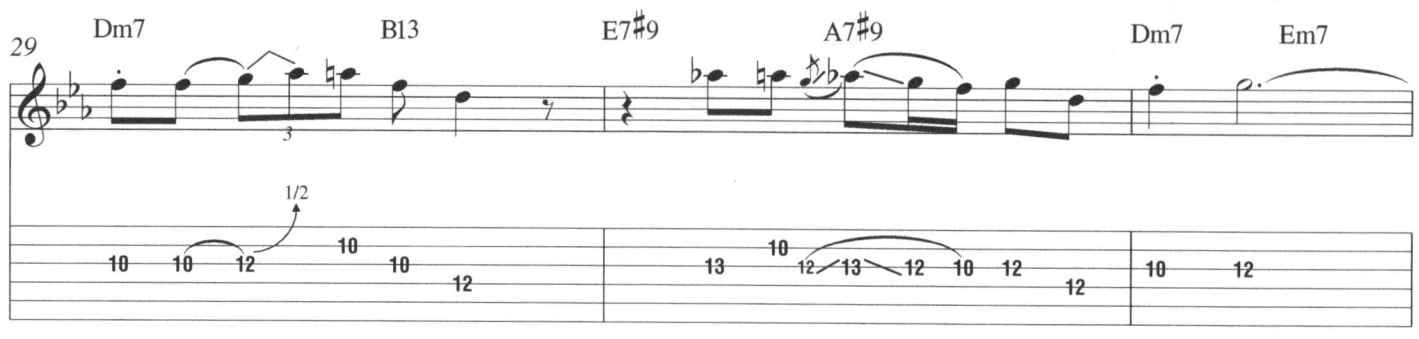
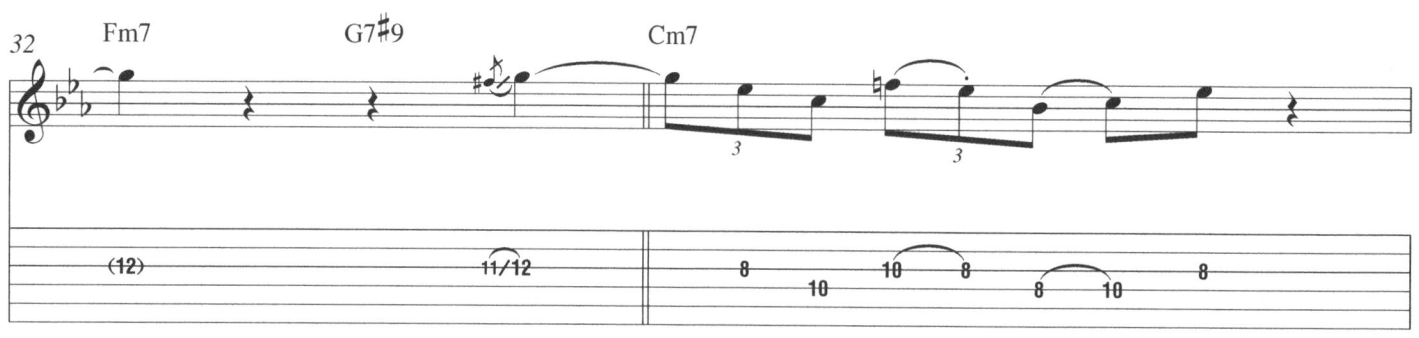
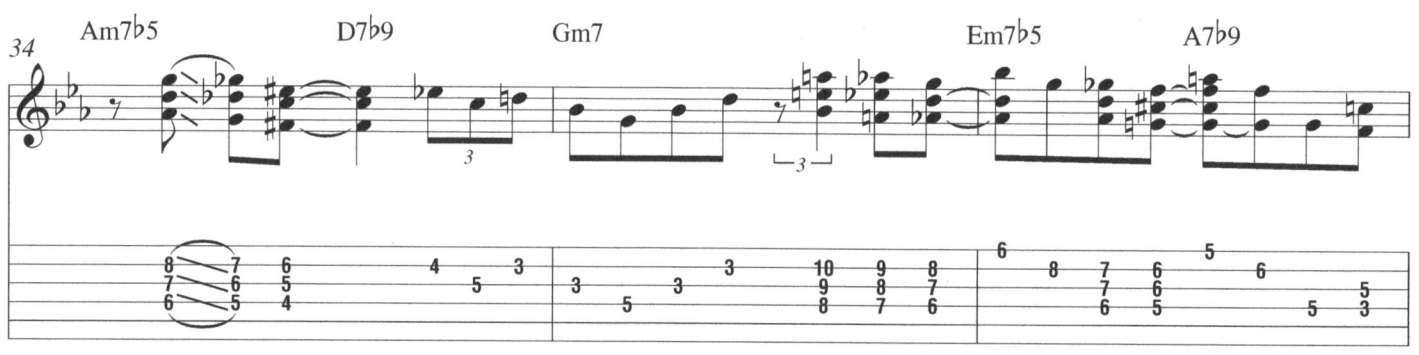
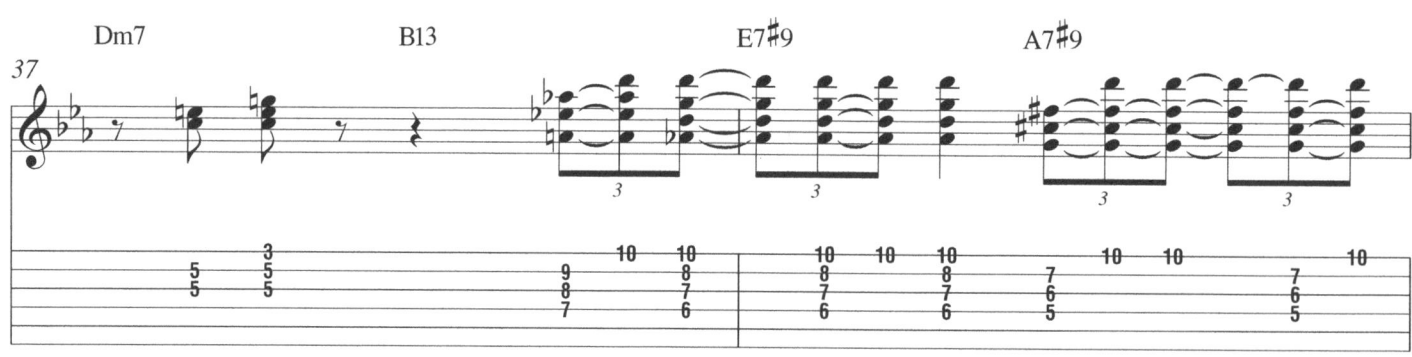
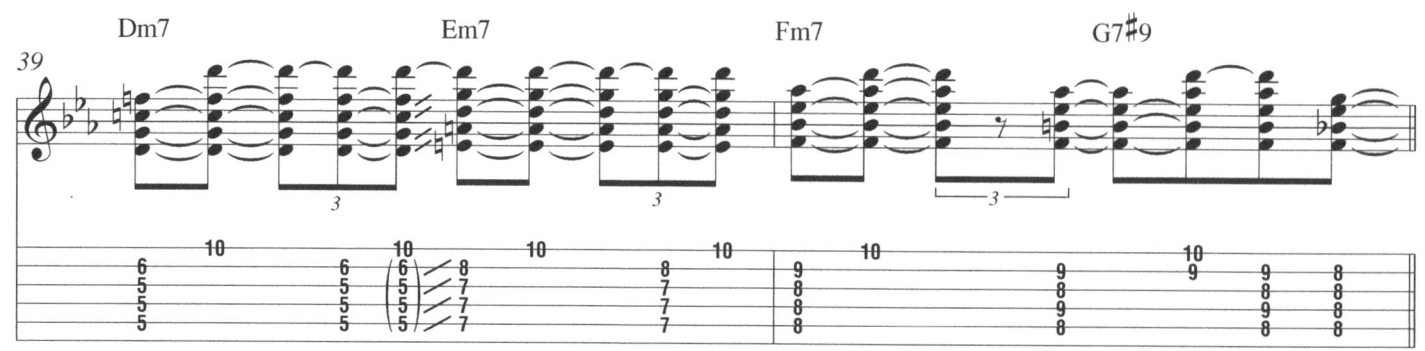

Whisper Not

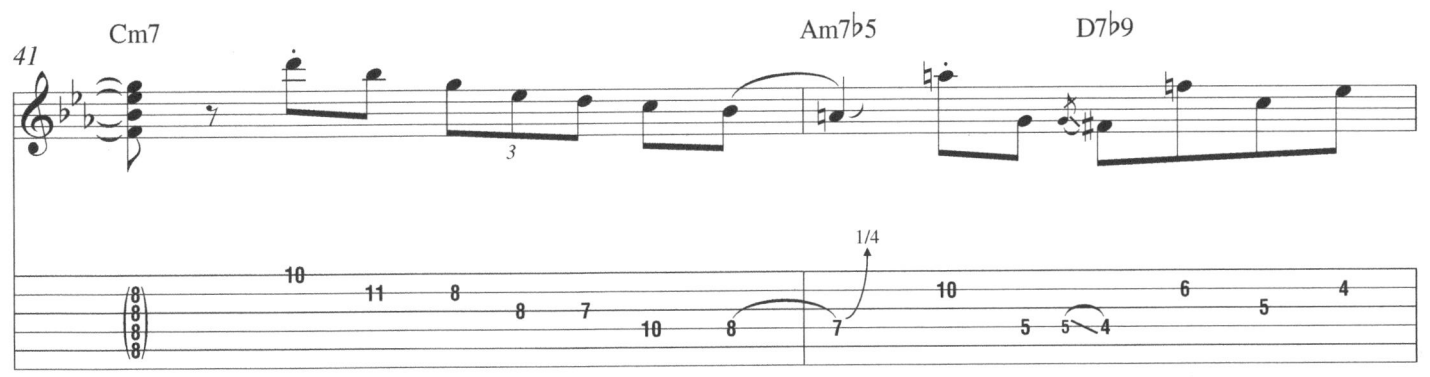

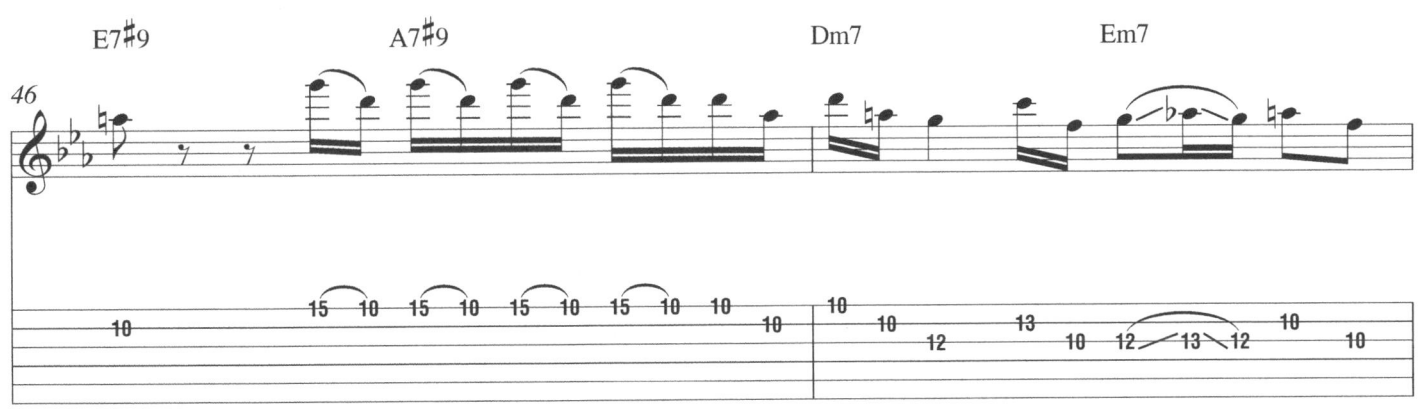

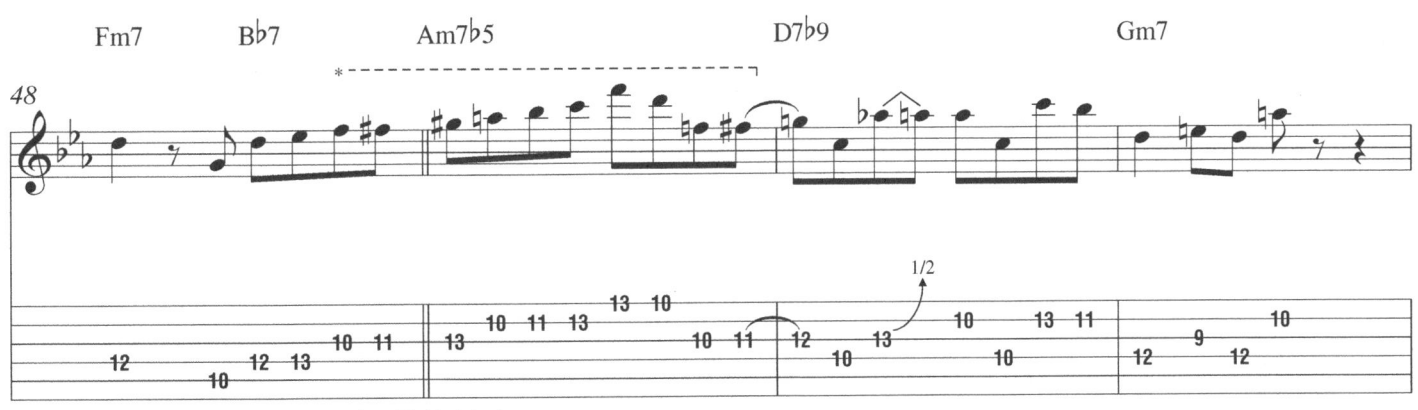

*Played behind the beat.

Whisper Not

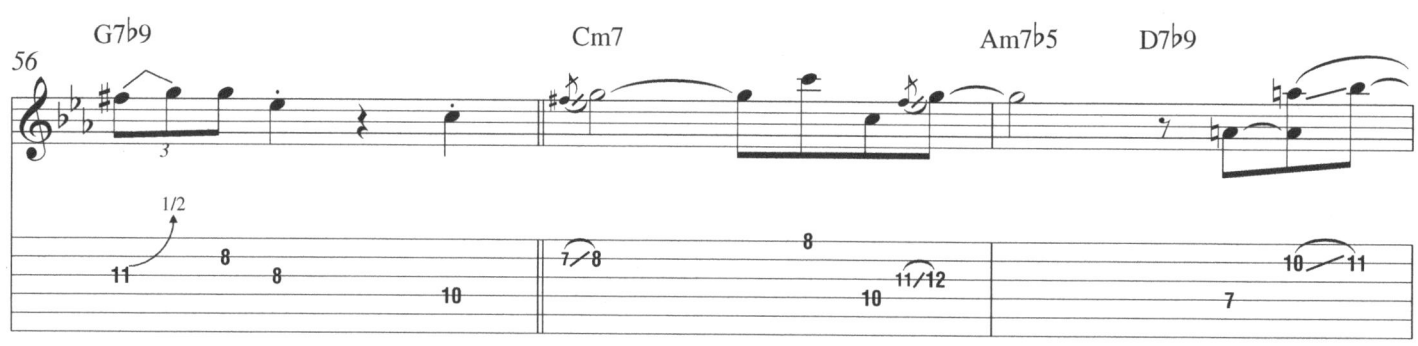
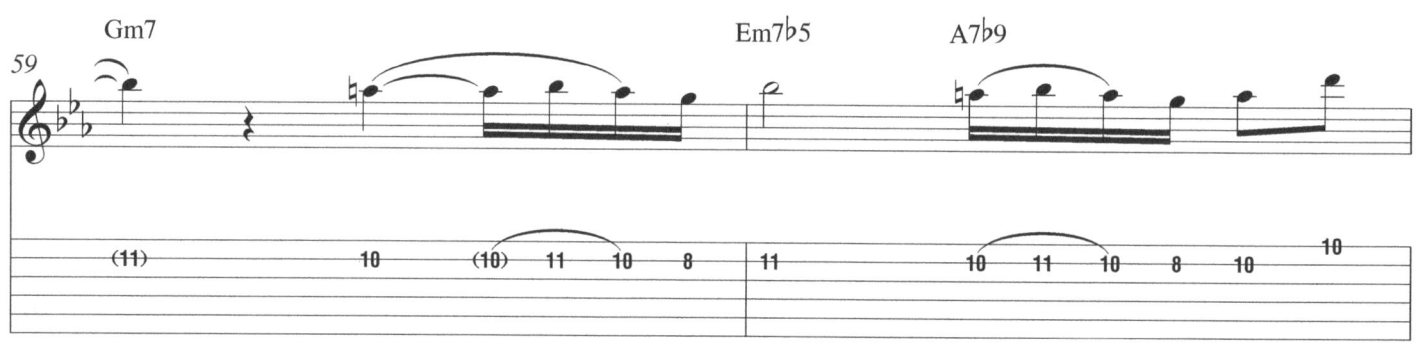

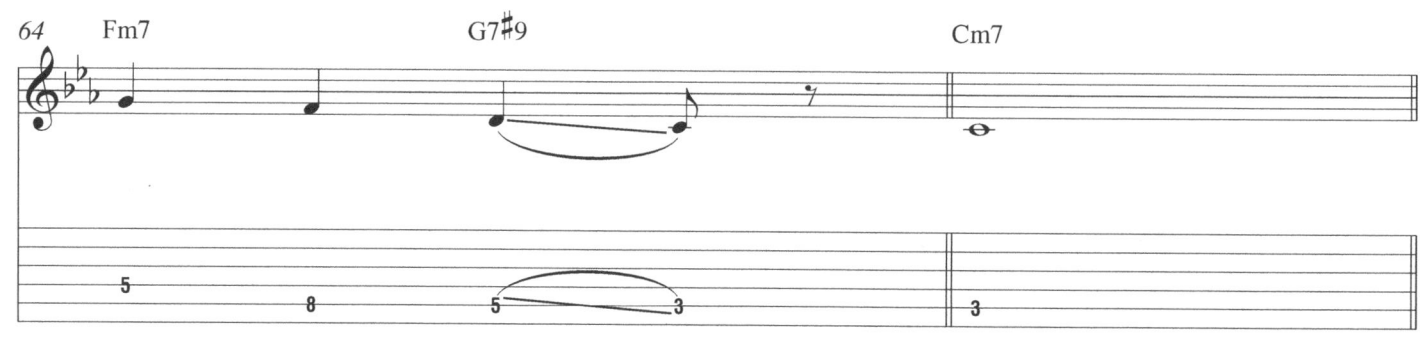

Lover Man (Oh, Where Can You Be?) 1978

Joe Pass

Courtesy Grubbit, Wikimedia

"What do I look like, a horse?!"
—Joe Pass (at Chicago's Jazz Showcase, upon hearing owner Joe Segal tell the audience that there would be three shows on Sunday)

In jazz guitar lore, the name Joe Pass has become synonymous with *Virtuoso*, the title of his first solo album recorded in 1973. Indeed, his greatest claim to fame may have been his groundbreaking demonstrations of how the music could be rendered on six strings alone. But throughout his career, he displayed virtuosity in many ways—from blazing single-note improv to tasteful accompaniment and excellent teamwork on the bandstand.

Born Joseph Anthony Passalacqua on January 13, 1929, he grew up in Johnstown, Pennsylvania, in a home filled with Italian-American cultural atmosphere, complete with live music from neighbors and relatives. He had no musicians in the immediate family, but his immigrant steel-worker father bought him a guitar at the age of nine and insisted on constant practice. By age 14, he was gigging in the area, and soon began working with dance bands like those of Tony Pastor and Charlie Barnet. He began making inroads on the famous New York City jazz scene in the mid and late 1940s, rubbing shoulders with influential heroes such as Charlie Parker, Dizzy Gillespie, and Art Tatum. But during this time, he developed a serious heroin addiction and for more than a decade—between gigs in New Orleans, Las Vegas, and Los Angeles, or on the road—would spend much of his time strung out, in jail, and in relative obscurity. In the early 1960s, he finally went through treatment successfully at the Synanon rehab center in Santa Barbara, California. While still in the program, he was recorded with fellow musician inmates on the LP *Sounds of Synanon*, displaying his talent on a Fender Jazzmaster solidbody electric borrowed from the institution.

By 1963, Pass was back on his feet, beginning his own recording career as a leader with *Catch Me!* on the Pacific label and winning *DownBeat*'s New Star award. He soon received a Gibson ES-175 hollowbody, which would remain a main axe of his for decades, as a gift from a fan. He garnered further attention through his 1964 classic *For Django*, with a quartet including guitar compatriot John Pisano (Pass considered Reinhardt, Charlie Christian, and later Wes Montgomery to be his biggest inspirations on the instrument). In 1966, he visited more popular territory with *The Stones Jazz*—yes, Rolling Stones tunes rendered in groovy fashion with a medium-sized band. Through the mid and late 1960s, he also toured with the quintet of pianist George Shearing and kept busy with TV and session work in L.A., performing with many notable entertainers.

But things really took off in the 1970s. He played frequently with fellow guitarist Herb Ellis, and the two made the first record for the new Concord jazz label in the company of bassist Ray Brown and drummer Jake Hanna (simply titled *Jazz/Concord*, 1973). They partnered again for the duo effort *One for the Road* in 1974. He joined Oscar Peterson in a

Lover Man (Oh, Where Can You Be?)

rejuvenated version of the piano legend's famous Trio, together with Danish bassist Niels-Henning Ørsted Pedersen (Peterson hadn't used the guitar-piano-bass format since the 1950s, with Ellis on guitar and Brown on bass). The three maestros were well-matched for breathtaking flights of improvisational brilliance and ensemble showmanship, as evidenced on their landmark 1973 live album *The Trio* (on impresario Norman Granz's new Pablo label).

Granz had given Pass his own contract as well and encouraged him to try recording completely solo. The guitarist balked at first but went along with the idea nonetheless. The resulting albums in the *Virtuoso* series have become classics in the jazz world, with standards like "All the Things You Are" and "Cherokee" rendered in a dazzling blend of chord-melody material, bass lines, and single-note runs, often sounding as if played by more than one musician. In his efforts to cover so much ground at once on the guitar, he gravitated more and more towards fingerstyle playing and away from the use of his torn-in-half guitar pick (though never completely abandoning it, especially for faster melodies and improvised lines). He often involved at least some acoustic sound for these tracks in the studio (going nylon-string for a couple of later sessions) and would henceforth tend to spend some time performing solo even in the context of a group concert.

This period also saw recordings with bop trumpet icon Gillespie, vibraphone master Milt Jackson, and his own trio, as well as the first of his timeless duo albums with the great Ella Fitzgerald. He would venture into Brazilian music with *Tudo Bem!* (1978) and *Whitehall* (1985), and in his later years was reunited on many occasions with old guitar colleague Pisano and the *For Django* band.

Joe Pass won innumerable awards for his playing (dominating the *DownBeat* polls of the late 1970s and early 1980s), authored or collaborated on several instructional books and videos, and saw the production of signature models by Ibanez and Epiphone. He succumbed to liver cancer on May 23, 1994, but lives on as one of the most influential guitarists in history. Beyond all the virtuosity of his skills, and all the complexity of his solo work, there is something very straightforward about the man and his music that should not be lost on the listener: he was, in a way, a guitar player who simply swung hard, with a wonderfully natural sense of melody and harmony.

How to Play It

In Pass and Pedersen's duo performance of "Lover Man," the classic 32-bar ballad is converted into a 64-bar lively jazz waltz, though it's still a bit on the quiet and intimate side in this very spare setting. Pass's solo chorus is full of long, graceful lines that run beautifully through the chord changes, flowing seamlessly from one idea to the next. After the initial two short phrases of the first four measures, he doesn't take another substantial breath until he's gotten clean through the bridge at measure 50!

Harmonically, "Lover Man" could be said to be in the key of F major, with strong leanings towards its relative minor, D, which is where the progres-

Chops are only one ingredient in this duo album on which virtuosi Pass and Pedersen show their great musical simpatico, in the midst of their time together with Oscar Peterson.

sion starts out. Pass's first phrase plays on the motif of a chromatic descent from the root of a minor chord (the D heard on beat 1 of the first measure), which in a way presages the bass motion of the first few changes. He takes up this gesture again in measures 5 and 6, this time from a high G on the Gm chord, with more embellishment, and continuing into new territory.

His largely eighth-note lines are indeed embellished with plenty of hammer-on/pull-off ornamentations, typically in the form of a 16th-note triplet slurred together with the following eighth note, shaped as in measures 6 and 7. These are handy enough to play when the left-hand fingers are placed in the correct position, situated such that the index covers the lowest note of the bunch. Remember that this rhythmic figure in jazz still fits into a flow of swung eighths, such that the final note is on a late "and" count (just as if preceded by a single eighth note on the downbeat).

Pass makes ample use of chordal arpeggios within his improvisation to directly outline whatever harmony is at hand, an

Lover Man (Oh, Where Can You Be?)

approach that is exemplified in measures 9–12. An interesting feature of this song's progression is that the first time we arrive at a tonic chord for the key of F (resolving to what we could call I in the key), it's an F7#9, an altered dominant rather than a major chord. Pass's tones reflect this perfectly, especially in measure 9, before changing slightly for measures 11–12 to imply a B♭13#11 (including E♮ now instead of E♭, and also G). Heading towards the end of this section in measures 14–16, he enters into a loose pattern of mostly rising perfect 4th intervals, collectively descending by half step—here he prioritizes melodic shape over chord tones, letting the figure maintain its trajectory even through some dissonance on F major, before eventually bringing the line back into the changes where A7 (with an implied #5th) resolves to Dm (on its 9th).

A degree of vertical mobility is required to get around the fretboard in the manner of Pass, with quick jumps occasionally coming into play mid-stream. This is already apparent in measure 12, where on the third note, the left hand must shift quickly from the eighth to the twelfth position (with the index finger handling two notes in a row on string 1). A similar leap takes place in measure 19, where, after playing in the fifth position through the first two beats, he jumps up to the 10th by placing the ring finger at fret 12 for another decorative figure. This time two more of these figures follow immediately, requiring a quick shift down to the ninth position at the next measure and a downwards slide-slur into beat 3 coming out of the last pull-off.

In measure 27, he plays his first double stops of the mostly single-note solo in a blues-flavored gesture. Here the pinky holds down the note on string 1 while the other fingers are free to operate on the strings below. The bridge begins at measure 33, where the harmonic progression temporarily takes us to the key of G major. And in measures 35–39, he gives his biggest display of arpeggiated ideas yet, outlining Am11 as an extension of Am7, A♭7 as a tritone substitute for D7, an A major triad for Gmaj7 (which creates the impression of a Gmaj9#11), a G major triad for Cmaj7 (fits right in), and a G major triad again at the start of measure 39, as the chords head home to G for the moment. Before the end of the bridge, he has again moved effortlessly from single notes into double stops, this time the pretty 3rds of measures 45–48. Each one-and-a-half-beat grouping here involves a harmonic 3rd interval from the F major scale, which moves down a fret and back up again, until in measure 48 a D♭ comes in (equivalent to C#) to bring out the sound of A7 at the end of the bridge (treated as A7♭9#5).

[Editor's note: Pass just barely misses a few of these 3rd intervals on the original recording; this part of the transcription has been slightly modified to better reflect the intended notes.]

Twice more will Pass deviate from single strings for sonic variety, first by hitting three notes in octaves in the middle of his line in measure 52, jumping back and forth in fretboard position along the way. Then the bouncing melodic intervals of measure 63 become a harmonic-interval figure by measure 64, as the notes on alternating strings are sustained against each other for an elegant conclusion to the solo, morphing into octaves by the very end—after which Pass, on the original recording, will actually keep on playing quietly in octaves, creating a high-pitched backdrop for the beginning of a bass solo, before he smoothly moves into chordal accompaniment. The seamless connection of tones and textures continues even as his solo ends.

Vital Stats

Guitarist: Joe Pass

Song: "Lover Man (Oh, Where Can You Be?)"

Album: *Chops*, 1979 (recorded 1978)—Joe Pass and Niels-Henning Ørsted Pedersen

Age at Time of Recording: 49

Guitar: Gibson ES-175

Amp: Direct into board (or possibly a Polytone Model 102 or Mini-Brute)

Lover Man (Oh, Where Can You Be?)

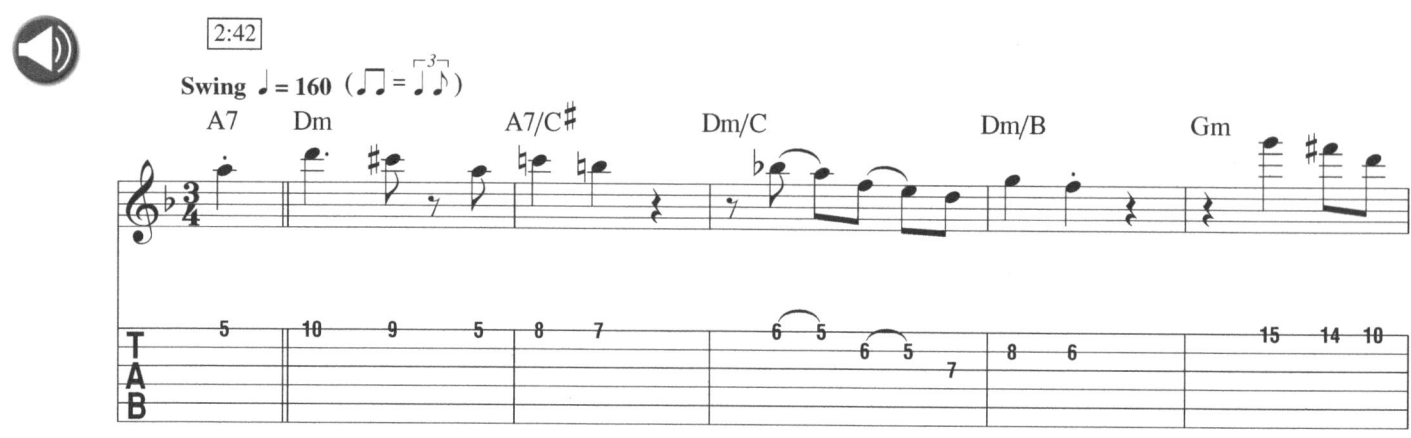
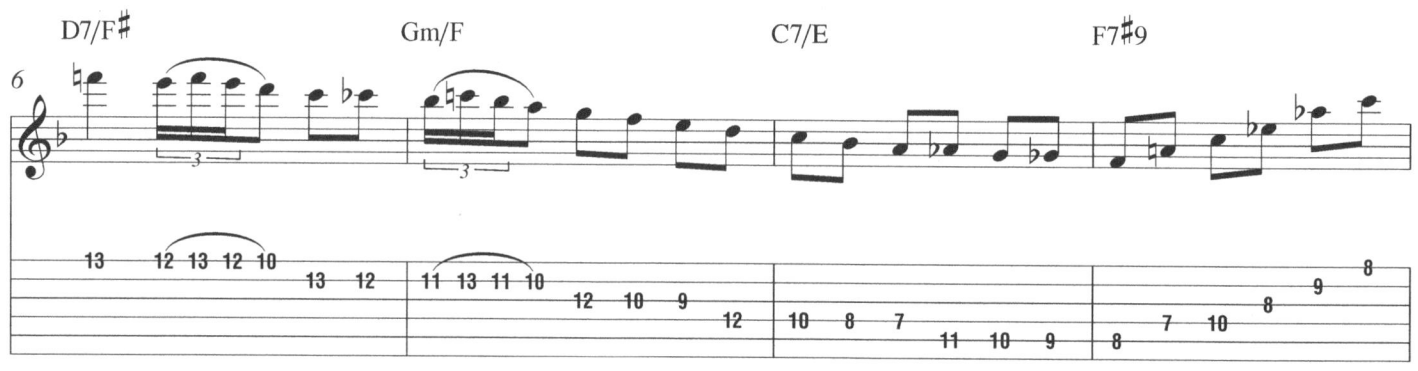
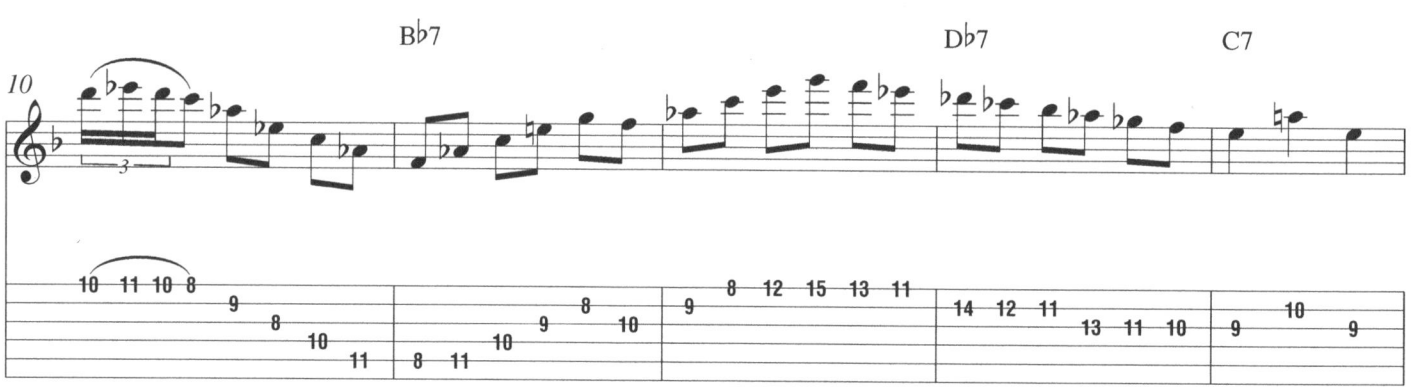
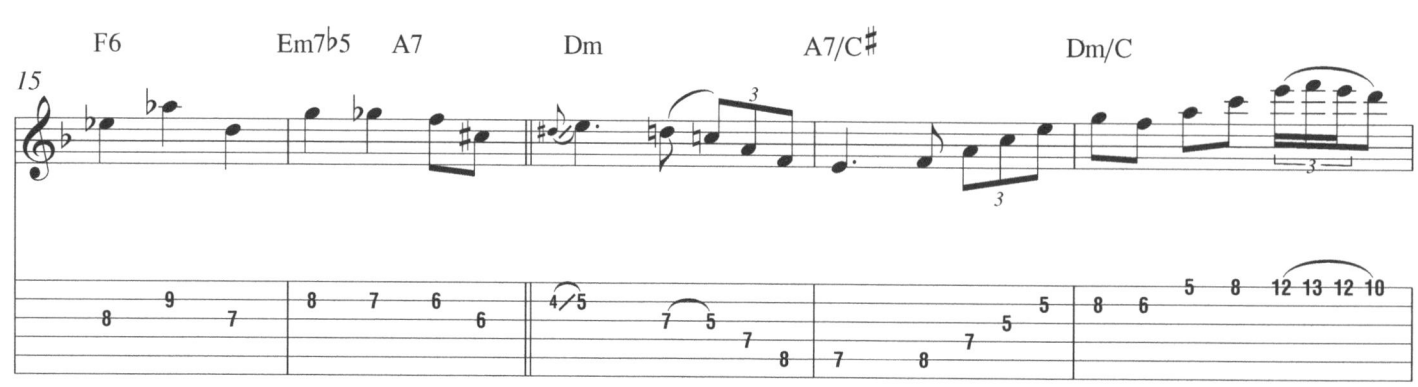

Words and Music by Jimmy Davis, Roger Ramirez and Jimmy Sherman
Copyright © 1941, 1942 UNIVERSAL MUSIC CORP.
Copyright Renewed
All Rights Reserved   Used by Permission

Lover Man (Oh, Where Can You Be?)

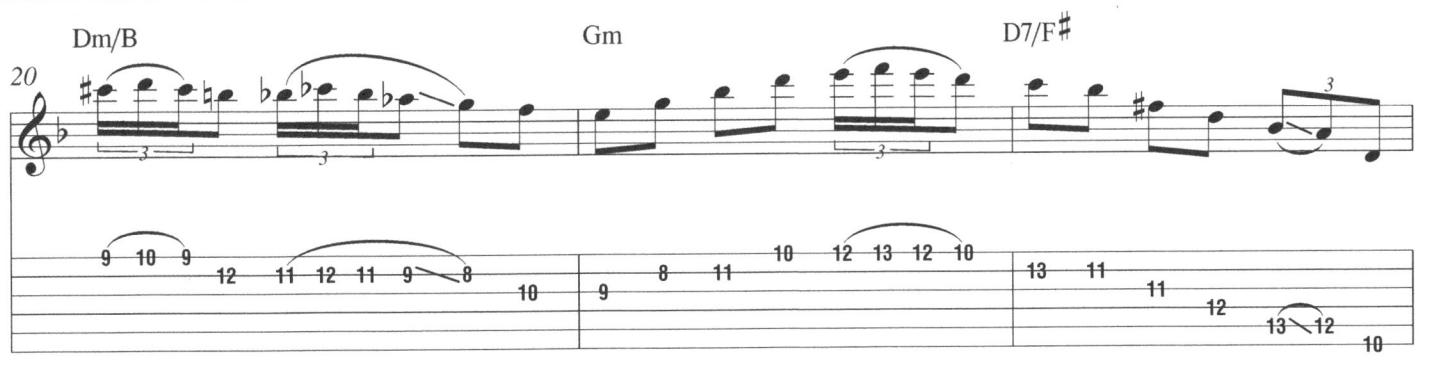

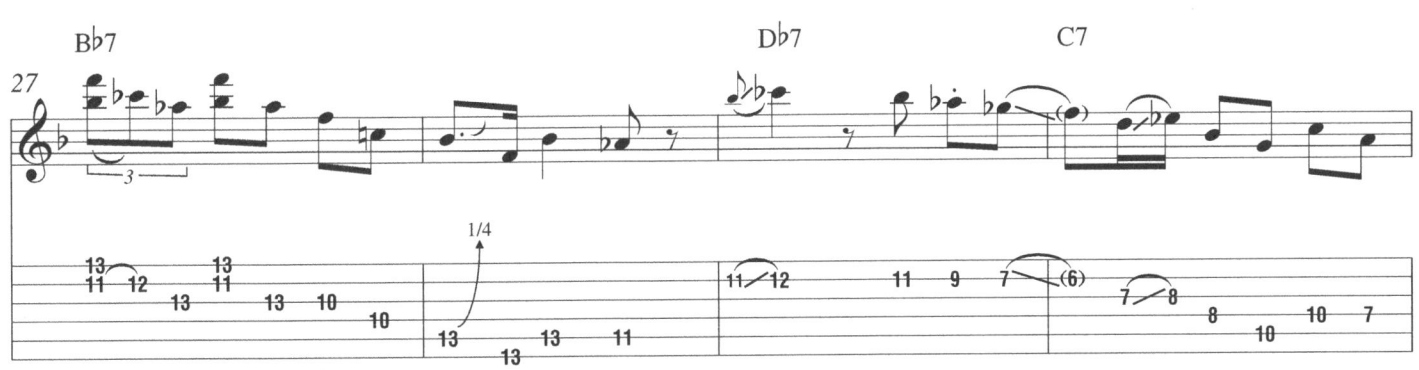
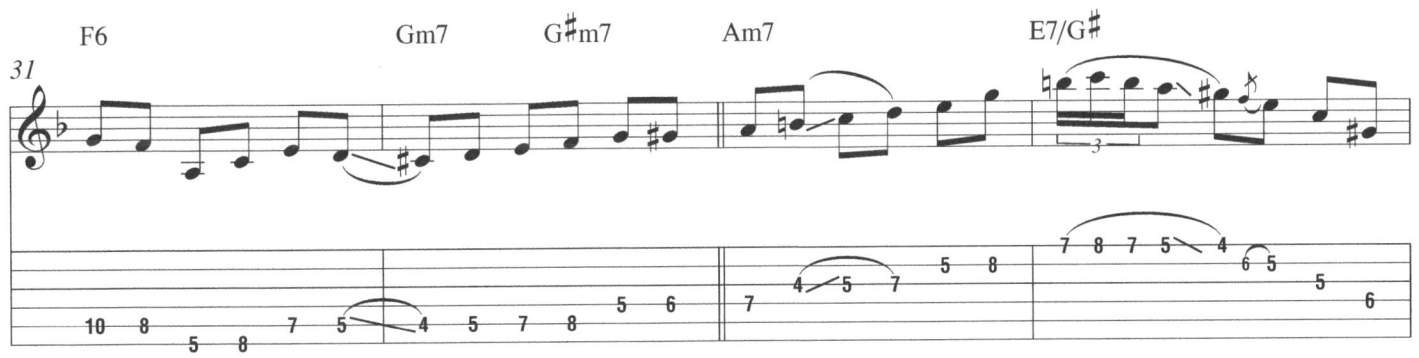
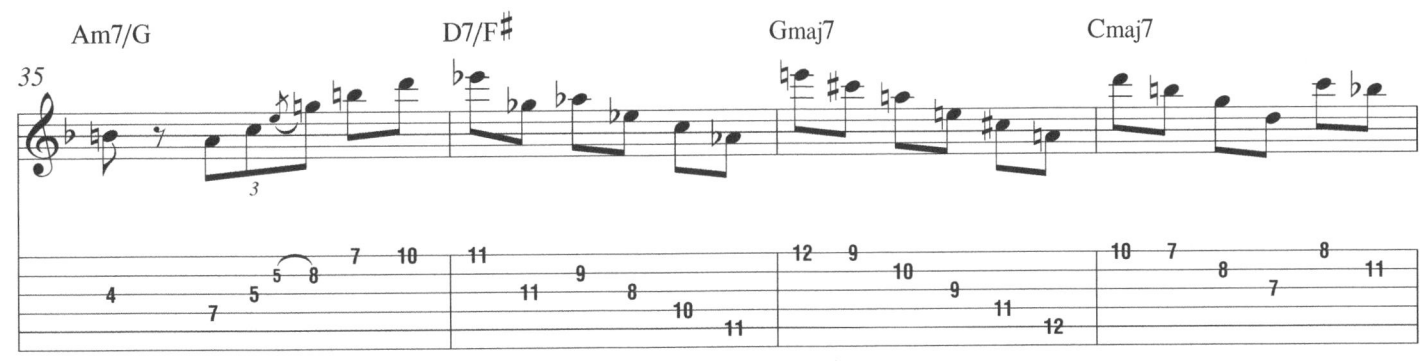

Lover Man (Oh, Where Can You Be?)

You Don't Know What Love Is 1986

John Abercrombie

"The idea is to be creative and spontaneous. To do that, you have to live with imperfection."
—John Abercrombie

© Alamy

Few guitarists are as hard to pin down stylistically as John Abercrombie. Consciously a jazzer, and a relatively quiet, subtle player at heart, he has most often chosen a solidbody instrument, has sometimes donned the screaming distortion of the fusion movement, was on the cutting edge of guitar synthesizer experimentation in the 1980s, and has occasionally been heard on the electric mandolin. While holding great admiration for the standard song (and for straight-ahead predecessors like Jim Hall and Wes Montgomery), he has pioneered wide areas of open texture and free improvisation within the broader jazz realm.

John Laird Abercrombie was born on December 16, 1944, and grew up in Greenwich, Connecticut, taking up the guitar at the age of 14. Initially inspired by Chuck Berry, he got his jazz awakening from the work of Barney Kessel and in 1962 headed to the Berklee College of Music in Boston to follow his passion. His Boston days led to professional connections with organist Johnny Hammond Smith and with the aspiring jazz-rock fusion band Dreams, which had the Brecker brothers (Michael on tenor sax and Randy on trumpet) and drumming powerhouse Billy Cobham in its lineup. Moving to New York City in 1969, he played with veteran drummer Chico Hamilton, joined a fusion outfit led by Cobham, and began life-long friendships with like-minded musical explorers such as pianist Richie Beirach, saxophonist David Liebman, and drummer Jack DeJohnette.

Abercrombie has for decades been associated with the ECM record label, famous for its leaning towards an often spacious, ambient, and experimental brand of jazz, whether based on swung or even-eighths rhythms (or neither). He credits its charismatic founder/producer Manfred Eicher with encouraging his exploration of unique timbral combinations and more open improvisational settings. His 1974 recording debut as a leader on the label, *Timeless*, involved DeJohnette, keyboardist Jan Hammer (mainly on organ), and a slate of expansive, hard-to-categorize original music, with tunes like Abercrombie's introspective title track and Hammer's high-octane "Red and Orange."

Since this time, he has toured extensively and cut countless albums both as leader and sideman on ECM and elsewhere, appearing with such trailblazers as trumpeter Kenny Wheeler, organist Lonnie Smith, and saxophonists Jan Garbarek and Charles Lloyd. His own bands have included a late 1970s/early 1980s quartet with Beirach, bassist George Mraz, and

This 1986 duo outing with pianist/bassist Don Thompson is a hidden gem in Abercrombie's catalog on which he plays almost entirely swingin' standards, all with a straight, mellow electric guitar tone.

You Don't Know What Love Is

drummer Peter Donald, a 1980s trio with bassist Marc Johnson and drummer Peter Erskine (in which he would often bust out the guitar synth), a 1990s trio with organist Dan Wall and drummer Adam Nussbaum, and a quartet in the 2000s with violinist Mark Feldman, bassist Marc Johnson, and drummer Joey Baron. He also made the solo recording *Characters* in 1978 (with the use of overdubbing), partook on and off for over twenty years in the jointly led trio Gateway with DeJohnette and bassist Dave Holland, and has collaborated with fellow guitarists Ralph Towner (on duo projects like 1976's *Sargasso Sea*) and John Scofield. Much of his output revolves around his own modern style of jazz composition, alternately simple or complex, and frequently inspired by John Coltrane or Ornette Coleman.

Within his personal aesthetic, Abercrombie has espoused the Jim Hall-derived practice of moving vertically on the fretboard in linear improvisation, usually on a limited number of strings, as a way to emphasize really listening for melodic ideas and not relying on rote patterns. He has also been influenced by Hall's comping style, with its varied textures and sensitive dynamics. In the early 1990s, he felt compelled to simplify his craft and return to a more natural sound, largely putting down the guitar synth and also putting down the pick in favor of his thumb (and occasional fingers).

Unfortunately, in late 2003, he needed to let go of far more yet, due to a fire at his Putnam Valley, New York home in which he lost the house, various instruments, his record collection, numerous manuscripts, and most sadly, his cat. Luckily, in light of this, he and his wife escaped unharmed, along with several guitars and his creative spirit. He continues to tour and record to this day, and among his recent releases are *Within a Song* (2012), featuring saxophonist Joe Lovano and a selection of post-bop classics, and *39 Steps* (2013), with long-time piano colleague Marc Copland on the roster. Abercrombie teaches at Purchase College and was a 1998 recipient of the Berklee Distinguished Alumni Award.

How to Play It

Here Abercrombie appears in about the most straight-ahead and intimate jazz setting possible, playing on a famous standard at proper ballad tempo, accompanied only by piano. Mixing simple, songful phrases with dazzling, intricate lines and a full dynamic range, he creates a beautiful compositional arc from start to end of his one-chorus statement.

Motivic development plays an important role throughout, and he starts off with a rising 5th interval that softly echoes the beginning of the song itself. Many a melodic idea is answered or built upon by the next one—compare the shapes found in measures 9 and 10, for example, or the fast material of measure 14 with the long line starting in measure 15. The three-note motif heard on each of the first two beats of measure 3 gives rise to the slightly longer descending phrase that follows and is reprised big-time during the bridge in measures 18–19.

Besides demonstrating Abercrombie's melodic creativity and prodigious technique, this solo provides a valuable lesson as to how an improviser might rhythmically handle a ballad. At a slow enough tempo where typical textures like swung eighths become unviable, more complex figures and finer division of the beat may come in handy.

He makes ample use of 16th-note triplets and speedy 32nd notes while still allowing plenty of breathing space and leaving the ballad feel intact. Notice that we often see a triplet grouping of an eighth note followed by a 16th, and that this particular figure actually represents swung 16ths, as if on an eighth-note pulse (this is noticeable especially where it is played in repetition, as in the last chunk of measure 29). These tend to blend in with the generally triplet-laden texture, and he and his accompanist never imply full-blown double-time. Other rhythmic devices can be more complicated, but perhaps easier to hear and feel than they appear in writing. For example, the figure from the third note of measure 5 (G) to measure 6, beat 2 is really just a series of eighth-note triplets that begins on the "and" of beat 1 rather than on a downbeat.

Abercrombie is remarkably fluid in his lines, with profuse slurring from hammer-ons, pull-offs, and slides. Add to this an ability to quickly shift positions within a phrase and his study (à la Jim Hall) of melodic movement along one or two strings, and we get the kind of fretboard mobility often seen here. In measure 5, the climb along string 4 involves only the index finger until fret 7, while towards the end of measure 6, the index takes three notes in a row on string 2 (at frets 8, 6, and 5), scooting down as needed. After the pull-off from pinky to ring finger going into measure 7, nudge the ring down one fret to get in place for the next segment. For the quick phrase at the end of measure 12, basically an ascent on string 3 that bounces off of lower tones on string 4 (a rather Metheny-esque device—see "Nothing Personal," measure 32), allow the hand to move up the neck as you go. In the subsequent dramatic climb along string 2, the middle finger frets all picked

You Don't Know What Love Is

notes on frets 8, 10, 11, 13, and 14. The 32nd-note run of measure 14 requires some shifting to let the pinky grab all pull-offs that start from frets 9 or 10. Begin the next long phrase with the ring finger, allowing the hand to gradually shift down to the first position before a final jump with the pinky to fret 6 on beat 2 of measure 16. Practice slowly and carefully to map these tricky lines out well and use alternate picking for the non-slurred parts.

In this rather somber F minor context, he often plays simply within the key (with flexibility between the natural and melodic variants of the F minor scale), but makes adjustments along the way for particular chords or shifts in key area, also throwing in a good deal of chromaticism (especially in faster runs like that of measure 15). The sound of C7 is frequently emphasized by the presence of E♮ (the chordal 3rd) in the line. The first halves of measures 4, 12, and 28 show an acknowledgement of the B7#11 chord (especially with A♮, its 7th), and A♭ Dorian material fills most of measure 7 as well as the first half of measure 31 to coincide with the A♭m7–D♭7 pairing. Occasionally Gm7♭5 gets a Dorian treatment as well, invoking a regular Gm7 sound (in measures 5 and 27), and the B♮ in measure 10 gives us a brief F blues scale inflection.

The bridge of the tune begins at measure 17 with a move to the relative major key of A♭, and though its scale consists of the same tones as F natural minor, Abercrombie makes use of them in such a way as to bring out the specific changes, highlighting the "sun coming out" mood of this modulation (note that the chromatic E♮ in measure 17 brings out the ♭9th color of E♭7). For measures 21–22, the progression heads to the distant key of C major, our soloist obliging with a G7#9 to C resolution. His next ideas revolve largely around the chordal shapes of D♭9#11 and C7 at the eighth position, reaching a high point of pitch, volume, and intensity in measure 24 as the tune prepares for a return to F minor at the last A section. Here, he mixes the mellow with the aggressive until bringing it down for good by measure 31, and finally ending with an F moving down to a sustained low C (an inversion of the very first two-note phrase of the solo), as if returning to the same quiet, melancholy place at which he began.

Vital Stats

Guitarist: John Abercrombie

Song: "You Don't Know What Love Is"

Album: *Witchcraft,* 1986—John Abercrombie and Don Thompson

Age at Time of Recording: 41

Guitar: Ibanez Artist solidbody

Amp: Roland Cube 60

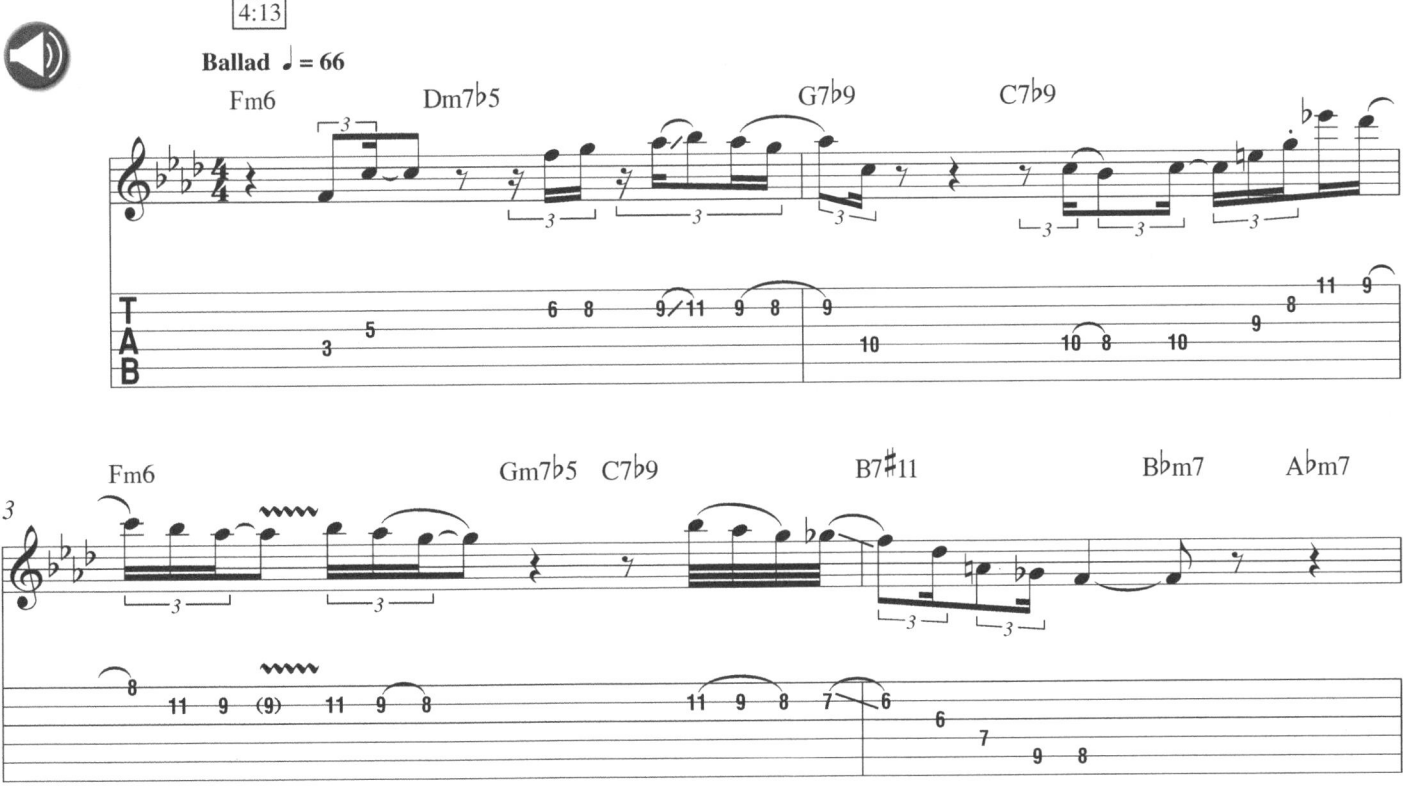

Words and Music by Don Raye and Gene DePaul
Copyright © 1941 UNIVERSAL MUSIC CORP.
Copyright Renewed
All Rights Reserved   Used by Permission

You Don't Know What Love Is

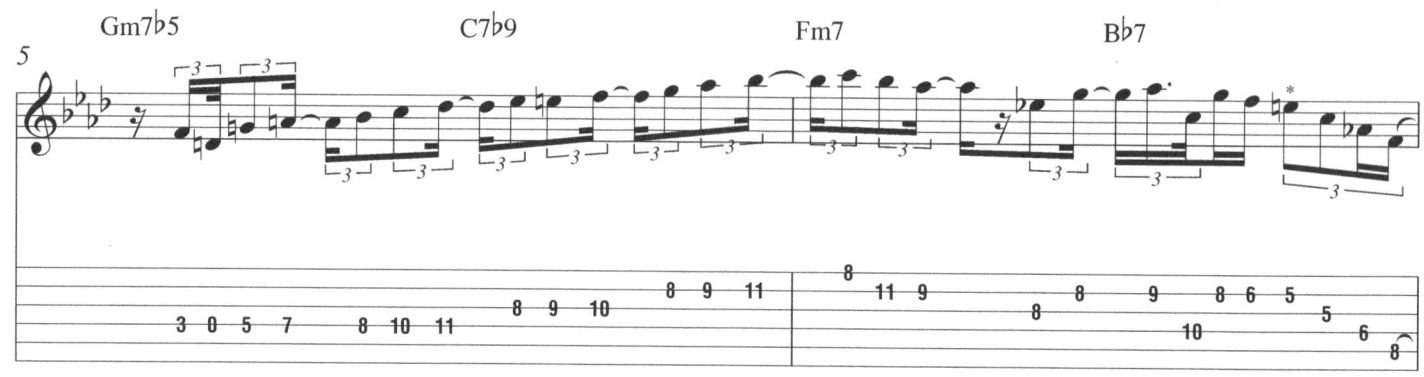

*Played behind the beat.

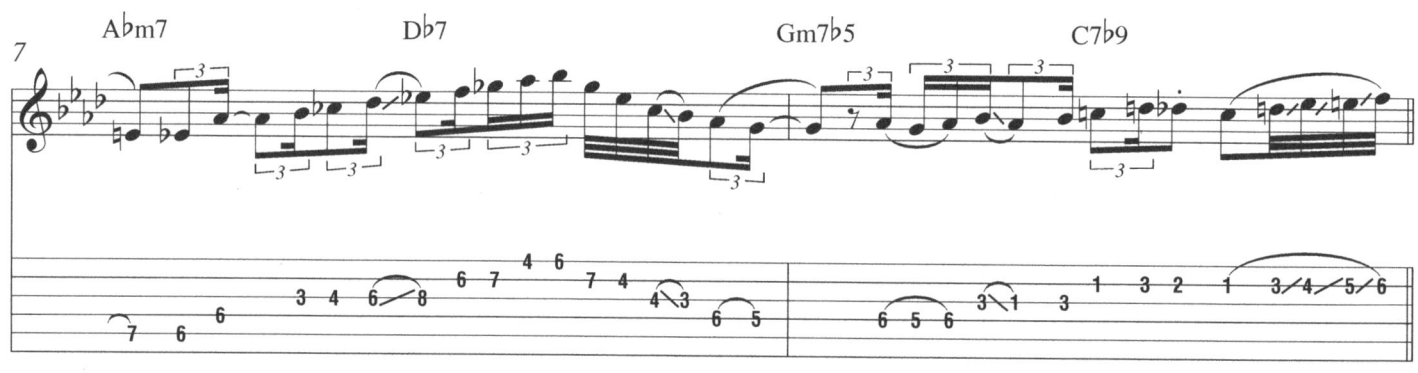

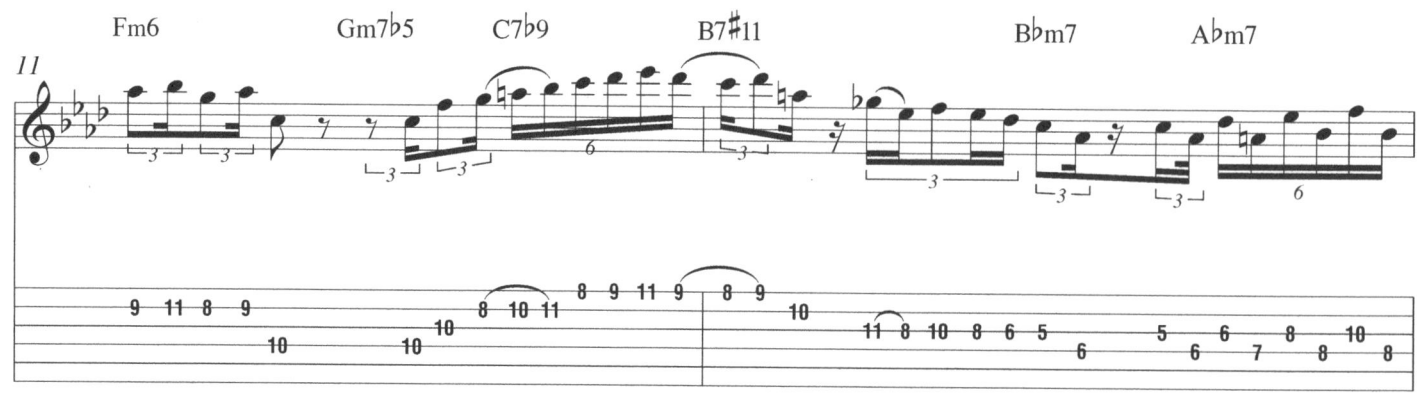

You Don't Know What Love Is

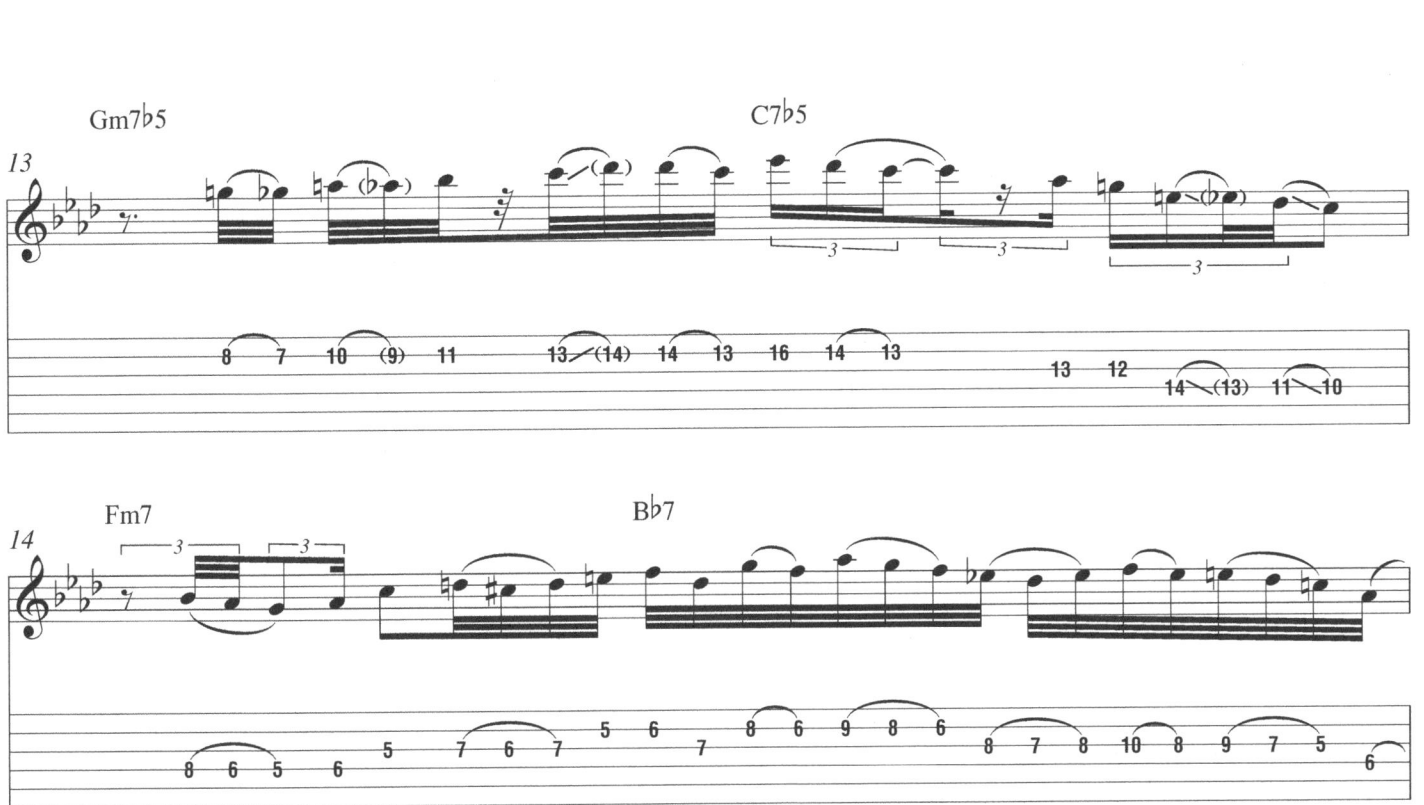
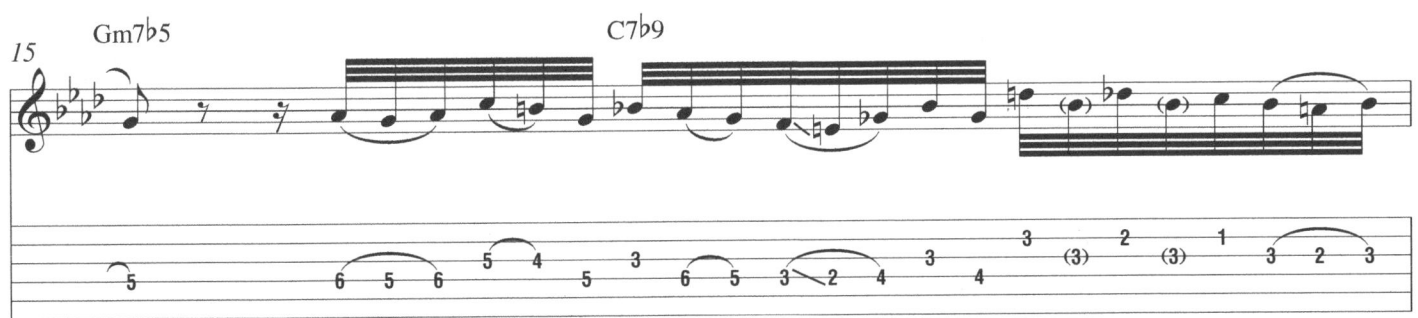

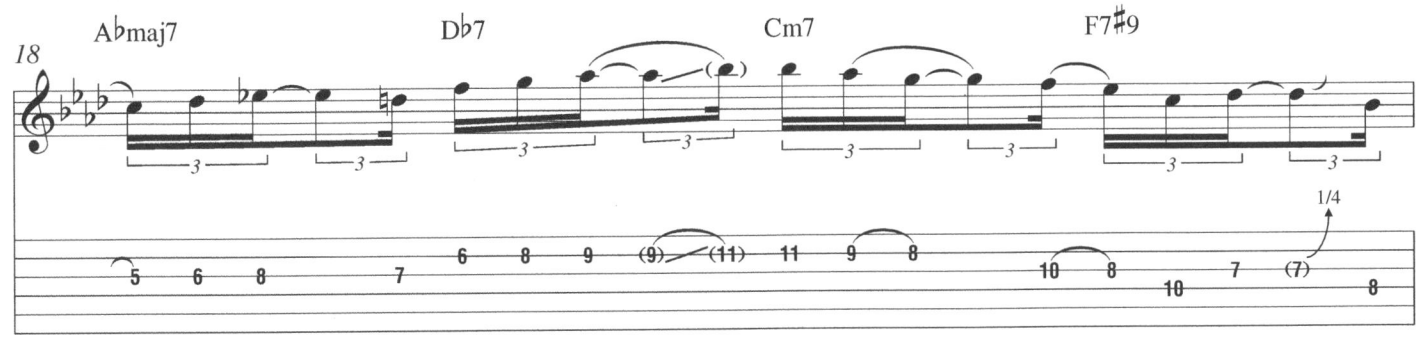

You Don't Know What Love Is

You Don't Know What Love Is

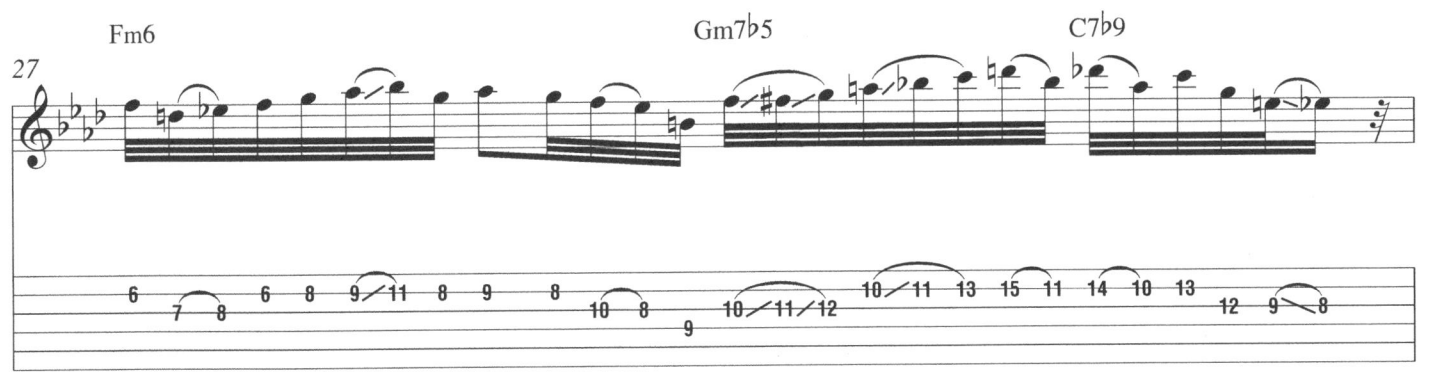

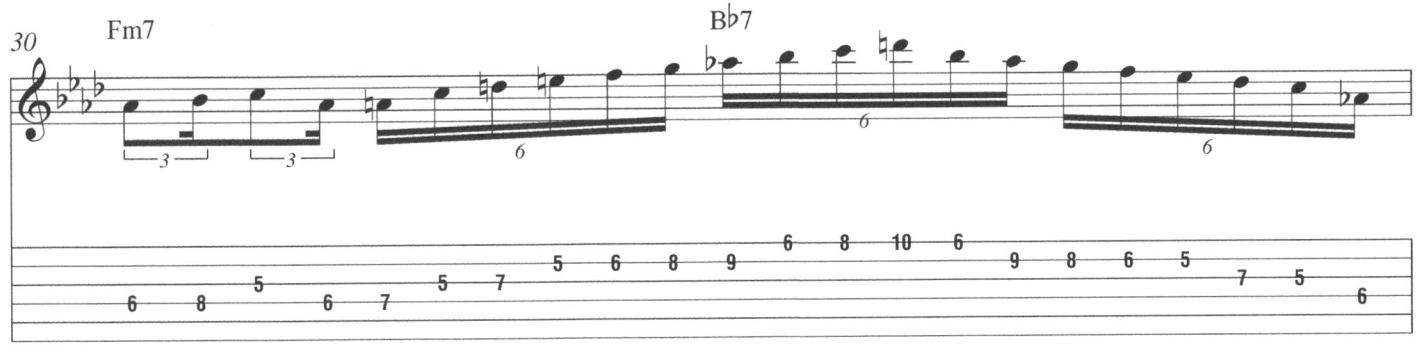
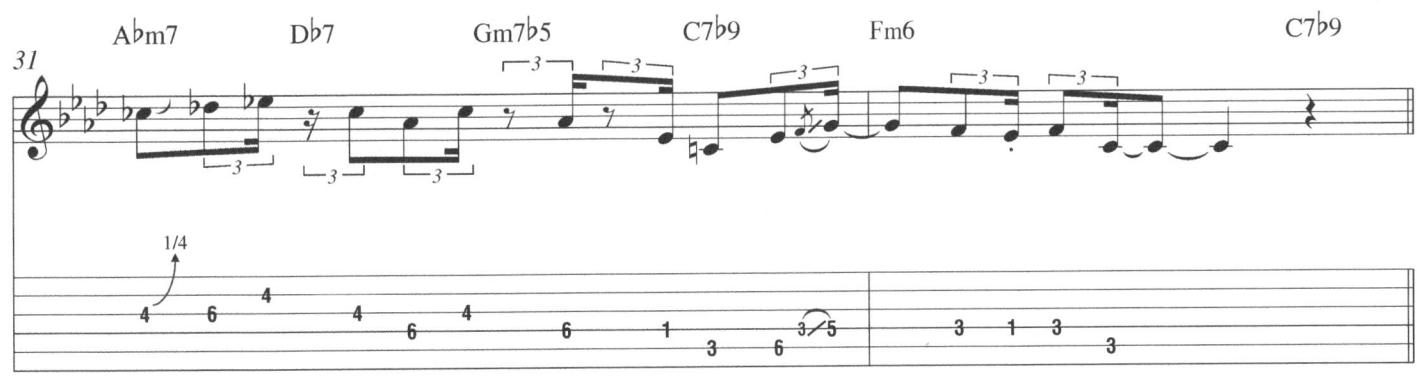

Nothing Personal 1987

Pat Metheny

"The quality that I admire in the musicians and music I love is something that always transcends the style it's played in."
—Pat Metheny

Courtesy Photofest

Considered by many to be the greatest jazz guitarist alive today, Pat Metheny is an artist who altogether defies category. Much of his most popular work mixes contemporary even-eighth-note rhythms with a jazz improviser's sensibilities, yet does not fit the mold of "fusion" in the usual sense. The ambient, other-worldly quality often heard in his music might sometimes invite the term "new age," but it is coupled with a rhythmic vitality and melodic/harmonic richness not typically associated with the genre. His tunes may play on the simplicity of a pop or folk aesthetic (particularly his Americana-flavored acoustic guitar pieces), while using a sophisticated chordal vocabulary. He can wail with a rockin' spirit, and at the same time venture into esoteric avant-garde territory. And through all his pioneering of new ground in composition and performance, he is still a guitar player who carries the torch of Wes Montgomery, Pat Martino, and Jim Hall, in his own innovative way.

With his especially low, round, non-twangy tone, processed with reverb and delay to a smooth finish, he has helped bring the sound of the amplified hollowbody guitar into the modern era. The Ibanez PM-100 jazz model was designed to his specs. He has also been at the forefront of guitar synthesizer music as a prominent player of the Roland GR-300 and early on embraced the arrival of digital workstation technology (namely the Synclavier). On the acoustic side, he has explored the use of unconventional instruments such as the baritone guitar and the four-neck, 42-string Pikasso guitar that he commissioned in 1984.

Born August 12, 1954 in Lee's Summit, Missouri, Patrick Bruce Metheny was a precocious young listener, player, and teacher. He took up the trumpet at age eight (a family habit—his brother Mike is a noted horn player), switched to guitar four years later, met his hero Wes Montgomery at age 13 while at the nearby Kansas City Jazz Festival, and by the time he was 15, was gigging with the pros in that town. Practicing ferociously, he devoted little time to schoolwork. Shortly after matriculating at the University of Miami in 1972 on a full-ride scholarship based on his playing ability, he felt compelled to drop out for lack of academic skills, but was asked to stay on as an *instructor*—their youngest ever at 18 years of age. Vibraphonist Gary Burton heard the up-and-coming guitarist at the Wichita Jazz Festival and offered him a position at Boston's esteemed Berklee College of Music, leading him to become the youngest-ever teacher there too at 19 (his star student at Berklee would be Mike Stern).

Burton soon brought him into his band, which already included modern jazz guitar maven Mick Goodrick, and three years with the group gave him world-class experience and wide exposure. Metheny made his first recorded appearance on *Jaco* (1974), the debut album by electric bass giant Jaco Pastorius (with whom he had played in Florida), which also involved pianist Paul Bley. His own debut as a leader, *Bright Size Life* (1976), was a trio effort with Jaco and drummer Bob Moses. Through this mostly originals set, his unique, often jubilant compositional style was already evident, as was the flowing sense of freedom in his virtuosic improvisation.

1977's *Watercolors* marked the beginning of his partnership with keyboardist Lyle Mays (a kindred spirit and frequent co-composer) as well as the origins of the famed Pat Metheny Group. This highly successful and influential outfit would become a major international touring act, releasing 14 albums from their self-titled LP in 1978 through *The Way Up* in 2005, and winning Grammys for 10 of them. With Mays as a constant, other long-term band members have included bassist Steve Rodby (also an important producer in Metheny's career) and drummers Danny Gottlieb and Paul Wertico, alongside numerous significant guest musicians, such as Brazilian percussionist/vocalist Naná Vasconcelos, Argentinian multi-instrumentalist Pedro Aznar, and trumpeter/vocalists Mark Ledford and Cuong Vu. The group's output has been colorful and varied, with wordless vocals often included in their palette of acoustic and electronic sounds. Their music video for the classic "Are You Going with Me" (from *Offramp*, 1982) received frequent play on cable channel VH1, with its mellow, trance-like vamp, a plaintive synthesized harmonica statement from Mays, and Pat in full flight through his trumpet-toned guitar synth solo. For one song on their soundtrack to the 1985 film *The Falcon and the Snowman*, they were partnered with David Bowie. 1987's *Still Life (Talking)* and 1989's *Letter From Home* attained gold record status and showed especially strong influence of the music of Brazil (where Metheny lived for a few years around this time). The compositionally ambitious *The Way Up* consists of one 68-minute-long piece.

Metheny's work outside the PMG is far-ranging, from solo acoustic projects (starting with the landmark *New Chautaqua* in 1979), to the sweeping sonic landscape of 1992's gold record-winning *Secret Story* and the quizzical distorted solo guitar (with overdubs) of *Zero Tolerance for Silence* (1994). He has shown a particular affinity for the music of saxophonist and free jazz innovator Ornette Coleman, recording several of his tunes over the years and collaborating with him on the remarkable *Song X* (1986). For the double album *80/81* (1980), he assembled an all-star team of Coleman alums Dewey Redman on tenor sax and Charlie Haden on bass—with additional tenor man Michael Brecker and drummer Jack DeJohnette—for a part hard-swingin' and part folky affair. Trio settings such as those on *Rejoicing* (1984, with Haden and drummer Billy Higgins), *Question and Answer* (1989, with bassist Dave Holland and drummer Roy Haynes), *Trio 99 > 00* (2000, with bassist Larry Grenadier and drummer Bill Stewart), and *Day Trip* (2008, with bassist Christian McBride and drummer Antonio Sanchez) find Metheny in the company of versatile modern jazz masters, swinging on standards like "All the Things You Are" as well as playing through a variety of his original music. He has made duo recordings with the likes of bassist Charlie Haden, guitar legend Jim Hall, and pianist Brad Mehldau, scored numerous films, and worked with the iconic Joni Mitchell, top-notch tenor saxman Josh Redman (son of Dewey), fellow guitar modernist John Scofield, and contemporary composers Steve Reich and John Zorn, among many others.

In recent years, Metheny has outdone himself in technological exploration with his Orchestrion project, which entails a massive collection of mechanically played acoustic instruments (piano, marimba, bottles, bells, cymbals, and more), all digitally controlled from his guitar, in solo concert performance or in the studio. He has also formed a new regular band with the Unity Group, featuring Sanchez, saxophonist Chris Potter, bassist Ben Williams, and lately also multi-instrumentalist Giulio Carmassi (as of the 2014 release *Kin*). All in all, he has sold over 20 million records, won 20 Grammy Awards (including two in the New Age category!), dominated the *DownBeat* Readers Poll as a guitarist through the 1980s and over the last decade, and been on tour between 120 and 240 nights annually since 1974. Publicly outspoken about the importance of the jazz tradition in our culture, he is known to be sharply critical of the most vapidly commercial forms of the music. He received an honorary doctorate from Berklee in 1996 and in 2013 was voted into the *DownBeat* Hall of Fame (the only guitarist to be inducted within his lifetime). A huge influence on younger generations of jazz guitarists, as well as on modern music generally, he remains a vital force in the art today.

How to Play It

Don Grolnick's minor blues "Nothing Personal," a spacious, modern take on a traditional form, is the perfect setting in which to check out the straight-ahead jazz talents of Metheny. His dark, reverberant guitar sound emerges from the tune's mysterious vamp to begin this three-chorus excursion, which ranges from low, quiet tones to high-pitched bursts of passion, from short phrases and mainly rhythmic gestures to seemingly endless virtuosic lines, and from simple in-the-key note choices to surprising substitutions and chromatic departures.

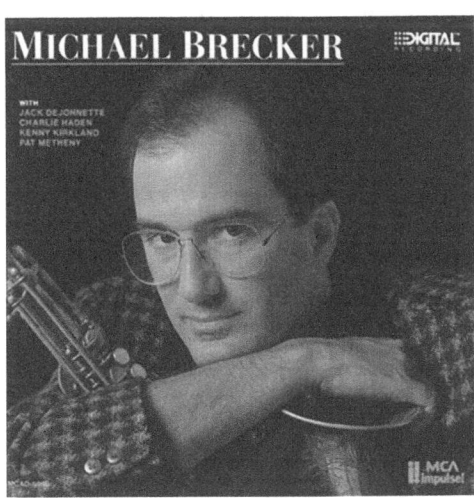

Michael Brecker's self-titled debut album, from 1987, is a great place to hear the jazz sideman aspect of Metheny, who also appears on the late, great saxophonist's posthumous release, Pilgrimage *(2007).*

Nothing Personal

Jazz guitar tone often entails the selection of the neck pickup, with the tone knob rolled towards the low end, and that is truer here than most anywhere else. Generous reverb and a touch of delay play a part as well in his silky smooth, slightly distant sound. Some of the muted mystery of his lowest notes is achieved by anchoring the picking hand at the near end of the bridge and letting the heel of the hand just touch strings 6 and 5 (and sometimes 4) for some light palm muting.

The chord progression here is at base a simplified, normal G minor blues despite the contemporary, fractured style put on it by pianist Kenny Kirkland, bassist Charlie Haden, and drummer Jack DeJohnette. However, it is metrically stretched out to a 24-bar form rather than the usual 12. Also, the tonic chord is a bit flexible in its minor type, as the initial bass line implies Gm6 or Gm(maj7) with the major 6th and 7th tones of the scale, while Metheny's early phrases tend to invoke Gm7 (with the note F♮, as at the end of measure 2). And where the iv chord would typically be a Cm of some kind, here the composer and most of the band treat it as a highly altered C7, with great variation in how it's voiced on the piano—but Pat often plays on it like Cm indeed, involving the note E♭ (its minor 3rd) as he does in measure 9 and again in measure 57, quite songfully (the divergent approaches seem to work out alright in the flow of things).

From the beginning through measure 28, his tone material relates largely to G Dorian, minor pentatonic, or blues scales, with some exceptions like the E♭ in measure 9 and the use of A♭ and B♮ to imply G7♭9 in measures 7–8 (for extra gravity towards Cm). But within the long line that begins at measure 29, Metheny starts to mix it up, allowing the momentum of melodic shapes to lead into "outside" notes that don't so obviously fit the chords. By the last half of measure 31, he is outlining an E6 chord before proceeding with a series of falling major 3rds, descending by half steps on strings 4 and 5, through measure 32. Even where he uses ideas that bring out the changes more clearly, they may be connected by such patterned chromatic motion: the tones of measures 41–42 make sense for E♭9 (except for the low note, E♮), and the line continues through brief dissonance on beat 1 of measure 43 into classic D7♭9 vocabulary as of beat 2 and on through a quick out-of-key moment at the end of measure 44 (with A♭ and B♮), before a clear return to Gm7-land.

Typical of Metheny's style are the short, quick, downward slides off of many notes (less aggressive in vibe than those of George Benson—see "Benny's Back"), heard especially within his trademark bouts of syncopated rhythm in measures 13–18 or 21–24. In the earlier of these segments, he creates a varied, bouncy groove on just four notes—well-suited to the flavor of the tune, the rhythmic interaction of the group, and his own musical personality. The mostly G minor pentatonic ascent of measures 21–24 is a recurring motif, especially at points of transition. Here, he uses it to move from low to high range on the guitar, raising the energy level on the way to his second chorus, where the rhythm section kicks into higher gear with walking-bass time (at measure 25). From measure 45 into measure 48, a similar climb leads to the energetic high point of the solo at the beginning of the third chorus in measure 49. Technical tip: these pentatonic runs originate in the third position and then work their way up string 1—you can scoot up to fret 8 with the pinky, but at the ends of measures 23 or 47, jump to the 10th position (sliding into fret 10 with the index).

During the electrifying rhythmic play of measures 49–56, Metheny dances on and around the high D on strings 1 and 2 alternately, accenting the basically single-note figure with the contrast in timbre (his own version of a device used by many guitarists—see "Benny's Back" again, measures 16–19, or Wes on "Full House," measures 56–62). He dramatically slides into, out of, or just past this note as he goes (echoing a particular element of the song's melody) before melodically soaring through the tones beyond. In a more than 10 measure-long, breathless run of eighth notes from measure 58 to nearly the finish, he lapses in and out of key, outlining various distant chords along the way: F6 at the end of measure 59 into measure 60, B♭m7 in the last three beats of measure 60, E6 with the last five notes of measure 62, and Gm7♭5 within measure 63. A tension-building fret-by-fret climb with diminished triad arpeggios in measures 65–66 precedes the return to G minor territory in measure 67 (the segment from beat 4 through the next measure really brings out the D7♭9, or V chord in the key). It then seems he is headed into another grand pentatonic climb, but this time he turns back to stay low and quiet things down, concluding with mellow, bluesy tones as the band returns to the opening vamp.

Vital Stats

Guitarist: Pat Metheny

Song: "Nothing Personal"

Album: *Michael Brecker* (self-titled), 1987

Age at Time of Recording: 32

Guitar: Gibson ES-175

Amp: Acoustic 134

Effects: Digital delay

Nothing Personal

By Don Grolnick
Copyright © 1987 Carmine Street Publishing (BMI)
International Copyright Secured All Rights Reserved

Nothing Personal

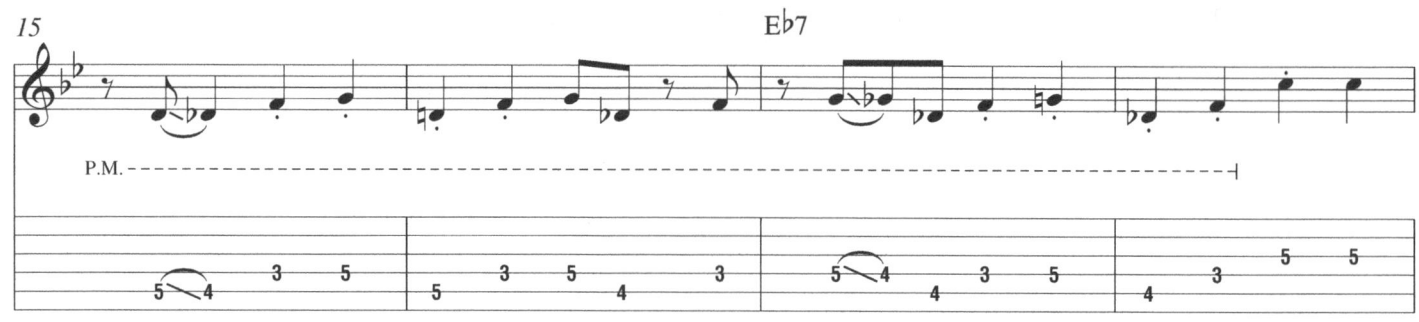
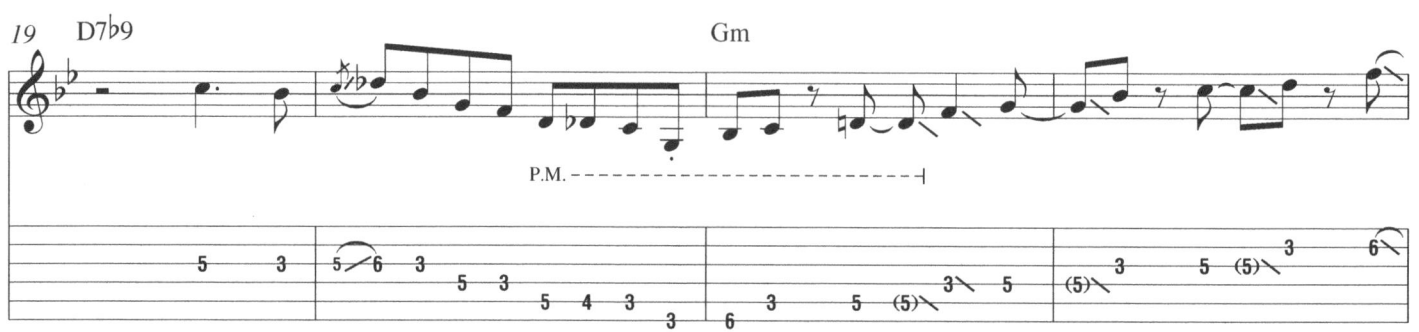
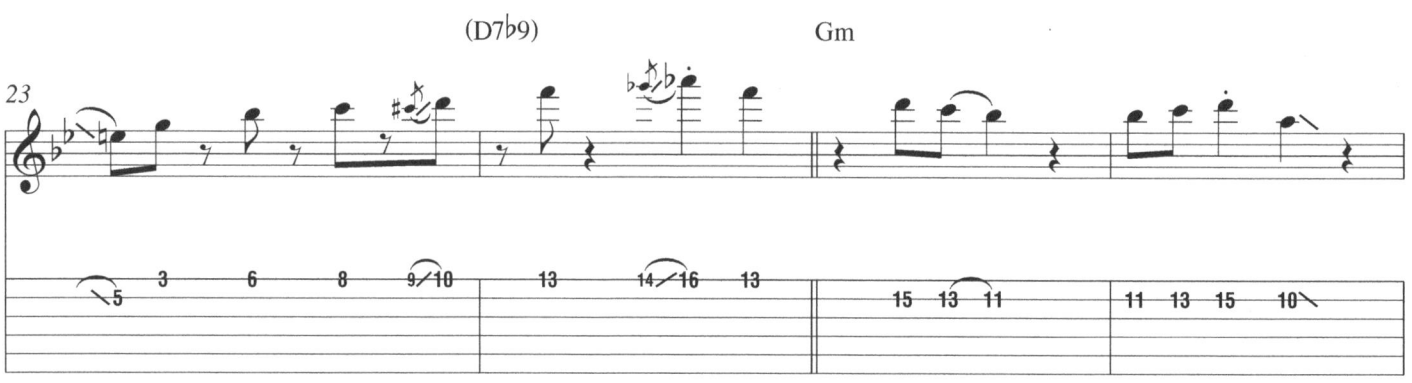

Nothing Personal

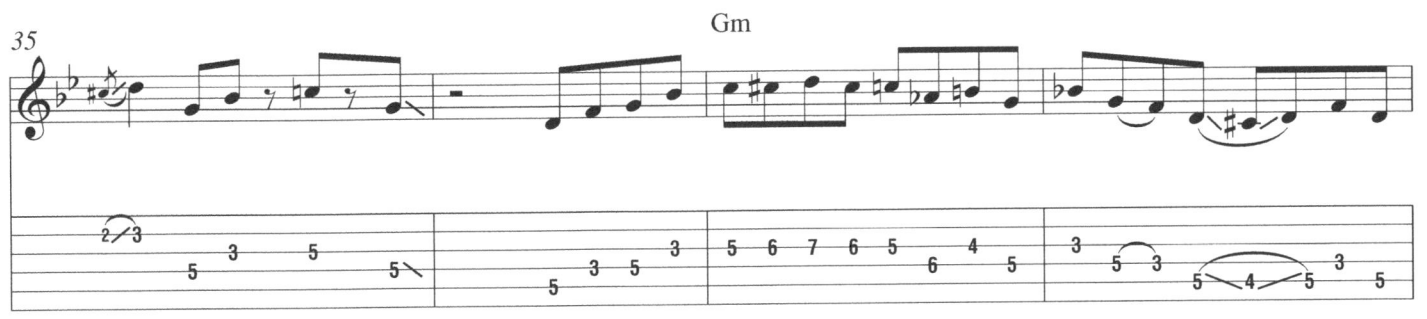
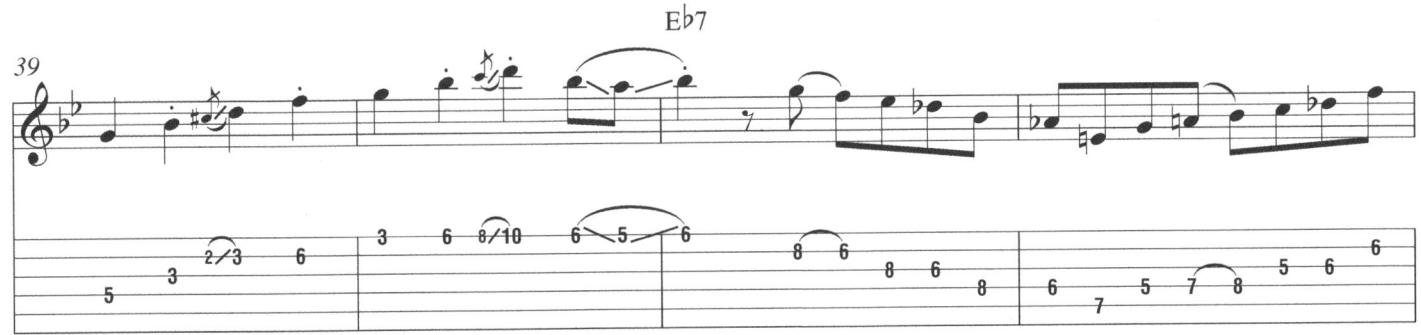

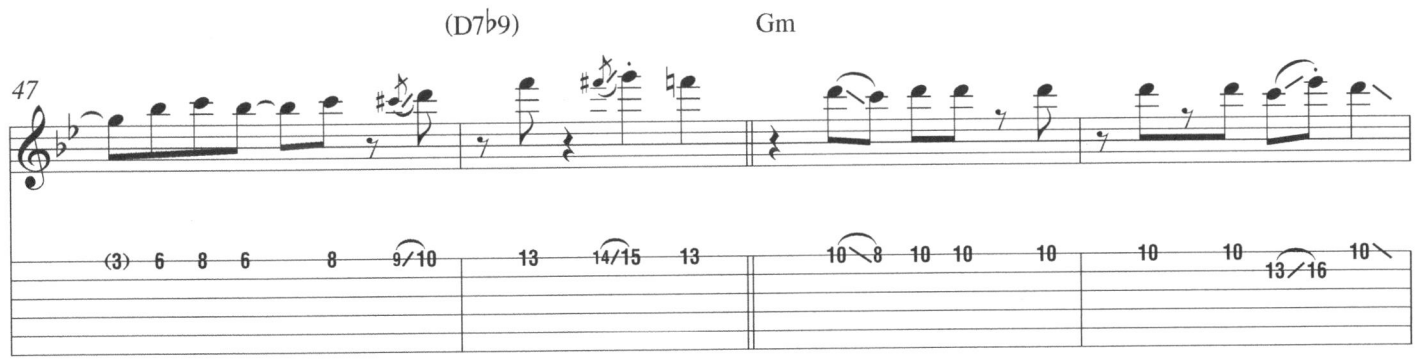
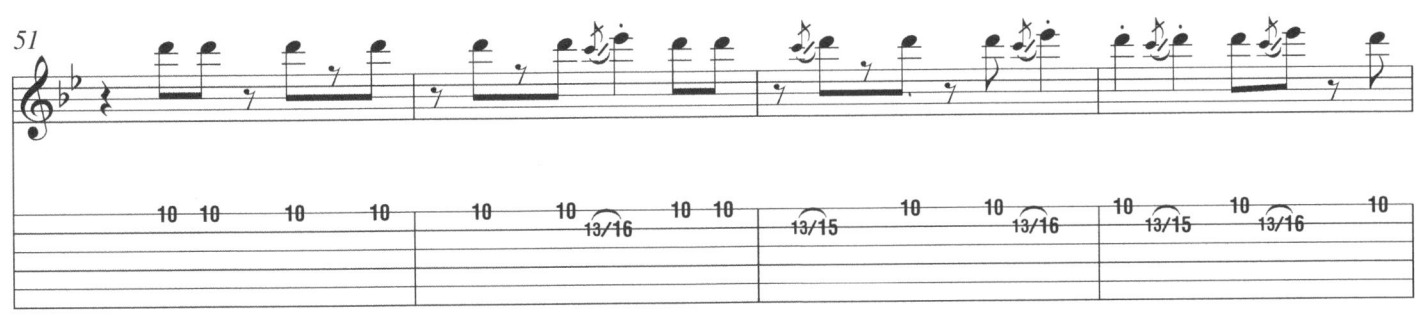

Nothing Personal

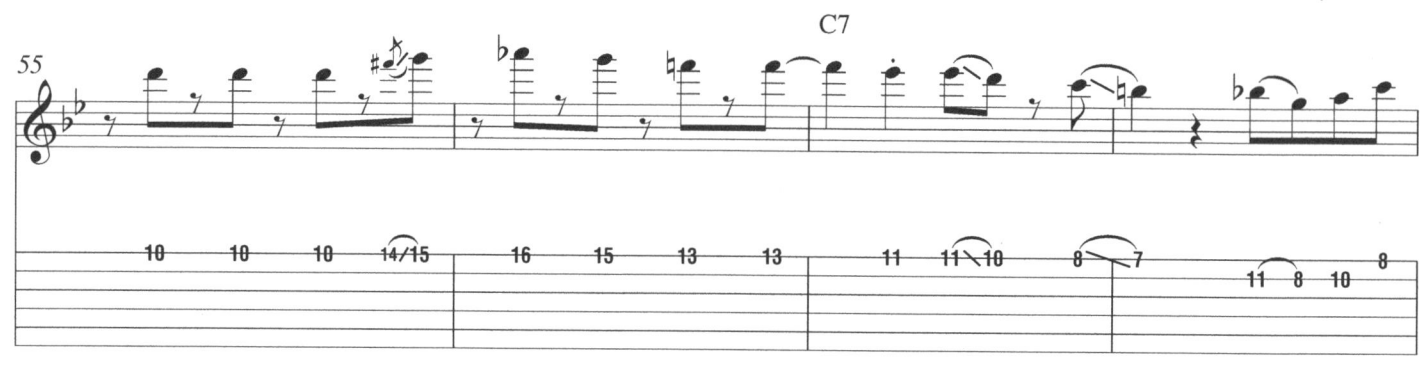
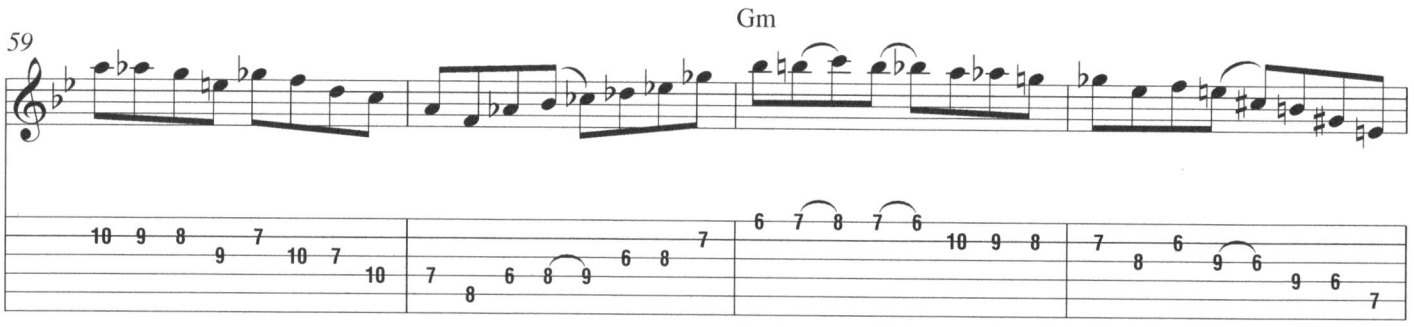

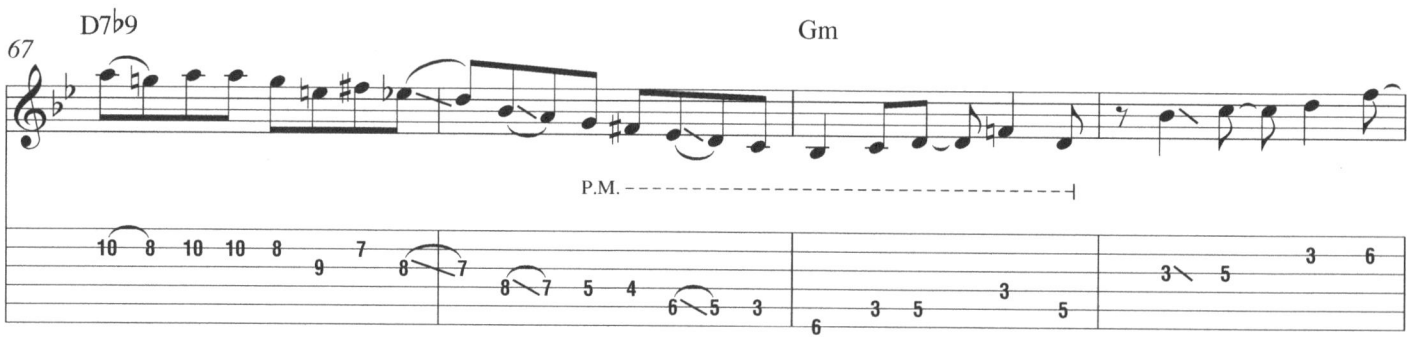
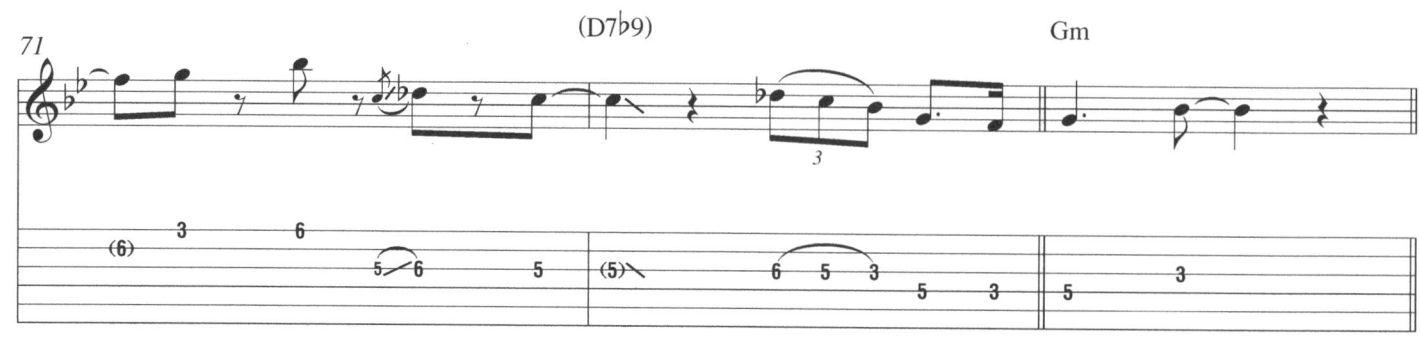

East to Wes 1988

Emily Remler

"You have to prove yourself every single time… you have to be twice as good as a man."
—Emily Remler

© Ray Avery CTSImages

One of the finest straight-ahead jazz guitarists to emerge in the 1980s was Emily Remler, born September 18, 1957 in New York City and raised in Englewood Cliffs, New Jersey. She began learning piano and guitar as a child, emulating early on the blues and rock stylings of Johnny Winter and Jimi Hendrix, on a Gibson ES-330 permanently borrowed from her older brother. While attending the Berklee College of Music in Boston from 1974 to 1976 (graduating at the precocious age of 18), she was captivated by the sounds of jazz and set in a new direction. A clear disciple of Wes Montgomery, she herself felt that she overly much bore the stamp of the giant from Indianapolis (as well as that of George Benson) well into her professional years. Still, her heroes and influences varied widely, from Ravi Shankar, Egberto Gismonti, and Leonard Bernstein to Paul Desmond, John Coltrane, and Pat Metheny, and in a career that lasted little more than a decade, she indeed found her own voice.

After Berklee, she relocated for a time to New Orleans, where she cut her teeth as a performer in a variety of genres, honed her skills through further study, and met jazz guitar legend Herb Ellis when he came through town. He became a mentor and key supporter, introducing her to the broader jazz world as a fill-in for Barney Kessel with the Great Guitars, and also as part of the Guitar Explosion at the 1978 Concord Jazz Festival (alongside such veteran masters as himself, Kessel, and Tal Farlow). She moved to New York in 1979 and began to work with the likes of jazz vocal star Nancy Wilson, famed bossa nova singer Astrud Gilberto, and bassists Eddie Gomez and John Clayton, making her recording debut on the Clayton Brothers' *It's All in the Family* (1980).

Remler soon had her own contract on the Concord Jazz label and in 1981 released her first album as a leader, *Firefly*, followed the next year by *Take Two*. These hard bop-oriented quartet sides featured a mix of her own music and compositions by jazz greats such as Montgomery, Duke Ellington, McCoy Tyner, Dexter Gordon, and Jamaican pianist Monty Alexander (her husband from 1981 to 1984). On *Transitions* (1983) and *Catwalk* (1984), she adopted a piano-less quartet format with trumpet in front, shifting towards original tunes and increasingly showing her modern jazz and Brazilian influences. *Together* (1985) was a tasty duo effort with notable fellow guitarist Larry Coryell. For 1988's *East to Wes*, she was joined by the world-class rhythm section of pianist Hank Jones, bassist Buster Williams,

East to Wes

and drummer Marvin "Smitty" Smith and sailed masterfully through originals, classic bop repertoire, and her own innovative arrangements of the standards "Snowfall" and "Softly, as in a Morning Sunrise."

She also played the Los Angeles production of *Sophisticated Ladies* (an Ellington revue) in 1982 and appeared through the mid and late 1980s on recordings by bassist Ray Brown, saxophonist Hank Crawford, fusion keyboardist David Benoit, and vocalists Rosemary Clooney and Susannah McCorkle. She shared her musical insights on two instructional videos made in 1986 (*Bebop and Swing Guitar* and *Latin and Jazz Improvisation*), offering a combination of encouragement and no-nonsense technical advice, and served in 1988 as Artist in Residence at Duquesne University in Pittsburgh. Around this time, even at the height of busy-ness as an avid teacher and globally touring performer, she strove to expand her knowledge, studying composition with the great Bob Brookmeyer and others. Honors bestowed upon her have included critic Leonard Feather's Golden Feather Award in 1981, Guitarist of the Year in the 1985 *DownBeat* Critics Poll, and Berklee's Distinguished Alumni Award in 1989.

In the male-dominated field of instrumental jazz, she is one of few female guitarists to achieve such stature (Mary Osborne, of the late swing era and beyond, and current players Leni Stern, Sheryl Bailey, and Mimi Fox are among other well-known jazzwomen on the axe). She preferred not to make a big issue of her gender, or of any sexism she encountered in the music business, but rather just to work towards excellence and gain recognition for her musical merits like anyone else.

With her final album, *This Is Me* (1990), she further stretched her musical boundaries, bringing guitar synth, electronic keyboards, auxiliary percussion, and wordless vocals into the picture, as well as more abundant Brazilian and contemporary rhythms. Sidemen like Benoit, Brazilian guitarist Romero Lubambo, and rock drummer Jeff Porcaro contributed to the change of flavor, and tracks such as "Carenia" and "Simplicidaje" display a newfound inspiration in her writing and playing. Tragically, this title was released only after her untimely passing—she died of a heart attack on May 3, 1990, while on tour in Sydney, Australia, certainly related to the drug problems from which she had suffered. That year, a large contingent of her comrades, among them Herb Ellis, David Benoit, and Leni Stern, recorded two volumes of a farewell tribute, *Just Friends*. At less than 33 years of age, her life and brilliant career were cut short, but she had helped to bring swingin' jazz guitar into the modern era, blazed a trail for women in the field, and left us with some good words about the art.

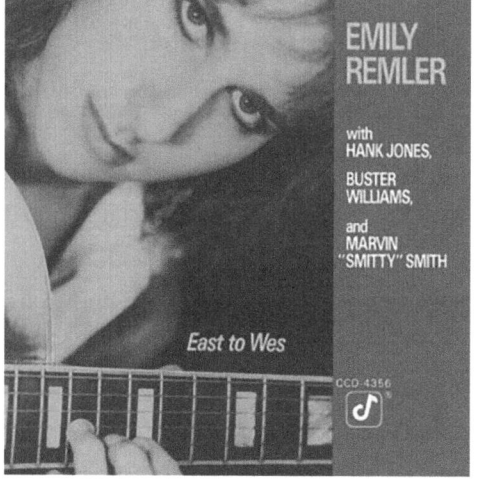

With a title track written in honor of all-time hero Wes Montgomery, Remler's last album for Concord also included her swingin' "Blues for Herb," dedicated to Ellis.

How to Play It

Remler's lovely tribute to her longtime hero is in the form of a medium-tempo Latin jazz tune, reminiscent in its even-eighths groove of Montgomery's later work. Upon entering her solo, she captures right off the bat the romance of a minor bossa with simple, lyrical phrases that embrace the G minor sound, gracefully embellished with subtle slides and quick hammer-ons/pull-offs. She brings a blues element to the table as well, as we hear in the phrase of measure 11 (which particularly invokes Wes's "Road Song"), the double-stop slide-ins of measure 12, or the blues scale-related figure in measure 15. Her timing is extra-expressive in both measures 21 and 22, as she holds back just slightly before sounding the note on beat 3 in either case (the high points in the melodic line).

"East to Wes" has a 40-bar AAB structure, with each chorus consisting of two 12-bar A-sections that center around Gm (with a visit to the relative major key of B♭), plus a 16-bar B-section which mainly vamps between E♭maj7 and an Am7/D7 pair. Remler takes two choruses total for her solo. Her first B-section begins at measure 25, and in the very next measure we hear the striking note choice of B♮ and E♮ (on beats 1 and 3 respectively)—a contrast to what our ears expect in the key of G minor. She makes it clear that she is treating these Am7/D7's mostly as *natural* ii–V pairs rather than altered. In other words, where the ii–V chords for this minor key would usually be Am7♭5–D7♭9 (or perhaps D7♯5)—which are indeed found throughout the A-sections—we get more of an Am9–D9 (or D13) effect here, the tone material of these measures lying within D Mixolydian (or A Dorian—modally related to G major in either case). An exception in this first B-section is measure 38, which features half-step movement down into each Am7 chord tone. To execute this lick, allow the index finger to *roll* through strings 1, 2, and 3 (rather than barring or hopping) while the middle finger performs its pull-offs.

At three distinct points within the solo, she ups the energy and the momentum with several measures of a dense, constant rhythmic pattern. This is in each case a *hemiola* in which a repeating figure creates a cross-rhythm against the 4/4 meter. The first of these begins in earnest with the last two notes of measure 34 and runs through the first half of measure 37, involving units of three 16th notes (three-quarters of a beat) in length, each made up of a pull-off on string 1 plus a single note on string 2. A similar device is employed at measure 52, this time feeling more syncopated yet with units of five 16th notes and using two pull-offs on string 1 for each repetition (the highest note alternates between the "blue"-sounding D♭ on fret 9 and the natural 5th of the key, D, on fret 10). In either of these cases, maintain a regular picking plan—such as all upstrokes on string 1 and downstrokes on string 2—and use the middle finger to fret the G on string 2 (this will help especially in exiting the second figure, in the middle of measure 54). Practice these slowly at first, especially to get in the groove with the asymmetrical picking rhythm.

After her second chorus begins at measure 41, Remler shifts into higher gear, skewing the texture towards well-articulated scalar and chromatic 16th-note runs and bringing to mind another big influence, Pat Martino (see "Days of Wine and Roses"). These fast segments call for alternate picking, and most of them can be fingered in or near a single position on the fretboard. The line from measure 44 to the beginning of measure 47, for example, is nearly all at the third position—but use the middle finger for the first two notes, use the index for the remaining slide-slur in that measure, let the pinky move up and back to cover both frets 6 and 7, and reach with the index for the A on string 3, fret 2 without taking the hand out of place. Pay attention in measure 58, though—here we jump quickly to the fifth position on beat 1, shifting up one more fret yet for beats 2 and 3. In measure 59, the pull-off on string 2 initiates a Metheny-esque chromatic descending figure on strings 2 and 3 fretted by index and middle fingers (the index will quickly hop from string 2 to string 3 at the beginning of beat 3).

Most of these note-packed phrases fit the corresponding chords in a quite logical scalar fashion, with some chromatic connecting tones in between. We largely hear altered dominant material for the 7♭9 chords (as in measures 42 and 44), as well as through most of measure 46 (implying F7♭9 or F7♯9 on the way to B♭maj7), C Dorian tones for Cm7 as in measure 45, and tones of B♭ major (modally related to C Dorian, or G natural minor) for the B♭maj7 and E♭maj7 chords in measures 47–48 and elsewhere.

Right at the beginning of her second B-section in measure 65, Remler launches into one more grand hemiola figure. The main theme to the tune's written melody, heard earlier in the original recording, was rendered partly in Wes-style octaves, and here she performs a special, fractured take on this texture. In a Benson-like pattern, each 16th note on an upper string is echoed by another one an octave lower, which then slides up or down to yet another 16th that presages the next note above. She uses hybrid picking to smooth out the tone of the whole passage, sounding strings 1 and 2 with the right-hand middle finger and strings 3 and 4 with the pick (going back to normal picking by the end of measure 70). She plays it a bit loosely, as regards movement of the lower note, and there are seemingly some stopping points along the way, but the essential rhythm remains intact throughout. She follows this with some climactic bends and vibratos, a briefly repeating bluesy figure in measures 72–73, a further barrage of 16ths, and then a very songful slow-down, culminating in the pretty double stops and rootless chord voicings of her conclusion.

Vital Stats

Guitarist: Emily Remler

Song: "East to Wes"

Album: *East to Wes*, 1988

Age at Time of Recording: 30

Guitar: Borys B120 HollowBody Electric

Amp: Polytone (or possibly Roland Jazz Chorus or Fender Twin Reverb)

East to Wes

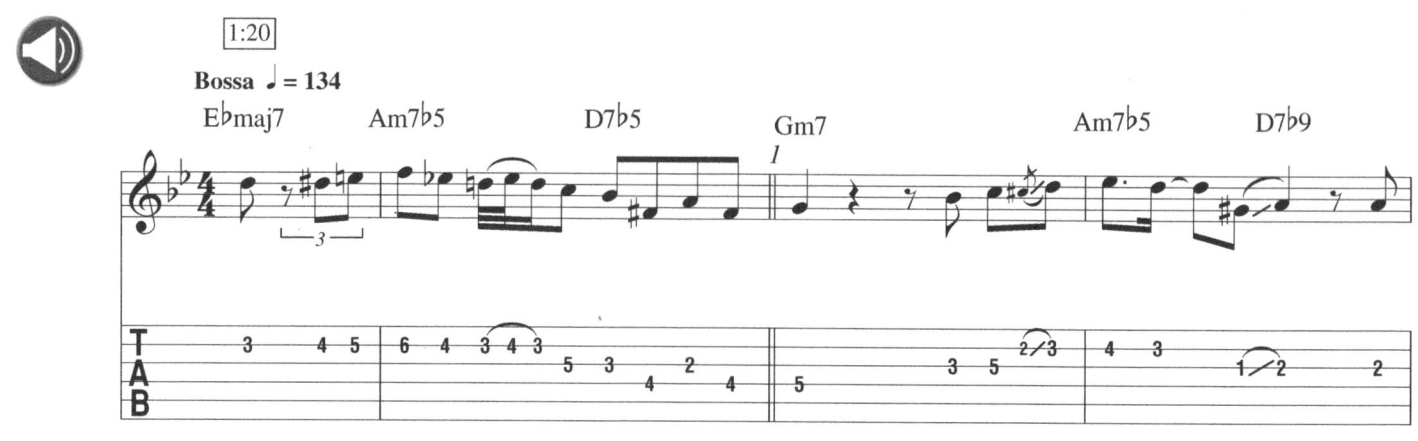
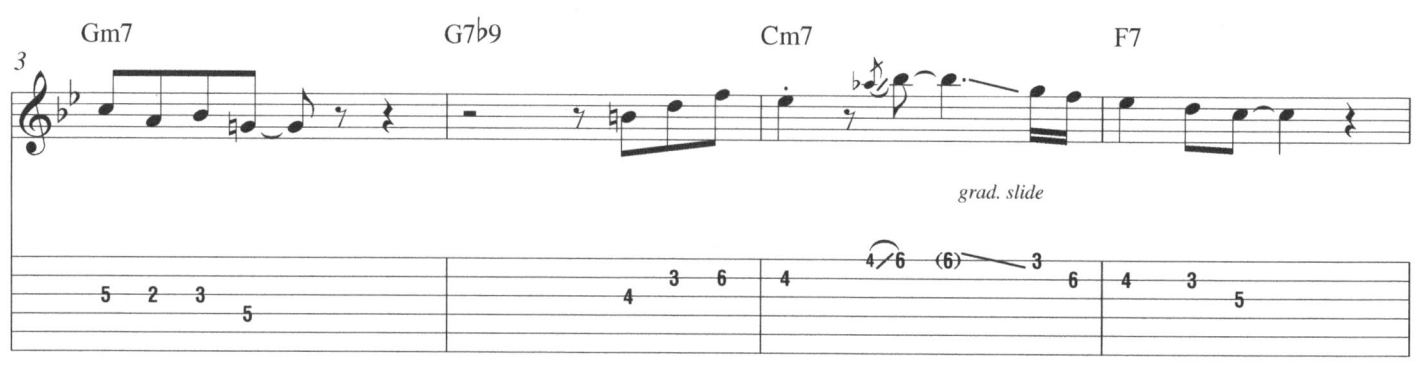

By Emily Remler
Copyright © 1989 Edson Publishing
International Copyright Secured   All Rights Reserved

East to Wes

*Played behind the beat.

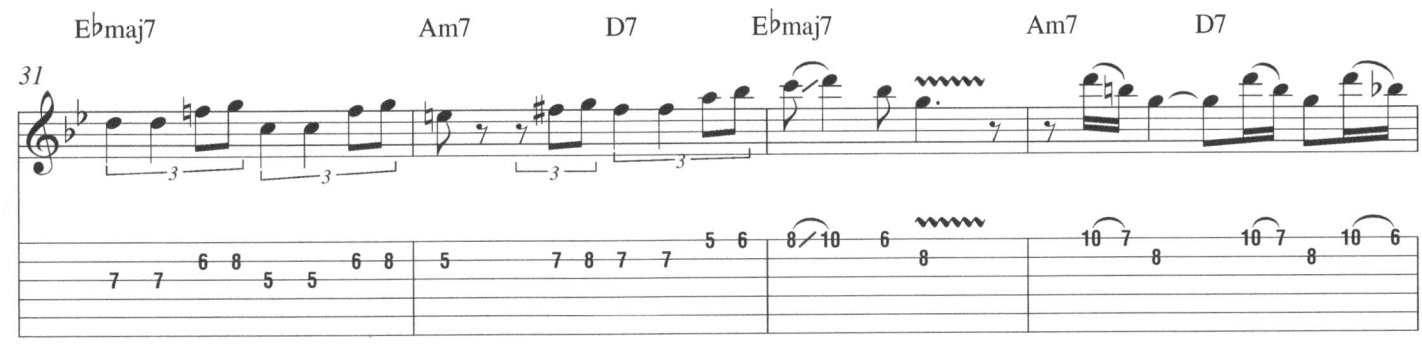

East to Wes

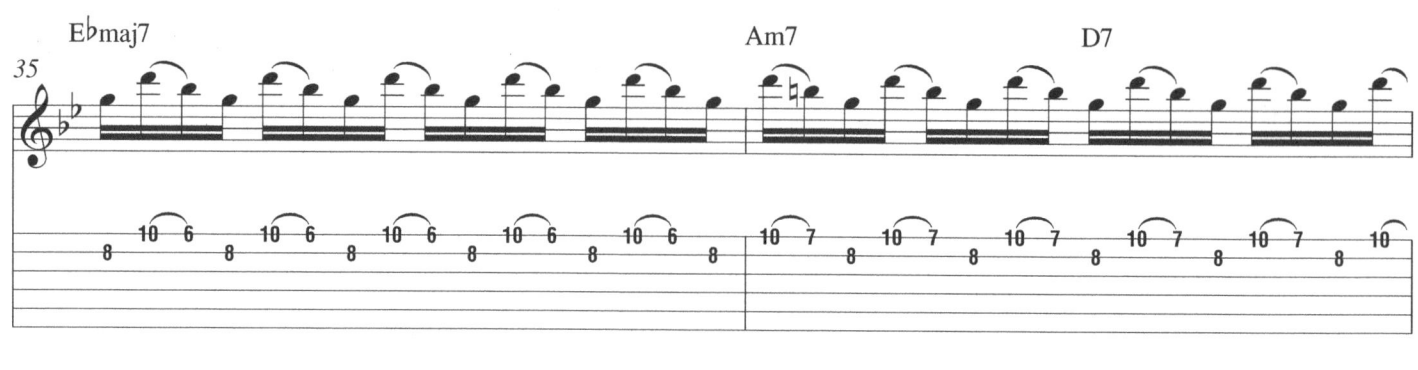
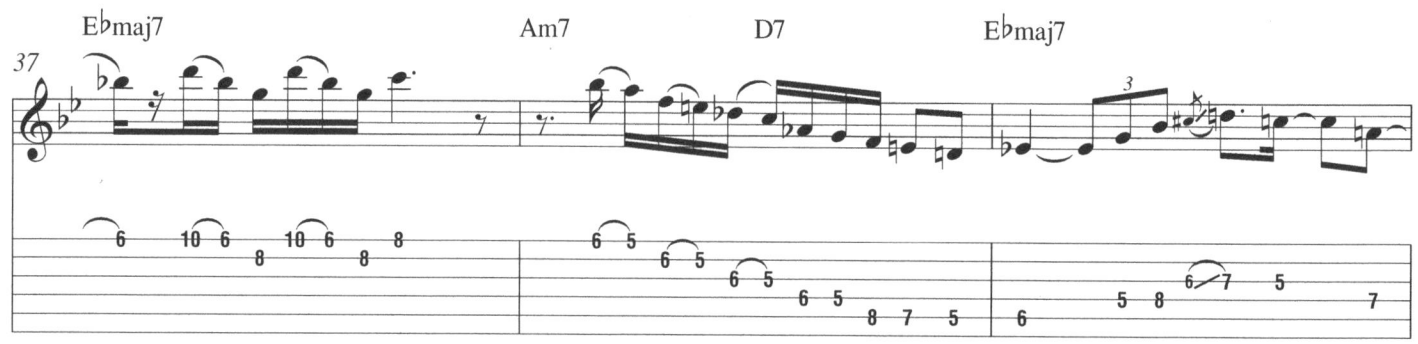
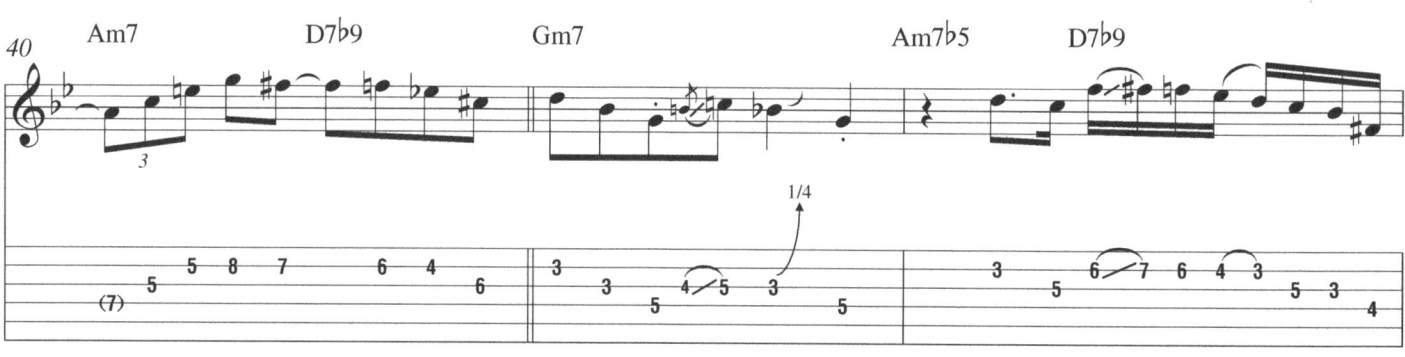

East to Wes

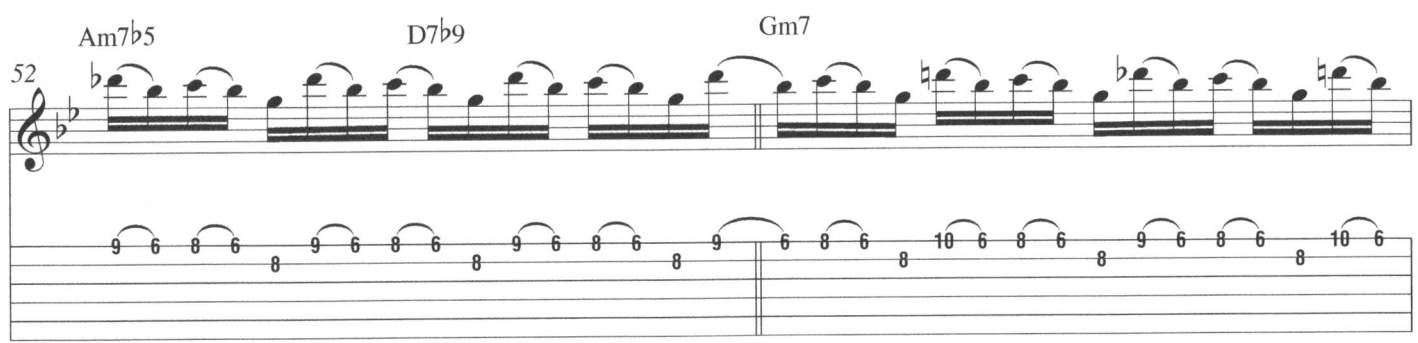
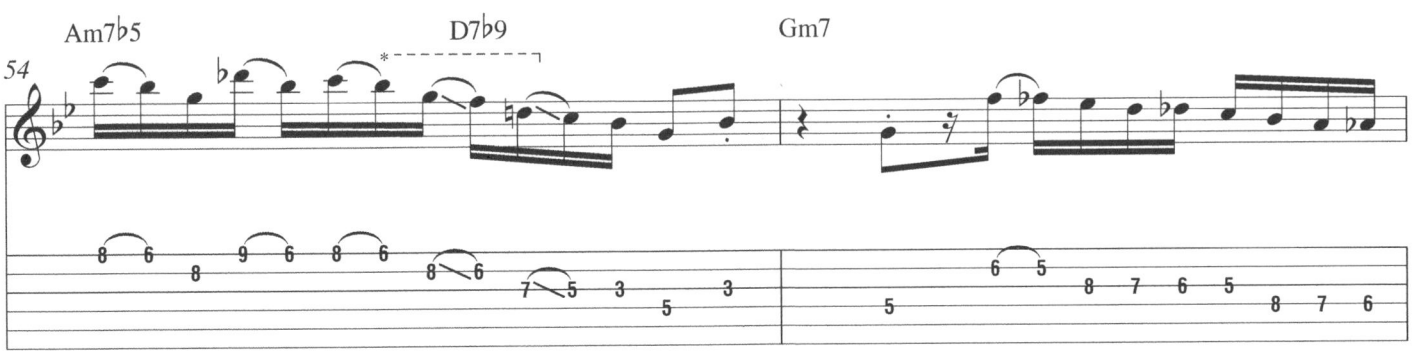

*Played as swung 16th notes.

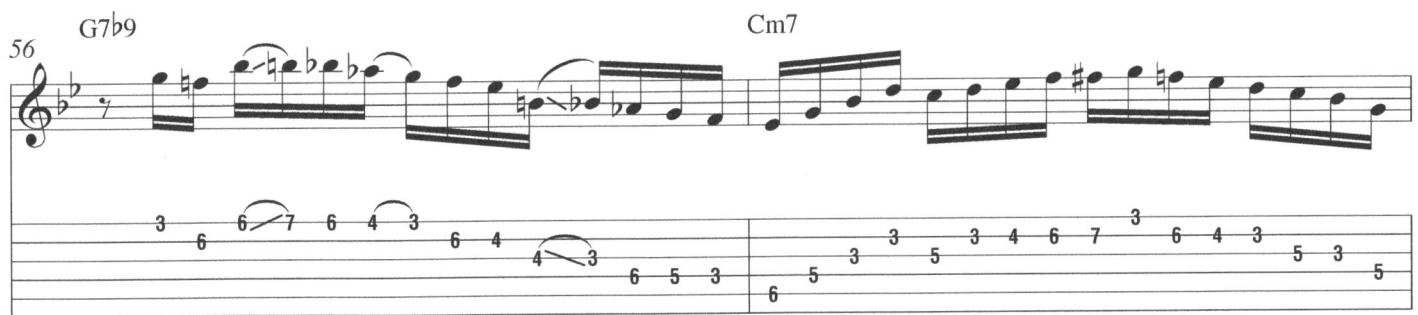

East to Wes

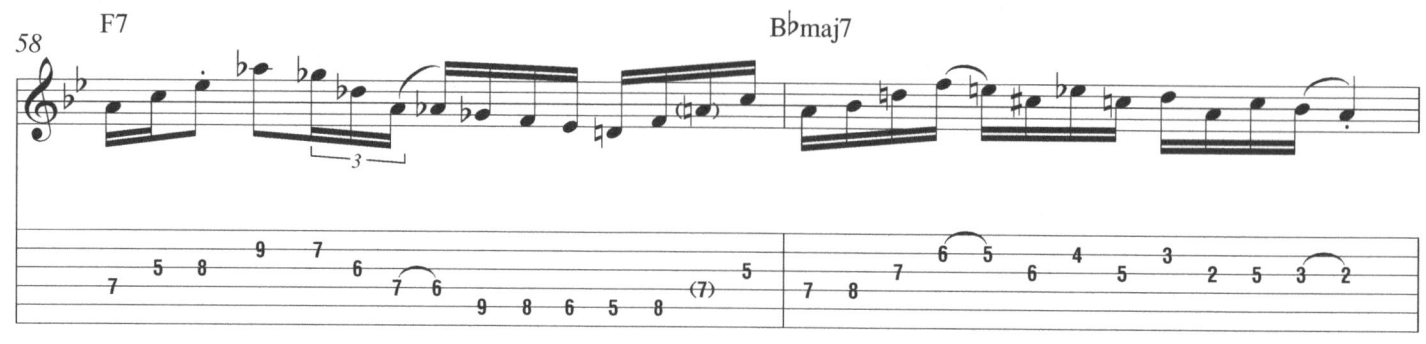
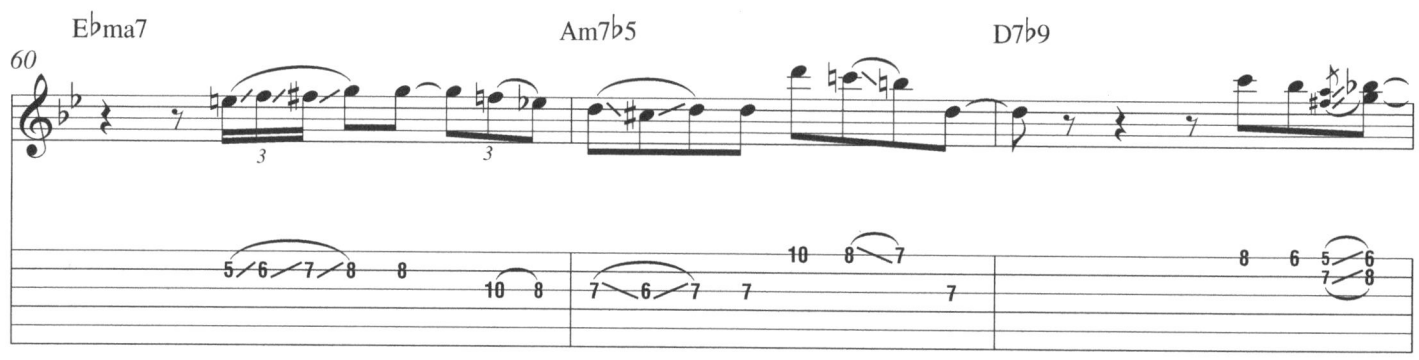
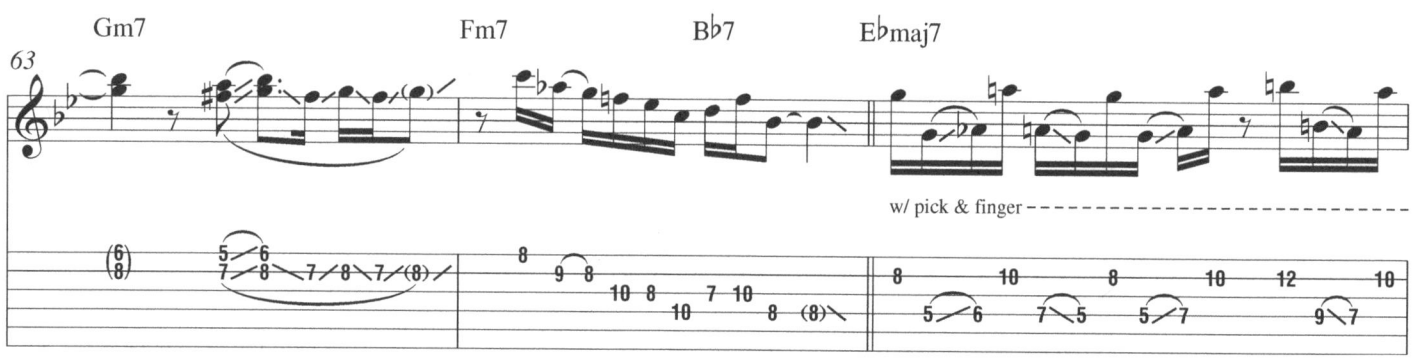

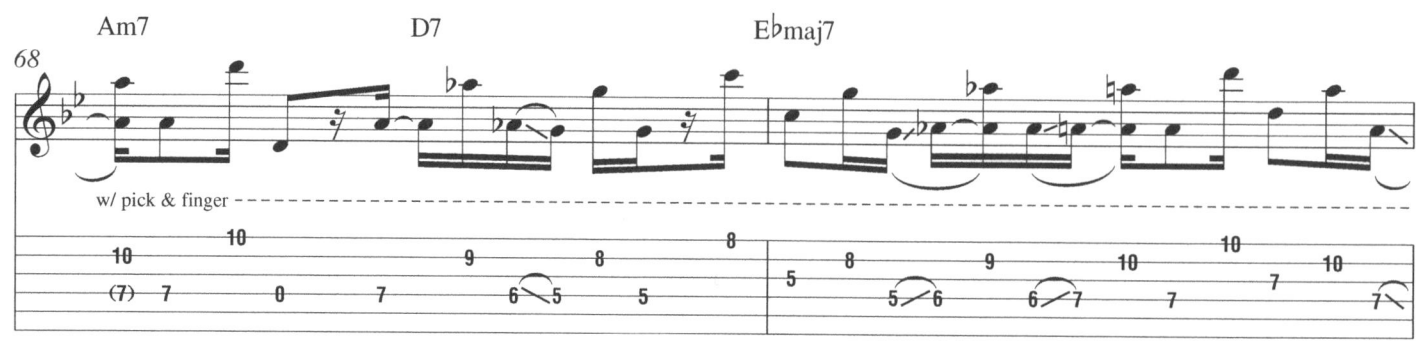

East to Wes

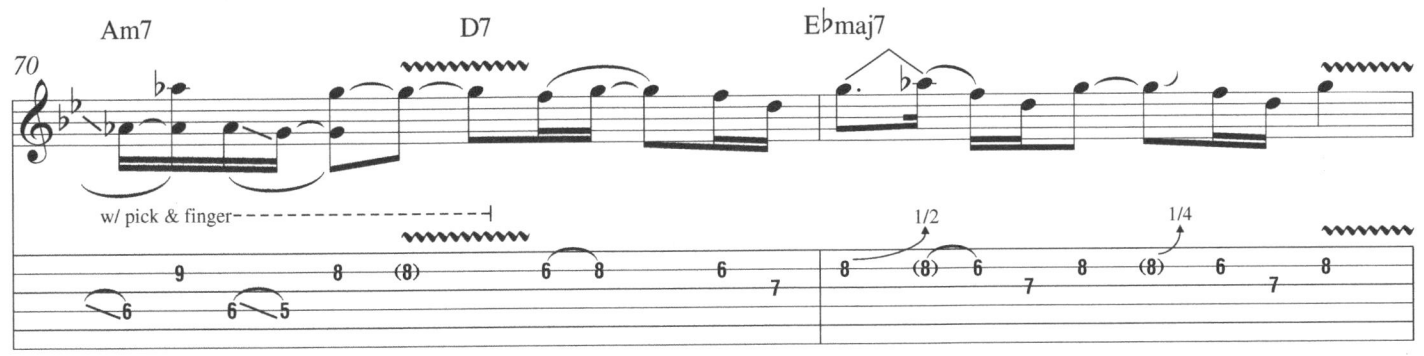
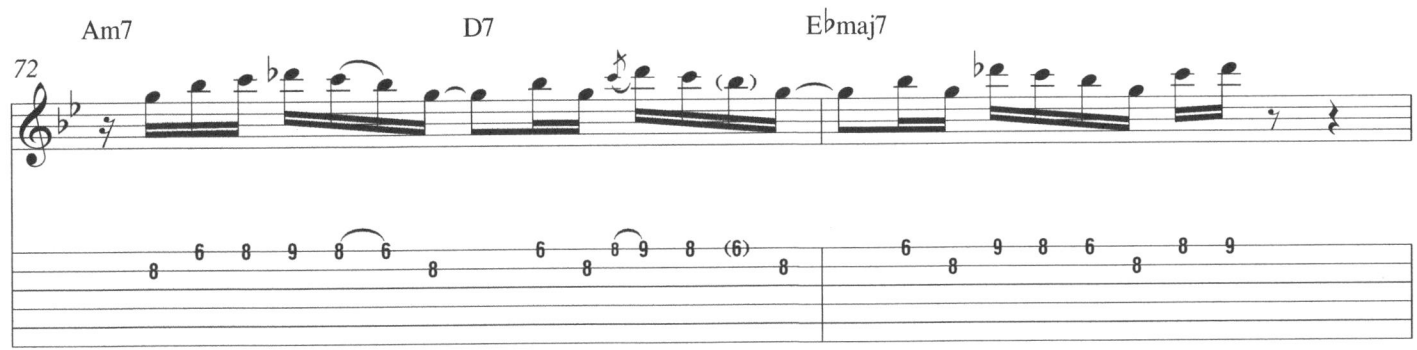
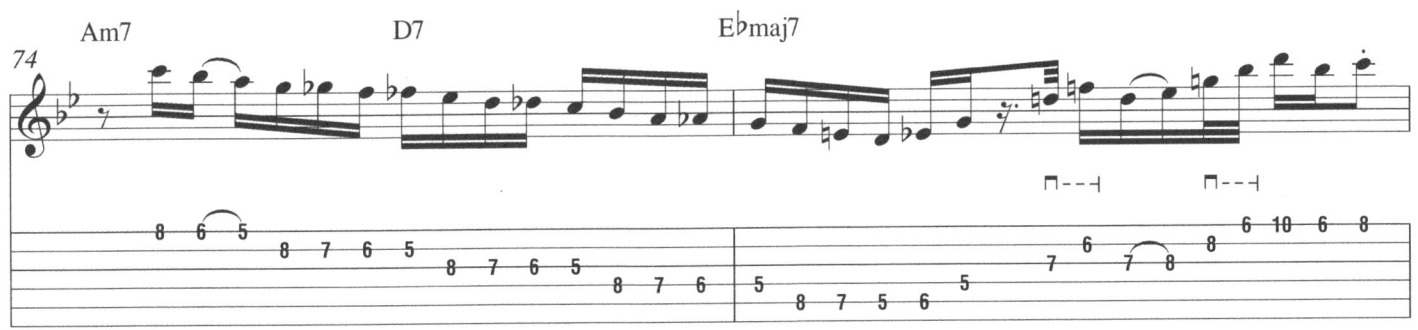
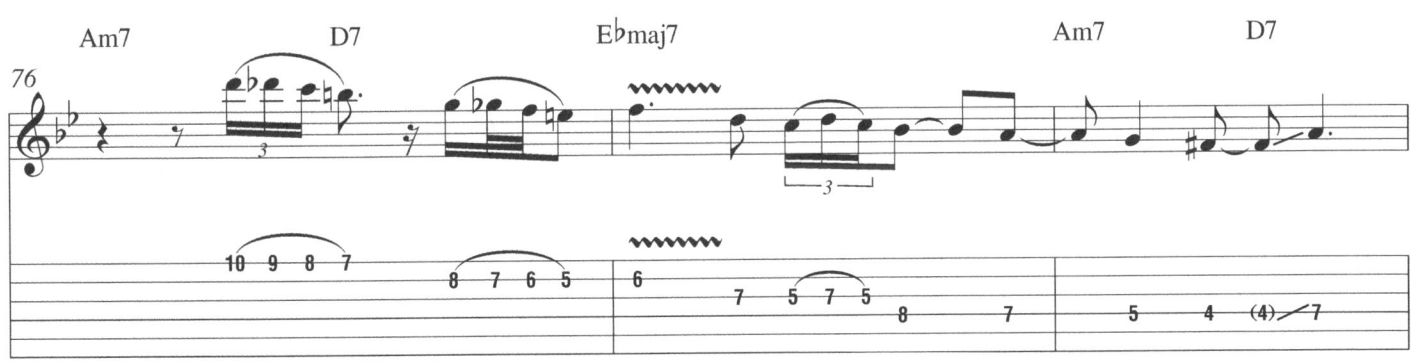
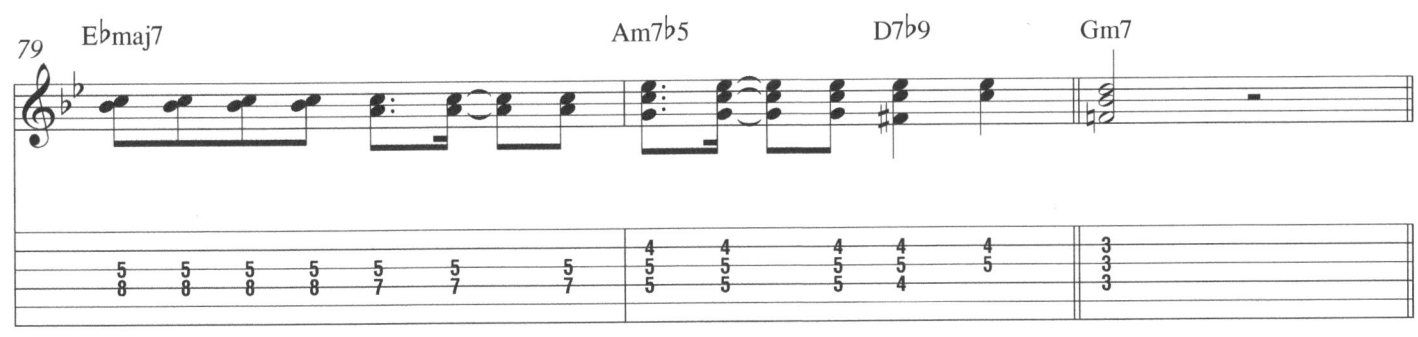

Nardis 1992

Mike Stern

Fittingly for a guy who has named his cats Wes and Jimi, Mike Stern is a guitarist who indeed bridges the gap between jazz and rock. Largely associated with the fusion genre, he plays with a strong sense of bebop language and swung feel while also delving into contemporary rhythms and the screamin' aspects of the instrument. He rose to prominence with legendary trumpeter Miles Davis's comeback band of the early 1980s and has been helping to establish a place for the modernized electric guitar in jazz ever since.

Born Michael Sedgwick on January 10, 1953, in Boston, Massachusetts, he grew up in Washington, D.C., took up the guitar at age 12, and in the early 1970s returned to Boston to attend the Berklee College of Music, studying there with guitar guru Mick Goodrick and a very youthful Pat Metheny. In 1975, Metheny encouraged him to pursue the gig with jazzy popular group Blood, Sweat & Tears, which he landed and stuck with for two years, becoming close friends with electric bass virtuoso Jaco Pastorius during that time. He moved further into the fusion realm with the band of high-octane drummer (and Miles alum) Billy Cobham from 1979 to 1981.

Miles, meanwhile, was preparing to return to the scene after a long hiatus (and dark period of seclusion and addiction) that followed his revolutionary jazz-rock experiments of the late 1960s and early 1970s. Stern was recruited for one tune on *The Man with the Horn* (1981), Davis's first album of new material in six years. The track was entitled "Fat Time," after the iconic bandleader's nickname

> *"All these musicians have one thing that's very important to me... the groove and the heart of the music is the first thing that you feel."*
>
> —Mike Stern (on Miles Davis and other greats playing complex music)

for the hard-grooving (and then over-weight) young guitarist, who garnered attention with his chorus-laden chords and counter-lines, as well as a famously blistering solo. Staying on with Miles' new lineup, which included saxophonist Bill Evans (not to be confused with the pianist of the same name), bassist Marcus Miller, drummer Al Foster, and percussionist Mino Cinelu, he appeared on the celebrated *We Want Miles* (recorded live in 1981), as well as on the intricate *Star People* (1983). This unit had a rather open texture that prominently featured his guitar work, but by 1983 his friend and fellow cutting-edge jazz-rocker John Scofield had been taken on as a second guitarist, presumably to safeguard against Stern's decreasing reliability (due to increasing substance abuse problems).

Parting ways with Miles in 1983, he joined Pastorius's Word of Mouth orchestra and soon made his recording debut as a leader with *Neesh* on the small Japan-based Trio label. The energetic album featured alto sax great David Sanborn and was produced by good friend Hiram Bullock, another ace of the electrified jazz guitar. Finally managing to clean up from the drinking and drugging in which he had engaged since his teens, he reenlisted with Miles for close to a year upon Scofield's departure from the band in 1985. He released *Upside Downside*, his major label debut (on Atlantic), in 1986, surrounded by a who's-who cast of prominent fusion players like Pastorius, Sanborn, tenor saxophonist Bob Berg, and drummer Dave Weckl. That same year, he began working with acoustic and electronic sax man Michael Brecker, both within and apart from the influential Steps Ahead group, and toured with Sanborn. He co-led a quartet with Berg from 1989 to 1992 and then played for two years with a reunited Brecker Brothers Band (including Michael and brother Randy on trumpet).

Continuing as a leader, Stern has had the company of many of the same bandmates recurrently over the decades, such as the Breckers, saxophonist Bob Malach, keyboardist Jim Beard, bassist Lincoln Goines, and drummers Weckl and Dennis Chambers. His albums are replete with his own compositions—from the hard-hitting fusion anthem "Chromazone" to the poignantly pretty "Bird Blue"—though he makes a nod to classic straight-ahead jazz repertoire on 1993's *Standards (and Other Songs)*

Stern's acclaimed 1993 release finds him swingin' and burnin' on an assortment of standard tunes, originals, and jazz compositions.

and 1997's *Give and Take*. He brought in fellow guitar luminaries Scofield and Bill Frisell for *Play* (1999). As of *Voices* (2001), he has used wordless vocals in much of his music, often to a rather Metheny-esque effect (covering voice himself as needed in live performance). Within his palette of sound and rhythm, he has also shown some world music influence and frequently thrown in a nylon-string guitar ballad as well.

More recent releases have reflected a growing fondness for wide-ranging collaborative projects. Through *These Times* (2004), *Who Let the Cats Out* (2006), *Big Neighborhood* (2009), and *All Over the Place* (2012)—all aptly titled—he has teamed up with a tremendous array of musical personalities, among them banjoist Béla Fleck, bassists Will Lee and Victor Wooten, bassist/vocalists Richard Bona and Esperanza Spalding, saxophonist Kenny Garrett, trumpeter Roy Hargrove, and guitarists Eric Johnson and Steve Vai. Stern and Johnson also joined efforts for 2014's *Eclectic*, which finds both Hendrix devotees singing on one cut. His later sideman appearances include the 2004 venture *Four Generations of Miles* (with fellow esteemed Davis alums) and *Lifecycle* (2008) with the fusion-oriented Yellowjackets.

A joyous performer with a sunny demeanor, Stern still maintains a busy touring schedule. He lives in New York with his wife, Leni, a noted guitarist in her own right, to whom he was introduced by Frisell in the late 1970s. While in town, he enjoys gigging at the intimate 55 Bar, where he has held forth for the last three decades (he had a similar home base in the early 1980s at the similarly-named 55 Grand Street). Voted Best Jazz Guitarist of 1993 in *Guitar Player* magazine, he was thusly honored also at the 1997 Orville H. Gibson Awards. He has a Pacifica signature guitar model from Yamaha, based in its design on his long-favored custom Telecaster copy.

How to Play It

In this epic journey through his old boss's mysterious tune, Stern both swings like Wes and rocks like Hendrix (with a touch of Jim Hall subtlety), starting out with quiet, well-spaced lines and building into lush chordal passages and high-pitched wailing. He makes the effected electric sound of his Tele-style axe fit beautifully into a modern jazz environment, wherein his rhythm section—Gil Goldstein on electric piano, Larry Grenadier on bass, and Ben Perowski on drums—loosely breaks up the groove atop a constant underpinning of swung rhythm.

"Nardis" has a 32-bar AABA structure like so many jazz standards but makes distinctive use of an ambiguous tonic chord. In what sounds mainly like an E minor setting, the E-rooted chord is often treated more like a major-with-♭9th sonority, especially during the melody at the end of the A-sections (or whenever this phrase is referenced in improvisation). The original tune makes use here of the fifth mode of harmonic minor—a.k.a. Phyrgian dominant or Freygish scale—built on E, including both F♮ and G♯ (the ♭9th and major 3rd of an E chord, respectively). As Stern concludes the melody on the way into his solo, he gives

Nardis

it a slight variation in tones, equally exotic-sounding, with the minor 3rd G♮ between F and G♯. And even though he improvises on the tonic chord with a straightforward Em approach most of the time, he invokes this spooky melodic paraphrase in places like measure 31 or at the very end of his solo. Elsewhere, tones suggesting an altered B7 may be temporarily imposed on these Em areas, as in measure 15 (really just accentuating the eventual resolution to Em).

His flowing, logical, largely scalar lines have an almost Bach-like quality to them, as he weaves through the changes with gracefully rolling shapes, like those in measures 2–9, or with a melodic-leap motif as found in measures 17–19 (where his first bridge begins) and echoed in measures 25–27 (the start of the next A-section). Occasionally laying back on the beat in spots like measure 9, beat 1 or measures 85–86, he maintains a relaxed feel for much of the way, especially towards the beginning (and even sometimes when the atmosphere heats up). Still, his blazing chops and energetic intensity are always just around the corner—his sheer speed and accuracy are foreshadowed in the triplets of measure 10 and fully brought to bear in the virtuosic ascent and rapid downwards arpeggios of measures 39–41, before he sings out passionately way up high on string 1 for the first time in this outing. Practice these speedy segments slowly with alternate picking and a light enough touch such that you can navigate even while moving quickly across strings (it may help here to arrange your picking so that measure 41 begins with an upstroke).

While some of his improvised material can be found in or near one position on the neck (especially during the faster parts), Stern motivates way up and down the fretboard for many of his linear ideas. Right off the bat, he exits the solo break in the second pickup measure with a slidey/stretchy move from fifth to second position. In measures 18–19, the fretting hand slides and jumps up to let the pinky grab fret 12, then 15, and then 17 in an ascent along string 1. In measures 44–46, the remarkable descent on string 3 involves efficiently shifting to allow the index finger to reach fret 10 (just before a slide down to fret 9 for the next note) and then fret 7 at the start of measure 46. A quick slide down from there to fret 4, followed by an immediate hammer-on at fret 5, results in a brief smear of pitch that sounds as if it were a bend (due in part to a bit of lateral tug created on the unwound third string).

He plays substantially with the elements of texture and density through these four choruses, as does his band. Through the bridge of his second chorus in measures 49–56, he gives us a layered figure of simple, sustained tones on string 1 plus chordal accents on the three strings below (reminiscent of a favorite Jim Hall device—see "Whisper Not"). The pinky frets all the single notes, aside from the initial grace note in the pickup; the chords are all on upbeats and initially clipped short in their delivery. The combined tones yield a colorful set of variations on the basic changes, as he uses Am9 for Am7, F6/9 for Fmaj7, Dm9 for Dm7, G13♯9 for G7, C6 for Cmaj7, and Bmaj♭9 for B7.

His third chorus begins and ends with blistering triplet runs in measures 65–67 and 89–90, respectively, culminating in a sonic blur of 16th notes in measures 91–92, before he proceeds to just plain rock out with bluesy bends and vibrato at the top of the fourth chorus (measure 97). From measure 113 on, he spends nearly the entire last half-chorus in chordal territory, this time with a thicker sound altogether, more rhythmic punch through part of the bridge, and more sustain and arpeggiation by the final section. Special voicings used here include forms of Am11, F6/9 (with a brief half-step-up departure in measure 116), Dm11, G13♭9, C6/9, B13♯9, and Em11 (grandly imposed on Cmaj7 in measure 124). Stern then tastefully winds down his solo in the last four measures with peaceful reference to the melody.

Vital Stats

Guitarist: Mike Stern

Song: "Nardis"

Album: *Standards (and Other Songs)*, 1993 (recorded 1992)

Age at Time of Recording: 39

Guitar: Michael Aronson custom Telecaster style w/ 1950s Broadcaster neck

Amp: Fender '65 Twin Reverb (or Yamaha G100-2x12)

Effects: Yahama SPX90 processor (for chorus), digital delay

Nardis

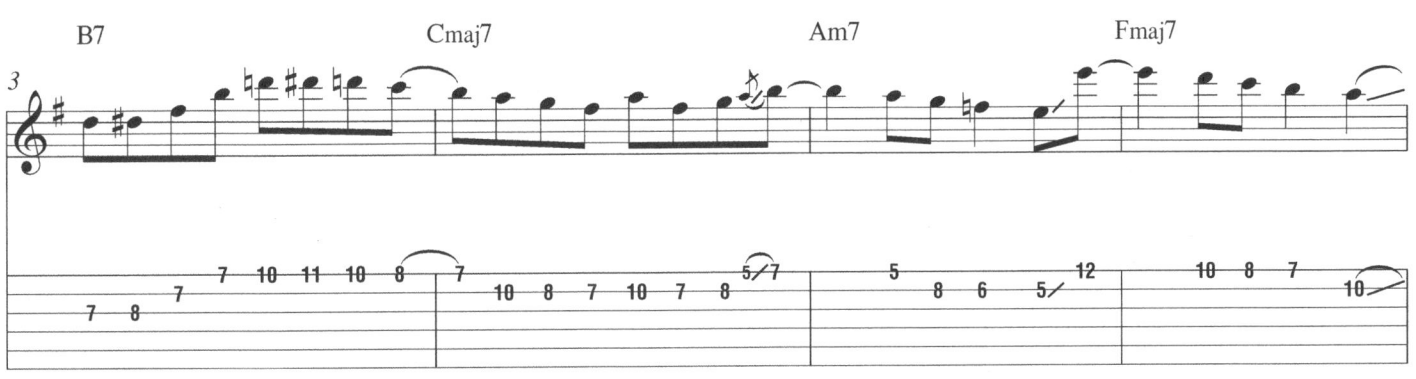

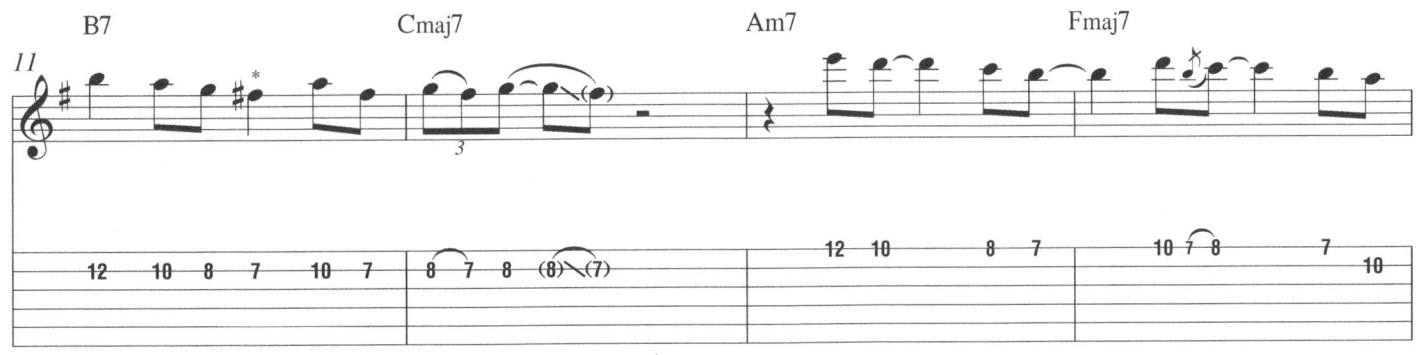

*Played behind the beat.

By Miles Davis
Copyright © 1959 Jazz Horn Music Corporation
Copyright Renewed
All Rights Administered by Songs Of Kobalt Music Publishing
All Rights Reserved Used by Permission

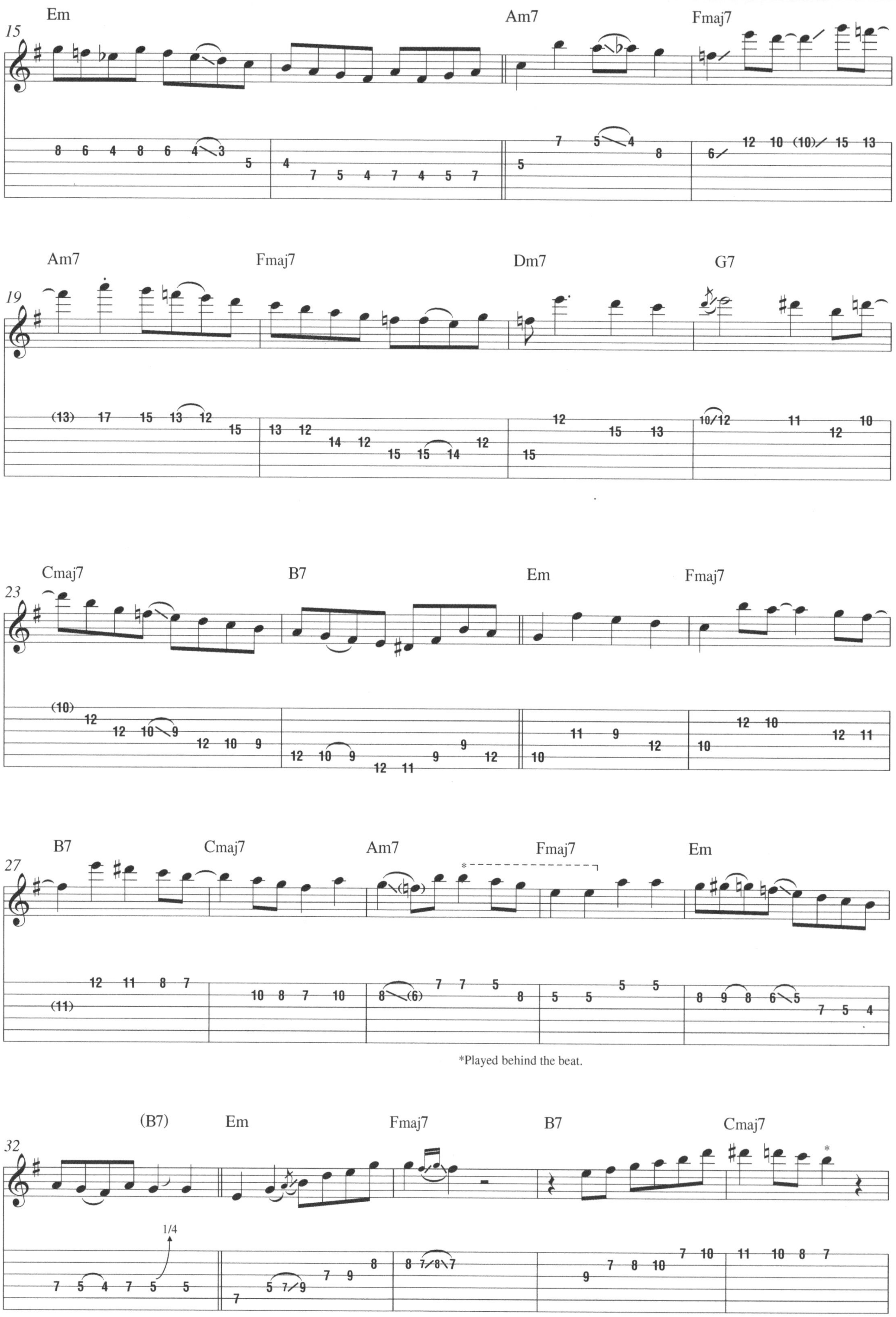

Nardis

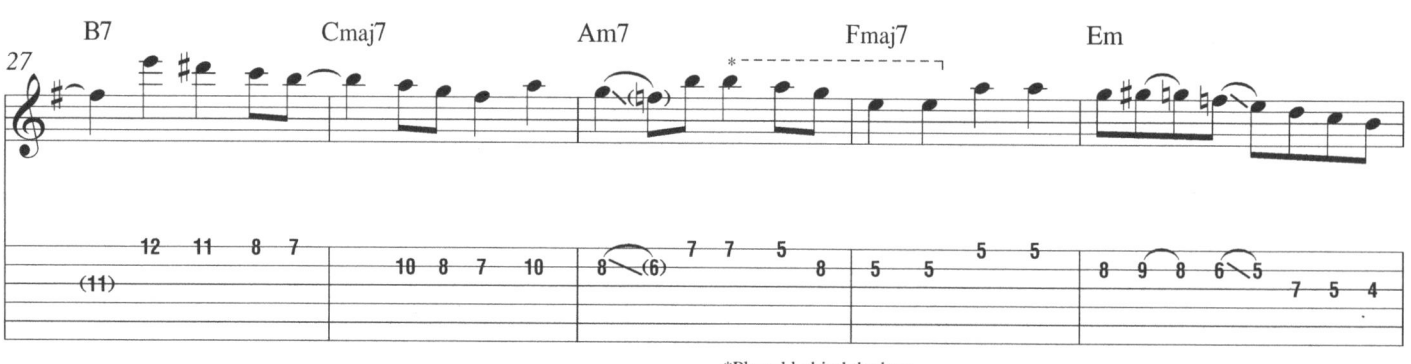

*Played behind the beat.

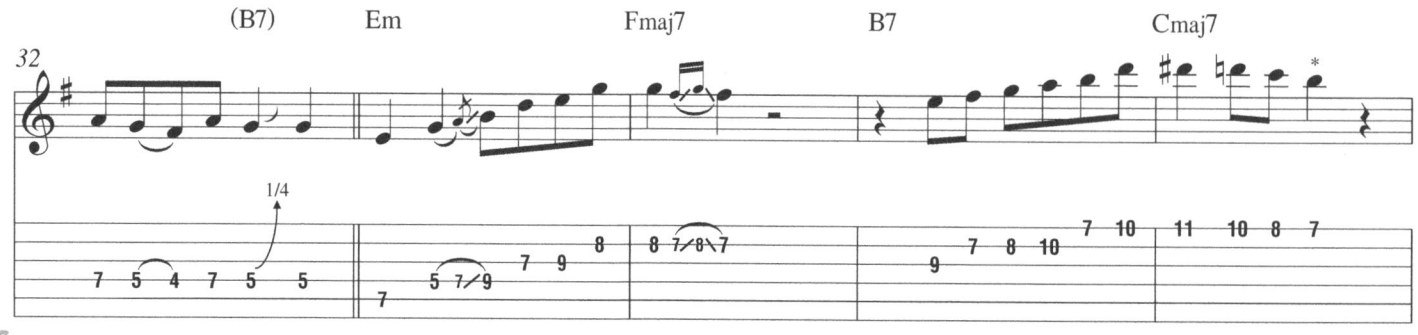

Nardis

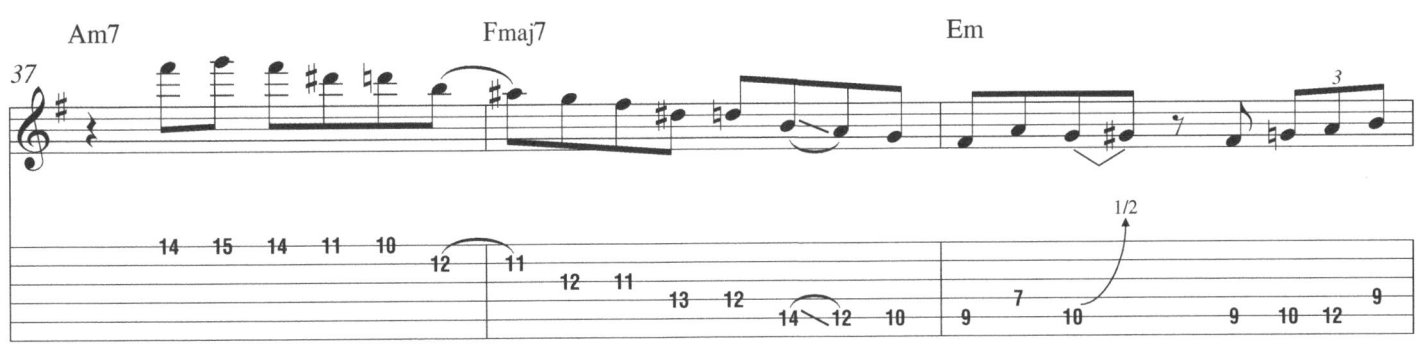
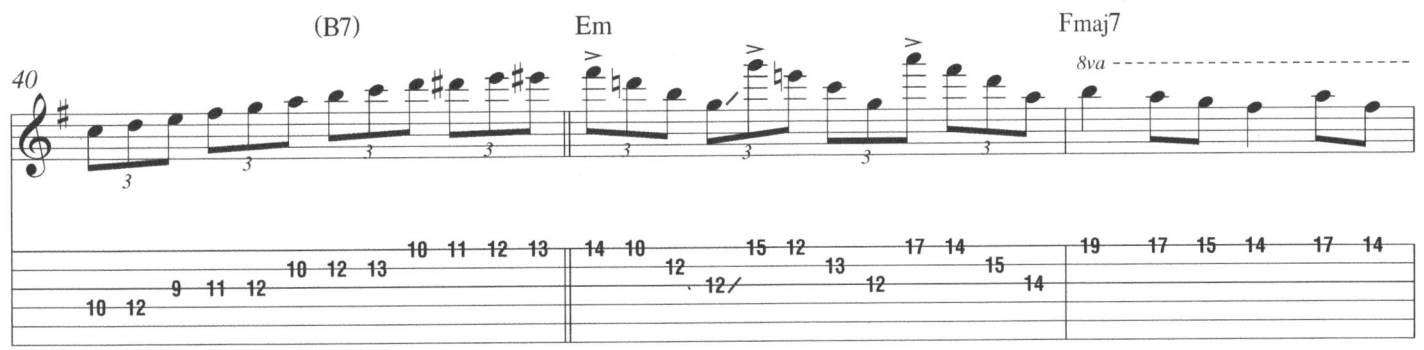

*Played as even eighth notes.

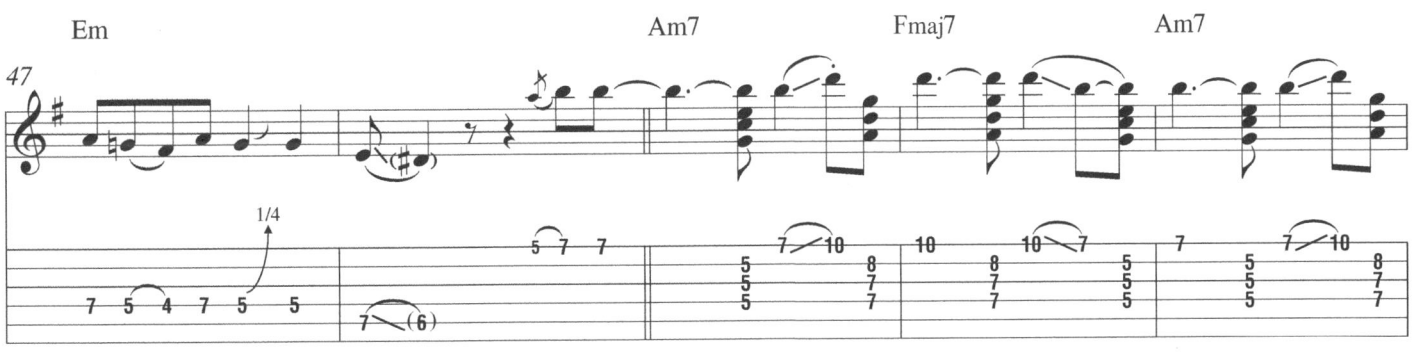

Nardis

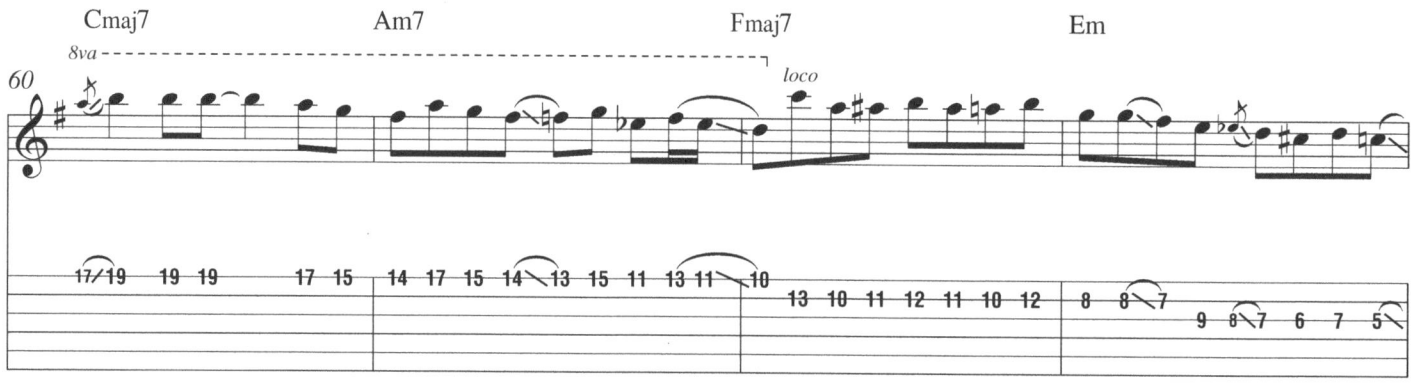
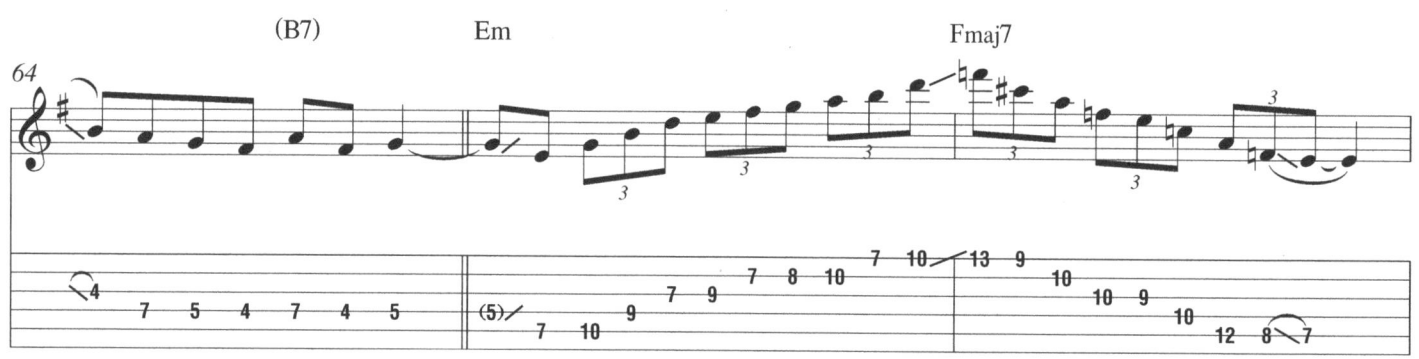

*Played behind the beat.

Nardis

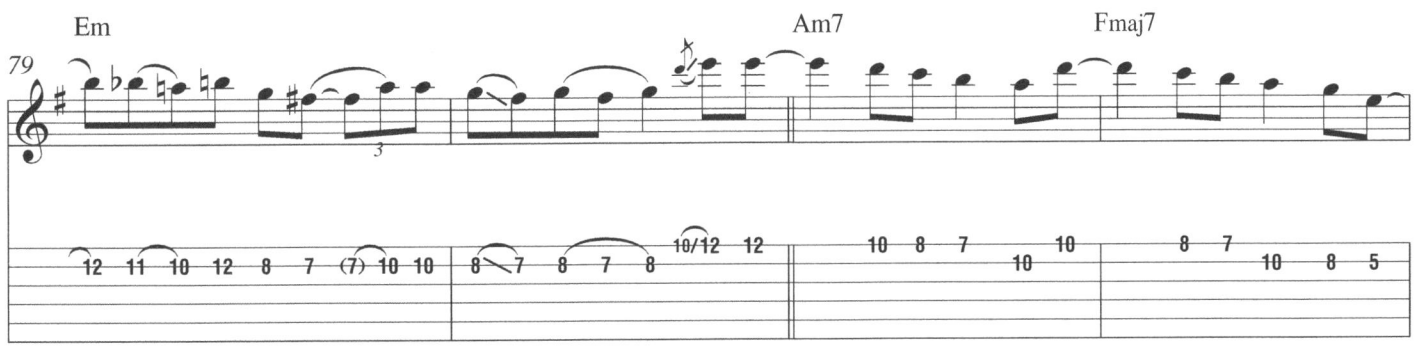

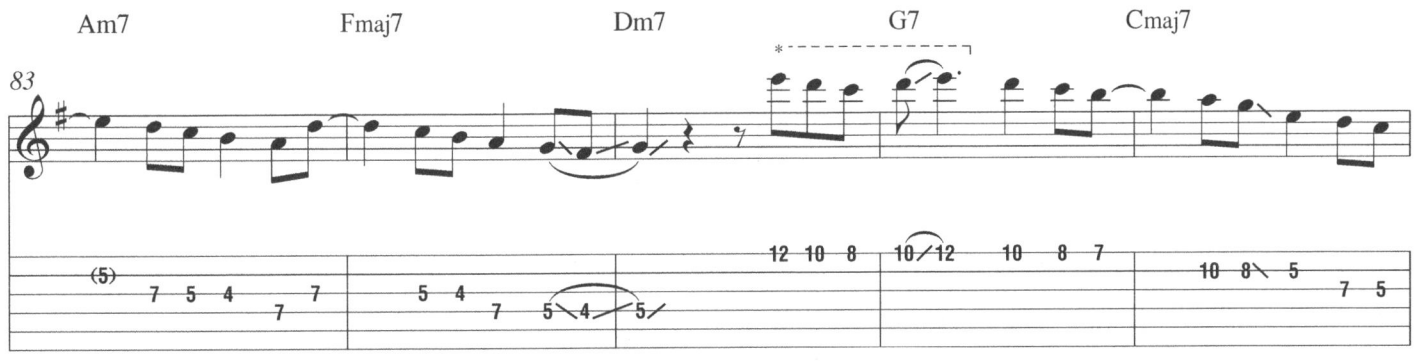

*Played behind the beat.

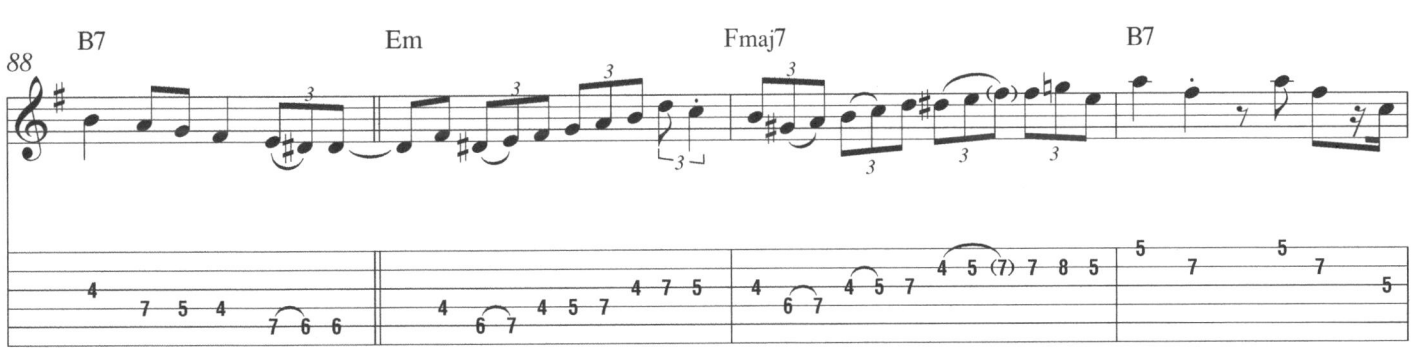

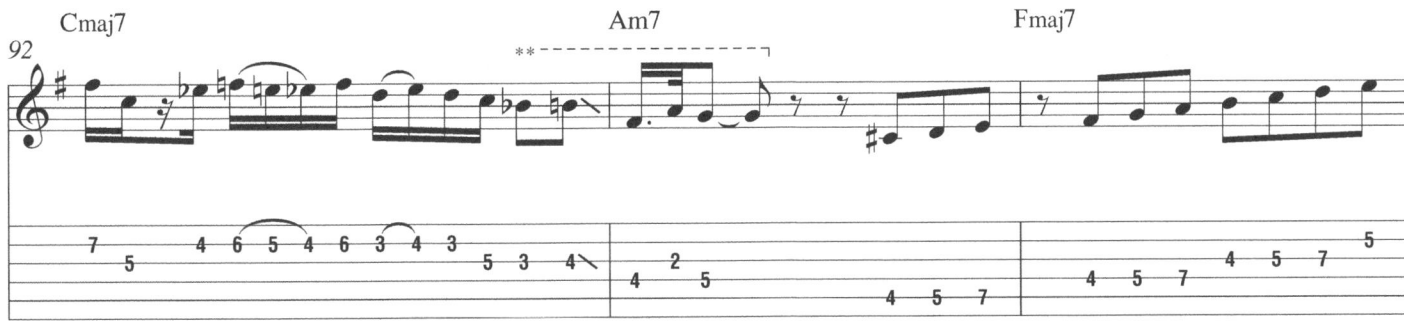

**Played as even eighth notes.

Nardis

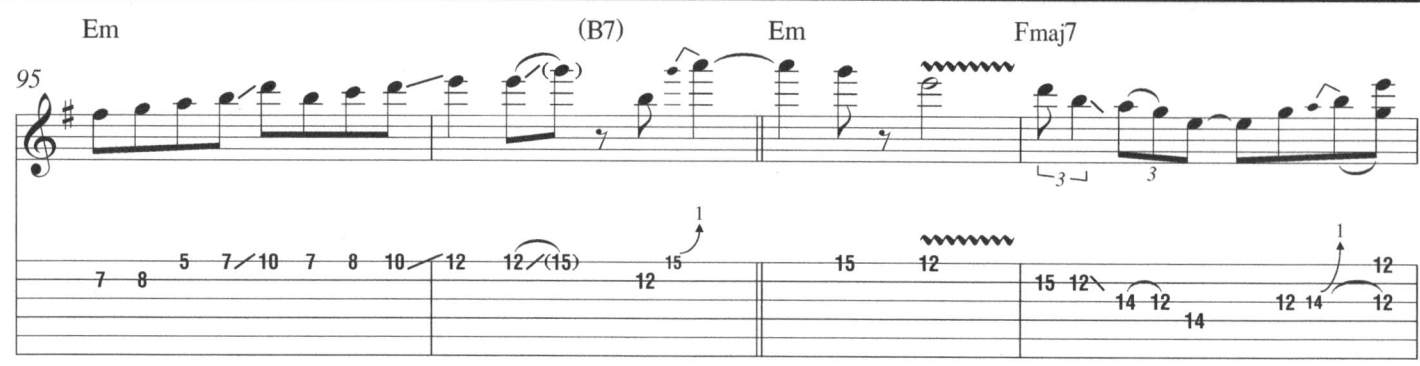
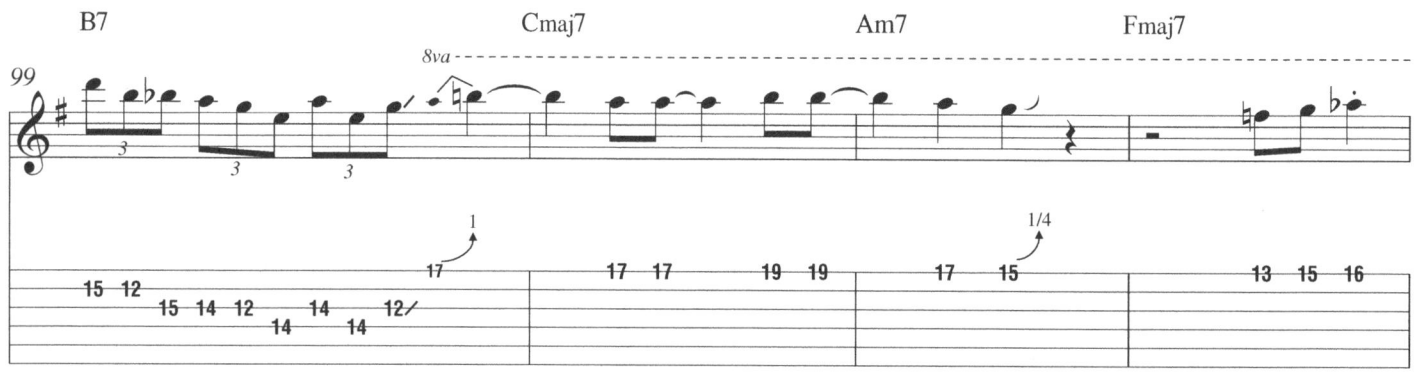
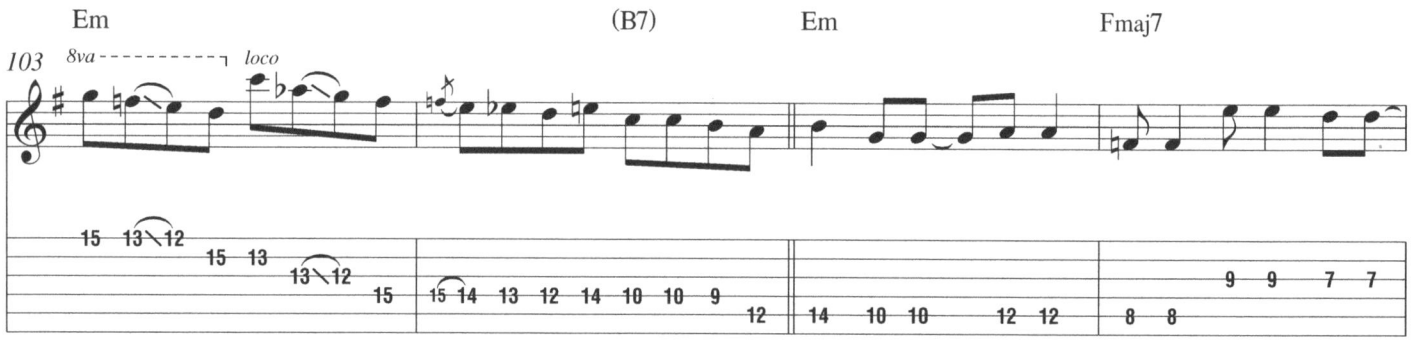

Nardis

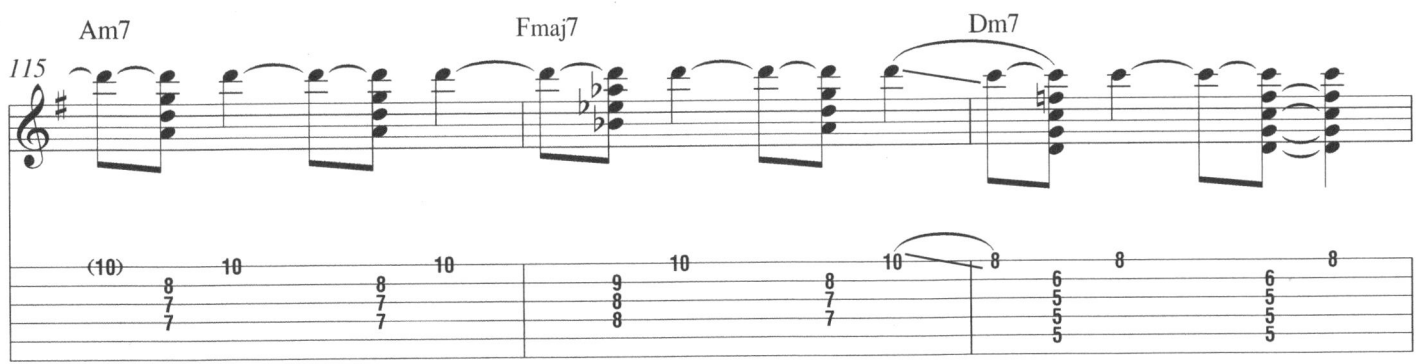
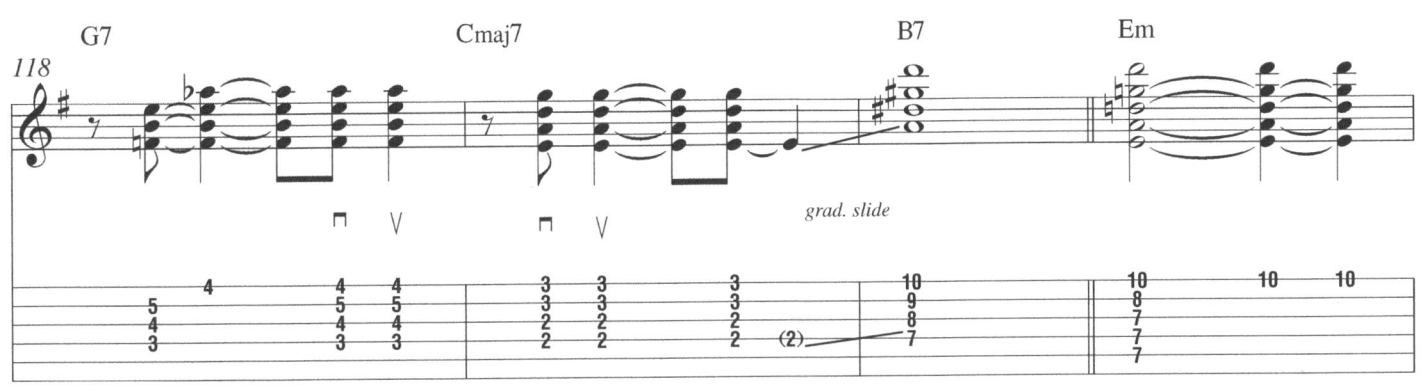
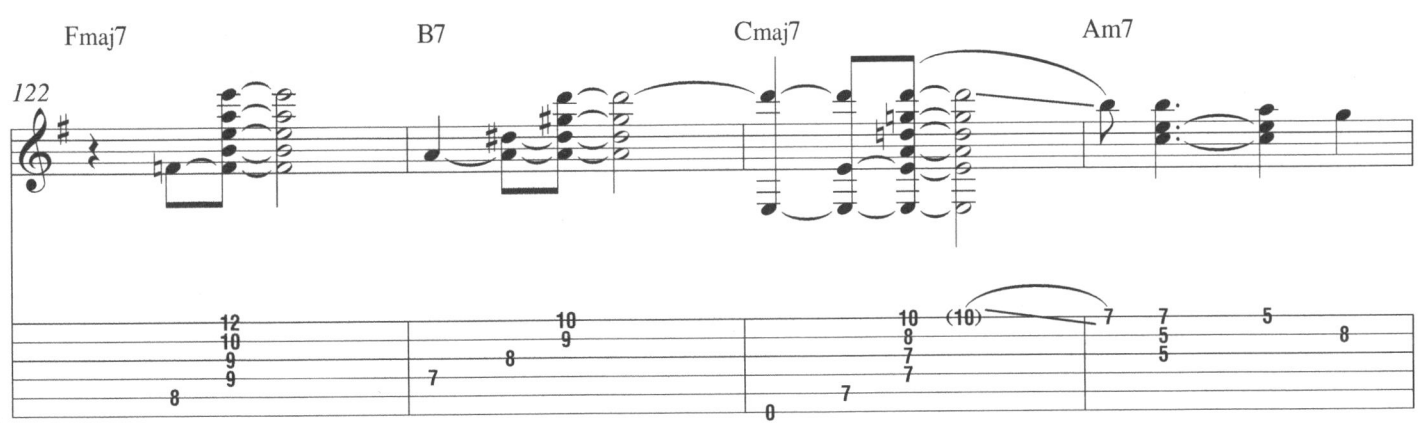
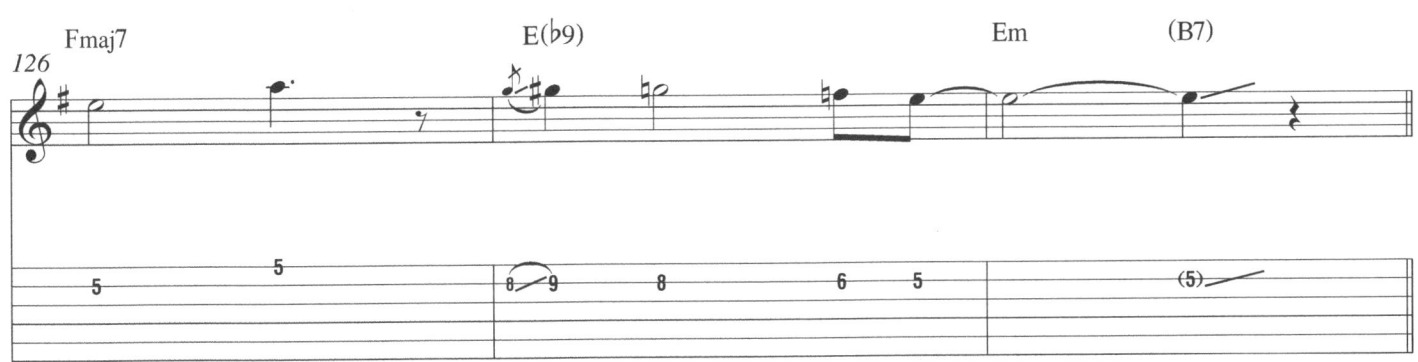

John Scofield

> *"I would feel guilty if I played exactly like somebody else… to me, the great thing in jazz has been 'have your own sound.'"*
>
> —John Scofield

© Alamy

Among the great modern guitarists who straddle the line between fusion and straight-ahead jazz, John Scofield (born December 26, 1951) is especially unabashed about letting his rock and blues roots hang out. In a career that keeps shifting between funky soul jazz and post bop-oriented ventures, "Sco" always sounds like his unique self, with his distinctive phrasing and idiosyncratic comping style. He avails himself plentifully of electronics and has often used chorus as part of his trademark not-too-dark semi-hollowbody sound, as well as a touch of distortion. At once angular, complex, songful, and earthy, in both his playing and his writing, he consistently shows how tasty, swingin', and sensitive one can be with twang and crunch.

Growing up in suburban Wilton, Connecticut and starting on guitar at age 11, he was taken early on with blues masters Otis Rush and B.B. King, as well as with Clapton and Hendrix. A local teacher introduced him to the music of jazz masters like Wes Montgomery and Jim Hall, and in the early 1970s he pursued this line of study at the Berklee College of Music in Boston. Among his important mentors during this time, in or out of school, were Hall, guitar luminary Mick Goodrick, bassist Steve Swallow, and vibraphonist Gary Burton. His recording debut came when filling in for Goodrick at a live date with cool jazz icons Gerry Mulligan (baritone saxophone) and Chet Baker (trumpet), which was released as their *Carnegie Hall Concert* (1974). In 1975, he replaced John Abercrombie in the intense jazz-rock fusion band of drummer Billy Cobham, and in 1977 followed Pat Metheny as the guitarist in Burton's group. He soon cut his first album as a leader, a self-titled 1977 release (later reissued as *East Meets West*), and played on sessions for legendary bassist/composer Charles Mingus, old school Kansas City jazzman Jay McShann, and bass phenomenon Niels-Henning Ørsted Pedersen. Continuing to make his own records, which began to incorporate more fusiony sounds, he joined the quintet of saxophone modernist David Liebman in 1979. He also formed a trio with Swallow and drummer Adam Nussbaum that same year.

But it was with the band of the great Miles Davis, from late 1982 to 1985, that Sco first came to widespread public attention. He was initially brought on board as a second guitarist, to be a backup for strung-out friend and colleague Mike Stern, and both players appeared on Miles' 1983 release *Star People*. With Stern's subsequent departure, Scofield held down the guitar role himself through extensive touring, as well as the recording of *Decoy* (1984) and *You're Under Arrest* (1985). In this period, Davis was moving from a more loose and raw brand of fusion to a greater emphasis on synthesizers, contemporary funk rhythms, and occasional covers of pop artists such as Michael Jackson and Cyndi Lauper. Scofield lent a bluesy element to the outfit, making important contributions as a soloist and receiving co-composer credits as his improvised ideas were turned into new tunes by Miles. When he left in 1985, his replacement was a cleaned-up Stern, rejoining his old boss for a while (Sco and Stern have often crossed paths elsewhere, as Berklee classmates, as co-leaders of a quartet at 55 Grand Street in early 1980s New York, and on tour together in 2013).

After Miles, he led a hard-hitting, funky fusion unit centered around electric bassist Gary Grainger and drummer Dennis Chambers, often referred to as his *Blue Matter* band, for their initial 1986 album by that name. He moved in a more straight-ahead direction with *Flat Out* (1988), which included his creatively fractured take on "All the Things You Are," as well as some poppin' New Orleans grooves courtesy of drummer Johnny Vidacovich. The early 1990s found him fronting a cutting-edge jazz quartet with tenor saxophonist Joe Lovano, and after the release of the landmark *Time on My Hands* (1990), with Lovano, bassist Charlie Haden, and drummer Jack DeJohnette, the band would evolve in its lineup to include bassists Marc Johnson or Dennis Irwin and drummer Bill Stewart. They recently reunited (now with Larry Grenadier on bass) for 2015's *Past Present*. For the jazz-funk-flavored *Hand Jive* (1993), he brought in soulful stylist Eddie Harris on tenor sax, as well as Larry Goldings on piano and organ. Goldings, like Stewart, has continued to work with Scofield in many settings through recent decades.

With 1997's *A Go Go*, he began his association with jam-band-meets-jazz trio Medeski, Martin & Wood (a partnership which continues sporadically to this day). In another group, involving rhythm guitarist and sample technician Avi Bortnick, he delved into newer electronics and rhythms (including the drum and bass style), releasing *Überjam* in 2002, followed by *Up All Night* (2003) and the reunion album *Überjam Deux* (2013). Meanwhile, 2000's *Works for Me* featured the very hip, swingin' crew of saxophonist Kenny Garrett, pianist Brad Mehldau, bassist Christian McBride, and drummer Billy Higgins.

Along the way, Scofield has also enjoyed collaborations with his fellow guitarists, recording *Solar* (1983) with Abercrombie, *Grace Under Pressure* (1992) with electronic colorist Bill Frisell, and *I Can See Your House from Here* (1994) with Metheny. He experimented with small-group horn arrangements on *Quiet* (1996, playing exclusively acoustic guitar) and *This Meets That* (2007), created a star-studded tribute to Ray Charles in 2005, played an assortment of gospel tunes for 2009's *Piety Street*, and joined the Metropole Orchestra in the Netherlands for *54* (2010), an album of his own tunes arranged by conductor Vince Mendoza. As a sideman, he has made significant appearances with bassist Marc Johnson, trumpeter Tom Harrell, saxophonist Joe Henderson, pianist Herbie Hancock, jam band Gov't Mule, and Grateful Dead alum Phil Lesh, among many others. He is an adjunct teacher at New York University, endorser of Ibanez guitars (makers of the JSM100 in his honor), and winner of numerous *DownBeat* polls for Best Guitarist.

How to Play It

Though swingin' like a jazz man throughout much of "Swing Spring," Sco creates a collage of highly varied elements on his journey through these four choruses, with rock and blues licks, bebop lines, simple song-like phrases, and slick "outside" ideas—not to mention musical gestures that are closer to pure sound-coloration. His overall statement is one of both down-and-dirty groove and heady sophistication, all mixed in with a sense of humor.

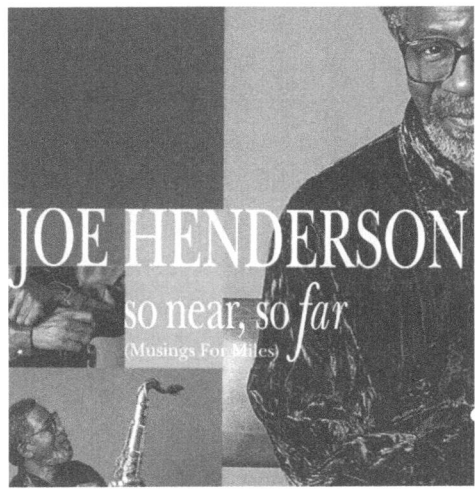

This classy Miles Davis tribute from tenor sax titan Joe Henderson was DownBeat's Jazz Album of the Year *for 1993 and a great showcase for the talents of Scofield, bassist Dave Holland, and drummer Al Foster (all Miles alums).*

The chord progression is that of "rhythm changes"—i.e., the changes to "I Got Rhythm," second only to the 12-bar blues form in its frequent use for jazz tunes (see Herb Ellis on "Orange, Brown and Green" for a more traditional swing/bop approach to the same basic progression). The structure is 32-bar AABA, with the A-sections largely based on turnaround chords (the I–VI–ii–V motion of B♭maj7–G7–Cm7–F7). "Swing Spring," however, has a specific set of substitutions for the bridge consisting of chromatically descending ii–V's (Am7–D7, A♭m7–D♭7, Gm7–C7, F♯m7–B7). Like the blues progression, rhythm changes may be treated with a high degree of flexibility by jazz musicians—in particular, the IV chord (E♭) in the sixth measure of any A-section may easily move to either A♭7 (akin to E♭m) or E°7. Sco's improv ideas and Dave Holland's bass lines may imply one or the other of these options (or neither!) in any instance. For example, Sco invokes A♭7 (or E♭m) in measure 30 by moving down to a G♭ in his line, while in measure 70 (and all around it, for that matter) he lays down an E diminished scale run, much more suggestive of E°7. Here Holland latches onto a pedal figure with E in the bass, to boot.

Swing Spring

Stylistic inflections of rock guitar are prevalent right off the bat, with plenty of little bends and shakes, abundant slurring and sliding, and phrases that are right out of a twangy blues playbook. Scofield blends his picking with hammer-ons and pull-offs much more than most jazzers, often to create an extra-legato feel as in measures 9–13. These two very scalar lines also show an interesting contrast in note choice, as the first one sits in the home key of B♭, while the next one takes us outside the changes with tones from the distant key of D♭, setting up a certain tension. The first half of this first chorus is capped off by the simple, down-home motif of major 6th intervals in measures 14–16. The ii–V's of the bridge are often treated as just the "V" part (a dominant chord)—the quick phrase from measure 21 through measure 22, beat 2 is a straight-up C7 idea, while the oblique-sounding tones that follow actually trace a B7 (compare them with familiar B7 shapes at the seventh or ninth positions), anticipating this change two beats before F♯m7 even arrives. But by the last beat of measure 23, Sco has slyly morphed his line into good ol' B♭ blues material, with which he will skate into the next section. In measure 21, start with the middle finger on fret 6, and use a stretchy hand position to navigate the next couple of measures.

The lick from measure 32 through measure 34, beat 3 would be a fairly common one if not for its unusual placement in time, straddling the double bar line rather than starting one measure later on the downbeat of the new section (and here its high note is stretched out two beats longer than normal). Notice the occasional "hammer-on from nowhere," where a note is subtly sounded by the left hand only, as at the end of measures 6 or 35. The descending figure of measures 39–40 is a total Scofield device, a striking sonic effect through patterned movement, here bringing out the tritone interval of B♭–E within a B♭7♭5 arpeggio. Start with the ring finger and use a new finger each string, so as to leave the pinky open for the big bends at the end of this run in measure 41. These represent another special Sco trick, in which he rapidly bends string 6 back and forth clear off the fretboard (this technique works better or worse on different guitars).

The crunchy A♭maj triad at the beginning of the second bridge (measure 49) serves as a tritone sub for the impending D7, creating an altered D7 sound right off the bat. The basic melodic shape here simply goes down a half step for measures 51–52, implying a D♭7♭9 as well. The next two measures exemplify the bluesy mixed minor/major 3rd treatment he often gives to dominant chords in the bridge, with both E♭ and E over the C7, while measures 55–56 are handled more like Cm7–F7♯9 (a variant of the ordinary ii–V in the key). In measures 60–63, the surprising clash of a harmonic minor 9th interval is just a foreshadowing of what's around the corner. For these double stops with a silent string in the middle, use the pick on the lower string and a finger to sound the upper string.

Scofield often works with factors of pure dissonance and density, and the somewhat "out there" third chorus is the peak of tension in this regard, starting with the profuse discordant intervals of measures 65–68 (which actually by and large fit into the concept of B♭13♯11♭9). The Hendrixian trills of measures 73–74 consist of minor-ish blues material, but this is based on a tonal center of E (a tritone removed from our key of B♭). Technical tips: jump up with the index finger for the last note of measure 78 (so as to be in the right spot after the slide down from there), be ready for a big jump up with the pinky a measure later, and strategize your fingerings carefully through the bridge in measures 81–88, which will involve some stretching and shifting. More off-neck bending is followed by tones in measures 90–92 that outline a quick cycle of A♭7–D♭7–G♭7—natural enough on its own but quite off-the-wall in this context. Then a lick of pure western twang, picked near the bridge of the guitar, begins to lighten the mood.

The overall sunnier final chorus starts off in measures 97–100 with straight-up linear bop material, thoroughly addressing the changes (though as if C♯°7 replaces the first F7) in a chunk of the progression where a more general major-key or bluesy approach had often been used. On the downbeat of measure 101, use the ring finger so as to be in better position for the move down string 2. And at the end of measure 108, let the middle finger slide subtly up string 3 until the index can access fret 6 on string 2. Amid the rockin' double stops of the bridge, measures 115–116 are treated as simple G7 territory. Sco playfully alludes to "Down by the Riverside" going into measures 105–106 and quotes his own tune "Flat Out" in the high-low call-and-response of measures 121–124. After one more taste of the blues, he dramatically strikes and slides up from different octaves of F (the 5th tone in the key), dissonantly concluding with a melodic minor 9th interval and fading on a sporadic trill before the bass solo begins.

Vital Stats

Guitarist: John Scofield

Song: "Swing Spring"

Album: *So Near, So Far (Musings for Miles)*, 1993—Joe Henderson

Age at Time of Recording: 41

Guitar: Ibanez AS-200

Amp: Mesa Boogie Mark I (or Vox AC30)

Effects: Ibanez Analog Chorus, Pro Co RAT distortion

Swing Spring

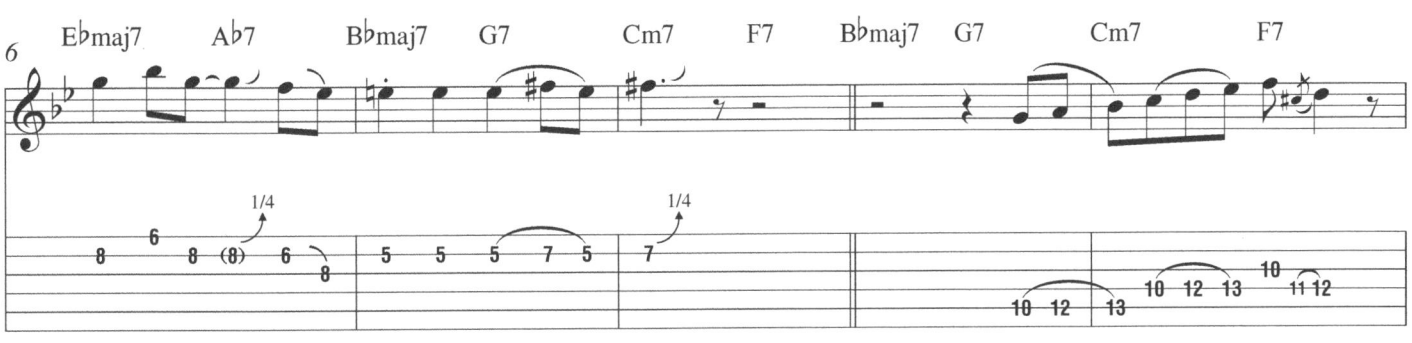
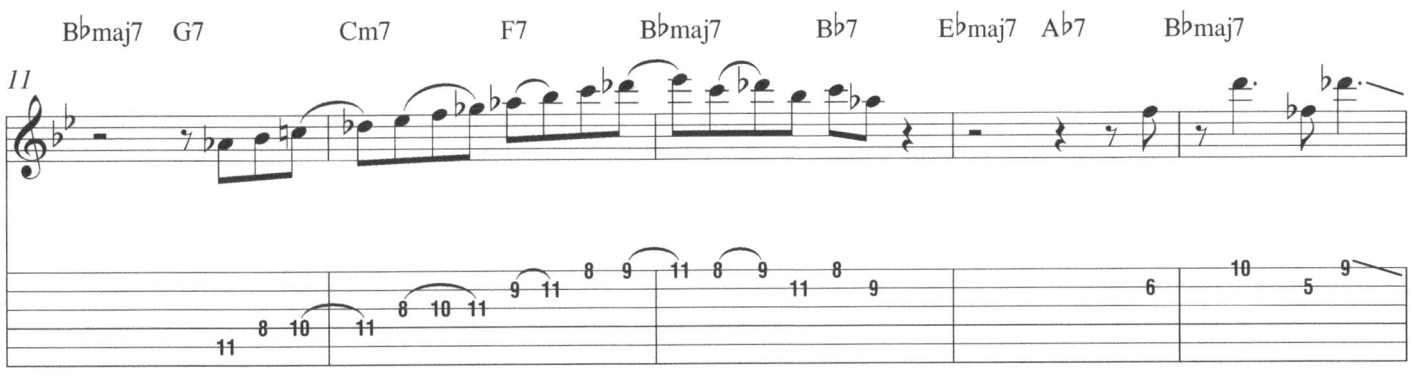
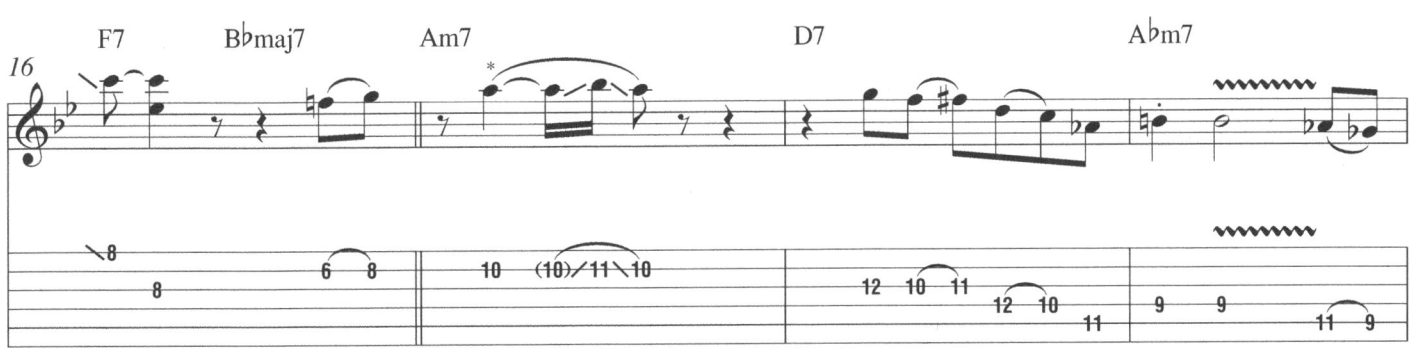

*Played behind the beat.

By Miles Davis
Copyright © 1954 Jazz Horn Music Corporation and Second Floor Music
Copyright Renewed
All Rights for Jazz Horn Music Corporation Administered by Songs Of Kobalt Music Publishing
All Rights outside the U.S. Controlled by Prestige Music
All Rights Reserved Used by Permission

Swing Spring

Swing Spring

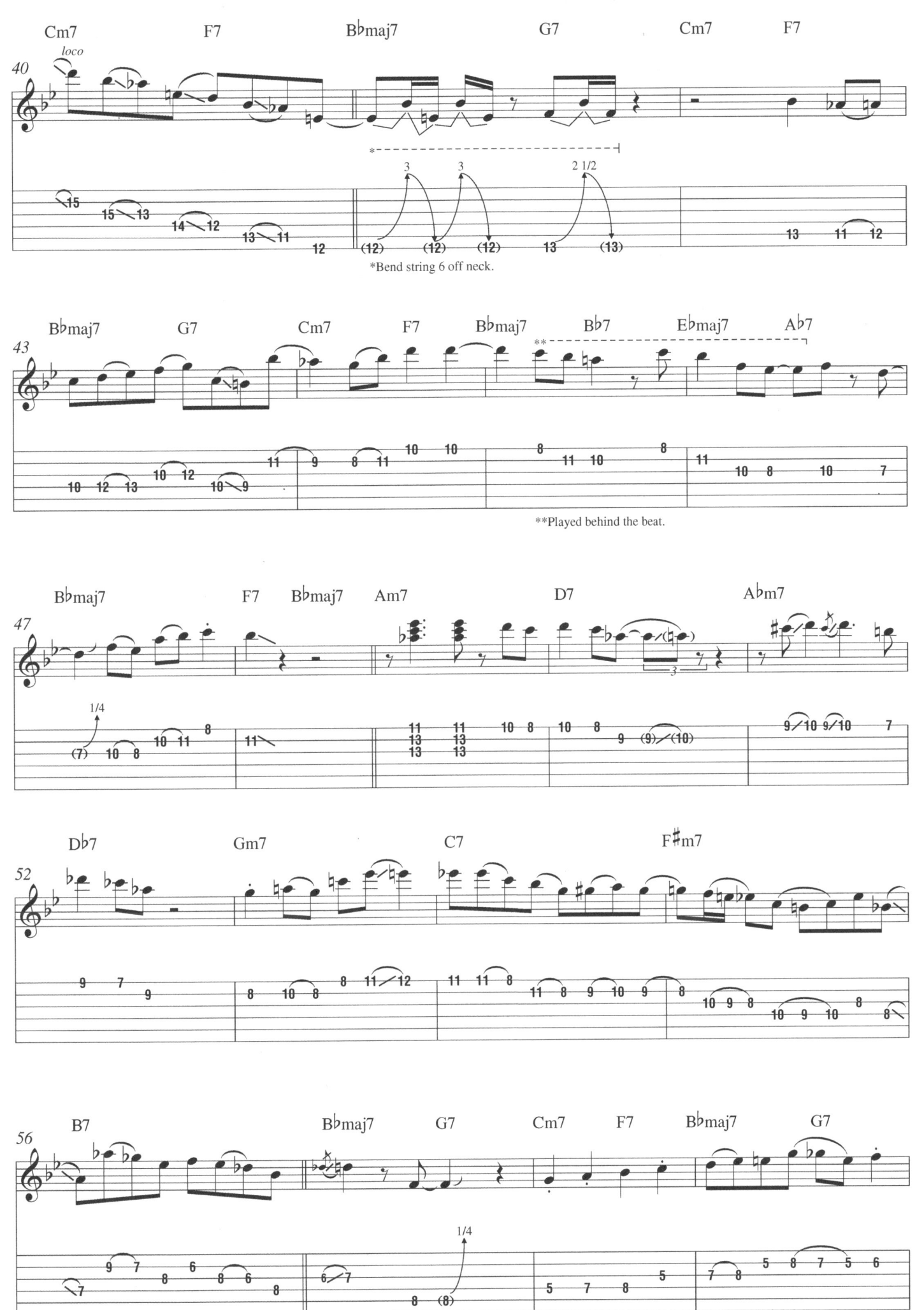

Swing Spring

Swing Spring

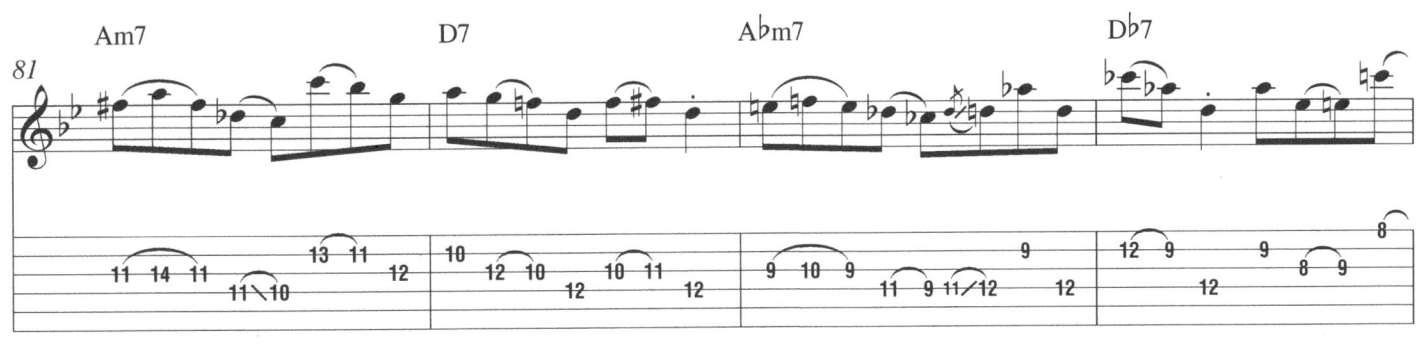
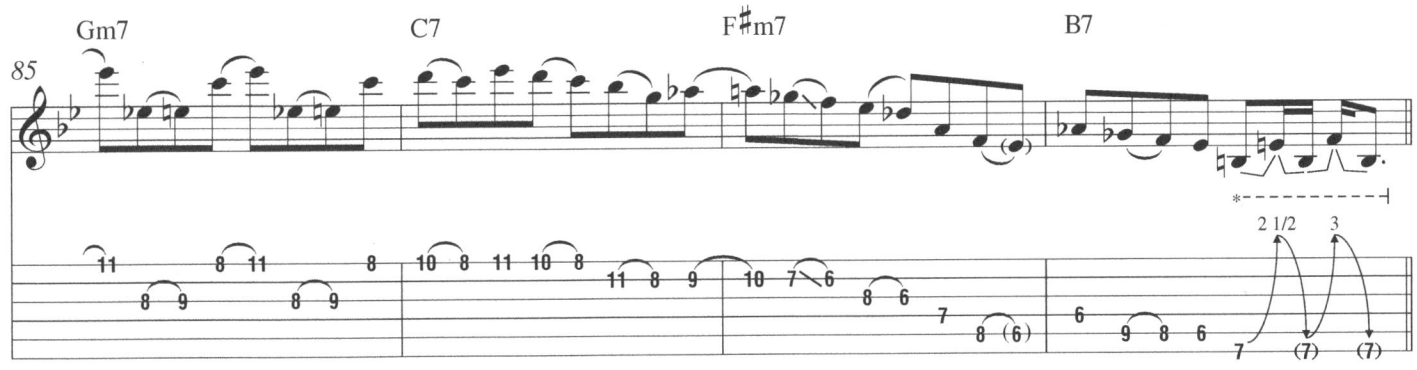

*Bend string 6 off neck.

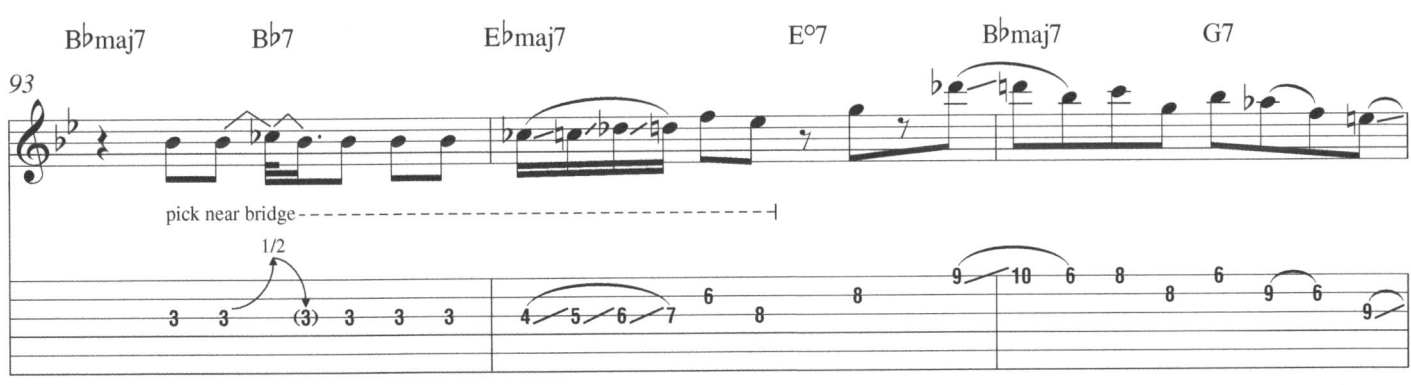
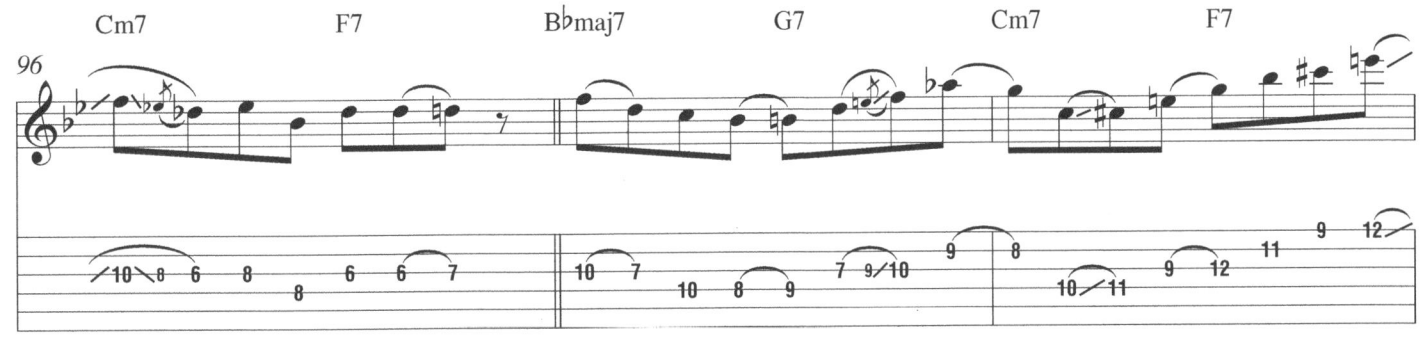

Swing Spring

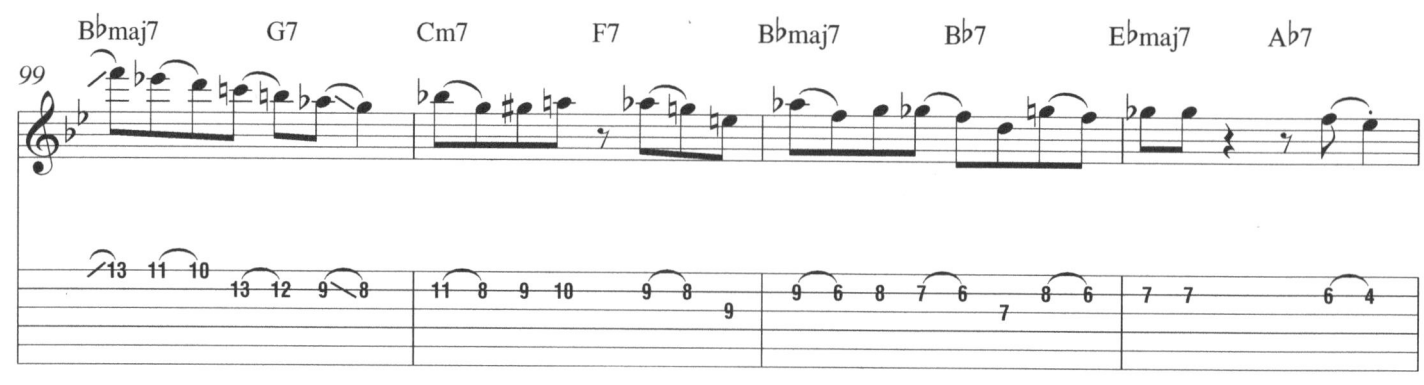
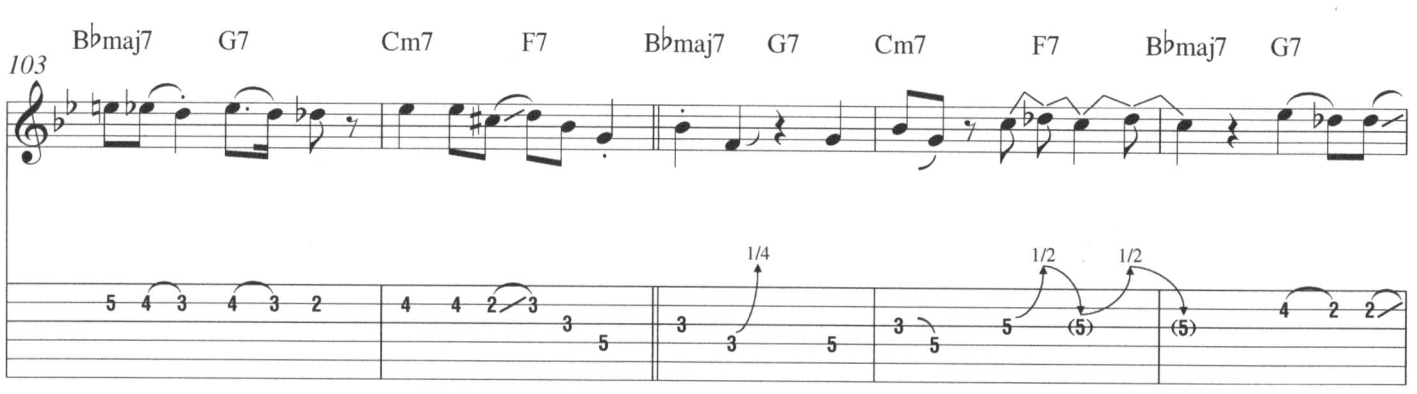
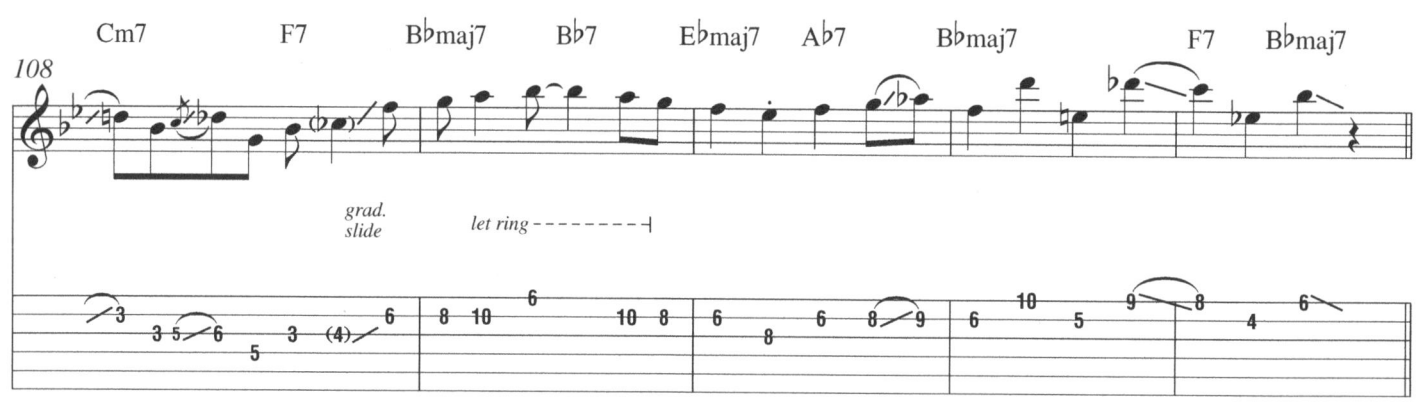
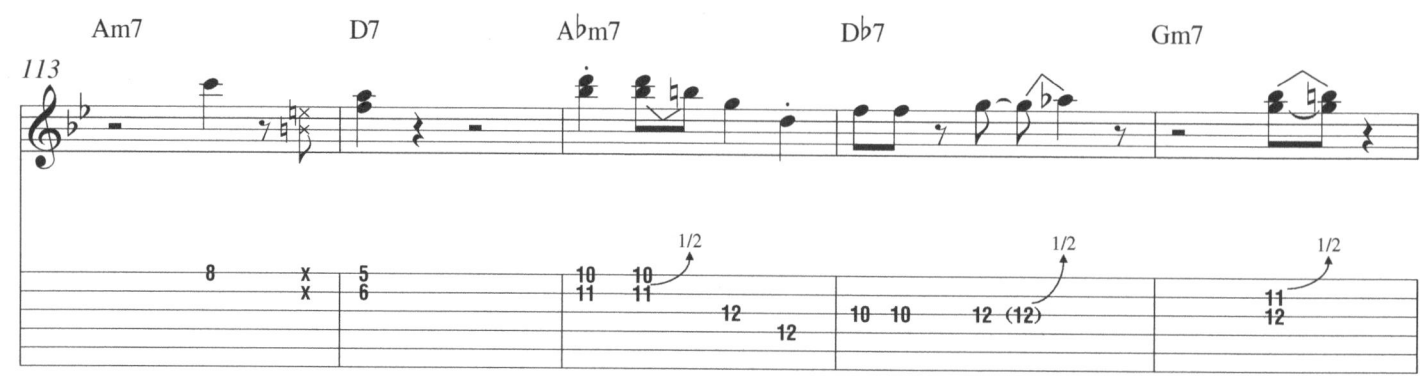

Swing Spring

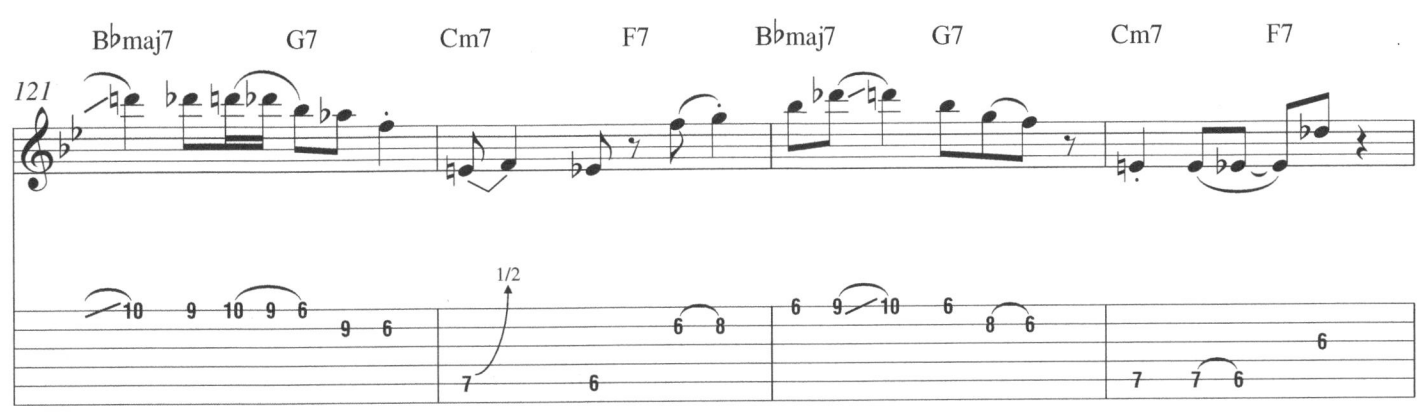
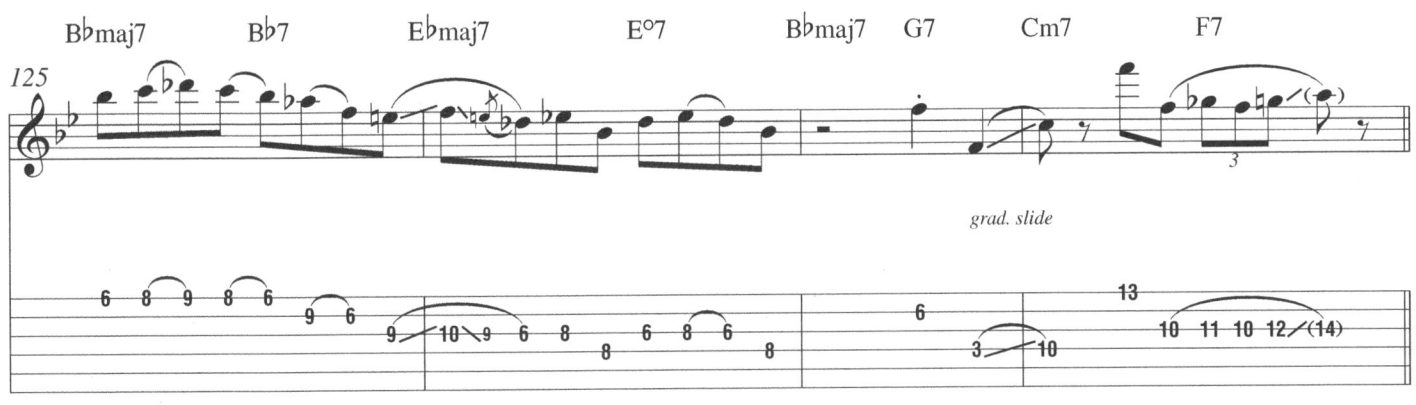
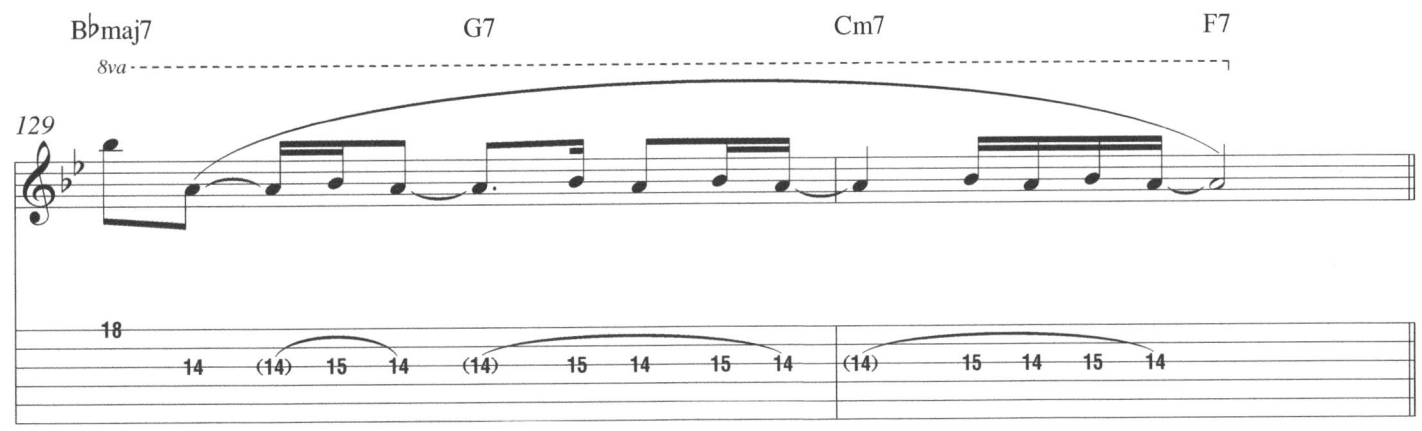

No Blues 1993

John McLaughlin

*"**What** isn't *fusion*?"*
—John McLaughlin

Courtesy Photofest

It's easy enough to identify John McLaughlin as one of the fathers of jazz-rock fusion, early as he was in the forefront of the genre. It's tougher to put in a stylistic nutshell exactly what else he has been throughout his rich and varied career. His explorations have ranged from pure acoustic tones to screaming electric passion, and from the traditional sounds of India to the most current digital technology. In any case, he is recognized across the board as one of the speed and precision monsters of modern guitar and has been a major influence on legions of players both in and outside of the jazz world.

McLaughlin learned violin and piano as a child and had plenty of exposure to classical music while growing up in Yorkshire, England (where he was born on January 4, 1942). He took up the guitar at age 11, inspired by blues and flamenco, and later by the work of Django Reinhardt and Tal Farlow. Making his way professionally on the London scene of the early 1960s, he played with successful, jazz-leaning R&B bands like Georgie Fame and the Blue Flames and the Graham Bond Organisation (alongside future Cream members Jack Bruce and Ginger Baker). He also did session work as the decade progressed—including tracks with Mick Jagger and Jimmy Page—and played straight-up jazz, much influenced by the music of Miles Davis and John Coltrane. In early 1969, he made his recording debut as a leader, *Extrapolation*, with a modern, slightly avant-garde jazz quartet and a set of his own tunes. The famously aggressive attack of his fast lines and short-clipped chords was already in evidence.

That same year, he came to the States to join the Tony Williams Lifetime, a seminal band in the fusing of jazz and rock, led by the legendary young drummer and rounded out by organist Larry Young (and soon also bassist Jack Bruce). During this exciting time, he also recorded on Miles Davis' groundbreaking forays into electrified territory—initially the aptly titled *In a Silent Way*, and subsequently the psychedelic *Bitches Brew* and the crunchy guitar-laden *Tribute to Jack Johnson*, among others. He appeared on record with a remarkable range of musicians, including Wayne Shorter, Carla Bley, popular singer/songwriter James Taylor, and fellow fusion guitar innovator Larry Coryell. In addition, he had the chance to jam with another of his clear influences, Jimi Hendrix.

This was the only full album by McLaughlin's slammin' early-1990s trio, the Free Spirits, with organist Joey DeFrancesco and drummer Dennis Chambers.

No Blues

McLaughlin's interest in both the music and philosophy of India would have a profound, lifelong effect on his art. He became a follower of spiritual leader Sri Chinmoy, who gave him the name Mahavishnu, and his landmark 1970 recording *My Goals Beyond* was dedicated to his new teacher. It featured strictly acoustic guitar, partly in ensemble with both Western and Indian instruments, and partly alone (with overdubbed self-accompaniment). Among its tracks were his guitar renditions of the Charles Mingus classic "Goodbye Porkpie Hat" and his own "Follow Your Heart." He collaborated with fellow Chinmoy devotee Carlos Santana on the highly spiritual *Love Devotion Surrender* (1973), inspired by their guru and honoring the late John Coltrane.

In 1971, McLaughlin started his own band, the Mahavishnu Orchestra, a high-powered quintet involving Jan Hammer on keys and fellow Miles alum Billy Cobham on drums. Regarded as one of the defining groups of the fusion movement, they played with tremendous intensity and could range in texture from the spacious and serene (with tunes like "A Lotus on Irish Streams") to the fast, dense, and complex, sometimes within one piece. Here he generally chose as his main axe a Les Paul or a double-neck electric (for the 12-string option), often making use of odd meters and exotic scales. Personality conflicts within the band brought the original lineup to an end by late 1973, but he kept it going another couple of years with new personnel—most notably violinist Jean-Luc Ponty. This newer group recorded *Apocalypse* (1974) with the London Symphony Orchestra. In 1975, he further pursued his love of Indian music with Shakti, an acoustic quintet with sidemen from India on percussion and violin. For this venture, he procured a custom-made Gibson acoustic with a scalloped fretboard and seven resonator strings, modeled after the Indian vina, to allow for drone sounds and extra bending.

Since the time of these revolutionary groups, McLaughlin has led or played in an amazing array of ensembles, among them the One Truth Band in the late 1970s, a new version of Mahavishnu in the mid-1980s (which sparked his first substantial use of guitar synthesizer), an acoustic guitar trio with fellow virtuosi Paco de Lucía and Al Di Meola (releasing three astounding albums and occasionally touring from 1980 to 1996), a trio involving Indian percussion master Trilok Gurtu in the late 1980s and early 1990s, and the Heart of Things in the late 1990s. In more recent years, he has recorded and toured with a reformed Shakti as well as with his current electric fusion band, the 4th Dimension, with whom he has released several albums including the colorful and spirited *Black Light* (2015).

Special projects along the way have included his concerto for guitar and orchestra (*The Mediterranean*, premiered in 1985 with the L.A. Philharmonic), an appearance in the 1986 epic jazz film *Round Midnight*, the multi-guest-artist albums *Electric Guitarist* (1979) and *The Promise* (1995), the tribute albums *Time Remembered* (1993, for Bill Evans) and *After the Rain* (1995, for Coltrane), and the instructional DVD *This Is the Way I Do It* (2004). He shared the 2010 Grammy Award for Best Jazz Instrumental Album with Chick Corea for their *Five Peace Band Live* and has been recognized by *Rolling Stone* as one of the 100 Greatest Guitarists of All Time.

How to Play It

McLaughlin's rendering of his famous old boss's simple 12-bar blues, recorded live with his Free Spirits band, offers a relatively modern look at jazz improv on this form. Through the seven choruses of his solo, he mixes basic, more traditionally bluesy-sounding gestures with complex, angular lines that go beyond the usual harmonic boundaries (compare and contrast to George Benson's earthy but bop-related playing on "Benny's Back").

Between the use of chorus effect and a whammy bar on an archtop guitar, the whole performance is characterized by a rather tremulous sound. The bar is not used for extreme dives or shakes but rather for slight dips akin to the quarter-step bends that frequently embellish the work of many players—just going the other direction in pitch. McLaughlin feels that these add a more life-like, plaintive quality than rising inflections alone, and he executes them with a quick touch of his right-hand pinky and ring finger on the wide handle of the Bigsby, either while holding a note, as in measure 5, or just before silencing it, as in measure 29 (resulting there in a dip with no upward release).

His rhythmic approach throughout is based on firm, aggressive swung eighth-note timing, whether in long, unbroken, flowing lines, or short bursts of a few notes with plenty of space in between. Indeed, for all his speed-demon chops and harmonically advanced material, many of his statements here are mainly about rhythm—from the sparse, bouncy ideas of the first chorus (through measure 12) to the percussive muted strings and double stops of his conclusion. At times

No Blues

like these, he plays with the placement of accents on different beats of the measure by way of where he interjects an isolated note or two, or abruptly stops a phrase. He often makes use of the open first string as a nearly muted percussive tool while grooving on a couple of notes higher up on the same string, as in his solo entrance or the figure of measures 53–54. In his fifth chorus especially (measures 49–60), he creates space for improvisatory call and response within the band, leaving long gaps that are wide open for organ fills.

Much of McLaughlin's tone material is right out of the old-school blues playbook. The segment from measure 5 through measure 11, beat 2 is all G blues scale-related and, more importantly, is made up of direct quotes and variations of Miles' melody, a theme that inspires many of the rhythmic and melodic shapes in the solo and which will be heard clearly again from the end of measure 60 through measure 63. Other phrases, like that of measures 56–57, play on the mix of B♭ and B♮, the minor and major 3rd of the key (found here on string 2, frets 11 and 12), as well as involving the 6th (E on string 1, fret 12). Listen also to his first four measures for this kind of sound.

Elsewhere, he tends to play in an "outside-in" fashion, following melodic shapes and patterns that may neatly fit the chord progression but which may also diverge from it with surprisingly oblique tones (sometimes implying alterations or substitutions). The notes of measures 15–16 may seem a bit "out there" but mostly make sense for an altered G7 chord (with ♭5th and ♯5th, ♭9th and ♯9th). We head into clear C Mixolydian territory for C7 in the next two measures and G Mixolydian for a straightforward G7 right afterwards. But by measure 21, the notes of this passage become very chromatic and difficult to analyze vis-à-vis the regular chords. We're left with a feeling of unresolved tension by the end of this line in measure 23, fittingly enough for the general harmonic direction at this point, as we're in the middle of a turnaround waiting to come back home to the tonic chord. The last four notes here, in 4th intervals that are played with the pinky and then middle finger rolling between strings 1 and 2, could actually be interpreted as the ♭5th, ♭9th, and 3rd of E7, plus an anticipated ♭5th of A7 (or as tones of an altered D7, implied early).

In places like measures 31–32 or 43–44, he launches into a new phrase with dissonant tones right off the bat, using an altered tone for G7 and "outside" material for the chords that follow. With the largely chromatic ascent of the four-note melodic cell found from measure 67, beat 3 through measure 69, McLaughlin demonstrates clearly how such patterned movement can be prioritized over chord-specific notes, highlighting his common ground with Pat Metheny in this area (see "Nothing Personal," measures 65–66). This long line culminates with the energetic high point of the solo in measures 73–75 as his final chorus begins, with abundant bends, whammy dips, and a return to good old G7 tones.

Be aware that McLaughlin's longer lines generally involve some shifting of fretboard position along the way, whether in gradual, fret-by-fret movement (as in most of measures 68–69), or trickier reaches and jumps. Note in particular: in measure 67, where the left hand has moved down to the second position, the index finger reaches for fret 1 while the middle finger stays ready to take fret 3 again, and the upward shifting begins when the pinky grabs the E♭ at fret 6 (the index then takes fret 3 and slides up). Also, the slide at the end of measure 38 with the ring finger precedes a quick jump to fret 8 with the pinky to take up the fifth position in measure 39.

Vital Stats

Guitarist: John McLaughlin

Song: "No Blues"

Album: *Tokyo Live*, 1994 (recorded 1993)— with The Free Spirits

Age at Time of Recording: 51

Guitar: Gibson Johnny Smith with Bigsby tremolo

Amp: Direct into P.A. (through Sony M7 signal processor)

Effects: Chorus and delay (from Sony M7)

No Blues

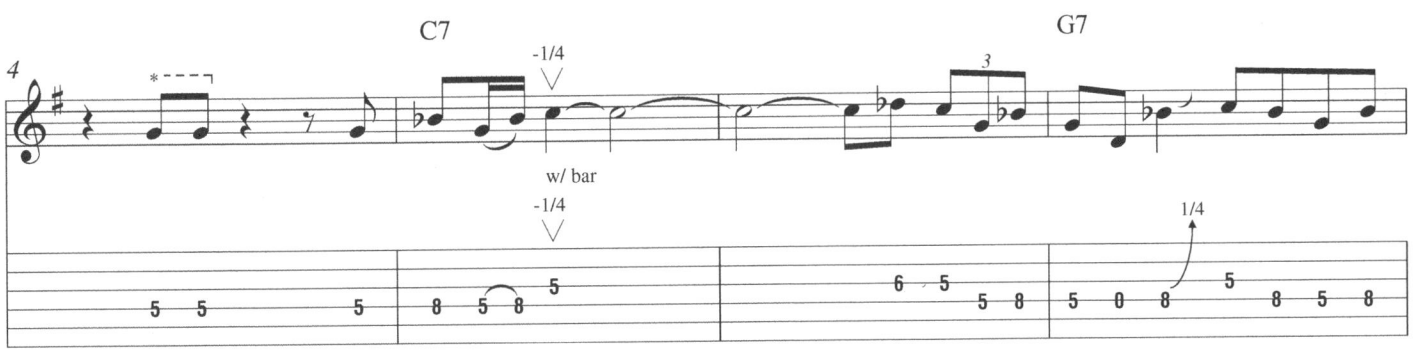
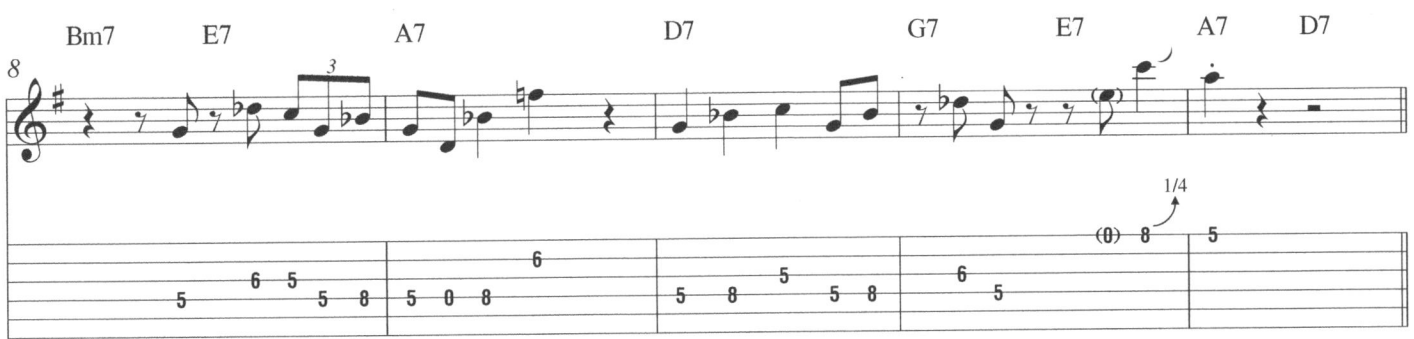
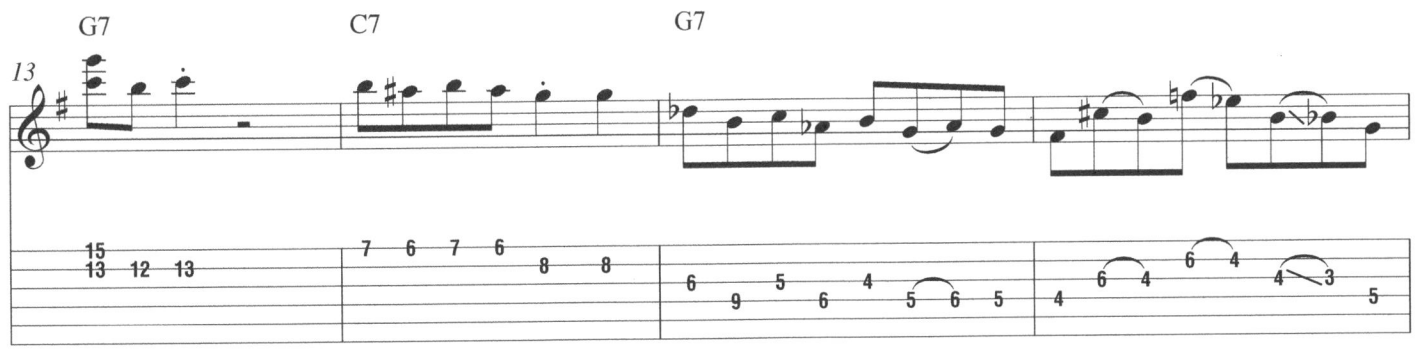

By Miles Davis
Copyright © 1961 Jazz Horn Music Corporation
Copyright Renewed
All Rights Administered by Songs Of Kobalt Music Publishing
All Rights Reserved   Used by Permission

No Blues

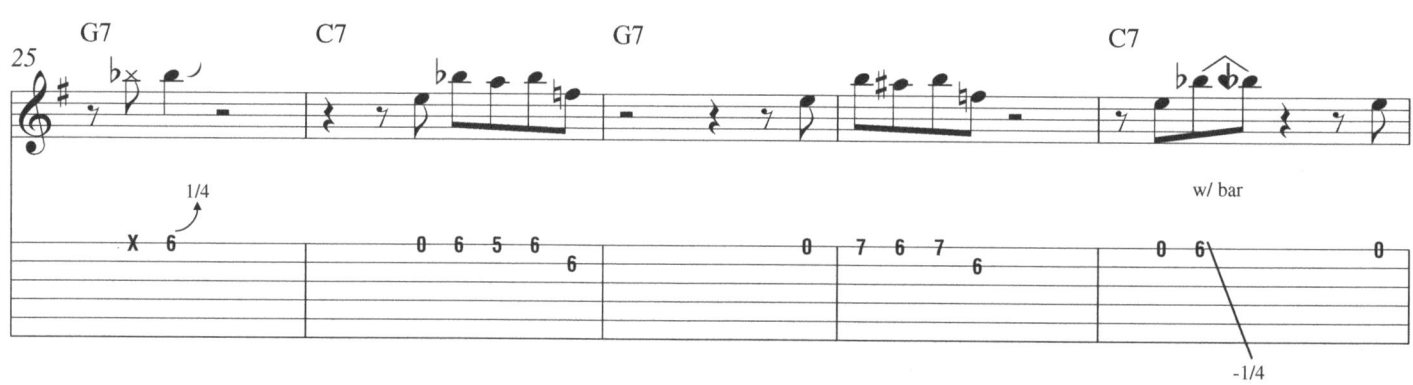
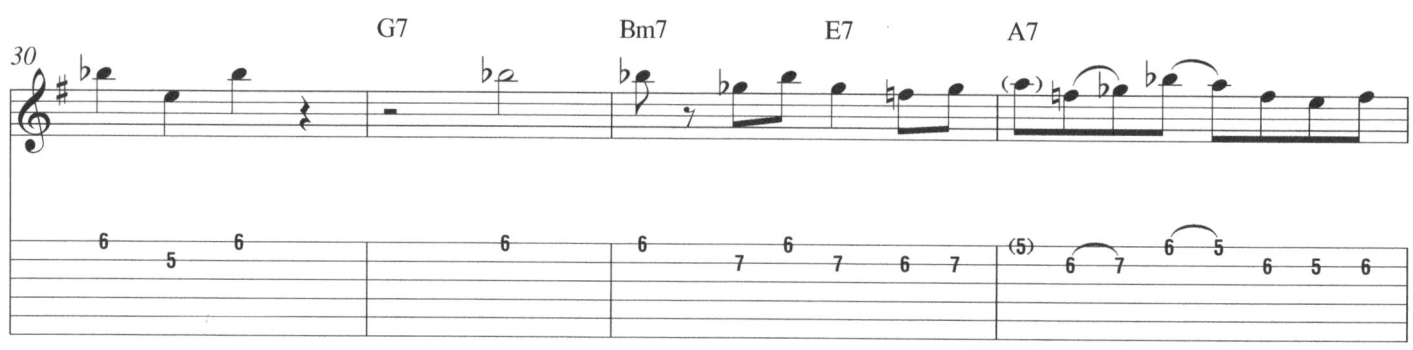
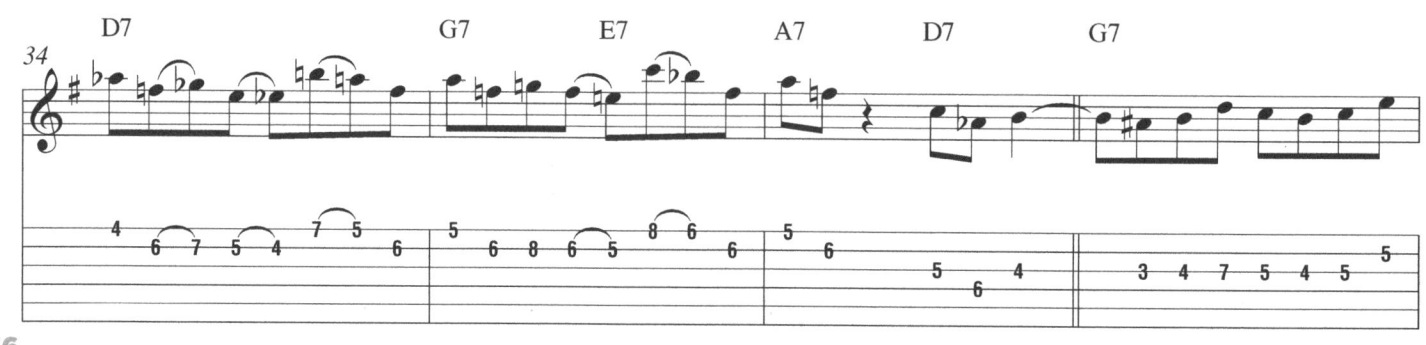

No Blues

No Blues

The Acrobat 1997

Peter Bernstein

© Alamy

"It's not about the guitar, it's about your ear... if your ear's getting better, you're a better musician."
—Peter Bernstein

Peter Bernstein has been the key guitarist of his generation in amalgamating the influences of classic jazz masters such as Wes Montgomery, Grant Green, and Jim Hall, and bringing their art into the current era. While highly capable on the instrument, he is more recognized for his taste, subtlety, refined tone, and knowledge of the music than for pure chops. He swings hard but always with a relaxed lyricism and a mature sense of space, and his resumé reads like a who's-who list of historical and recent greats.

Born right into the Big Apple on September 3, 1967, Bernstein learned piano at first, switching to guitar by age 13. He attended Rutgers University in New Jersey, benefitting there from the instruction of noted guitarist Ted Dunbar and revered pianist Kenny Barron. Continuing his studies at the New School in New York, he became a protégé of hero and mentor Jim Hall, who in 1990 invited him to participate in his star-studded guitar event within the JVC Jazz Festival, resulting in the young guitarist's inclusion on *Jim Hall and Friends—Live at Town Hall, Vol. 2*. That same year, he began working as part of legendary alto saxophonist Lou Donaldson's regular band, and it was all uphill from there. His performance and recording credits have since included drumming icon Jimmy Cobb, popular jazz vocalist Diana Krall, tenor sax phenom Joshua Redman, cutting-edge trumpeter Tom Harrell, and Hammond organ wizards Jack McDuff and Lonnie Smith.

Two other organ-based groups have been of special significance and longevity in his career. He has played for over a quarter century with contemporaries Larry Goldings on organ and Bill Stewart on drums (both top-flight players and major influences in their own right), in a state-of-the-art version of the classic organ trio lineup. They have made numerous acclaimed recordings together along the way, starting with Goldings' debut release, *The Intimacy of the Blues* (1991), on which a rendition of his tune "The Acrobat" initially appeared. Bernstein also had a long association with the late, great organist Melvin Rhyne (of Wes Montgomery fame) that began in 1991, when both were on a session with trumpeter Brian Lynch for the Criss Cross label. The rapport between them was clear, and the guitarist wound up effectively in Wes's old chair well into the 2000s for various live shows and some outstanding studio dates with the electric organ master (appearing on most of Rhyne's albums from 1992's *The Legend* to 2007's *Front and Center*).

Bernstein's own recordings as a leader started on Criss Cross with *Somethin' Burnin'* (1993) and continued with titles such as *Brain Dance* (1997) and *Heart's Content* (2003), involving sidemen like Cobb, modern piano maestro Brad Mehldau, and tenor sax titan Eric Alexander. Known as a wonderful inter-

The Acrobat

preter of standard repertoire, his albums also tend to include a healthy dose of his own writing, with such originals as "Blues for Bulgaria," the sophisticated and swingin' "Metamorphosis," or the relaxedly funky "Carrot Cake." Among more recent efforts, *Monk* (2009) is a guitar-bass-drums trio outing devoted entirely to Thelonious Monk compositions, and *Solo Guitar—Live at Small's* (2013) captures his well-received venture of the last few years into unaccompanied performance, replete with his creative and intricate chord-melody work, at the intimate Greenwich Village club.

In 2008, he joined forces with high-profile colleagues, including trumpeter Nicholas Payton, to form the Blue Note 7, a group honoring the legacy of the great jazz label on its 70th anniversary. They released *Mosaic: A Celebration of Blue Note Records* in 2009, with fresh arrangements of classics from the catalog. Bernstein continues to be widely in demand as a concert artist and clinician, and in recent years he has enjoyed working with all-time tenor sax giant Sonny Rollins as well as teaching at NYU and the New School.

Of many fine albums from the longtime trio with organist Larry Goldings and drummer Bill Stewart, 1997's Earth Tones *is the only one so far under Bernstein's name as the leader, aside from a 2005 live DVD.*

How to Play It

Through three choruses of this lively minor waltz by bandmate Larry Goldings, Bernstein shows how to *cook* with a relaxed feel and fluid phrasing. His lines are colored throughout by frequent sliding slurs, slight bends and vibrato on sustained notes, and behind-the-beat timing. He picks near the neck pickup for a warm tone, and for tremolos may anchor the picking hand lightly with its free fingertips. A reminder to readers of notation in this transcription: being in E♭ minor, the tune has six flats in the key signature, so stay on your toes! Keep in mind also that C♭maj7 is the enharmonic equivalent of Bmaj7, and is being used here as the theoretically correct ♭VI chord of the key.

Much of the fairly complex harmonic progression lends itself well to skating through with E♭ minor pentatonic or blues scale material, as well as using melodic ideas tailored to the specific changes, and Bernstein avails himself of both approaches. He begins with tones that imply a B♭7♭9♯5 (or E13♯11) as a turnaround chord in the solo break pickup and then continues in an E♭ minor pentatonic vein. Even when his lines stick largely to this scale, little exceptions abound, adding color or reflecting the chords at hand—the E♮ in measure 6 brings out the sound of the D♭m7 (E♮ = F♭, the 3rd of D♭m7), and the first two notes of measure 74 are E7-friendly. The F diminished scale material of measures 14–16 relates most of all to the B♭7♭9 at the end of this segment, generally setting up tension before the resolution back to E♭m. He tends to use more chord tone-oriented ii–V–I lines for the D♭m7–G♭7–C♭maj7 sequences in spots like measures 46–47 and 62–63. The ghosted F in measures 33–34 is non-harmonic to the D♭m7–G♭7 chords but is just being quickly bounced off of for rhythmic purposes.

For three measures towards the end of each bridge (the tune has a 56-bar AABA structure, with 16-bar A-sections and an eight-bar bridge), the chords make a decisive visit to the distant key of A major, which requires an adjustment by the soloist. You can hear (and see) how he alters his note choice to suit these ii–V–I's in A (Bm7–E7–Amaj7) found in measures 37–39, 93–95, and 149–151, with linear content that lies mainly within the A major scale.

Bernstein has a frequently *vertical* approach to the fretboard, often moving up and down the neck with quick shifts, slight reaches, or short slides, as in the movement from the high note of measure 69 into the mid-neck area of measure 71 (tip: use the middle finger for the slide into measure 70). In measure 135, a change of position is effected by allowing the ring finger to slide up into fret 11 on string 2 after the index slides down from the same fret on string 1 (the middle finger will take fret 11 on string 3). The line of measures 61–65 starts out in a more compact position, requiring the index to roll across strings 4, 3, and 2 for consecutive notes on fret 9 (followed by a roll of the ring finger on strings 2 and 1) but then elongates to span frets 7 through 14, even presenting the same G♭ twice in a row in two different places towards the end (string 3, fret 11 and string 2, fret 7). Altogether, he tends to avoid the use of the pinky for single-note lines, like Wes before him, although not to the same

The Acrobat

absolute extent. This entire solo is indeed playable without that finger, especially if adopting a somewhat stretchy fretting-hand posture (fingers angled a bit more like those of a violinist) and being prepared to move.

His use of rhythmic variation is a key component of the overall statement here. In a rather modern touch of timing, common to many of today's jazz guitarists, he often holds back just a little before sounding a note on the downbeat of a measure, as in measure 12 (see Mike Stern on "Nardis" or Bobby Broom on "I Thought About You"). He takes after Grant Green in frequently saying a lot with a little, continually rephrasing what would otherwise be quite repetitive material, especially during long blues-scale stretches like the one in measures 104–119. The gesture of measures 104–105 in particular is total Grant, and he sings on from there into a segment of boldly leaned-back phrasing, joined by the extra intensity of his bandmates in setting up the dramatic third and final chorus (which starts at measure 113).

From measure 126 to the beginning of measure 131, he swoops between rising major 6th intervals in a colorful, rolling hemiola figure comprised of 1-1/2-beat rhythmic units against the 3/4 meter (compare to the similar pattern Emily Remler uses in 4/4 time on "East to Wes," measures 65–70). It works well here to use the middle finger on strings 4 or 3, while the ring finger frets the higher notes on strings 2 or 1 (the index slides into measure 126 and takes the double slide of measure 131). He gets a lot of mileage out of few tones again in measures 137 through 140 and creates great momentum with plain old quarter notes through the last five measures of the bridge (measures 148–152), scooting up string 2 with the ring finger by the end of this line. Then in the climactic final section, after some more easy-paced high wailing in E♭ blues territory, he begins the wind-up with a reference to the tune's melody in measures 161–166, while the band soon reprises the kicks and changes that belong to the end of the tune.

Vital Stats

Guitarist: Peter Bernstein

Song: "The Acrobat"

Album: *Earth Tones*, 1998 (recorded 1997)

Age at Time of Recording: 30

Guitar: Gibson L-5

Amp: Fender (possibly Vibrolux)

By Larry Goldings
© 1991 Larry Goldings/Largold Music (ASCAP)
All Rights Reserved Used by Permission

The Acrobat

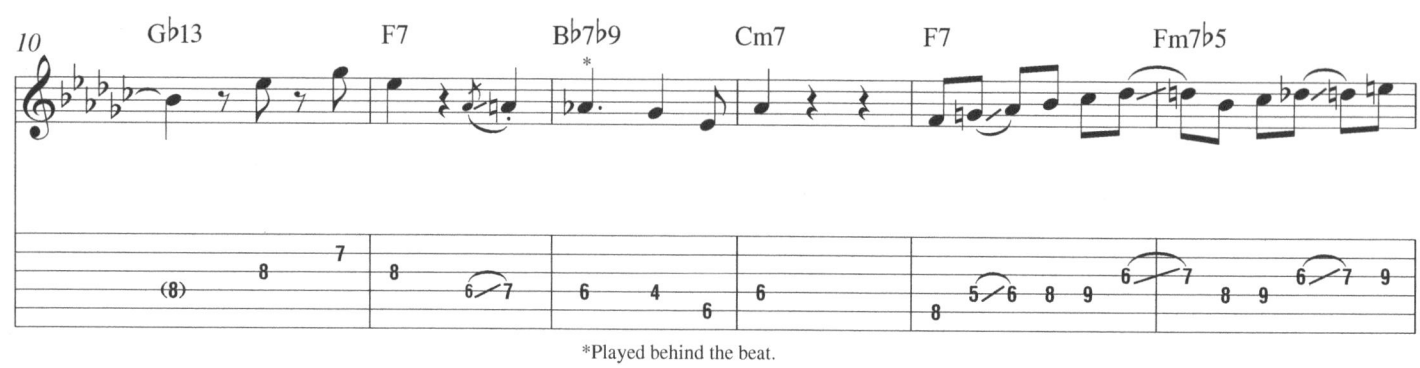

*Played behind the beat.

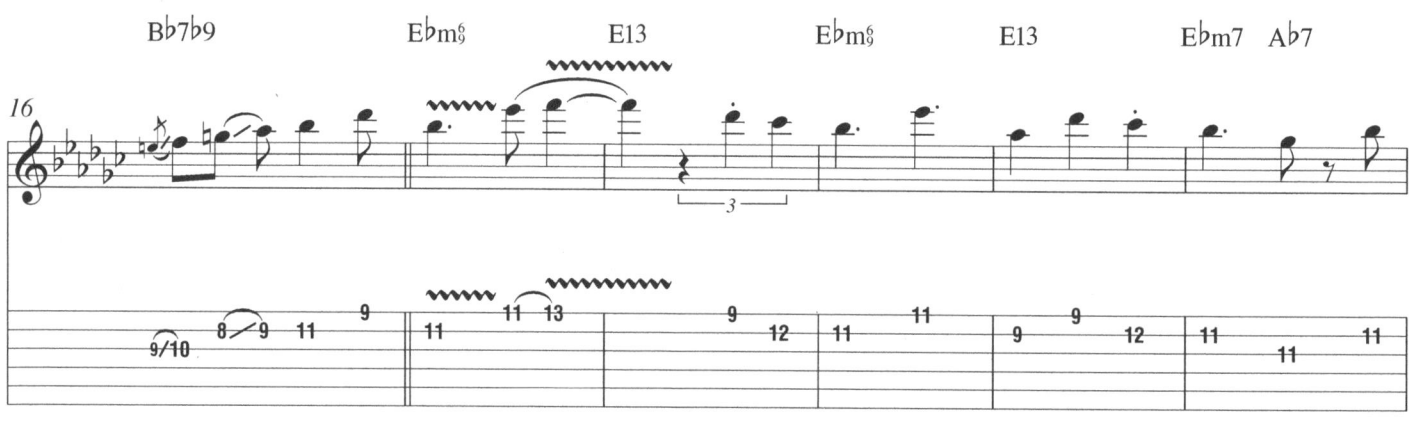

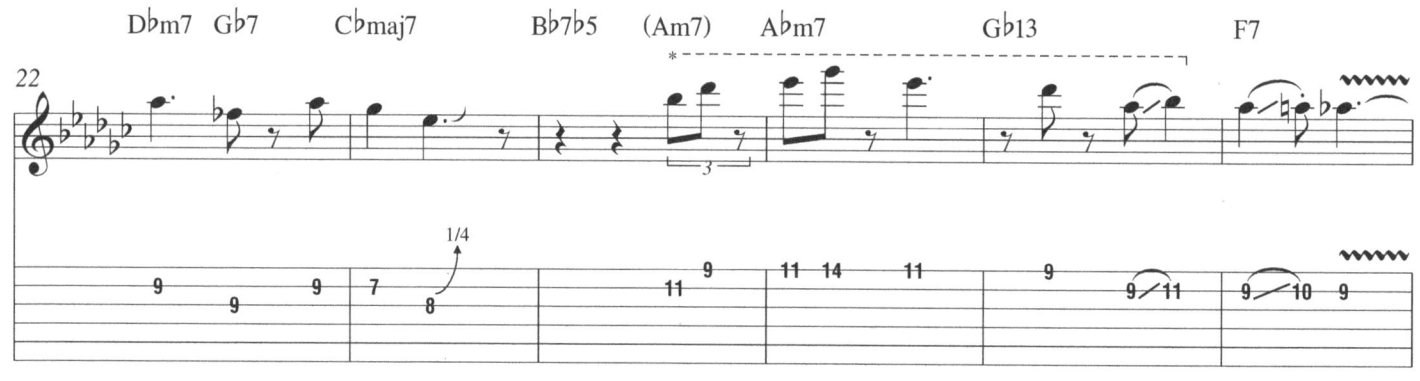

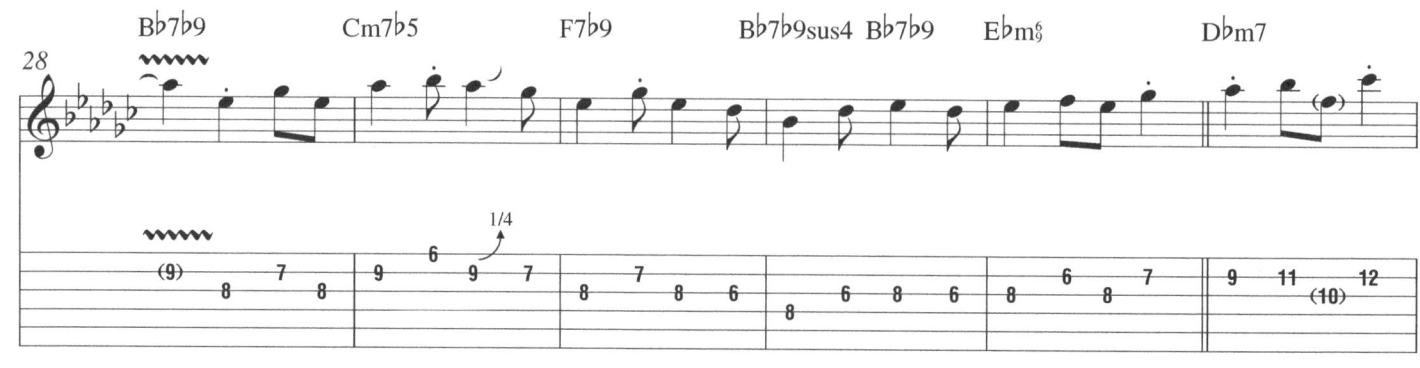

The Acrobat

The Acrobat

*Played behind the beat.

The Acrobat

The Acrobat

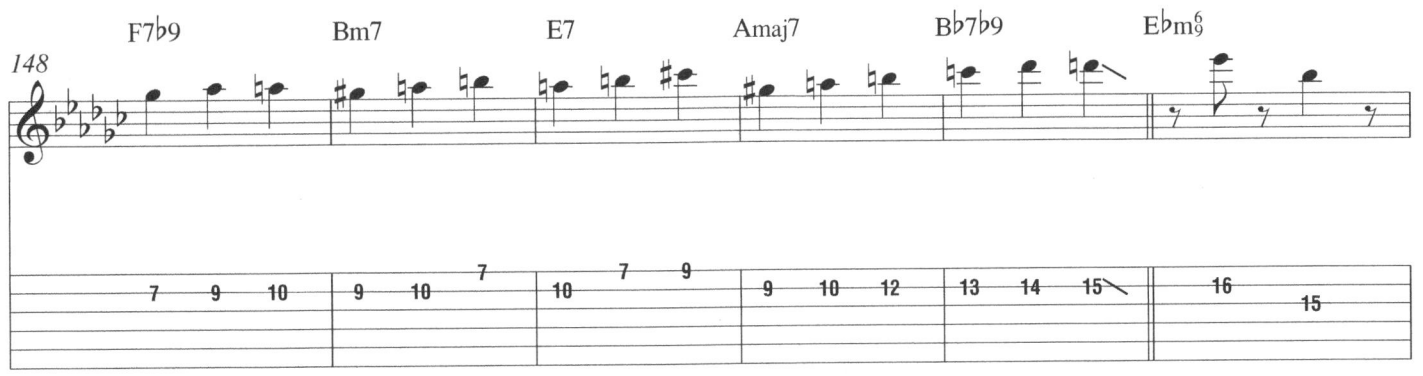
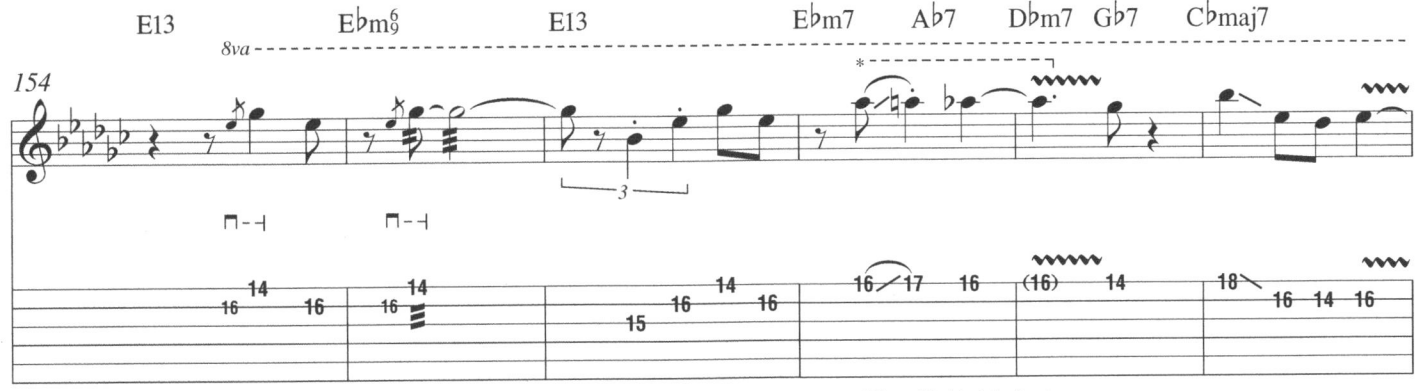

*Played behind the beat.

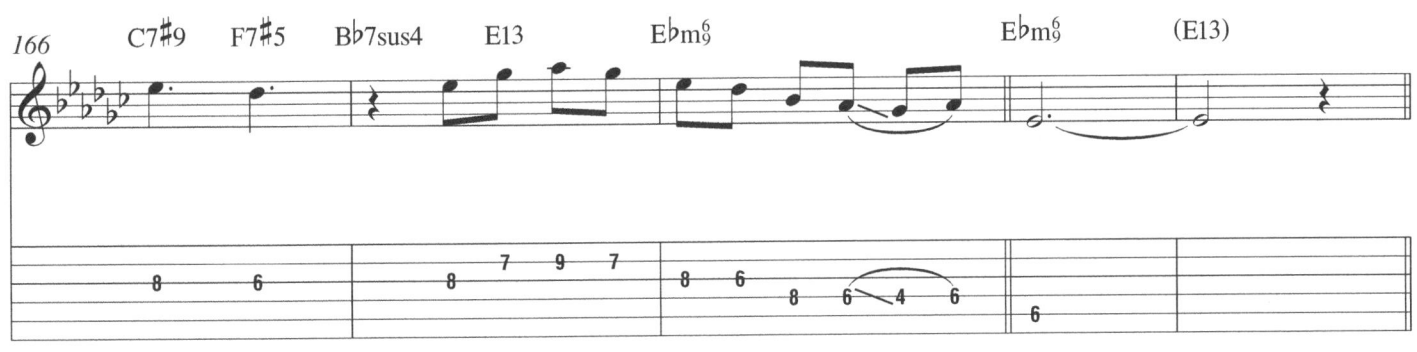

If I Should Lose You   2005

Kurt Rosenwinkel

"I really don't care about self-expression in music... I want to dissolve and disappear into the wave of the universe."
—Kurt Rosenwinkel

© Alamy

More than anyone else in recent times, Kurt Rosenwinkel is seen as blazing new territory for the sound of the guitar in jazz. He has long been the "it" guitarist for a large contingent of the jazz scene, and his influence is audible in the tone, the tunes, and the improvisation of countless younger players. In keeping with his eclectic nature as an artist, his own primary inspirations cover a wide range of periods and genres, with such heroes as Allan Holdsworth, Tal Farlow, John Coltrane, Led Zeppelin, Pat Metheny, Arnold Schoenberg, Keith Jarrett, David Bowie, George Van Eps, and Bud Powell.

An individualistic and sometimes mystical artistic thinker, he aims to be in touch with the impulses of the universe around him as he plays and often relates his music to his dreams. He has been known to randomly tune his strings to non-standard pitches in order to make himself listen harder within a musical search. With great concern for sonic detail, frequently demonstrated in his ample use of electronics, he has helped launch a resurgence of the pedalboard as an essential component of the instrument for many jazz guitarists. And his long-standing practice of wordlessly singing along with his guitar work is no mere gimmick, but rather a vehicle for feeling more connected to the music. This voice element (more ethereal and non-syllabic than George Benson's famous unison vocalizing) has become a fundamental part of his sound, miked and subtly mixed in, whether onstage or in the studio.

Rosenwinkel was born October 28, 1970 to piano-playing parents and grew up with the rich musical legacy of his hometown of Philadelphia. A pianist himself at first, he took up the guitar at age 12 and soon participated in local jazz jam sessions. He attended the High School for the Creative and Performing Arts, where he made connections with future luminaries like bassist Christian McBride, organist Joey DeFrancesco, and drummer Ahmir "Questlove" Thompson. After two and a half years of study at Boston's Berklee College of Music came high-profile engagements with famed vibraphonist and Berklee dean Gary Burton (from 1991 to 1992) and with veteran drummer Paul Motian's Electric Bebop Band (throughout the 1990s).

In early 1990s New York City, he began his long associations with tenor saxophonist Mark Turner, bassist Ben Street, and drummer Jeff Ballard, fellow cutting-edge players who would become his working band for some time, helping to forge a new direction in jazz through their performances at Small's in Greenwich Village. Rosenwinkel's debut recording *East Coast Love Affair* (1996, in a trio with Street and Ballard) focused on standard jazz repertoire, as did his 1998 follow-up *Intuit*, which really began to alert listeners to his fresh and unique approach. For 2000's *The Enemies of Energy*, he moved to a format of all original music, and *The Next Step* (2001, with his regular quartet) was a true break-out album, showing a more fully developed personal sound and style and introducing such other-worldly signature compositions as "Zhivago" and "Use of Light." In 2003, he created the further-afield *Heartcore*, an at once ambient and rhythmic mixture of jazz and electronica, co-produced by hip hop star Q-Tip and involving numerous guest musicians.

The makeup of his band began to change with 2005's *Deep Song*, which included new treatments of two standards and of some older originals, along with a number of brand new tunes. He has since released *The Remedy: Live at the Village Vanguard* (2008), *Reflections* (2009), a newer trio effort emphasizing jazz standards, *Our Secret World* (2010) with the Portuguese big band Orchestra Jazz de Matosinhos, and *Star of Jupiter* (2012), which features

For 2005's landmark Deep Song, *Rosenwinkel was joined by the formidable cast of tenor saxophonist Joshua Redman, pianist Brad Mehldau, bassist Larry Grenadier, and alternately drummers Jeff Ballard and Ali Jackson.*

the lineup of pianist Aaron Parks, bassist Eric Revis, and drummer Justin Faulkner. Through his illustrious career, he has also played with the Brian Blade Fellowship, tenor saxophone legends Joe Henderson and Pharoah Sanders, pianist Danilo Pérez, tenor sax-wielding contemporaries Seamus Blake, Chris Potter, and Joel Frahm, and guitarists Eric Clapton and Allan Holdsworth (both of these at Clapton's 2013 Crossroads Guitar Festival), among many others. He moved to Zurich, Switzerland in 2003 and from there to Berlin in 2007, where he is currently on faculty at the Jazz Institute Berlin.

How to Play It

In this highly inventive 21st-century treatment of a well-worn standard, Rosenwinkel brings out the monumental emotion of its title and lyrics in a whole new way. The tune is cast here as a Latin-tinged near-ballad using a groove that allows some flexibility between swung and even eighth notes and a spacious texture created by the rhythm section. The arrangement stretches what was a very symmetrical 32-bar song form into an 80-bar structure by way of the cut-time meter (two measures for every one of the original), an elongated section towards the end, and a built-in intro and tag. It has been slightly reharmonized to add to the mysterious aura and, of all things, placed in the key of E—infamous as a preference of rock and blues guitarists, but certainly not of jazz horn players! In any case, this allows

him to eventually make a striking arpeggiated run all the way down to the lowest note on the axe (the E of the open sixth string) for a deep, resonant tonic tone at a dramatic point in the solo (measure 77).

A factor to note regarding Rosenwinkel's unique sound is the wordless singing with which he doubles his melodic lines. Though faintly heard on the original recording, it blends significantly with his tremulous guitar notes to create an especially distinctive tone (this vocal aspect is not included on the accompanying audio for this book). Another expressive device used often throughout the solo is a quick downward slide into the intended note, as heard in measure 1 or especially measure 99. These can be so short that it's hard to say there's a grace note involved, and the effect can be achieved by placing your finger just on the other side of the fret and picking the string just as you slide down into position.

With the preliminary line in the pickup measures, he shows right away his penchant for diminished scale patterns—in this case with a sequence that belongs to the G# half-whole diminished scale, implying G#13♭9 as a specific version of the G#7♭9 at hand. The pattern is a very particular one on the fretboard that requires some down-the-neck mobility. To execute it, each time you are about to go back to string 1, hammer the last note on string 2 with the middle finger but then use the ring finger at the same fret on string 1, getting the index finger in place further down for the ring-finger pull-off. Agile shifting up, down, or across the fretboard is needed in other instances as well, including the patterned descent that starts with the last two notes of measure 43. The first three fingers can handle everything here, but be prepared

If I Should Lose You

to reach or jump along strings 1, 3, and 5, while the notes on strings 2, 4, or 6 are fretted by the ring finger. This is largely an arpeggiated A minor triad—the odd Am(maj7)/C♯ chord in the progression is really akin to an altered G♯7, which moves to C♯m in a V–i relationship (but which doesn't usually have C♯ in the bass). Tones of the A melodic minor scale (heard through most of this run, and also in measure 11) typically relate well to either Am(maj7) or G♯7alt.

Rosenwinkel's handling of time and rhythm is an important element in the solo. He leaves lots of breathing room at this easy tempo and beautifully mixes the sparse and simple with the dense and complex. This is aptly demonstrated when moving from the relaxed, in-key phrases of measures 25–28 into the twisty material of measures 29–34. In a manner that is prevalent in modern jazz guitar, he frequently lays back a bit on a single note that feels as though it belongs on a downbeat, placing it just a tad later (see Peter Bernstein on "The Acrobat" or Bobby Broom on "I Thought About You"). Here, this particular stylistic inflection is notated with a short rest right on the beat, as in the triplet figures of measures 12, 17, or 19 (remember that such an eighth rest goes by pretty quickly in cut time).

In measures 59–60, he plays the whole line behind the beat, actually lingering on the first note of measure 60 until the next note is a full half a beat late and then catching up by beat 1 of the next measure. Generally, as he pushes and pulls on time with his remarkable phrasing, the overall rhythm of a segment must really be *felt* to be played—and yet it is often quite definable in terms of mixed triplet and syncopated figures, as in the sweeping statements of measures 19–23 or 32–34. In this latter case, he puts a new spin on a typical diminished pattern (especially with the last eight notes)—one that's been heard for decades now in the practice halls of the jazz academy. The scale used is a near-fit for the F♯9♯11 but creates a little extra tension with the ♭9th and ♯9th tones (G♮ and A).

After Rosenwinkel's graceful entrance into the final stretch of the tune (at measure 57), Joshua Redman re-enters on tenor sax to play a counterline to the guitar phrases, as he did throughout the initial presentation of the melody on the original recording. The two instrumental voices entwine as the band dynamically builds to the climactic final vamp at measure 73, heralded by Rosenwinkel's sweeping arpeggio and pentatonic runs (B augmented triad tones in measure 72, E major pentatonic in measure 74, and C major pentatonic in measure 76), which all declaratively land on the tonic E. His impassioned soloing continues as the alternating E and C major chords are repeated freely, now beyond the bounds of the rearranged form, until he brings the performance to a close with a dramatic ritard and hold on Cmaj7. After briefly tremolo picking a low C triad here, he makes one last quiet comment while the tune fades into the ether.

Vital Stats

Guitarist: Kurt Rosenwinkel

Song: "If I Should Lose You"

Album: *Deep Song*, 2005

Age at Time of Recording: 34

Guitar: D'Angelico NYSS-3

Amp: Polytone (or Harry Colby-modified Fender Twin Reverb)

Effects: modulated delay

If I Should Lose You

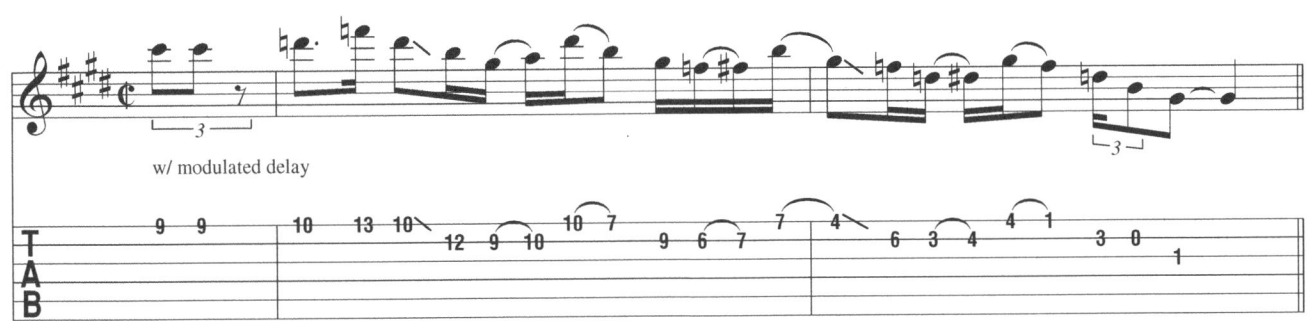
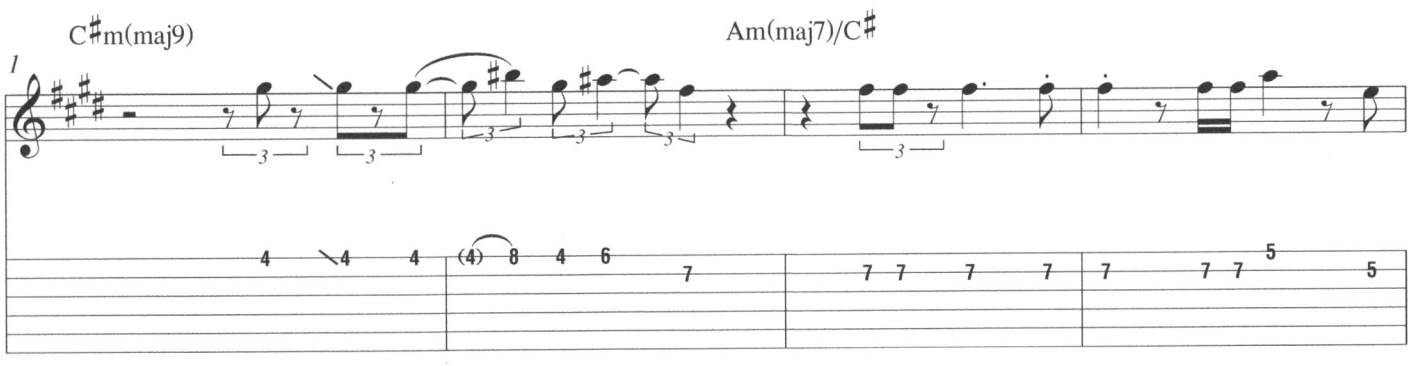

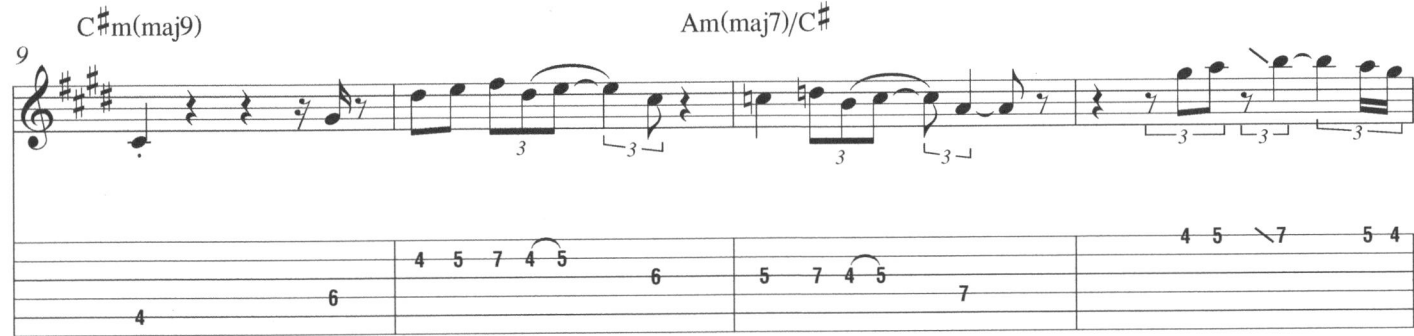

Words and Music by Leo Robin and Ralph Rainger
Copyright © 1935 Sony/ATV Music Publishing LLC
Copyright Renewed
All Rights Administered by Sony/ATV Music Publishing LLC, 424 Church Street, Suite 1200, Nashville, TN 37219
International Copyright Secured   All Rights Reserved

If I Should Lose You

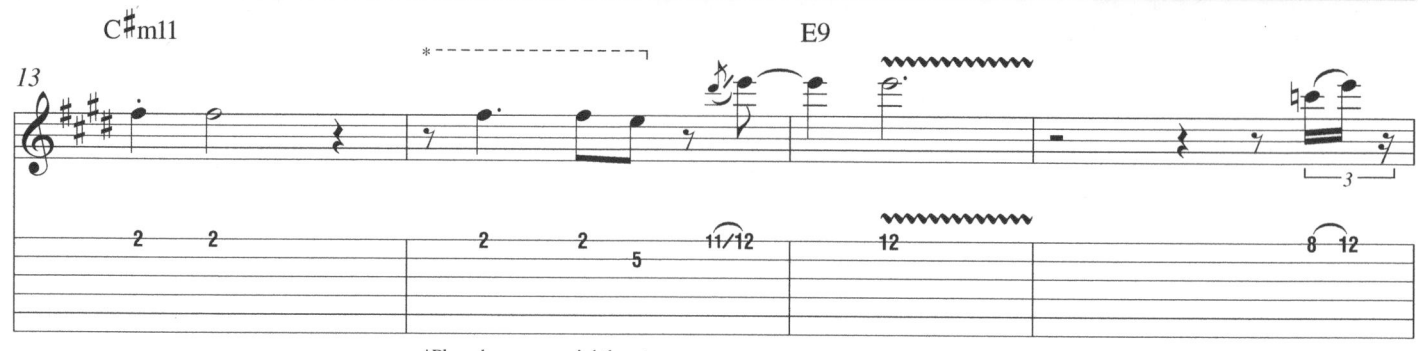

*Played as swung eighth notes.

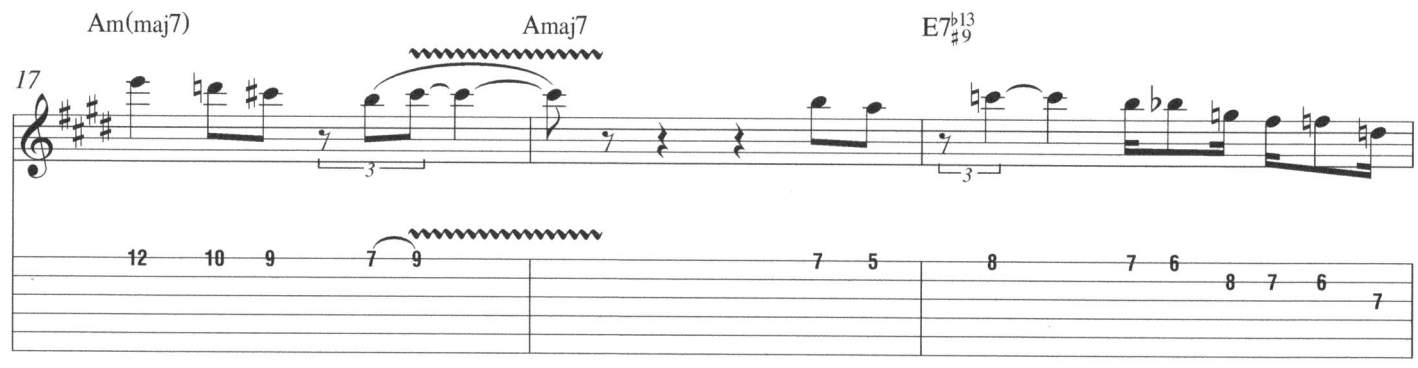

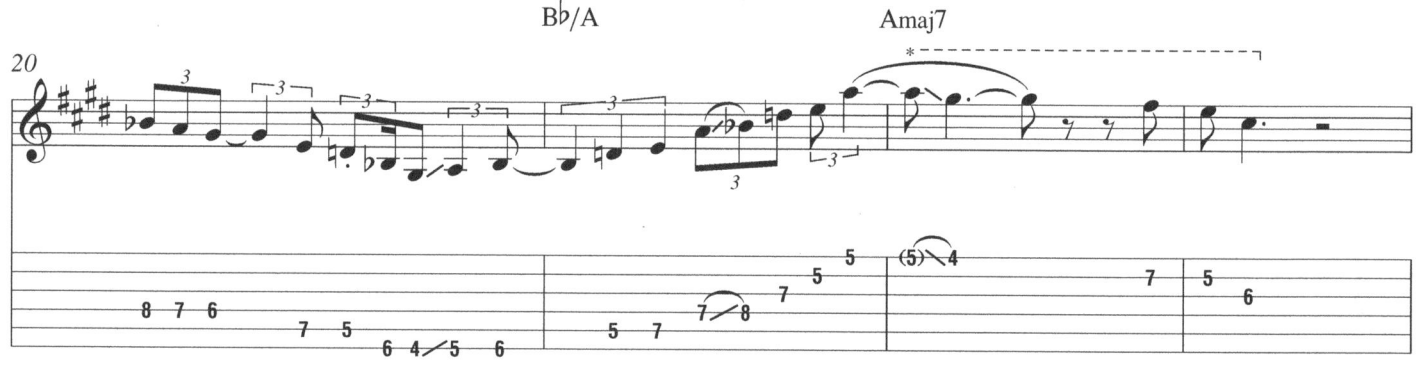

If I Should Lose You

*Played as swung eighth note(s).

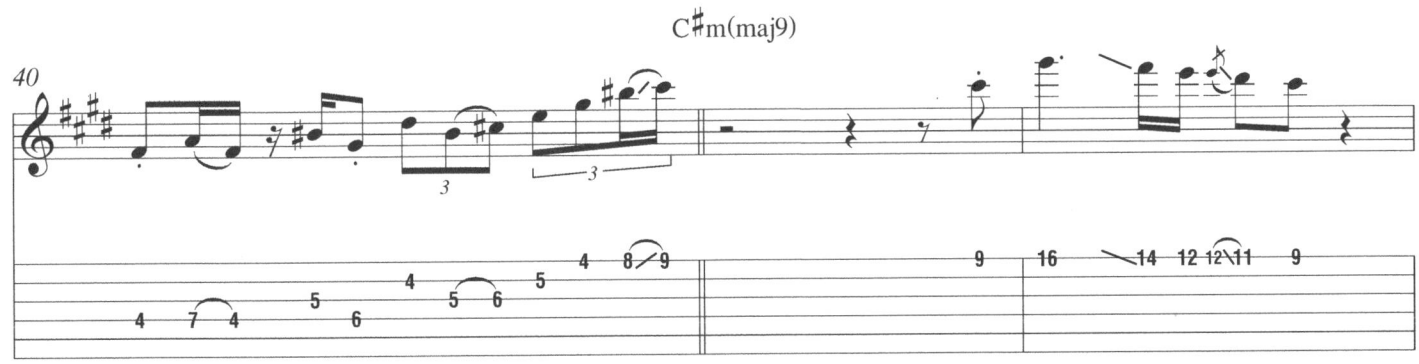

173

If I Should Lose You

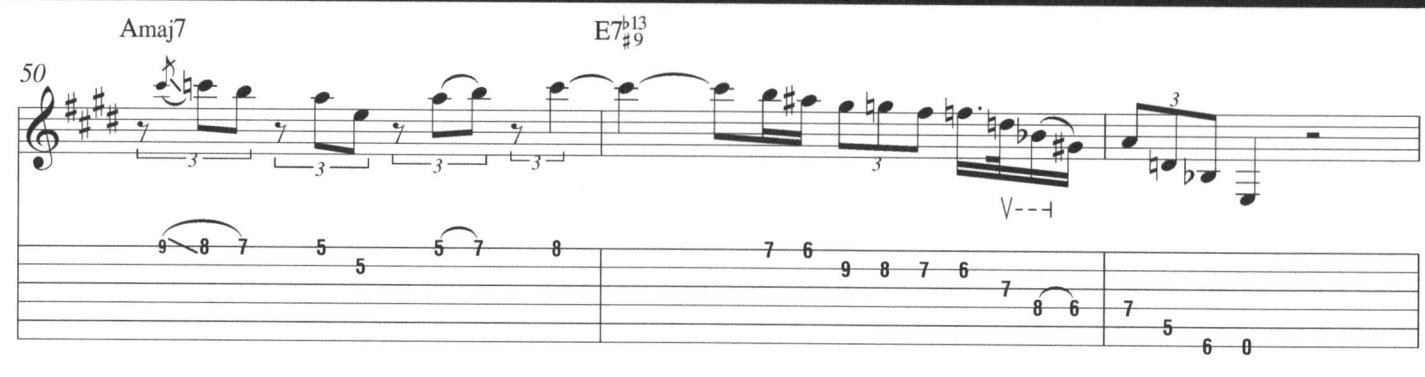

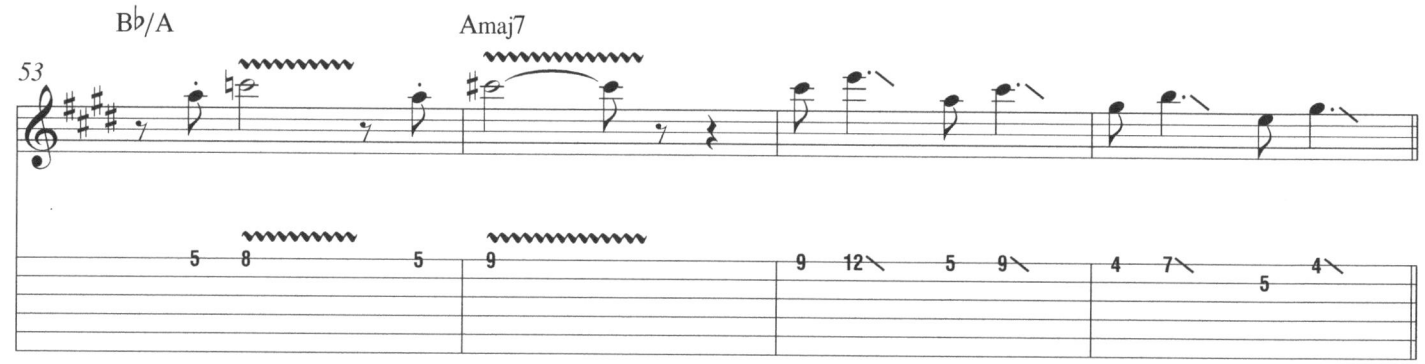

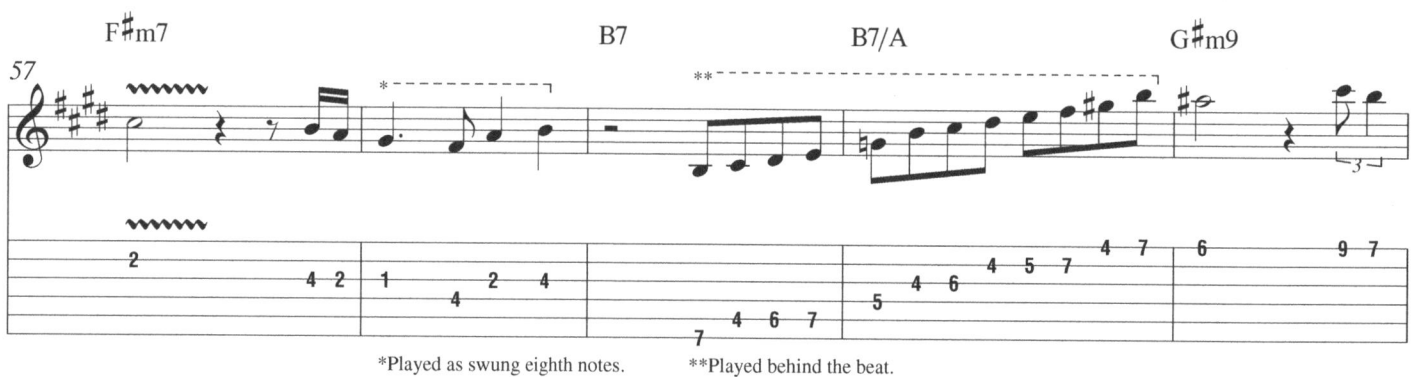

*Played as swung eighth notes.   **Played behind the beat.

If I Should Lose You

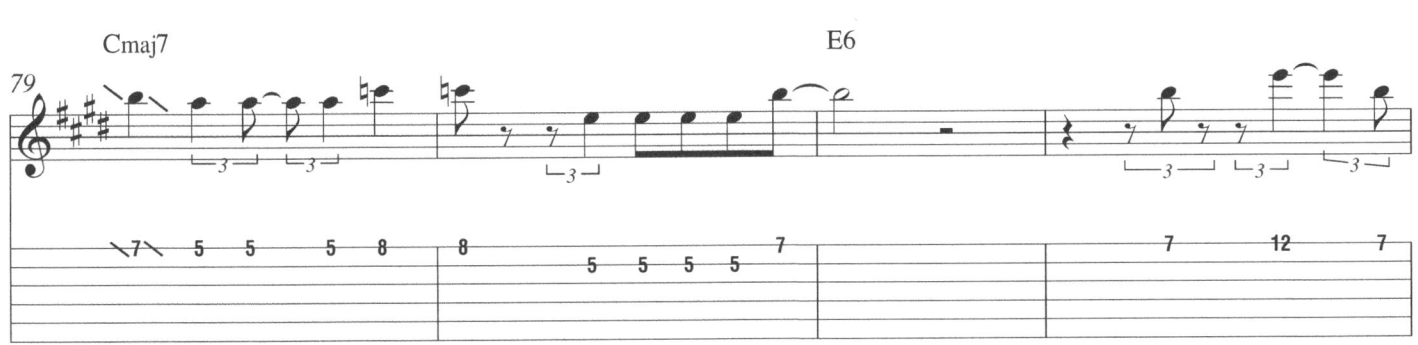

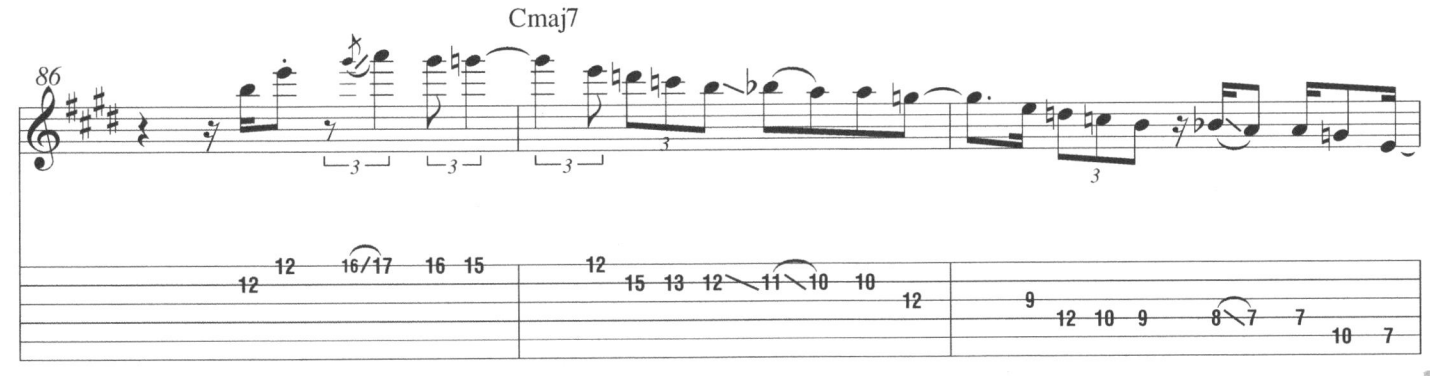

If I Should Lose You

I Thought About You   2007

Bobby Broom

Photo by John Broughton

"Really, playing music is something that a person is compelled to do beyond all reason."
—Bobby Broom

New York City born and bred, but making Chicago his home base since 1984, Bobby Broom is a defining force in the sound of contemporary, clean-toned, straight-ahead jazz guitar. He has taken the impulse of influential heroes like George Benson, Wes Montgomery, and Pat Martino, and stretched the limits of their language with his sophisticated sense of chordal substitution and creative handling of rhythm.

Born January 18, 1961, and taking up the guitar at age 12, a precocious Robert Broom, Jr. realized not much later that jazz was his calling upon hearing Benson's 1974 LP *Bad Benson*. While attending New York's High School of Music and Art (since renamed LaGuardia High School), his dedication to the music earned him some tremendous opportunities, including the chance to routinely sit in with veteran pianist Al Haig (an alum of bop innovator Charlie Parker's band in the 1940s) and an invitation to go on the road from none other than tenor sax icon Sonny Rollins—which young Broom had to decline so as to stay in school. But while still only 16 years of age, he indeed played with Rollins at Carnegie Hall in a special concert also featuring trumpet legend Donald Byrd.

After only one year at the Berklee College of Music in Boston, he returned to his hometown in pursuit of the wide-ranging gig opportunities there. Then, in order to play in the band of jazz-funk crossover trumpeter Tom Browne, he was once again compelled to turn down an offer from an all-time great—this time drummer Art Blakey, who asked the young guitarist to join his Jazz Messengers (at the same time as budding trumpet prodigy Wynton Marsalis was getting on board). Also working during this period with pianist Dave Grusin and trumpeter Hugh Masekela, Broom soon got his own recording contract on GRP and released his smooth jazz-leaning debut album *Clean Sweep* (1981), complete with his own vocals, in a George Benson/*Breezin'*-style effort.

Stardom in this more commercial vein might have awaited, but his career took a different path as he hooked up with Rollins for real from 1982 to 1987 (appearing on the tenor titan's early 1980s records *No Problem* and *Real Life*)—and in 1984 made the unusual move, for an up-and-coming jazzer, of leaving New York and heading to Chicago, for personal reasons. As much of a jazz mecca as the Windy City has been, it was not as central as NYC to the world scene, but he feels in hindsight that this distance from the epicenter may have helped him maintain his own natural voice in the increasingly electronic jazz guitar environment of the 1980s. And he has certainly managed to be a global player from his Midwestern base, appearing with the likes of saxophonists Stanley Turrentine and Kenny Garrett, and popular New Orleans-styled songster Dr. John. In 1986, he was asked by the legendary Kenny Burrell to participate in his Jazz Guitar Band, a

I Thought About You

2007's Folk Music *was the third release from the Deep Blue Organ Trio featuring a mix of jazz compositions and pop tunes, as well as the standard "I Thought About You."*

quintet in which the elder guitar master featured younger players Broom and Rodney Jones and which made a notable live recording at New York's Village Vanguard (released on *Generation* and *Pieces of Blue and the Blues*). Around the same time, Broom had a brief stint in the band of Miles Davis—clearly requiring him, in this era, to bring out the electronics!

He also became a mainstay of the Chicago scene itself, working with many of its star players, like organist Charles Earland (a favorite artist of his since childhood) and saxophonists Ron Blake and Eric Alexander, who each resided for a time in the area. An increased recorded output as a leader has documented his creative work over the last couple of decades, starting in 1995 with *No Hype Blues*. Since 1991, he has led the Bobby Broom Trio, involving a succession of top-flight Chicago-area drummers over this long span, including George Fludas, Dana Hall, Kobie Watkins, and recently Makaya McCraven, while the superlative bassist Dennis Carroll has long held down the fort. Among his titles with this outfit are *Waitin' and Waitin'*

(1997), *Stand!* (2001, showing his flair for jazz adaptation of 1960s and 1970s pop songs), *Bobby Broom Plays for Monk* (2009), the all-originals *Upper West Side Story* (2011), and the standards-laden *My Shining Hour* (2014). Another long-running group (under his co-leadership) was the Deep Blue Organ Trio with organist Chris Foreman and drummer Greg Rockingham. Putting a modern touch on the traditional bluesy, soulful, and swingin' sound of such a lineup, they made several fine albums, among which 2011's *Wonderful!* gives special treatment to the music of Stevie Wonder. Both Deep Blue and the more recent Bobby Broom Organi-Sation have toured as an opener for Steely Dan.

While still in his early twenties, Broom was encouraged by famed alto saxophonist Jackie McClean (then teaching at the University of Hartford) to share his experience with students. He has since taught at various Chicago-area institutions, such as Roosevelt and DePaul Universities, and he completed his master's degree in jazz pedagogy at Northwestern University in 2006—basically just in time for another tour of duty with Rollins, from 2005 to 2010.

How to Play It

Broom's solo on "I Thought About You" is a beautiful example of a modern, individualistic statement on an age-old, favorite standard, delivered within the classic swingin' groove of the organ trio setting. Throughout these two choruses on the 32-bar tune, he plays on the chord progression with both a simple, straightforward melodic sensibility and an edge of harmonic complexity and chromatic departure. All this is done while profusely pushing and pulling on the beat in his adventurous manner of laid-back timing, and wringing as much expression as possible from each note through careful touch and tasty slides and bends.

He begins with a relaxed, groovy, and understated solo break in the pickup measures, by the end of it implying $B\flat7\flat9\sharp5$ before moving into $E\flat maj7$ at the top of the first chorus. The solo is full of playful quotes, starting in measure 1 with the opening tones of "I Had the Craziest Dream" (a lesser-known old gem that remarkably resembles the song at hand). Later, he references the Mercer Ellington blues "Things Ain't What They Used to Be" (measure 11 plus the next two notes) and uses a motif recalling the ballad "It's Magic" in measures 29 and 30. He displays his signature behind-the-beat phrasing in measure 2, landing on one of his subtly bent ending notes. Many in-the-key phrases like those of measures 4–5 lie within $E\flat$ major pentatonic and evoke a gospel-blues feel, sometimes with a call-and-response aspect—the last three notes of measure 5 roughly echo the preceding phrase, though in a lower octave (see measures 12–13 for a similar effect). He subtly delays his attack on some individual notes, as heard on the downbeat of measure 8, in a way that is stylistically characteristic of numerous current players (see Peter Bernstein on "The Acrobat" or Kurt Rosenwinkel on "If I Should Lose You"). As he launches into 16th notes in measure 14, he enters the phrase behind the beat and then

I Thought About You

accelerates to catch up again by the start of the next measure.

He is often quite harmonically specific in his note choice, as in measure 14 with tones of the D altered scale (implying D7♭9 throughout), measure 15 with an ascent through a Gm11 arpeggio for Gm7 (from the 3rd), or measures 19 and 20 with mainly F Mixolydian material for the F7 (with a couple of chromatic connectors). From measure 21 through the first beat of measure 22, he moves a three-note motif down strings 4 and 5 to suit the descending minor seventh chords (lumping the Dm7♭5 in with the others), putting bold bends on the string 5 tones. He arpeggiates an A♭maj9 in measure 41 and presents a contrast to it right away with the G♭ of measure 42, bringing out the change to A♭m7 with its chordal 7th. From there, he moves chromatically down to E♭, the chordal 5th. Other examples abound of such half-step motion to connect chord tones, including the descent through the last half of measure 16 (G♯ = A♭, the 7th of B♭7, and he finally lands on C, the 3rd of Am7♭5).

Broom also uses distinct chordal substitution in places. He plays on the B♭7 of measure 6 as if it were E7, its tritone sub, which has the effect of making it a fully altered B♭7 and creating extra momentum on the way to E♭7. For the first half of measure 16, he plays an arpeggiated figure that actually implies F♯m7 rather than the present Fm7. He is here invoking a common bebop substitution of an extra ii–V pair, a half step higher than normal, snuck in before the regular ii–V chords (which are indeed Fm7–B♭7 in this key). Measure 39 is a doozy, as he starts with a rising B♭m11 arpeggio from the 3rd (which relates to an E♭7sus4) before moving through tones that outline A and C major triads along the way—compare the line with the shape of those barre chords at the fifth and eighth frets on the top three strings—as well as the note E♭. This all makes sense for an E♭13♭9 treatment of the E♭7, but the overall impression is rather "out there." Though many of his lines are playable in one area of the neck, this segment in particular requires some quick shifting up the fretboard, with a jump from the third to the fifth position after three notes and a slide up to the eighth position by the end. Some passages seem a little further out altogether, with tones less clearly related to the official changes (even if they support the overall harmonic direction), as heard at the end of measure 22 and the beginning of measure 23.

With two grand descending figures mid-solo, Broom at once shows the full intensity of his pulling back on the beat and floats adventurously outside the chords. The melodic pattern starting with the last note of measure 28 begins diatonically (in the key), but by measure 31, descends through a B♭ whole-tone scale until reaching bottom (this could be seen as relating to the final B♭7 here, implying B♭7♭5). Through this segment he leans back against the pulse until the eighth notes become broken-up triplets and lets the index finger drift farther and farther down string 3 before he leads declaratively into his second chorus at measure 33. Measures 37–38 consist almost entirely of one long chromatic descent, covering the better part of two octaves in half steps (while bouncing off of a few lower notes in between and finishing with a whole step). He plays behind the beat through measure 38, jumping back into sync with it just by the "and" of beat 4. Once again, the index finger is ultimately allowed to keep shifting down one string.

By measure 45, as he approaches the climactic final half-chorus, he heightens the tension with his unpredictable and expressive phrasing, while drawing on sudden blues scale tones imposed over the changes. The plaintive bendiness and sliding in and out of notes intensify at measure 49, leading to flat-out blues gestures from the end of measure 53 through measure 55 (where the ring finger covers a lot of ground in a soulful back-and-forth slide on string 2). In measures 57–59, he paraphrases the melody of the tune itself before heading to a subdued and graceful conclusion, recalling the end of his initial solo break with the final few notes.

Vital Stats

Guitarist: Bobby Broom
Song: "I Thought About You"
Album: *Folk Music*, 2007—Deep Blue Organ Trio
Age at Time of Recording: 46
Guitar: Höfner Jazzica
Amp: Peavey Special 130

I Thought About You

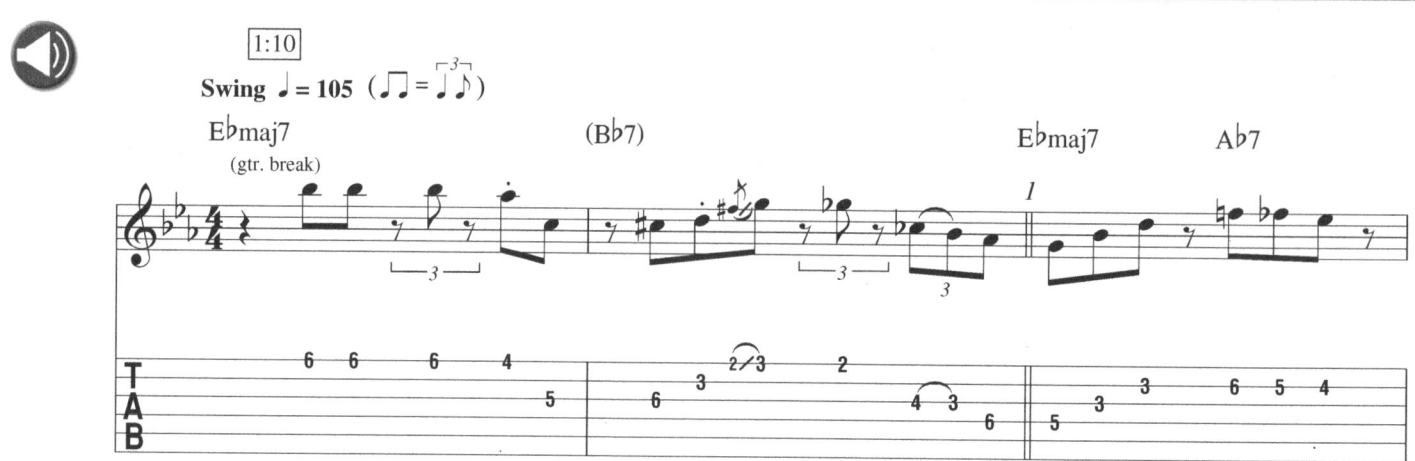

*Played behind the beat.

Words by Johnny Mercer
Music by Jimmy Van Heusen
Copyright © 1939 by Range Road Music Inc., Jerry Leiber Music, Mike Stoller Music and The Johnny Mercer Foundation
Copyright Renewed; extended term of Copyright deriving from Jimmy Van Heusen assigned and effective
October 13, 1995 to Range Road Music Inc., Jerry Leiber Music and Mike Stoller Music
All Rights for Jerry Leiber Music and Mike Stoller Music Administered by Range Road Music Inc.
All Rights for The Johnny Mercer Foundation Administered by WB Music Corp.
International Copyright Secured   All Rights Reserved
Used by Permission

I Thought About You

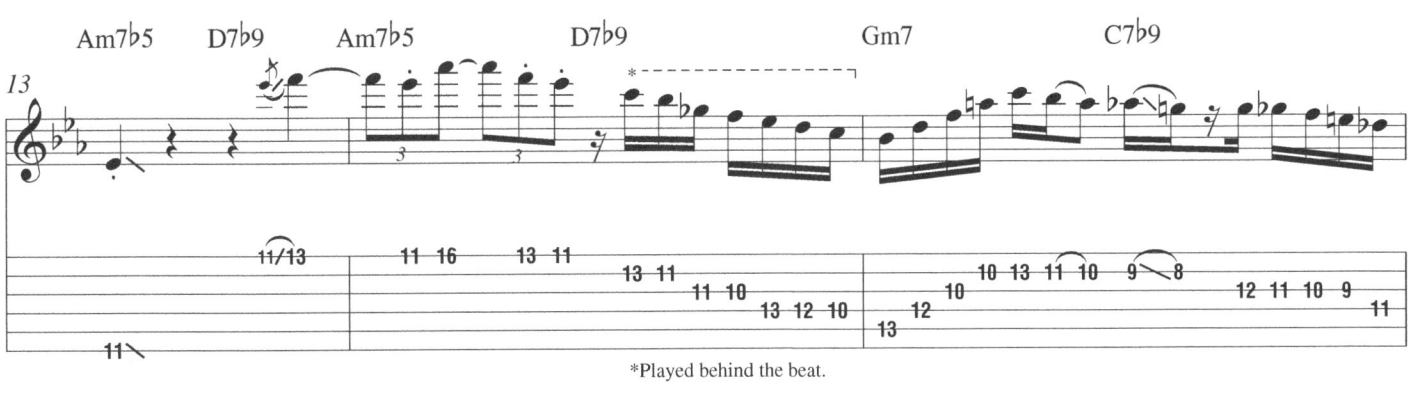

*Played behind the beat.

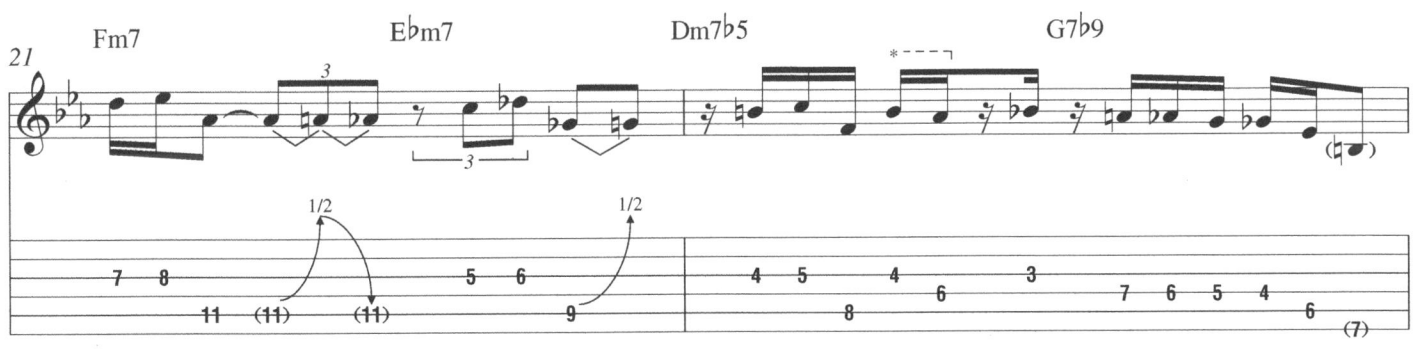
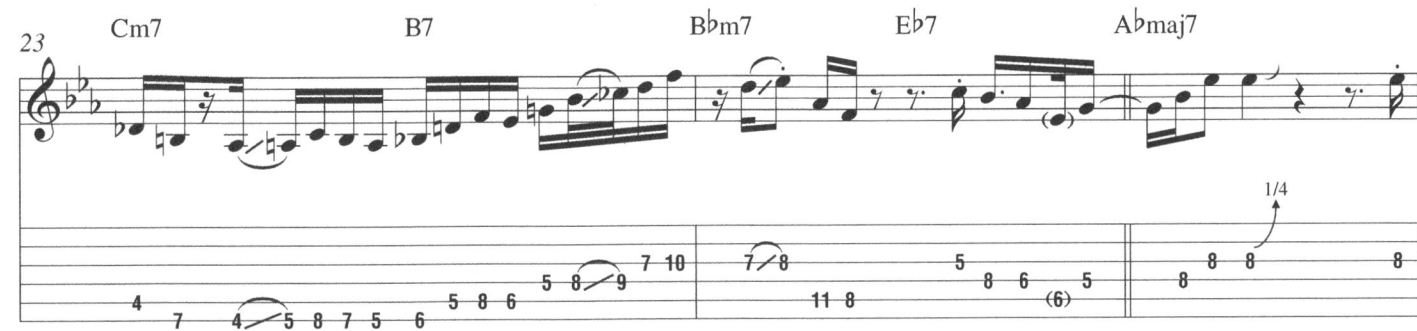

I Thought About You

*Played behind the beat.   **Played as even eighth notes.

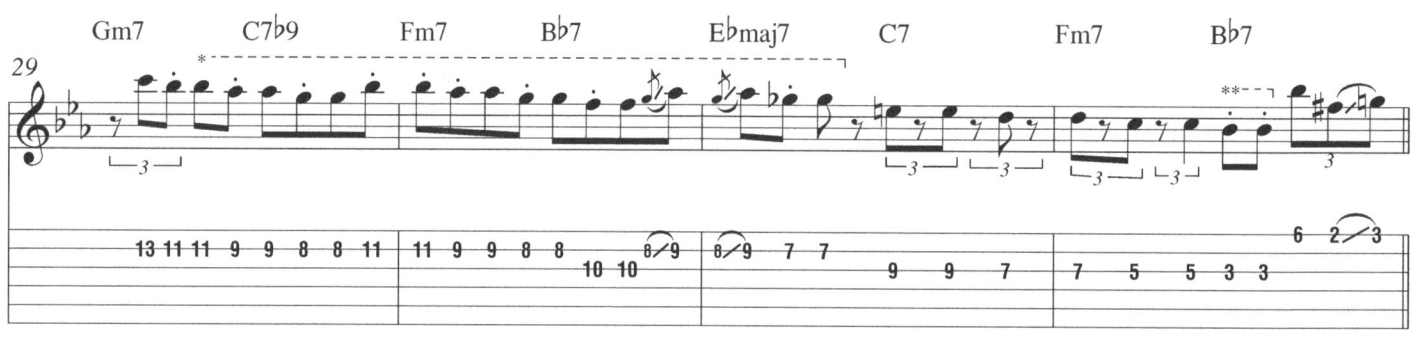

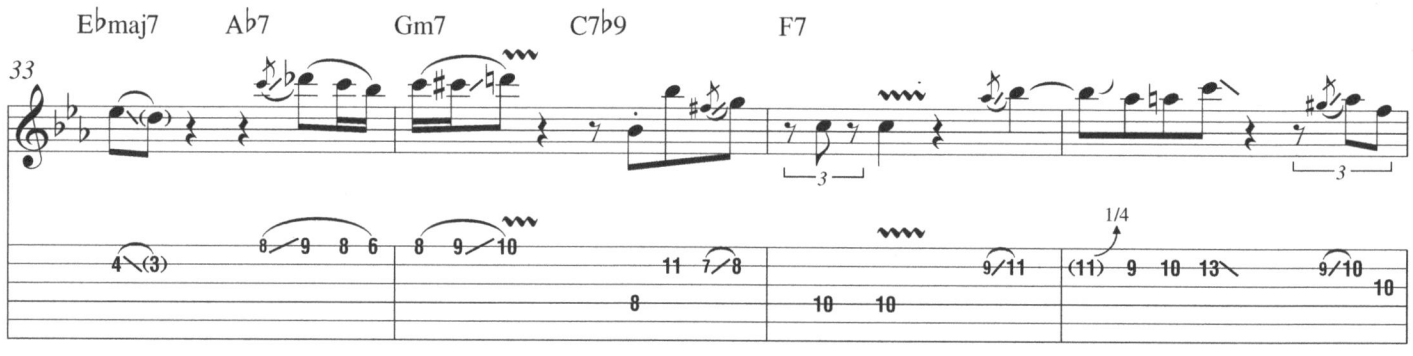

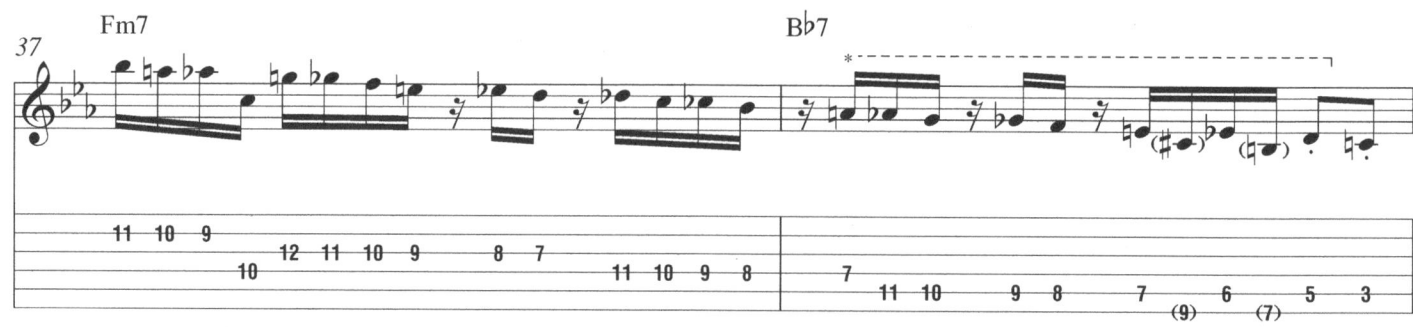

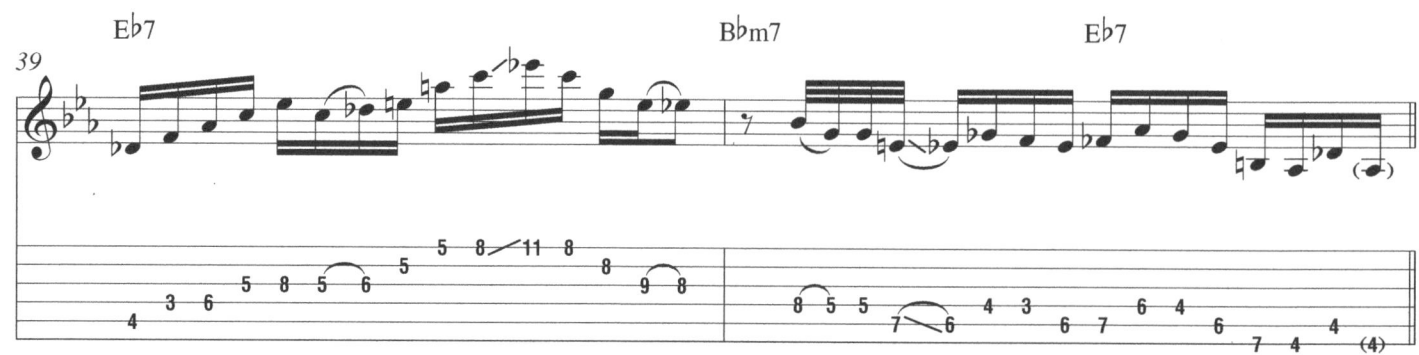

I Thought About You

*Played behind the beat.

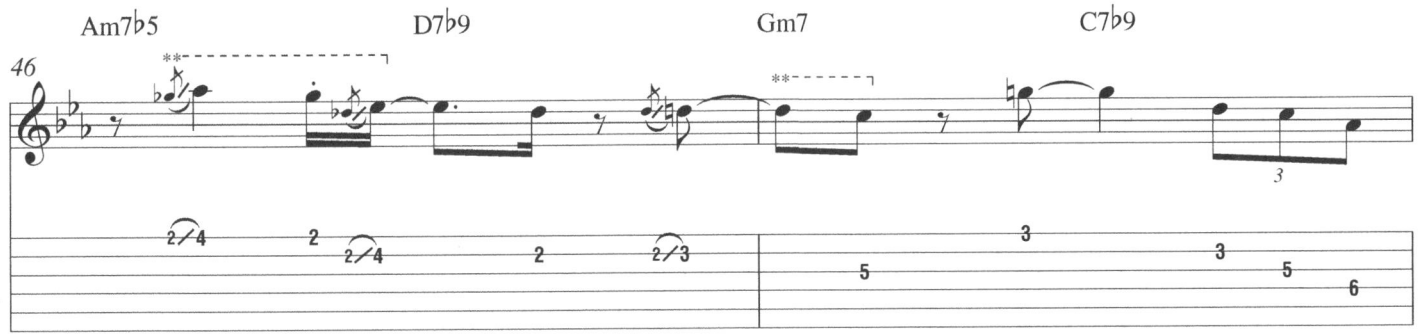

**Played as even eighth notes.

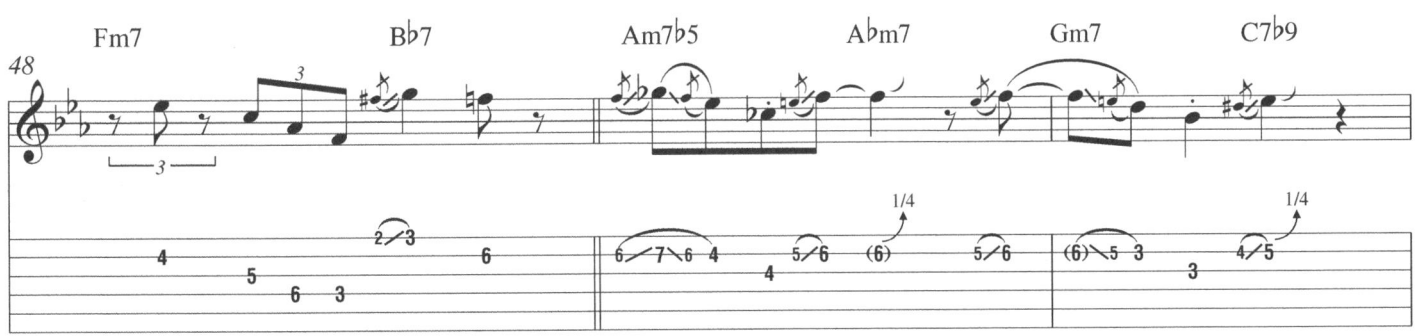

***Played behind the beat,
as even eighth notes.

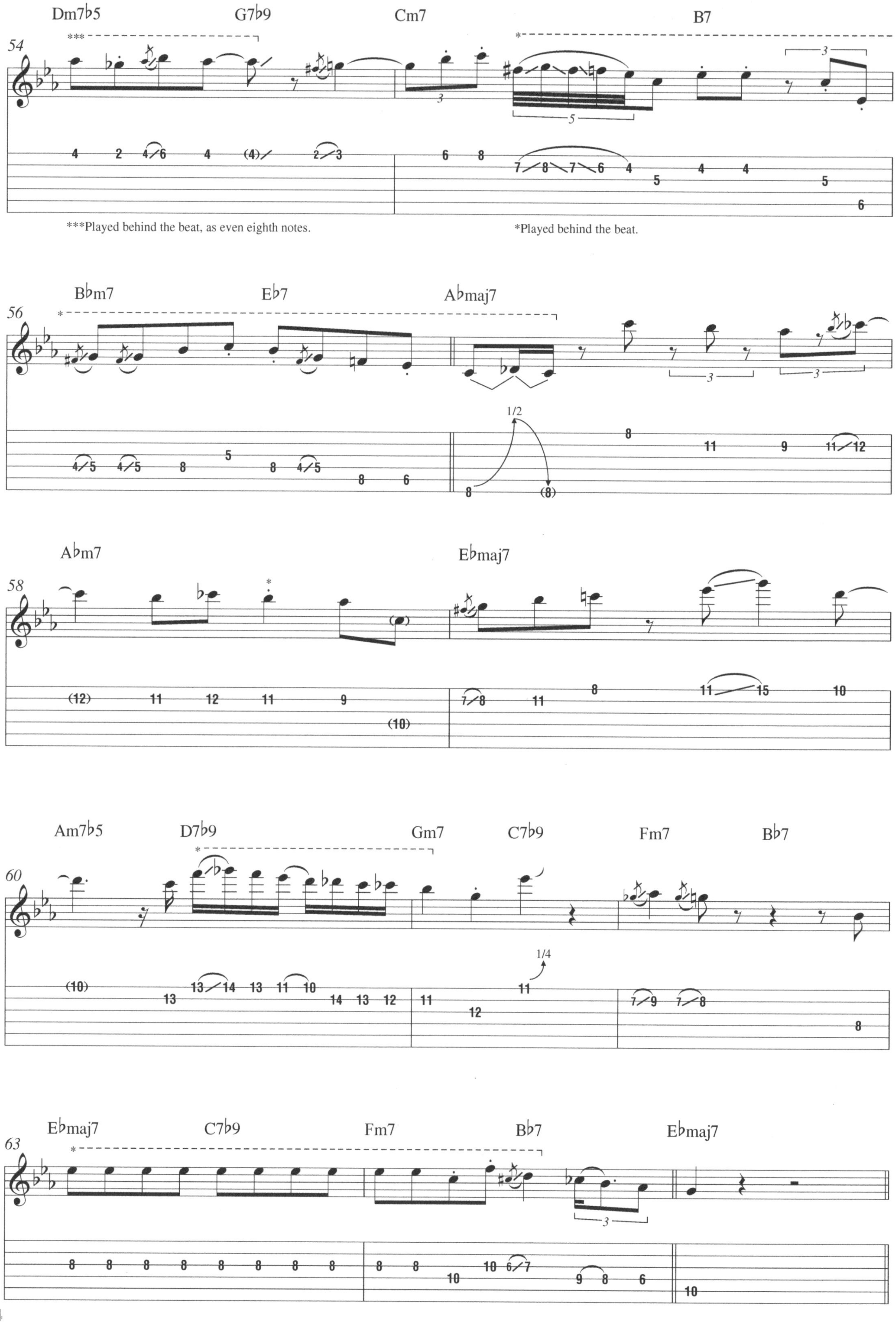

Dm7♭5
G7♭9
Cm7
B7
***Played behind the beat, as even eighth notes.
*Played behind the beat.
B♭m7
E♭7
A♭maj7
A♭m7
E♭maj7
Am7♭5
D7♭9
Gm7
C7♭9
Fm7
B♭7
E♭maj7
C7♭9
Fm7
B♭7
E♭maj7

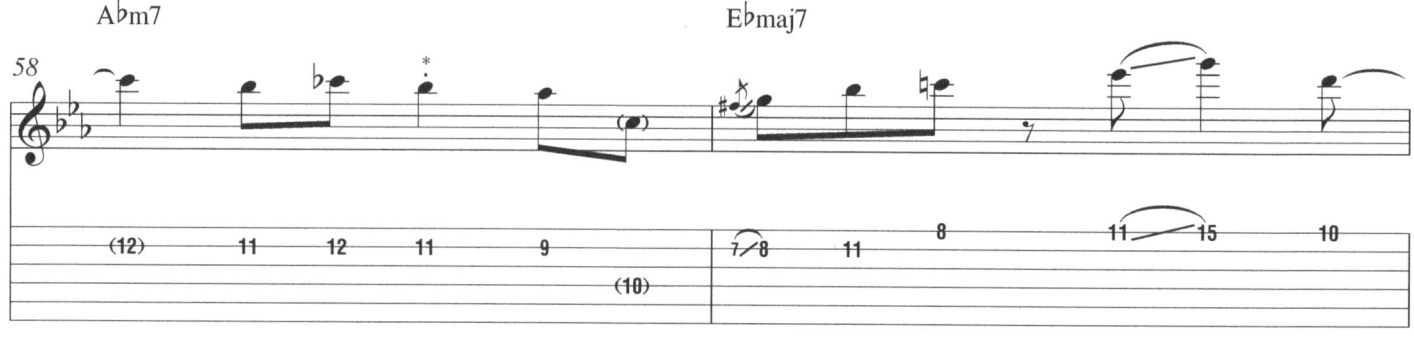

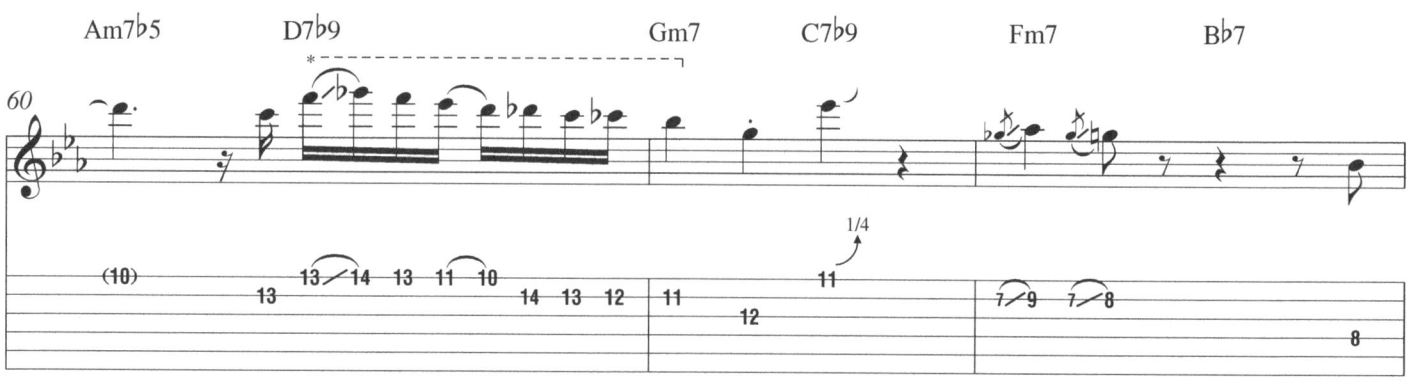

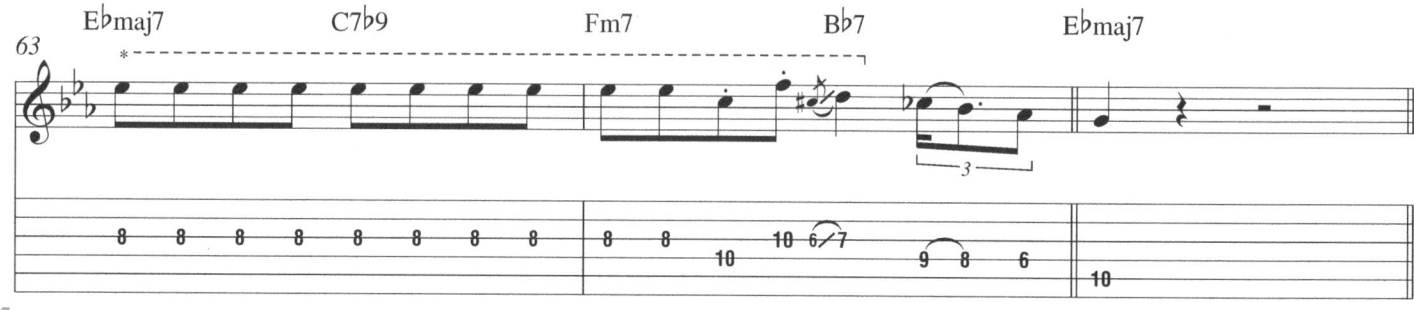

Conclusion

Soulful and sophisticated, astounding both in terms of fretboard chops and spontaneous compositional finesse, the work of the great jazz guitar improvisers is a joy for the ears to behold. There is great benefit to us as players in putting these 25 masterful statements under our own fingers, whether trying them in small samples or tackling them in their entirety. Besides the tremendous technical workout that some of them provide, they all give us insight into the melodic, harmonic, and rhythmic vocabulary of the artists themselves, which has reflected and affected the changing styles of jazz through the ages.

Of the soloists whose tones grace these pages, some are still here exploring new territory, and others are with us in the recorded legacy they left behind— and in their enduring spirit and influence. Still other gifted, dedicated, and diverse guitarists, including Howard Alden, Gene Bertoncini, Larry Coryell, Kevin Eubanks, Bruce Forman, Bill Frisell, Fareed Haque, John Hart, Rodney Jones, Biréli Lagrène, Russell Malone, Jack Wilkins, and so many more, have long been helping to carry on the tradition. And more recent bright stars on the scene, such as Jonathan Kreisberg, Julian Lage, Ben Monder, Mike Moreno, Jeff Parker, Adam Rogers, Anthony Wilson, Lage Lund, and Gilad Hekselman, continue to broaden the instrument's horizons in the music. With a hip, inspiring, and hard-swingin' heritage, the art of the jazz guitar solo lives on, bound to keep moving forward in ways we can only begin to imagine.

About the Author

Paul Silbergleit is a Milwaukee, Wisconsin-based jazz guitarist, composer, author, and educator. He has played with Jack McDuff, Phil Woods, Melvin Rhyne, Richie Cole, Tierney Sutton, Brian Lynch, David Hazeltine, and the Milwaukee Symphony Orchestra, among many others. Previously for Hal Leonard, he appeared on *200 Jazz Licks* in the *Guitar Licks Goldmine* DVD series, and co-authored *100 Jazz Guitar Lessons* in the *Guitar Lessons Goldmine* collection. He performs frequently with his own trio, with We Six, and as a solo guitarist, and has enjoyed nationwide airplay through his albums *Silberglicity* and *My New Attitude*. A graduate of Oberlin College, he is currently on faculty at the Wisconsin Conservatory of Music and Cardinal Stritch University.

GUITAR NOTATION LEGEND

Guitar music can be notated three different ways: on a *musical staff*, in *tablature*, and in *rhythm slashes*.

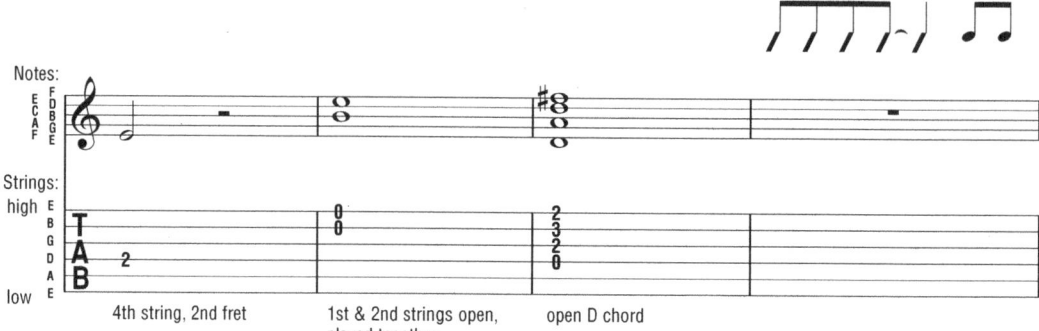

RHYTHM SLASHES are written above the staff. Strum chords in the rhythm indicated. Use the chord diagrams found at the top of the first page of the transcription for the appropriate chord voicings. Round noteheads indicate single notes.

THE MUSICAL STAFF shows pitches and rhythms and is divided by bar lines into measures. Pitches are named after the first seven letters of the alphabet.

TABLATURE graphically represents the guitar fingerboard. Each horizontal line represents a string, and each number represents a fret.

HALF-STEP BEND: Strike the note and bend up 1/2 step.

WHOLE-STEP BEND: Strike the note and bend up one step.

GRACE NOTE BEND: Strike the note and immediately bend up as indicated.

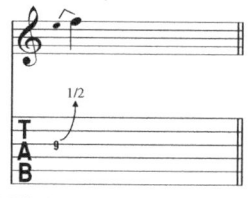

SLIGHT (MICROTONE) BEND: Strike the note and bend up 1/4 step.

BEND AND RELEASE: Strike the note and bend up as indicated, then release back to the original note. Only the first note is struck.

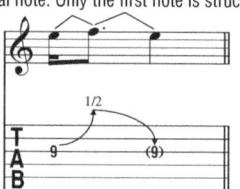

PRE-BEND: Bend the note as indicated, then strike it.

VIBRATO: The string is vibrated by rapidly bending and releasing the note with the fretting hand.

WIDE VIBRATO: The pitch is varied to a greater degree by vibrating with the fretting hand.

HAMMER-ON: Strike the first (lower) note with one finger, then sound the higher note (on the same string) with another finger by fretting it without picking.

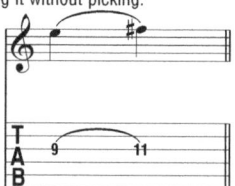

PULL-OFF: Place both fingers on the notes to be sounded. Strike the first note and without picking, pull the finger off to sound the second (lower) note.

LEGATO SLIDE: Strike the first note and then slide the same fret-hand finger up or down to the second note. The second note is not struck.

SHIFT SLIDE: Same as legato slide, except the second note is struck.

TRILL: Very rapidly alternate between the notes indicated by continuously hammering on and pulling off.

TAPPING: Hammer ("tap") the fret indicated with the pick-hand index or middle finger and pull off to the note fretted by the fret hand.

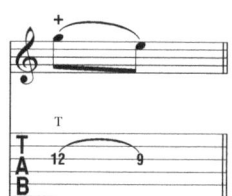

NATURAL HARMONIC: Strike the note while the fret-hand lightly touches the string directly over the fret indicated.

PINCH HARMONIC: The note is fretted normally and a harmonic is produced by adding the edge of the thumb or the tip of the index finger of the pick hand to the normal pick attack.

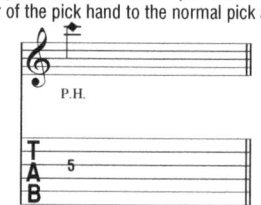

PICK SCRAPE: The edge of the pick is rubbed down (or up) the string, producing a scratchy sound.

MUFFLED STRINGS: A percussive sound is produced by laying the fret hand across the string(s) without depressing, and striking them with the pick hand.

PALM MUTING: The note is partially muted by the pick hand lightly touching the string(s) just before the bridge.

RAKE: Drag the pick across the strings indicated with a single motion.

TREMOLO PICKING: The note is picked as rapidly and continuously as possible.

VIBRATO BAR DIVE AND RETURN: The pitch of the note or chord is dropped a specified number of steps (in rhythm), then returned to the original pitch.

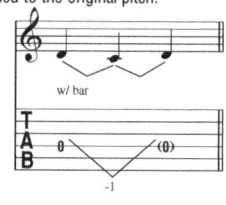

VIBRATO BAR SCOOP: Depress the bar just before striking the note, then quickly release the bar.

VIBRATO BAR DIP: Strike the note and then immediately drop a specified number of steps, then release back to the original pitch.

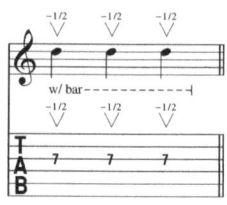